INTERPRETING MODERNITY

INTERPRETING MODERNITY

Essays on the Work of Charles Taylor

EDITED BY
DANIEL M. WEINSTOCK,
JACOB T. LEVY, AND
JOCELYN MACLURE

McGill-Queen's University Press
Montreal & Kingston | London | Chicago

ISBN 978-0-2280-0143-0 (cloth)
ISBN 978-0-2280-0144-7 (paper)
ISBN 978-0-2280-0282-6 (ePDF)
ISBN 978-0-2280-0283-3 (ePUB)

Legal deposit third quarter 2020
Bibliothèque nationale du Québec

Printed in Canada on acid-free paper that is 100% ancient forest free
(100% post-consumer recycled), processed chlorine free

We acknowledge the support of the Canada Council for the Arts.

Nous remercions le Conseil des arts du Canada de son soutien.

LIBRARY AND ARCHIVES CANADA CATALOGUING IN PUBLICATION

Title: Interpreting modernity : essays on the work of Charles Taylor / edited by Daniel
    Weinstock, Jacob T. Levy, and Jocelyn MacLure.
Names: Weinstock, Daniel M., editor. | Levy, Jacob T., 1971– editor. | Maclure, Jocelyn,
    1973– editor.
Description: Essays collected in this volume were originally presented at a conference
    organized in Charles Taylor's honour on the occasion of his eightieth birthday. |
    Includes bibliographical references and index.
Identifiers: Canadiana (print) 20200247379 | Canadiana (ebook) 20200247557 | ISBN
    9780228001447 (paper) | ISBN 9780228001430 (cloth) | ISBN 9780228002826
    (ePDF) | ISBN 9780228002833 (ePUB)
Subjects: LCSH: Taylor, Charles, 1931– | LCGFT: Festschriften.
Classification: LCC B995.T3 I58 2020 | DDC 191—dc23

Set in 11/14 Sina Nova with Futura and Caecilia Std
Book design & typesetting by Garet Markvoort, zijn digital

CONTENTS

PART SIX

Political Philosophy, Recognition, and Multiculturalism

PART SEVEN

Canadian Politics

ACKNOWLEDGMENTS

This volume arises out of a 2012 conference "Charles Taylor at 80"; most of the papers here were presented in draft form there. The conference was the culmination of a four-year grant from the Fonds de recherche du Québec, Société et Culture (FRQSC) to Montreal's Groupe de Recherche Interuniversitaire en Philosophie Politique (GRIPP). We thank our colleagues in GRIPP for their contributions and participation, and the FRQSC for financial support for the conference and for GRIPP's ongoing programs. The conference and subsequent work toward publication was also supported by grants from the Templeton Foundation to the Research Group on Constitutional Studies at McGill, and from Quebec's Secrétariat aux affaires intergouvernementales canadiennes, and by additional contributions from l'Association des études canadiennes; the Centre de recherche en éthique de l'Université de Montréal and the Vice-rectorat à la recherche, à la création et à l'innovation, l'Université de Montréal; the Centre for Global Challenges at York University; McGill's Faculty of Arts, Department of Political Science, and Research Group on Constitutional Studies; the Canadian Federation for the Humanities and Social Sciences; le Groupe de recherche interuniversitaire sur la normativité; and le Groupe de recherche sur les sociétés plurinationales. Pierre-Yves Néron did the primary organizational work for the conference. Maud Gauthier-Chung, Martin Blanchard, and Louis-Philippe Caron Lanteigne contributed valuable additional organizational support.

We wish to thank Michel Bastarache, Guy Laforest, and Julius Grey who, along with Daniel M. Weinstock, contributed thoughts at the conference on professor Taylor's important role as a public intellectual, in a public discussion ably chaired by the late Gretta Chambers.

We especially wish to thank professor Taylor for his memorable willingness to engage extemporaneously with the speakers, and to discuss issues ranging from the philosophy of mind and language to Canadian politics.

This book would not have come to fruition without the indispensable research assistance provided by Muhammad Velji, Éliot Litalien, and

Alice Everly. Thanks for additional assistance to Abbie LeBlanc and Ewa Nizalowska.

We are grateful to the following publishers for permission to reprint material that was initially published in whole or in part in the following works.

Richard Bernstein. "Taylor's Engaged Pluralism." In *Pragmatic Encounters*, 87–99. New York: Routledge, 2016.

William E. Connolly. "Third Interlude: Fullness and Vitality." In *The Fragility of Things*, 140–8. Duke University Press, 2013.

Cécile Laborde. "Protecting Freedom of Religion in the Secular Age." In *Politics of Religious Freedom*, edited by Winnifred Fallers Sullivan et al., 269–79. Chicago: University of Chicago Press, 2015.

Tariq Modood. "State-Religion Connections and Multicultural Citizenship." In *Religion, Secularism, and Constitutional Democracy*, edited by Jean L. Cohen and Cécile Laborde, 182–203. New York: Columbia University Press, 2015.

INTERPRETING MODERNITY

Charles Taylor: A Biographical Sketch

DANIEL M. WEINSTOCK, JACOB T. LEVY, AND JOCELYN MACLURE

The essays collected in this volume were originally presented at a conference organized in Charles Taylor's honour on the occasion of his eightieth birthday. They are by former students, colleagues, and academics who in one way or another have been influenced by his work, and also by the way that Taylor has, throughout his career, been able to write works that have placed him at the very pinnacle of academic achievement with a deep and ceaseless commitment to public engagement.

Taylor was born in Montreal in 1931 in a bilingual family. He obtained a BA in history at McGill University and received a Rhodes Scholarship to study at Oxford, where he received a BA in philosophy, politics, and economics, and a DPhil in philosophy in 1961. During his time at Oxford, he was awarded a prestigious fellowship from All Souls' College. Taylor began his academic career in the department of philosophy of the Université de Montréal, where he taught from 1963 to 1971. He moved to McGill University in 1973 and was a professor in the departments of both political science and philosophy. From 1976 to 1981 Taylor held the Chichele Chair in Social and Political Theory, one of the most prestigious chairs in political theory in the English-speaking world. He has also held numerous visiting appointments at universities in North America, Europe, and beyond.

Throughout his academic career, Taylor maintained a commitment to civic engagement. At Oxford, he was one of the founding editors of the *Universities and Left Review*, which would eventually become the *New Left Review*, to this day one of the most important vehicles for progressive ideas and arguments. Upon returning to Canada in the early 1960s, he became a frequent contributor to *Cité Libre*, a public affairs magazine that published the works of intellectuals who would go on to become leading public figures in Quebec and Canadian public life – including Pierre Elliott Trudeau. Taylor is a lifelong member of Canada's federal social-democratic party, the New Democratic Party. He ran for Parliament under the banner of the NDP in three elections between 1961 and 1965, losing the last of these elections to his longtime friend Pierre Elliott Trudeau, who would go on to become Canada's longest-serving prime minister (1968–79 and 1980–84).

Taylor has been not just a commentator, but an *engagé* public intellectual in all of Canada's political dramas since the 1970s. He was a passionate defender both of federalism during the referendum campaigns of 1980 and 1995, arguing to his fellow Quebeckers that their aspiration to self-determination could be realized within the context of Canadian federal institutions, and of attempts in 1987 and 1992 at constitutional amendment that would have created institutional space within the Canadian constitution for Quebec to function as a self-determining nation within a federation whose other members did not harbour the same national aspirations. Though these attempts at instituting "asymmetrical federalism" ended up being defeated, they inspired a generation of Canadian political philosophers, including James Tully, Will Kymlicka, and Guy Laforest.

Taylor's public engagement in the '00s and '10s have turned to the cause of defending religious and ethno-cultural diversity against attacks levelled at the Canadian multiculturalist model in his home province of Quebec. After a series of high-profile incidents led to demands by many Quebec voters and politicians for an inquiry into the practice of religious and cultural accommodation in the province, Taylor co-chaired a commission from 2007 to 2009 that heard widely from Quebeckers about their views on the increasing diversity of Quebec society, but also more broadly about the changes that Quebec society was undergoing, and the anxieties raised in many quarters by these changes. The final report that the commission produced sparked furious debate throughout the province, and is still widely referred to and read by all sides of the debate concerning the extent to which laws and institutions should adapt to accommodate citizens with religious and cultural practices that diverge from those of the majority. Most recently, Taylor was an unrelenting critic of a controversial proposed piece of legislation put forward by the short-lived (2012–14) government of the Parti Québécois, known as the *Charter of Values*, that would have prohibited employees in Quebec's public sector from wearing "conspicuous" religious symbols.

Across the decades and across this range of issues, Taylor's public engagement has been marked by the attempt to "reconcile solitudes," whether Canada's constitutive linguistic solitudes, or the ethno-cultural solitudes that have developed in Quebec and throughout Canada as a result of immigration and of the diversification of the society's religious landscape. He has always sought to act as an "honest broker," providing interpretations of the motivations and aspirations of all sides to a political struggle, and allowing for the values and goods that are at stake to emerge. Taylor thus avoids the tendency toward caricature that too often takes hold in the cut and thrust of political conflict.

As we shall see, Taylor's philosophical work has also ranged across an impressively broad range of issues while at the same time being unified by a single underlying preoccupation.

A Brief Overview of Charles Taylor's Writings

The range of Charles Taylor's philosophical writings is truly remarkable. There is scarcely an area of contemporary philosophy to which he has not devoted his attention, and to which he has not made a significant contribution. He has written on the philosophy of mind, of language, and of action; he has also published works in moral and political philosophy that have become standard texts both for students and for professional researchers seeking to contribute to these areas. One cannot today write on issues to do with multiculturalism, with secularism, or with the nature of liberty without attending to the powerful arguments developed by Taylor throughout his long and prolific career. The major works Taylor wrote in the latter part of his career attempt nothing less than an interpretation of modernity, and of the ways of defining oneself as a "self" and of relating to a realm of spiritual transcendence that modernity has given rise to.

Taylor's range can be appreciated in other ways as well. For example, he has always refused to situate himself squarely within one or the other of the philosophical "camps" that have characterized academic philosophy throughout the twentieth century and into the twenty-first. Though his writing is immediately recognizable and legible by "analytical" philosophers through its mobilization of clear and rigorous argument and distinctions in short essay form, it is also in continuity with the more ambitious reach that characterizes what is sometimes referred to as continental philosophy. Taylor converses with Donald Davidson and W.V.O. Quine just as readily as he does with G.W.F. Hegel, Martin Heidegger, and Maurice Merleau-Ponty. Indeed, one of the unstated methodological ambitions of Taylor's work is to show that philosophical questions are best treated when the resources of diverse philosophical traditions that have heretofore been kept apart are brought into fruitful dialogue.

Despite its wide range, Taylor's work is characterized by a very deep unifying concern. He aims to help philosophy resist the reductive pressures of the aspiration, explicitly professed by some philosophers, inherited in a sometimes unreflective and unintentional manner by others, to integrate into philosophy a vision of human agents, and a set of associated methods of inquiry, inherited from the natural sciences. That aspiration – one that Taylor has wrestled with across the full range of philosophical domains – is to remove from the purview of philosophical discourse, and even more broadly from that of the human sciences, ways of considering the human that invoke notions that are not easily quantifiable or observable.

Much of Taylor's early work can be seen as an attempt to identify and to criticize this tendency in apparently unrelated areas of modern philosophy, particularly of the kind of philosophy practiced in the Anglophone academic context, a style that was in its heyday at Oxford. His first major philosophical work, *The Explanation of Behaviour*, was a book-length attack on the then-fashionable theory of behaviourism, pioneered by the psychologist B.F. Skinner. Skinner argued that human behaviour can be understood according to a very simple stimulus-response model, one that leaves values and aspirations on the basis of which humans purport to act in a "black box," unnecessary from the point of view of serious scientific exploration. Taylor argued in that work that the explanation of behaviour cannot be carried out without representing humans as "telos" driven, that is as motivated by the pursuit of certain ends. Taylor's work in the philosophy of mind and action continued into the 1970s through seminal papers such as "The Concept of Human Agency" in which Taylor shows that the attempt to understand human agency in terms of a simple "belief-desire" model such as that put forward in Davidson's influential writings in the philosophy of actions leads to absurdities. Human agents are characterized by the fact that they inevitably affirm or reject their "first-order" desires on the basis of second-order evaluative commitments, what Taylor famously called "strong evaluations." These evaluations make it the case that human agents do not only act on the basis of the strongest occurrent desire, but rather that they evaluate their desires on the basis of a rich evaluative vocabulary that identifies different desires as noble or base, as involving the pursuit of values or not. This notion is introduced in Taylor's magisterial interpretation of the modern self, *Sources of the Self*, as that of "hypergoods."

Taylor has also been concerned with the proper philosophical understanding of the linguistic capacity of humans. Here, he inveighed against what he saw as a radically incomplete view of language, one that would exhaust linguistic meaning in terms of truth-conditional semantics, in other words, of the conditions under which linguistic utterances can be said to be true. Such reductive understandings of the linguistic behaviour of humans, Taylor has argued, cannot account for the full way in which humans use language. They use it not just faithfully to report on their observations of the world or of their inner states. Rather, they also express who they are and what they value through it, through the use of metaphor, through the use of tone and inflection that is such a pervasive aspect of human communicative behaviour. *The Language Animal*, published in 2014, is a summation of Taylor's work on the subject, and it is a clear instance of his ability to bring diverse philosophical sources to bear on the considerations of a philosophical topic, bridging as it does the analytic philosophy of language of such thinkers as Davidson and Robert Brandom, and the accounts of language present in thinkers such as Johann Georg Hamann, Johann Gottfried von Herder, and Heidegger.

Taylor's critique of a reductive conception of human action and of human linguistic behaviour meant that he found himself at odds with many of the philosophical assumptions underlying much of the social sciences of the post-war period. The aspiration of these sciences was to bring to the study of human societies and of their political institution's scientific methods analogous to those that had been deployed in the natural sciences to telling effect. While Taylor understood the emancipatory potential latent in the attempt to understanding the laws that underpin the collective life of humans, Taylor argued in highly influential essays such as "Interpretation and the Sciences of Man" that the positivist attempt to equate the understanding of human societies with the discovery of causal regularities present therein was doomed. If human agency is a function of the strong evaluations that human agents deploy when they act (whether consciously or not), then the human sciences cannot simply be about the uncovering of causal regularities that can be spelled out independently of the meanings and values that are constitutive of human agency. Rather than seeking explanations that will ultimately yield natural science-like predictability, social scientists should be involved in the business of interpreting: recovering and attempting to articulate the horizon of meanings that are fundamental to the self-understandings of those that they attempt to understand. Taylor's work in this area has been of great importance in bringing to light the importance of those he sees as interpretive social scientists *avant la lettre* such as the Baron de Montesquieu and Alexis de Tocqueville. It also brought the hermeneutical ideas of philosophers such as Hans Gadamer into the purview of modern social science.

As important as his work in action theory, as well as in the philosophies of mind, language, and social science, has been, it is probably as a contributor to debates in moral and political philosophy that Taylor has achieved the greatest academic renown. (It was after all a chair in political theory that Taylor was awarded at Oxford University). His work in these fields has been continuous with the arguments that he formulated in other areas of philosophy. In moral philosophy, Taylor argued in essays such as "The Diversity of Goods" against the dominant families of theories that would reduce the sources of moral obligation that apply to human agents to one overriding normative consideration. He argued against the utilitarian aspiration to reduce all objects of human aspiration to one monistic value such as utility, and has also devoted critical attention to the formalistic understanding of morality and of moral reasoning that in his view has characterized the Kantian tradition, from the works of Immanuel Kant himself all the way to the writings of the philosopher who has been one of his most faithful interlocutors, Jürgen Habermas.

In political philosophy, Taylor has been associated with the "communitarian" current of thought (in our view wrongly), which emerged in reaction to the works of such liberal theorists as John Rawls and Ronald Dworkin. Communitarians argued that liberals placed too much emphasis on the protection of individual rights, and not enough on community, and that they failed to appreciate the degree to which the self that liberalism portrays is a fiction. According to communitarians individual agents are thickly "encumbered" with values and normative commitments that they inherit from their social milieu. Taylor did not so much argue against the liberal focus on rights and on the protection of the individual. Rather, he held that many liberals tended to ignore the rich moral sources that the kind of moral individualism that is expressed through rights theories draws its inspiration from. Liberal theories are in Taylor's view not so much wrong as they are blind to their dependency on a conception of the good. This blindness has led liberals to emphasize notions such as value-neutrality that in Taylor's view led liberals to holding philosophically suspect positions. For example, he famously argued that the privilege accorded to a purely negative conception of liberty, according to which liberal theory and liberal institutions should emphasize the breadth of the freedom from interference that liberal citizens enjoy (as opposed, say, to their ability to exercise rational control over their desires, the hallmark of what Berlin termed "positive" liberty) does not allow us to account for the very great value that has traditionally been ascribed to liberty. Similarly, Taylor has questioned the emphasis placed by some liberal political theorists on the ideal of neutrality, since liberalism in his view embodies a conception of the good, rather than being neutral among such conceptions.

None of this should be taken to imply that liberal norms and principles should on Taylor's view be rejected. For example, in the report to the government of Quebec that Taylor co-authored in order to provide a framework for the granting of accommodations to cultural minorities, Taylor insisted on the importance of state neutrality with respect to religious (and non-religious) conceptions of the good, but he insisted at the same time that neutral political institutions can only be justified relative to the good that they facilitate the realization of.

Taylor's most widely discussed and influential essay in political philosophy has perhaps been his paper on multiculturalism, originally delivered as the inaugural lecture for the *Centre for Human Values* at Princeton University. In that essay, Taylor distances himself in a manner that is of a piece with his other contributions to political philosophy from interpretations of the theory and practice of multiculturalism that would ground it in value skepticism or in relativism. Multiculturalism is on Taylor's view best interpreted in the need for recognition that is a basic requirement of human subjectivity. In earlier periods, this requirement was satisfied by a cosmology and a corresponding social ontology in which the identity of human agents was tightly tied to their social status. Taylor recognized a modern period that has rid itself of belief in such orders is now tied to the cultural identities of agents. Far from undergirding an uncritical multiculturalism, Taylor's oft-misunderstood position is that cultures are worthy of protection to the degree that they allow for the flourishing of worthwhile identities, but that relations between cultural groups must be guided by the presumption of equal worth, since we lack anything like an Archimedean point from which to judge them.

The philosophical positions that Taylor has spent his career arguing against, philosophical positions according to which one can fully account for the human condition "scientifically," without adverting to a realm of meaning and significance, are ultimately in Taylor's view all poisoned fruits of certain trends within modernity. This trend has been in a sense associated with the rise to cultural dominance of the natural sciences. Appreciating the power of these sciences, and of the techniques of prediction and control of what had previously been seen as an "enchanted" but ultimately unknowable natural realm, many thinkers associated with the Enlightenment project have sought to import these methods into the understanding of human agents, of the societies that they inhabit and the institutions that they construct. But unlike some of the thinkers, such as Alasdair MacIntyre, who have also diagnosed many contemporary ills as rooted in intellectual trends born in the Enlightenment and who have recommended the rejection of many aspects of that project, Taylor is no anti-modernist or anti-rationalist. He has devoted much of the last thirty years of his intellectual career to reclaiming an understanding of modernity that, while it gives the scientific outlook its due, attempts to make room within it for a non-reductive conception of human agents. It is no accident that Taylor's first "big book" was an attempt to come to terms with, and to make intelligible to an Anglo-American audience, the thought of a philosopher who had fallen into disrepute in those philosophical quarters: G.W.F. Hegel. Hegel searched for a way to understand the development of the modern consciousness, and of modern institutions, that viewed them as resulting from the unfolding of rational spirit, and thus as imbued with meaning. Taylor's Hegel book provides us with a reading of Hegel's work that takes its systematic aspirations seriously while at the same time making a case for its philosophical plausibility (unlike, say, the work of Robert Solomon – who argued that Hegel could only be taken seriously if the systematic nature of the work was read ironically).

In a sense, the two volumes that together represent Taylor's prodigious attempt at vindicating modernity, *Sources of the Self*, published in 1989, and *A Secular Age*, published in 2007, can be read as his attempt at actualizing the Hegelian project. Throughout both, Taylor wants to make plausible through the intellectual narratives he weaves in the two works:

neither the rise of individualism, nor that of secularism, in the West, are best viewed "subtractively," that is as involving the negation of values and of dimensions of human life with which they are usually contrasted. Rather than being grounded in the denial of substantive values, modern individualism should, Taylor argues in *Sources,* be seen as the instantiation of a view of the modern individual as the locus of the aspiration for an "authentic" life inspired and guided by substantive sets of values, a view that found its definitive formulation among the thinkers of the Romantic period in Europe. Secularism, Taylor argues in *A Secular Age,* can be understood not along the lines of the kind of "disenchantment" narrative articulated by Max Weber, but rather as a process through which human agents find myriad ways to express their sense of the sacred through various forms of expression, be they aesthetic or spiritual.

A Summary of the Volume

The essays collected in this volume engage with the full range of Charles Taylor's philosophical contributions, from the philosophy of action and mind to political philosophy. They amply demonstrate that even Taylor's earliest writings still provide a rich source of philosophical inspiration. They show that Taylor's writings have been sources of inspiration for generations of philosophers and political theorists, as the volume brings together both Taylor's peers and younger academics who continue to find Taylor's work a necessary point of departure for their own, even when they find themselves disagreeing with it. The volume also importantly includes a conversation between Taylor and the editors, focussed on the themes and topics of the chapters.

The first section of the book brings together contributions by leading contributors to the philosophy of mind and the philosophy of action. In "To Follow a Rule: Lessons from Baby Logic," Shaun Gallagher identifies intimations of contemporary theories of the embodied mind. He shows that this conception of the mind, which locates the mind not just "in the head" but in the "minded" actions of the body as a whole, and of the rich socio-culturally constituted set of affordances through which the embodied mind develops, we are better situated to solve certain enduring puzzles in developmental psychology, and are in a better position to account for the "joint" attention which infants already manifest. This conception of the mind, Gallagher shows, is present in Taylor's earliest writings, as well as in his most recent *The Language Animal*.

In "Charles Taylor's Conception of Language and the Current Debate about a Theory of Meaning," Hans Schneider points to a limitation of Taylor's expressivist theory of language as expressed in his earlier writings as well as in *Language Animal*. Such theories, Schneider argues, are incapable of accounting for the structural features of language. Drawing on the work of the later Ludwig Wittgenstein, and siding with those who have come to be referred to as the "resolute readers" of Wittgenstein, Schneider argues against those theorists of language that would account for language in terms either of "pictures" or of "logical calculus." In line with Wittgenstein's view that there is no firm line in language between sense and nonsense, he argues for a creative, non-rule governed theory of linguistic structure along the lines of the one he defended in his book *Phantasie und Kalkül*.

In "Taylor's Engaged Pluralism," Richard Bernstein endeavours to pin down Taylor's distinctive epistemological stance. Bernstein claims that Taylor's work can be read as criticizing the dichotomy most often set up between universalism and relativism because "swinging between these unsatisfactory extremes distorts and obscures the real social, political and personal problems that we have to confront." Taylor's engaged pluralism is a more nuanced position. On the one hand, and contrary to the universalist approach, Taylor recognizes that there are incommensurabilities between our cultures, religions, politics, and morals; on the other, and unlike relativists, he acknowledges that those incommensurabilities do not constitute rigid epistemological or metaphysical barriers. Bernstein traces this epistemological commitment to a non-relativistic form of pluralism through a range of Taylor's arguments, including his embrace of Gadamerian "fusion of horizons," in his interpretation of secularism, and in his nuanced stances on political debates and controversies such as those that he provided nuanced interpretations of throughout his writings as a political commentator.

Tariq Modood and Ronald Beiner both engage with Taylor's contributions to the philosophy of religion, and of religious accommodation. In "State-Religion Connections and Multicultural Citizenship," Modood, engaging with Taylor's latter writings on multiculturalism and on state-religion relations, argues that there are apparent tensions between multiculturalism and liberalism and between multiculturalism and secularism, but that those tensions dissipate if we recognize that state-religion connexions are not, by themselves, normatively problematic. He thus argues those connexions are, in some contexts, integral to a historical and reasonable version of secularism. Echoing Taylor's arguments about state neutrality developed in *Secularism and Freedom of Conscience*, Modood argues that an approach of "multiplex privileging" – the complex arrangements of multiple privileging (of multiple values or goals) – is the way to integrate concerns for religion in the secular and multicultural state.

In "Taylor, Rawls, and Secularism," Ronald Beiner argues that Taylor's conception of secularism is excessively marked by his engagement, and by his at times backhanded integration, with normative requirements that have been argued for by liberals such as John Rawls. Rather than trying to show how his conception of religion's place in the public sphere can be made to cohere with Rawlsian neutrality, Beiner argues for a conception of a conception of the good articulated around a notion of citizenship that implies secularism as he and Taylor understand it.

The contributions by John Christman, Nancy Hirschmann, and Kwame Anthony Appiah engage with Taylor's conception of human agency and with his influential account of the self. In "What, If Anything, Is Wrong with Positive Liberty? The Struggles of Agency in a Non-Ideal World," John Christman develops a critique of some theorists' recent attempts to "resuscitate" a purely negative model of freedom. Instead, inspired by Taylor's own thoughts on the matter, Christman sketches a positive view of freedom that avoids the pitfalls of both a strictly negative approaches and perfectionist accounts of positive liberty that fail to abide by liberal strictures. In this paper Christman builds on Taylor's influential critique of a purely negative conception of liberty; he also develops a conception of "freedom as effective agency," which he argues avoids criticisms that have been heaped upon positive conceptions of freedom by liberal critics.

Hirschman endorses Taylor's views on positive freedom and concludes that he was right to rescue it in face of dichotomist and caricatured conceptions of freedom like those of Berlin but also of more recent authors such as Kateb and Flathman. The author argues that positive liberty improves upon negative liberty in three ways, of which Hirschmann argues that Taylor is not always aware. First, she argues, it allows us to see that the enjoyment of negative liberty often involves positive provision in order to overcome conditions such as disability and poverty. Second, it involves the overcoming of internal barriers, an aspect of positive liberty that Hirschmann defends against critics such as Berlin. Finally, Hirschmann argues that it opens the door to a social constructionist account of the self, one that fully acknowledges the interpenetration of self and social structures and culture. Hirschmann argues that Taylor does not sufficiently allow for external determinants to the self's constitution, operating as he does with a fairly self-contained picture of the human agent.

In "Self-Creation or Self-Discovery?" Kwame Anthony Appiah is at one with Taylor's rejection of the Humean account of the self that ascribes primacy to brute desires. He argues that Taylor's interpretivism allows us to formulate plausible answers to the question of how human agents develop answers to the question "Who am I?" These answers can split the difference between a Wittgensteinian approach that focuses on rule-following – but that does not in Appiah's view leave room for interpretation – and a view that sees identity as pure, unfettered self-creation. Taylor's work shows we always ask this question against a background of cultural values and within a "web of interlocution," one in which the resources upon which we draw in the interpretive exercise of self-making are always provided from those with whom we entertain dialogic relations.

Michael Rosen and William Connolly both engage with dimensions of Taylor's interpretation of modernity. In "Whatever Happened to the Ontic Logos?" Michael Rosen offers a different narrative for secularization to that deployed by Taylor in *A Secular Age*. Whereas Taylor concentrates on countering the subtraction theory and views secularization as an unforeseen consequence of Christianity's attempt to reform itself, Rosen emphasizes the problem of theodicy, the reconciliation of the existence of God with the presence of evil in the world. Rosen emphasizes Kant as the pivotal figure who transformed the traditional question of theodicy into that of justice, and whose conception of the Kingdom of Ends lays the grounds for the transformation of the question of theodicy into a political one. Rosen sees Johann Gottlieb Fichte as the figure who radicalized this argument of Kant's, and whose rejection of an otherworldly reconciliation of goodness and happiness opens the door to the figure of the modern revolutionary who identifies his own good with that of his community.

In "Taylor, Fullness and Vitality," William Connolly engages with the notion of "fullness," a notion that is central to Taylor's account of secularism in *A Secular Age*. Fullness as construed by Taylor is meant to convey the subjective experience of one's life as reflecting or sensitive to transcendent sources of meaning and value. Connolly in his engagement with Taylor aims to elucidate a concept, "vitality," which is meant to take on the same centrality in his account of lived experience as Taylor ascribed to "fullness," but without invoking a conception of transcendence. Connolly's objective is to introduce a master concept, borrowed from Whitehead, that can have the depth, richness, power, and feeling we have of admiration with the concept of fullness (and the absence we feel without it) while still remaining committed to immanence. Vitality is linked with spontaneous creativity and newness in the act of creation. Of course, this is not Kantian spontaneity; it is constituted by preconditions and restraints and emerges from them, but never in a way we could have predicted. Vitality, for Connolly, exceeds fullness. It is the strand linking other concepts such as "agency, creativity, and freedom," which animates arguments between both traditions of positive and negative liberty.

Essays by Joseph Heath and by Nigel DeSouza engage with the implications of Taylor's interpretivism and of his distinctive form of naturalism (one that does not assume that the natural sciences have come up with the most perspicuous conception of nature) for ethical theory. In "An Explicative Conception of Moral Theory," Joseph Heath identifies and critiques a number of ways in which moral theory practiced by moral philosophers can be said to lie in an interpretive relation with the conventional moral practice and understandings of ordinary moral agents. Heath argues that the most adequate account, one which should guide the practice of moral philosophers, is explicative. That is, he holds that moral theorists should aim to explain the patterns that obtain in ordinary moral judgment, without assuming that these explications will give rise to single principles. For example, conventional moral judgment seeks to find a place both for deontological and for consequentialist moral reasoning. Moral theorists should therefore not seek to jettison the one in favour of the other. Heath argues that his explicative view is not bereft of critical purchase, as it can involve holding a community accountable before the principles that best explain its moral practice.

In "Charles Taylor and Ethical Naturalism," Nigel DeSouza uncovers some of the commonalities that unite the work of Taylor on the one hand, and David Wiggins and John McDowell on the other, commonalities which Taylor himself does not always acknowledge. These commonalities underpin a distinctive form of ethical naturalism, one that resists the reduction of naturalism to scientism. Where De Souza sees real differences between the three thinkers is in Taylor's phenomenological method, one that allows him to go beyond the genetic accounts to be found in

McDowell and Wiggins. What is missing from McDowell and Wiggins' account of values on DeSouza's reading is what Taylor captures with the expression "the phenomenology of the incommensurably higher." This difference gives rise to a more robust conception of agency, one that emphasizes human agents' connection to something that transcends them, which Taylor calls "fullness."

Cécile Laborde and Rajeev Bhargava engage with Taylor's political philosophy. In "Protecting Freedom of Religion in the Secular Age," Laborde takes aim at the arguments put forward by Taylor in his co-authored work with Jocelyn Maclure. In her view, Taylor and Maclure collapse freedom of religion into freedom of conscience, a philosophical move that gives rise to three undesirable consequences. First, she argues, such a move fails to provide any way in which to counter fundamentalist and rigid interpretations of religious dogma. Second, by emphasizing the individual conscience, it makes it difficult to account for the value of religious community and of cultural membership. Third, it does not provide us with a way of distinguishing between the kinds of beliefs and convictions that are worthy of protection, and those that are comparatively trivial. Recourse to the notion of "strong evaluation," which is central to Taylor's conception of agency, is not adequate to the task of addressing this flaw.

In "Two Conceptions of Indian Secularism," Rajeev Bhargava emphasizes the pluralism inherent in the very notion of "secularism." Secularism, Bhargava argues, has to do with the separation of organized religion from political power, a structural feature that can be realized in many different ways, and whose manifestations throughout the world are highly path dependent. Bhargava argues that the notion of "separation" inherent to the concept of secularism needs to be disambiguated. Separation can have to do with the ends of the state, with its institutions, or with its laws and policies. Investigating Western models of secularism, which he identifies respectively with France, the United States, and Europe (excluding France), Bhargava shows that there have been great differences between secularisms as to the levels at which they deem separation to be most important, and as to the question of whether some entanglement of religion with politics precludes a state from calling itself secular. Turning to India, Bhargava shows that there are two ways in which secularism has been understood, one which emphasizes the even-handedness of the state in relation to all religions, and one which constitutionally entrenches powers of self-determination over such areas as education for religious groups. Bhargava's plea is for a more nuanced conception of secularism than many political philosophers have worked with, one that is alive to the plurality of values that underpin its various instantiations.

In "Memory, Multiculturalism and the Sources of Democratic Solidarity," Michele Moody-Adams engages with Taylor's notion of "modern social imaginaries." While she agrees with Taylor that we need a richer account of the bases of social solidarity in modern democracies marked by the "fact of pluralism" than that found, for example, in John Rawls's account of "overlapping consensus," she holds that Taylor's account is insufficiently sensitive to the challenges of social solidarity over time. She argues that Taylor needs to take into account the "deep horizontal comradeship" or "fraternity" involved in healthy democracies since synchronically, democracies are communities of memory that persist over time. Moody-Adams proposes to supplement Taylor's theory with the addition of the idea of a civic ethos that coheres a democracy into a true community yet does not exclude minorities in the act of political identity formation. She argues this civic ethos must include three civic virtues that must be inculcated into the citizenry. She terms these values "civic trust" (which has to do with the fund of "social capital" upon which a diverse citizenry can draw), "civic sacrifice" (for example the willingness to make mundane material sacrifices from which one does not then immediately benefit), and "civic grace," the latter concept referring to the willingness to treat political opponents with civility.

Finally Jeremy Webber, in "Recognition in Its Place," distinguishes two conceptions of recognition that are, in his view, possible interpretations of the views Taylor put forward in his famous essay on "Multiculturalism and the Politics of Recognition." One conception, labeled "Recognition 1" by Webber, emphasizes differential state rules to accommodate cultural diversity, while the second, "Recognition 2," emphasizes symbolic recognition and affirmation. Webber critiques this latter conception, arguing that it unhelpfully psychologizes the concept of recognition, and is implicitly based in a static and de-politicized view of minority cultural groups. Though he argues that there is much in Taylor's writing that seems to point toward this second, deficient view, Webber also claims that the resources exist within Taylor's work to mount a successful argument in favour of the first of these two conceptions.

No single book could do justice to the full richness of Taylor's *oeuvre*, to which Taylor continues to add important instalments well into his eighties. But the essays collected here show that almost all domains of philosophy can benefit from a deep engagement with the work of Charles Taylor.

PART ONE

Epistemology, Philosophy of Mind, and Philosophy of Language

1

To Follow a Rule

LESSONS FROM BABY LOGIC

SHAUN GALLAGHER

In his essay "To Follow a Rule,"[1] Charles Taylor begins with Wittgenstein's considerations about the kind of understanding involved in rule-following, and ends with Bourdieu's idea of habitus. Taylor supports the idea that the kind of understanding involved in following a rule is a form of embodied, pragmatic understanding rather than something like a higher cognitive comprehension favoured by intellectualism. Thus, an agent can be guided by a rule without comprehending a large number of problems that seemingly must be solved from an intellectualist perspective. Taylor acknowledges throughout his essay that these issues have much to do with intersubjective relations and how we understand others.

For Taylor rules should not be understood in terms of causal regularities. Neither is it the case, however, that they belong exclusively to the space of reasons. If they do represent patterns of reasons for actions, he suggests, "reason-giving has a limit" – or as we might say, rules do not provide reasons all the way down. At some point they translate into embodied practices.

> A rule that exists only in the practices it animates, and does not require and may not have any express formulation. How can this be? Only through our embodied understanding. This is what Bourdieu is trying to get at with the habitus. It is "a system of durable and transposable dispositions," dispositions to bodily comportment, say, to act, to hold oneself, or to gesture in a certain way. A bodily disposition is a habitus when it encodes a certain cultural

understanding ... Children are inducted into a culture, are taught the meanings which constitute it, partly through inculcating the appropriate habitus.[2]

One can take this as a starting point for further and productive discussions about habitus and institutions in the larger social/cultural environments, as Bourdieu and Taylor do. For my purposes here, however, I want to stay with some of the issues just mentioned – issues that concern embodiment, intersubjectivity, and enculturation. To do this, I first want to ask what position Taylor occupies on issues raised in the recent debate between Hubert Dreyfus and John McDowell – a debate that involved Taylor in an indirect and implicit way, and that resulted in his essay "Retrieving Realism."[3] Second, I then want to take a 180-degree turn and look back on the developmental timeline to ask about where and how precisely for the child the process of habitus building starts.

Let me note that for my purposes, embodiment, dialogical interaction, and the background are three important and interrelated aspects in Taylor's analysis. The notion of background, or what Bruner and Kalmar[4] call the "massive hermeneutical background," however, will for the most part stay in the background in the following discussion. This is not to deny that it plays a large role in our pragmatic understanding of rules, and in our intersubjective understanding of others – especially going forward into the larger framework of social and cultural institutions.[5] It derives from and helps to constitute the meaning of embodied and dialogical interactive practices in which children are already involved when they begin to attain a narrative competency (at around three to four years of age); something that further expands the background and carries it forward. The notion of background is also tied to discussions of both phronesis and language in the Dreyfus-McDowell debate.

Between Dreyfus and McDowell

In his APA Presidential Address, Dreyfus,[6] with McDowell in mind, rejects the idea that perception is conceptual and defends his long-held views on non-conceptual embodied coping – we are in-the-world primarily in terms of embodied skills. He rejects the "myth of the mental" – the idea that the mind is pervasive in perception and action – and holds that perception and action most often occur without mental intervention.

At the same APA conference, I participated in a panel discussion Dreyfus organized on just these topics. The discussion focused on the work of Samuel Todes,[7] who greatly influenced Dreyfus by providing an analysis of perception and action with an exclusive emphasis on embodied practices. Todes's analysis lacks any reference to intersubjectivity. He assumes that object perception can be adequately analyzed without introducing any considerations about our interactions with others. Following Todes's strategy, we would come to understand the fullness and complexity of human perception and action by first understanding how an isolated body, moving alone in the world, perceives non-living objects. Then we would have the option to add to this an analysis of how others enter into the picture. I suggested, during the panel and in subsequent publications,[8] that the type of approach taken by Todes, and by Dreyfus himself, is pragmatically solipsistic, insofar as it leaves the effects of intersubjectivity on action and perception out of account. Similar criticisms of Dreyfus have been made by Young,[9] Sheets-Johnstone,[10] and Collins,[11] all of whom suggest that social and cultural contexts play no part in Dreyfus's account of expertise, where one finds an overly exclusive emphasis on embodied practice. As we'll see, this raises some problems with Dreyfus's appeal to the concept of phronesis as a model for embodied coping skills.

McDowell[12] defends the idea that perception and embodied coping are conceptual/rational, and not as "mindless" as Dreyfus contends. Dreyfus[13] takes this to mean perception is "upper floor" all the way down, and that McDowell ignores non-conceptual, situated embodied coping. McDowell, Dreyfus claims, is taken by the myth of the mental, that is, the pervasiveness of detached or off-line cognitive, mental, and reflective attitudes throughout human action. McDowell insists, however, rationality does not have to be situation independent, and this can be seen in his own reference to the Aristotelian notion of phronesis as a model for situated rationality – one that Dreyfus himself takes for embodied coping. For McDowell, however, phronesis involves an initiation into conceptual capacities.

In contrast, Dreyfus refers us to Heidegger's concept of phronesis – a way of understanding that makes possible an immediate, non-conceptual, zuhanden response to the full concrete situation.[14] For McDowell this doesn't decide the issue of whether we should consider perception and action rational, i.e., conceptual. McDowell acknowledges Heidegger's influence on his understanding of Aristotle's view – something he had learned via his reading of Gadamer's Truth and Method. McDowell furthermore notes that it was Charles Taylor who had recommended Gadamer's text. From Gadamer he learns that "the practical rationality of the *phronimos* is displayed in what he does even if he does not decide to do that as a result of reasoning."[15] Reasoning is the activity of explicitly deciding which affordances to respond to and how to go about responding to them. McDowell calls this our "means-end rationality," which involves a "stepping back." Importantly, for McDowell the fact that we are able to give reasons for our action, even if we did not form deliberative reasons prior to the action, suggests that our actions/embodied copings have an implicit structure that is rational and amenable to conceptuality.[16]

For Dreyfus, following Heidegger, the idea of giving reasons for our actions, involves the detached, reflective rationality associated with language (*logos*) – propositional discourse, the space of reasons, and conceptual articulation. For McDowell[17] following Gadamer, language is what sets humans off from non-human animals. Language, importantly, expands the background that informs our actions and perceptions. For McDowell, language use is closely tied to situation – our openness to the world involves a situated categorial aspect – this allows us to register it linguistically (even if we don't always do so). Another way to put this: we are not "ready in advance" to put a word to every aspect of experience, but following Gadamer and Heidegger, we have a pre-ontological understanding that informs our experience – and McDowell would interpret this as a conceptual understanding. For McDowell, language provides the massive hermeneutical background that provides us with a world (a proto-conceptual structure, and not just the immediacy of the environment).

Dreyfus, however, while agreeing that we have freedom to step back and take a reflective stance,[18] insists on the difference between embodied coping and the reflective, language-informed attitude. He distinguishes affordances as facts (features of the world) from affordances as solicitations. When we step back and contemplate them, affordances can be experienced as features of the world; but when we respond to their solicitations they remain somewhat transparent. McDowell, according to Dreyfus, assumes that the world is already a set of determinate facts that can then be named and thought. But, "the indeterminate is not implicitly conceptual and simply waiting to be named. Our relation to the world is more basic than our mind's being open to apperceiving categorially unified facts."[19] Dreyfus has in mind here the phenomenological concept of motor intentionality, as found in Merleau-Ponty,[20] as a more basic, non-conceptual way of relating to the world. Accordingly, for Dreyfus, the background is more like the habitus; it doesn't have to wait for language since it is already acquired in the embodied practices that are capable of producing phronesis.

If Taylor recommends a Gadamerian view of phronesis and language, he may seem closer to the McDowell side of this debate; at the same time, the way that Taylor thinks about rationality and rule-governed behaviour, puts him closer to the Dreyfus position. If for Taylor our actions/embodied copings have a structure that is rational, he would likely want to insist on a concept of rationality that is, in the first place, an embodied pragmatic rationality. On this conception of what I would call an "enactive rationality," the world is laid out in perception, not in terms of a conceptual, or proto-conceptual meaning, but first of all, in terms of differentiations that concern action possibilities. Accordingly, the object is something I can reach, or not; something I can lift, or not; something I can move, or not; and our ability for making sense of the world comes, in part, from an active and pragmatic engagement with the world.

Rationality in Hand

I take this Taylorian position, between Dreyfus and McDowell, to be consistent with an embodied and enactive conception of the mind, where the mind is not something purely "in the head," but is distributed in our engaged activities in the world. As such, in contrast to Dreyfus, we could say that action and everyday coping is indeed "minded," but that the mind is not what either Dreyfus or McDowell seem to think it is. Consider the rationality implicit in the hand. Hands are action oriented and smart. As an agent reaches to grasp something, the hand automatically shapes itself into just the right posture to form the most appropriate grip for that object and for the agent's purpose. If I reach to grab an apple in order to take a bite, the shape of my grasp is different than when I reach to grab a banana, but also different from when I reach to grab the apple to throw it.[21] The hand does not do this blindly; it requires the cooperation of the dorsal visual stream to provide visual information about the shape of the apple and where in the near environment it is located. But the brain evolved to do *what it does* in this regard only because it had hands to work with, hands that evolved with the brain, and continue to work with the brain, in a holistic relation with other bodily aspects of (upright) posture. More generally, the brain is what it is, and does what it does, only because it is part of a human body that has certain capabilities tied to its anatomical structure.

Robertson and Treisman[22] reported on a patient with visual agnosia who was unable to recognize objects or say what they were. "When the patient was shown a picture of a clarinet, he hesitated in naming it, suggested it was a 'pencil,' but meanwhile his fingers began to play an imaginary clarinet." Our hands express this kind of wherewithal all the time in doing what they do, in gesture and in action. The body and its movement are characterized by a motor intentionality that can be more minded or rational than what is traditionally considered the mind.[23] Bodily behaviour is minded along the lines described by Horst Bredekamp[24] as a kind of manual thinking (*manuelles Denken*). The manual thinking of the hand has the potential to differentiate the manipulatory area of the surrounding environment in pragmatic terms (reachable, non-reachable; graspable, non-graspable, throwable, non-throwable, etc.) and to integrate its action in ways that link up to all perceptual modalities, including touch and haptic exploration, hand-mouth coordination, hand-eye coordination, shading the eyes, cupping the ears, holding one's nose, waving away a bad smell, and so forth.

The primary rationality of the hand not only facilitates perception and action; it transforms its movements into language (via gesture) and into thinking. Evidence from gesture studies suggests that there are close relationships between gesture, speech, and thinking – they are part of the same system, which David McNeill calls the hand-language-thought system.[25] Evidence of such connections can be found in experiments by Susan Goldin-Meadow[26] on solving math problems with and without gesture – where gesture improves speed and accuracy and, so to speak, adds to the rationality of one's problem solving. In this regard there is no break, no discontinuity, no "stepping back" that comes between this kind of movement (gesture) and spoken language – nor between manual thinking and minded thinking. They are part of the same system.

One might easily think, however, that this insight, moving from hand to gesture/language to thought, placing them in one system, plays directly into to McDowell's argument. McDowell seemingly makes this point when he accuses Dreyfus of treating minded/mental processes as disconnected from the body – the myth of the disembodied intellect. But as Zahavi[27] correctly points out, both Dreyfus and McDowell adopt an overly intellectualized (conceptualized, languaged) conception of the mind. In contrast to this traditional, internalist, and conceptualist conception of mind (which Dreyfus rejects, thereby ending up with something close to mindless behaviour, and which McDowell attempts to push all the way down into the structure of basic action), we should think of mind as instantiated in forms of embodied coping that emerge from a pre-predicative perceptual ordering of differentiations and similarities.

From the agentive perspective, there is no question here of rule following, unless, as Taylor indicates, it is "a rule that exists only in the practices it animates, and does not require and may not have any express formulation." It may (or, depending on circumstances, may not) be possible to stand back after the fact and describe or demonstrate a set of rules that may partially characterize such actions and engagements. The claim might then be made that the agent acts in accordance with such rules. Such rules, however, do not capture or explain the agent's motivation or how she sees the situation, which nonetheless does not mean that the action is irrational. The concept of rationality at stake here is closer to the notion of phronesis, or practical rationality, a form of rationality that develops in the habitus, in the world, in the action. It's a form of rationality that allows the agent to meaningfully differentiate A from B (e.g., apples from bananas), without necessarily having a concept of A or B.

For McDowell, if one can put this difference into words then conceptuality (a more traditional rationality associated with judging, deciding, reasoning, and spontaneity, in the Kantian sense) is already implicit, part of the very structure of the action. Even if words are unavailable or one is unable to describe the difference, an ostensive differentiation will do to signal a conceptual sense. The fact that we can reflectively push our skilful discriminations into conceptual categories, however, does not mean that our skilful discriminations are conceptual to begin with.

If we accept this enactive view we might think that this is the end of the story, and that we already have what we need to formulate a different conception of the mind (more embodied, more enactive) than either Dreyfus or McDowell proposes, and one not far from what Charles Taylor could endorse. But to stop here, as Taylor reminds us, would be to remain pragmatically solipsistic – and indeed, the hand does not fail to gesture and point us in a direction that suggests that something more is involved – namely, that action, gesture, language, and thinking are not things that happen without others.

It is true that the perceived world is laid out in a set of spatial (egocentric) and pragmatic distinctions relative to the body – up, down, left, right, reachable, not reachable, etc. But it also presents itself as a set of intersubjective differences between those things in the environment that count as, and that we perceive as agents and those that do not. We also perceive the world in terms of affective, hedonic, and value distinctions that are tied to what I see other agents do[28] – such things that I learn by way of a natural pedagogy.[29]

We should be able to recognize the importance of escaping the kind of pragmatic solipsism that characterizes Dreyfus's accounts of everyday coping and specialized cases of expertise by returning to the question of phronesis – of which both Dreyfus and McDowell want to make use – a certain kind of practiced excellence in pragmatically (action-oriented) knowing what to do. Phronesis is closely tied to the contextualized situation (we judge or act case by case). It can be either/both intuitive/automatic (Dreyfus) or reflective/deliberative (McDowell). On an enactive view, however, reflective deliberation is a skill continuous with embodied coping; and reflection itself may be intuitive or close to automatic or, if necessary, metacognitive and strategic. In this regard, phronesis itself can be expertly skilful only if it has been practiced sufficiently. In addition, however, and most importantly, phronesis is intersubjective.

Phronesis, as Aristotle tells us, is something that we learn from hanging around with others. Our worldly knowledge, and our ability to do and to reflect are gained in very basic, intersubjective interactions – seeing things as others see them, imitating, doing what others do, valuing what others value, in processes that involve enactive rationality, natural pedagogy, social norms, situated reflection, etc. Taylor helps us to see the importance of intersubjectivity at a basic embodied level. He suggests that "my sense of myself and the footing I am on with others is in large part also embodied,"[30] here with reference to even the physical postures and movements I make in my interactions with others. In such cases, the understanding involved (which, if rightly formed, I would identify with a form of phronesis), "is carried in patterns of appropriate action, which conform to a sense of what is fitting and right. Agents with this kind of understanding recognize when they or others have put a foot wrong. Their actions are responsive throughout to this sense of rightness, but the 'norms' may be quite unformulated, or only in fragmentary fashion."[31]

To the extent that phronesis involves formulation, or situated reflective deliberation, and to the extent that it can be taken as a model of rationality, it is a form of thinking *without thinking about it*, continuous with and cut from the same fabric as embodied coping – which is both action *and interaction*. The fact that we may be able to *step back* – to detach ourselves from the demands of the immediate environment, to have a second-order, conceptual, reflective thought – does not make thinking any less of an embodied/intersubjective skill. Reflective thinking, like perception, is an embodied performance, and in this regard we should think of concepts as affordances that allow us to do things, to solve problems, to communicate with others, to construct institutions, etc.

ToM and Behavioural Rules?

Now, making the 180-degree turn, let's ask about where all of this gets its start. Developmental studies provide evidence for such perceptual and action-related and intersubjective differentiations in very young infants – and such evidence counters all myths: the myth of the given, the myth of the mental (in Dreyfus's sense), as well as the myth of solipsism. Specifically I want to focus on questions pertaining to social cognition where, on some accounts, there seems to be a certain rule following involved. To help us focus on this issue I'll refer to recent experiments with young infants that purportedly show that thirteen- to fifteen-month-olds are capable of recognizing false beliefs. The relevance of this issue can be seen in frequent references in the Dreyfus-McDowell debate to "basic perceptual capacities we seem to share with pre-linguistic infants and higher animals,"[32] and the fact that there is a similar ongoing debate about the status of conceptuality and rule following centred around these experiments.

Standard false-belief tests have pointed to ages three to four years as significant since at around four years, on average, children begin to be able to recognize when another person has a false belief about a particular situation. One interpretation is that children around four years attain a theory of mind (ToM), which allows them to "mindread" the other person's mental states. The theory known as theory theory (TT) claims that at this age the child gains the ability to use folk psychology to make inferences (following rules of inference) about the other person's mental states. One version of TT proposes that individuals (or individual brains) have a cognitive mechanism, or set of mechanisms, that literally house the rules and representations that form the basis of our folk psychological mind-reading competencies. The relevant mechanism may be an innate module,[33] or something that acquires the rules through learning.[34]

Despite claims made by theory theorists about the implicit (or even sub-personal) nature of the theoretical inference involved, the standard false belief tests that are cited as evidence for such inferential processes are completely explicit. The child is asked to observe a situation and to make a conscious judgment about where some third person (or, usually, some puppet, doll, or cartoon character) will look for a toy that has been moved, unbeknownst to that person. Accordingly, such tests involve third-person observational strategies, and are designed to require a personal-level inference. On average, three-year-olds fail the test and four-year-olds pass it. What is tested in such experiments (namely, the child's ability to mindread the third person with whom they are not interacting), and the explanations of how this happens completely ignore the successful second-person interaction that happens between child (including the three-year-old child) and experimenter. As we'll see, this is an important point if we are to explain why the three-year old fails the test, while younger infants seemingly pass false belief tests.

Recent experiments[35] purportedly show that thirteen- and fifteen-month-old infants pass more implicit false belief tests. The infant witnesses an agent place a toy in location A and then either leave the room or turn away. The toy is shifted to location B when the agent cannot see the shift. The agent then returns to look for the toy. The information the agent has should lead her to look in location A, where she falsely believes the toy to be. The agent, however, looks in location B. The infant looks longer at this behavior indicating a violation of expectation (VOE) about where the agent would look[36] That is, the infant seemingly recognizes that the agent has a false belief about where the toy is located and is surprised when the agent unexpectedly looks in the other place. In other experiments,[37] the infants' anticipated looking (AL) at a specific target (in this case, A) indicates where they expect the agent to look for the toy. The experimental results are surprising precisely because the TT consensus had been that infants this young (thirteen to fifteen months) were thought not to have a concept of belief, and certainly not to be capable of representing (or engaging in the kind of metarepresentational process necessary to grasp) false belief.

Despite that, the theory theorists interpret the results in terms of TT: the infant is able to attribute a false belief to the agent. Carruthers, for example, sees this performance as "evidence of very early metarepresentational competence in infants, embracing false-belief understanding."[38] Baillargeon, Scott, and He conclude that the infant not only *infers* that the agent's mental state consists of a false belief, but that the child can reason about a complex set of mental states.[39]

An alternative interpretation is offered by the *behavioural rules* theory, proposed by Ruffman and Perner.[40] On this account, the infant is governed by knowledge of behavioural rules (e.g., "people look for objects where they last saw them") gained via statistical learning abilities.[41] This account, however, still requires some kind of inference on the part of the infant, and, obviously, some kind of rule following.

Baillargeon, Scott, and He[42] suggest that the behavioural rules explanation fails because of the large number of rules that would be needed in a variety of situations involving false beliefs. Low and Wang,[43] however, defend the behavioural rule view by pointing out that in many cases ToMistic mindreading may entail even more rules. Furthermore, it is not clear why infants should not be able to apply more general perception and action principles especially if infants spend their entire first year interacting with others and begin to engage in joint attention and joint actions starting around nine to twelve months.

On the one hand, TT – relying on mentalistic conceptions of inference to mental states – offers the kind of intellectualist (representationalist) analysis that Taylor rightly criticizes. It attributes to the infant a high level of meta-cognitive skills or a set of sub-personal representations that work mechanistically. On the other hand, behavioural interpretations require a mechanistic, causal process of abstraction to general rules, and then inference from rule to predicted action. Both approaches, as Low and Perner[44] make clear, are methodologically individualistic – they look for mechanisms within the individual subject – and they ignore the contribution of interaction, or the potential for interaction, settling for monological (pragmatically solipsistic) mechanisms (a theory-of-mind module or some equivalent brain mechanism) that can run conscious or unconscious inferences.

Taylor's citation of Bourdieu is relevant: "To pass from a regularity ... to a rule consciously and deliberately edited and respected or to an unconscious regulation of a mysterious unconscious brain or social mechanism are the two most common ways of shifting from the model of reality to the reality of the model."[45] In retrospective reflection, or from the perspective of a scientific observer, we can devise a rule to explain the behaviour. But this doesn't tell us how the infant understands *when*, and *how*, and *with whom* to apply the rule. Taylor calls this the "phronetic gap." Here we can return to our previous discussion of the intersubjective aspect of phronesis. There is a way to answer this question in the case of older children or adults – much as Aristotle proposes in regard to phronesis: our upbringing, in part, provides the proper kind of understanding – the massively hermeneutical background (which we get via our dialogical interactions and our learned narratives) needed to get the process of understanding others started. The thirteen-month-old is closer to the beginning of this process; she does not yet have the massive hermeneutical background; she is not yet to the point of having narrative competency – or, for that matter, a folk psychology. She remains outside of the space of reasons. But that does not mean that her behaviour is irrational or that it can be reduced to mechanistic causes. Rather, what is significant is that since birth she has been dialogically interacting with others in a strongly embodied and enactive way.

The No-Rules Alternative

One way to cash out Taylor's intuitions about the role of embodiment and dialogical interaction is to understand infants as applying perception-action principles in an enactive, and, as Dan Hutto[46] puts it, "unprincipled" way. On this view, infants understand others in terms of *how they can interact with them*, or in terms of the infant's engagement in what the other is doing or expressing or feeling. Merleau-Ponty[47] suggests that "the other's intentions somehow play across my body" as a set of possibilities for my action. I see the other's action as aimed at the world in ways that offer social affordances for interacting. This may apply even in cases where I am observing rather than actually interacting with the agent. The agent's involvement in the world, which I see, can influence my expectations in terms of the possible or potential interactions I can have with that person.

Experiments that involve dialogical interaction rather than just observation offer some insight into this idea.[48] Buttelmann et al. show that eighteen-month-old children attempt to help an agent retrieve a toy while taking into account the fact that the agent hasn't seen a switch of location (the false belief situation).[49] In that situation, when the agent focuses on the wrong location (A), the infant is ready to lead him to the correct location (B), but not in the situation when the agent knows about the switch, i.e., the true belief situation, and still goes to A. In the latter case the infant goes to assist the agent at A. The infant sees exactly the same in the case of true belief (when the agent knows there has been a shift from A to B) as in the case of false belief (when the agent does not know about the shift). The fact that the infant sees either that the agent has seen the switch or not, plus the agent's behaviour with respect to A (e.g., moving to the container at A and attempting to open it), is enough to specify the difference in the agent's intention – an intention that is built into the agent's movements within the situation. The intention signals a difference in affordance, i.e., a difference in how the infant can act, and thereby interact with the agent. The infant does not have to make inferences to mental states or consult a set of behavioral rules since all of the information needed to understand the other and to interact is already available in what the infant has seen of the situation.

The enactive approach to social cognition emphasizes embodied dialogical interaction.[50] On this view, the capacity for understanding social situations complicated by an agent's lack of information is closely intertwined with the infant's ability to deploy social competences that engage with those situations. Even in cases where the infant is allowed only to observe, the violation of expectations may be a violation of affordance expectation – the fact that the agent goes to B rather than A does not present the expected affordance for the infant's own potential action. Even in the case of observation, the agent's involvement in the world, which I see, can influence my expectations in terms of the possible or potential interactions I can have with that person.

I have suggested that this kind of enactive account is consistent with Taylor's position concerning rule following. Taylor points us towards an embodied understanding of rule following that exists only in the practices it animates. In contrast to McDowell, and in a move that is closer to Dreyfus, Taylor maintains that such rules do not require and may not have an express formulation. I have suggested that an interactive-enactive model provides for this unprincipled set of dispositions that guide bodily comportment to act and to interact. This tells us how the formation of a habitus begins and how an infant can be inducted into a culture, a set of norms, without an explicit rule following.

The strongest habitus is one that is set in intersubjective interaction, and this may help to explain why thirteen- to eighteen-month-old infants seemingly pass false belief tests while three-year-old children fail the standard variety of such tests. As Pierre Jacob[51] has pointed out, the tasks are quite different, and the difference between explicit requirements (in the standard tests) and implicit opportunities (in the young infant tests) puts the infants in a different situation. To be more precise, on Jacob's account, it is the difference in perspectives involved in the two kinds of tests. In the standard test, the infant is required to deal with two perspectives – the third-person perspective required to make a judgment about the other person (or puppet, etc.) that the child is *not* interacting with, and the second-person perspective required to interactively engage with the experimenter. In the young infant tests, the infant is required to engage only in a (real or potential) second-person perspective with the person with whom they are interacting, or potentially interacting. As I understand Jacob's explanation, it is the number of perspectives that makes for the complicating difference – a child dealing with only one perspective is less likely to become confused about what is required than a child (even at three years) who is required to deal with two perspectives at once. The standard task is complicated.

Rubio-Fernández and Geurts make a similar point.[52] On their view a number of factors (e.g., the number of characters involved, the disappearance of the agent during the experiment) in the standard false-belief tasks interfere with the three-year-old child's ability to track the perspective of the agent. In their experiment, the "Duplo task" (so called because it creates the test scenario using Duplo toys, i.e., large Lego toys for small children) certain aspects of the situation are redesigned to eliminate complexity and to support the child's ability to track the agent's perspective, which then allows three-year-olds to pass the false-belief test.

Let me offer a slightly different explanation. Rather than the number of perspectives, or the complexity of the task, per se, I suggest that in the case of the standard test which the three-year-old fails, the second-person interaction (with the experimenter) has a saliency that takes precedence over the third-person task, and biases the child's answer. Both the child and the experimenter have a common knowledge of where the toy really is, and in their real interaction with each other, this shared knowledge becomes the salient feature and motivates the (wrong) answer to the third-person task. In the standard experiment, the three-year-old more consistently provides the answer that is facilitated by the second-person interaction with the experimenter. The modifications introduced by Rubio-Fernández and Geurts in the Duplo task are consistent with this view since they rearrange the experiment in a way that makes the interaction with the experimenter support (rather than distract from) the child's ability to track the perspective of the agent. Indeed, in the Duplo task, not only does the child interact with the experimenter, she is also invited to interact with the agent.[53]

The saliency of the second-person interactive relation – building on the habitus that has already been established in the infant's earlier primary and secondary intersubjective relations with others – biases the child's response, one way or the other, in all of these tests. The four-year-old, for various reasons pertaining to the development of narrative competency[54] and reflective skills, is better able to step back from the interaction with the experimenter in the standard task, and to manage the conflict of perspectives. This doesn't mean that he stops interacting (with the experimenter), but that he is better able to integrate his reflective coping skills with this ongoing interaction.

Conclusion

Rather than following rules, Wittgenstein suggests that in many everyday circumstances one engages in practices; Taylor wants to add that in many such circumstances these are social practices. We do not follow rules mechanistically because we are hardwired to do so; and to follow a rule we do not require a top-down intellectualistic understanding that would allow us to give precise reasons for following a rule. Between these two positions we can find an account of social practices, and their development in infancy, that avoids pragmatic solipsism and allows for a conception of mind that is both enactively embodied and also capable of reflective thinking. This Taylorian position gestures toward a rich terrain that can be sketched out between Dreyfus and McDowell on the one hand, and between a top-heavy, monological theory of mind and a bottomed-out behaviourism on the other. Neither "top floor all the way down," nor "basement all the way up."[55]

2

Charles Taylor's Conception of Language

AND THE CURRENT DEBATES ABOUT A THEORY OF MEANING

HANS J. SCHNEIDER

Many years ago, Charles Taylor published a long paper[1] in which he pointed out limits and shortcomings in the standard theories of meaning, i.e., in the semantics of truth conditions in the tradition of Frege and Davidson. Taylor has returned to this subject a number of times,[2] and his insistence on this topic is fully justified since one cannot say that his critical comments have been heeded, as they should have been. On the contrary: what he had criticized in many quarters of philosophy still counts as common wisdom.

Taylor's complaint is twofold: the first point is that the standard theory *leaves out* important aspects of what is done in language, such as the articulation of something new, the opening of a social space, and the constitution or disclosure of characteristic human concerns. The second point is that the standard conception distorts the picture we have of our language-competence even in the domain it does treat, and thus distorts the picture we have of ourselves as human agents. Roughly speaking, the standard conception assumes that the process of sense perception itself provides the individual with *representations* and that the meanings of words basically are (or are formed of) these representations. In this way, representation (misleadingly) appears to be the core of all linguistic meaning, and to be (on the most basic level) the result not of a cultural, but of a natural process.

His own alternative Taylor calls the "expressive" or "expressivist" conception, and he finds important building blocks for it in the writings of Herder, Humboldt, and Hamann.[3] The term "expressivist" stresses the active side of speaking, the fact that it originates in the subject as an agent, as opposed to the idea of a passive process of mirroring. The coincidence that the first letters of these authors' names are the same, allows Taylor to speak of the "triple H theories." But one must hasten to add that he sees Ludwig Wittgenstein as an honorary member of this group,[4] and it is Wittgenstein who inspires most of what the current paper will have to say.

It will proceed in the following steps: the first part will treat the main point of Taylor's criticism, the role of representation. The second part will discuss what must be regarded as a regrettable blank spot in the early formulations of the expressivist conception. It becomes visible when we ask: How would a defender of this position account for the phenomenon of language structure? Taylor himself has not worked out such an account and at times can even be read as suggesting that as far as structure is concerned the Frege-Davidson approach can be kept in place, either because it is satisfactory as far as it goes, or because it is the only one we have so that there is no choice.[5] If it were indeed the case that the Frege-Davidson picture of language structure invites no further critical thought from the expressivist side, this would perhaps explain why only few logicians or linguists show a deeper interest in it. They can regard its contributions as optional additions to what they see as the formal core.

The current paper outlines an alternative. I claim that a close reading of Wittgenstein can provide us with an account of the structures of natural languages that harmonizes with the expressivist picture and at the same time makes visible the limits of a purely formalist approach. In this way it is able to complement the expressivist account, to fill out the blank spot, and at the same time to do justice to what is right in Frege's account. The third part of the paper will discuss what these considerations teach us for the debates about the possibility or impossibility of a "theory of meaning." The fourth and final portion of this paper is a personal remark.

The Role of Representation

Taylor has argued that representation is neither the most basic nor the most important trait of natural languages. When we take a glimpse at Wittgenstein's later work, we can see that he shows – on the very first pages of his *Philosophical Investigations* – that a practical understanding between individuals must be in place before they can begin to grasp a relation of the kind "the word x stands for (or 'represents') the object y." His well-known example is the social activity of erecting a building. Only after a person has understood this activity can we attribute to her an understanding of linguistic meaning.[6]

As Taylor has shown in his discussion of Herder's critique of Condillac,[7] to treat this relation as given amounts to begging the fundamental question of any philosophy of language. Wittgenstein makes the same point with regard to what he calls "the Augustinian picture of language." It is, he says, as if Augustine would describe how a second language is learned by a person who is already familiar with a first language and who therefore knows what linguistic meaning is (*PI* 32).

This primacy of a shared non-lingual practice is easy to see for single words. Also, we can understand how and in what sense talk of an abstract relation of representation can be introduced along Wittgenstein's lines: When a speaker has acquired a command of a multiplicity of words in a multiplicity of contexts, we can speak "in the abstract" of a representational relation between, for example, "the word 'slab'" and a "species of building material." But this ability presupposes the more basic ability to take part in the social activity of erecting a house. Without it, the expression "a species of building material" makes no sense; "knowing the species of slabs" *is* being able to use the word "slab" in an appropriate context.

So Wittgenstein recognizes ways of expressing ourselves with the help of sentences like "'slab' stands for slabs," "'five' stands for the number five," etc., but he regards them as secondary. He writes: "But assimilating the descriptions of the uses of words in this way cannot make the uses themselves any more like one another. For, as we see, they are absolutely unlike" (*PI* 10). "Assimilating the descriptions" would, as the case of the numerals shows, bypass important differences between kinds of meaning and would thus stay on the level of what Wittgenstein calls the "surface-grammar" of language (*PI* 664). We can add here that this kind of assimilation is what we find in truth-conditional semantics. For certain purposes this assimilation is useful, no doubt, but it should not be overlooked that, with respect to natural languages, it is also a distortion.

A parallel question can be raised for sentences. It is common usage to say that a sentence like "the cat is on the mat" represents a state of affairs. But what is a "state of affairs," and how and in what sense can a sentence represent it? For example, is the mentioned state of affairs to be thought of as a complex object consisting of a cat and a mat in a particular spatial relation? When writing the *Tractatus Logico-Philosophicus*, Wittgenstein seems to have been inspired by such a "picturing" idea of language.[8] It interprets the complexity of sentences as resulting from a projection of a complexity residing "in the world," waiting, as it were, to be apprehended and to be represented by language users. As an example for this type of complexity we can consider a group of buildings. Each building can be named and then their spatial relations can be specified with the help of appropriate relational expressions.

If this were a convincing account of the complexity we find in natural languages, the case of language would be similar to what we are familiar with from our traditional musical notation.[9] Here one can say that the complexity of the score mirrors or "maps" the complexity of a melody. The melody is constituted by a particular order of single sounds – of items, that is, that we can isolate and sing in any order we might choose. If this analogy were sound, sentences would "represent" in the same sense of "representation" as words do, only that words would represent "small" or "simple" state of affairs (we might say of a single note it would stand for a short and simple "melody," consisting of only a single tone), whereas sentences represent "complex states of affairs." Wittgenstein discusses and criticizes such an understanding of linguistic complexity in the *Philosophical Investigations*, for example in the paragraphs where he invents a "language" for representing complexes of coloured squares. He is able to show that the complexity of natural languages must be of a fundamentally different kind (PI 48–53).

It is indeed easy to see that this understanding of complexity does not fit to natural languages. One of the examples Wittgenstein uses to show this is a sentence like "Peter and Paul are not fighting."[10] This sentence does not represent a complex object in any straightforward sense, so that the complexity of the object would be mirrored in the complexity of the sentence. In cases in which we do speak of a complex object (for example in using a complex nominal phrase like "the continuous avoidance of Peter and Paul to fight out their conflict") it is only in a secondary sense. Only in a grammatical sense can we say that "the avoidance" is a complex object, meaning: something we talk about. It is an object of reference. But we come to grasp it and its alleged complexity only via language.

But how does structure arise in natural languages and how does it function there if it is not by mirroring a complexity in the "represented objects"? Any answer to this question must do justice to what has come to be known as the "Frege-principle" or "principle of compositionality." It says that we understand new sentences by means of (firstly) understanding their constituent words and (secondly) understanding the particular way in which they are composed in the given case to form a sentence. As Michael Dummett has rightly insisted, we do not learn the sentences of our language one by one; we are in some sense "deriving" the new meaning from the meanings we are familiar with.[11] The grammatical side of this aspect of language can be called its "calculus-side." Can there be an understanding of it other than the semantics of truth conditions?

Wittgenstein's Treatment of Language Structure as a Necessary Addendum to Taylor's Conception

It often happens that we encounter what we conceive of as a discrepancy between the structure of what we mean and the structure of the sentence we use. The best-known examples here are probably Frege's: when we say "the morning star is the evening star" and "Peter is married" we use the same linguistic complex-building device "is" to express two different ways in which the parts of the respective sentence make a whole. And when we say "Peter has two children" we are using the same word "have" as we do when we say "Peter has a job," although the kind of relation we want to express is quite different in the two cases. Again, the way a unitary meaning of a sentence is formed is different in the two cases, but this does not show in the forms of the expressions.

Since in any particular case, the speaker can give an account of the structure of what she means, it seems to be a straightforward move to try to write down, exhaustively, all the structures of what one can possibly mean. This is the project of Frege's *Begriffsschrift*: it is designed to be a means of expression with the help of which all possible (scientific) contents can be stated in an explicit and unequivocal fashion.[12]

A logician pursuing this project must be able to say what it is that guides him in doing so. For Frege this was an abstract realm of thought, in a non-psychological sense.[13] For most of us today, this is not a convincing answer anymore, but it is not easy to propose an alternative. Neither "structures of thinking" (as for example proposed by Wilhelm Wundt),[14] nor "the structure of the world" (as envisioned by the early Wittgenstein), nor biological structures (as proposed by Noam Chomsky)[15] seem to be plausible candidates. So our current situation is that we have the results of Frege's pioneering work, but we have no philosophical underpinning of them, no shared understanding of what logical structure is the structure of. Dummett's answer, namely, that we have nothing else to offer as an explanation for our understanding of an unlimited number of new sentences is no more than a default position, it is no proper justification.[16]

For pragmatic conceptions of language (like the expressivist one) it is natural to explore the idea that the structure of what we mean is a result of our own linguistic activities. In this case, structure would not be pre-existent to language. Instead, the proper question to ask would be how we can understand that our own activity of speaking leads us to structured sentences.

Applying this to Wittgenstein, we ask: what kind of two- or three-word utterances does he consider as possible verbal extensions of the simplest forms of his invented builder's language? What kinds of semantic relations are established by these steps? And in what light will a logical language, as it is used in truth conditional semantics, appear from Wittgenstein's perspective?

It is interesting to note here that the steps that Wittgenstein takes when he extends the signalling system of the builders in order to make it more like our familiar natural language are not leading to sentences of the kind "this slab is white" (or "the cat is on the mat"). The first complex utterances he considers are not "representations of states of affairs." Instead, we find (for example), three-word utterances like "four slabs over there" (PI 8). In explaining how they are acquired, Wittgenstein does not introduce the words of the two new types (i.e., numerals and expressions like "over here") as representations of new types of objects. Instead, he explains their functions by showing how they work as extensions of existing language games. The new expressions modify, they extend the respective language games, but in the way he describes their use, they do not do so by adding new means of representation for new kinds of things. For Wittgenstein, as for Taylor, representation is secondary.

There are three points here that deserve to be highlighted. The first is trivial; indeed it is a premise of the whole discussion: sentences of natural languages exhibit a structure. They are not unstructured concatenations of words, like shopping lists are. The second point is this: all the discussed examples of complex sentences show that their structures cannot be understood as the results of simple projections (or "mappings") of an alleged structure of corresponding "states of affairs."

And thirdly: in natural languages the kinds of semantic relations exhibited in their structures are manifold, whereas logical languages like Frege's *Begriffsschrift* reduce them. There are two aspects in this reduction. The first is well known and uncontested: in logical languages some of the relations expressed in our natural languages (for example the non-descriptive ones like the speaker-hearer relation) do not get into the picture in the first place. In Frege's case this is a deliberate decision.

For the current context a second restriction is more important. It concerns the kinds of expressions that are allowed (or provided for) inside the descriptive realm. Frege's concept script (and, consequently, truth conditional semantics) is not only narrow in the field it can treat, but also narrow in the scope of kinds of expressions it admits in its chosen field. Are there good reasons for this restriction when the topic is natural language? How should we interpret the fact that such a restriction is possible?

Frege thought that in a logical language all content can and should be expressed with the help of only a few forms, namely the object-concept form and its truth-functional combinations, together with the apparatus for quantification that he was the first to propose. Since he was of the opinion that in the process of developing his construction, he would be following structures in the "realm of thought," his results seem to have a certain dignity in that they exhibit the structures of "pure" thought, without any rhetorical or poetical (one might critically say: any "human") additions.

Wittgenstein's conclusions are the opposite of Frege's. He tried to show that the complex-building devices of natural languages are much richer than logicians had thought and that (outside quite particular contexts like, for example, those of formal derivations) it would lead to "injustices" to favour the logical notation in preference to an expression of natural language.[17] For Wittgenstein, the structures proposed by Frege and Russell constitute a particular language, they are neither "above" natural languages, nor hidden "in" them. Therefore, to opt for a logical language means to make a choice, to decide for a particular "form of expression" (PI 402).

What Wittgenstein has in mind here can perhaps most easily be grasped by considering an analogy he has worked out. He compares a sentence's grammatical form, in particular the subject-predicate scheme, with the result of projecting figures from one plane to a second plane. He notes that in such a projection one can proceed in more ways than one. One possible way would be to decide first for a certain method of projection, say the right-angle projection, and then to carry out this method for the projection of all the figures. In this case, when someone is considering the results of the projections, she will be in a position to determine, based on the form of the figures on plane II, at least one aspect of the form of the figures in the initial plane I: in the simplest case a rectangle in I appears as a rectangle in II, a circle as circle, etc.

The situation is different, however, if the one who controls the projection had the intention from the start to make all the figures, whatever their forms might be on plane I, appear as circles on plane II. This could be achieved by changing the method of projection from case to case. Instead of having one method of projection and the corresponding varied forms we would have *various* methods of projection and as a result figures of a single form. In concluding these considerations Wittgenstein writes: "In order in this case to construe the circles in II as representations of the figures in I, I shall have to give the method of projection for each circle; the mere fact that a figure in I is represented as a circle in II by itself tells us nothing about the shape of the figure copied. That an image in II is a circle is just the established norm of our mapping. Well, the same thing happens when we depict reality in our language in accordance with the subject-predicate form. The subject-predicate form serves as a projection of countless different logical forms."[18]

The last two sentences, which introduce the theme of the functioning of language-forms, echo earlier ideas of the *Philosophical Remarks*, as this somewhat longer passage shows: "It is like this with reality if we map it onto subject-predicate propositions. The fact that we use subject-predicate propositions is only a matter of our notation. The subject-predicate form does not in itself amount to a logical form and is the way of expressing countless fundamentally different logical forms, like the circles on the second plane."[19]

And in another passage it becomes clear that Wittgenstein is speaking here not only about grammatical structures, but also and especially about the structures of Frege's logic. He says: "When Frege and Russell talk of concept and object they really mean property and thing; and here I'm thinking in particular of a spatial body and its colour."[20] And later: "If a table is painted brown, then it's easy to think of the wood as bearer of the property brown and you can imagine what remains the same when the colour changes."[21]

So we see that for Wittgenstein the universality even of Frege's object-concept form (as well as the subject-predicate form in English or German) is the result of a decision that a particular form should serve as a standard, even though that form is taken from contexts in which it served to express a particular type of content. This has the result that this standard form is now used for (or one might say "forced upon") all contents.[22] A consequence of these observations is that the idea of a logical form as something above or behind our natural languages, something that we grasp and try to follow in our thinking and that could be spelled out comprehensively in a logical language, is misguided. This in turn means that the discrepancy between what we mean, on the one hand, and what the expressions of our respective languages suggest by the forms they exhibit, on the other, cannot be resolved once and for all. It will never be the case that in all sentences we use, their forms will match what we would like to call the "forms of what we mean." Rudolf Carnap's idea that we could, by sticking to the rules of "logical syntax," stay in the realm of sense "automatically" has to be given up.[23] In a living language, a discrepancy between the "structure of what we mean" and "the structure of what we say" (the grammatical or the logical structure) is the standard case. The fact that we can always comment on or explain the structural aspect of what we wanted to say does not allow the conclusion that it is possible to characterize a totality of the structures of what can be meant by constructing a new medium like Frege's concept script.

So the direction of projection has changed: not the world (plane no. I) determines the structure of our sentence (plane no. II), the projection does not go from world to language. But it is the other way around: we project structures that have been developed according to the steps of extending language games as discussed above onto ever new fields of articulation. For example, we use the object-concept form when we speak "of numbers" and say that the number four is even. So it is for our forms of representation that numbers (and places, and moments of time, and "mental states") are called "objects." They are "objects of reference" in the (surface-) grammatical sense.

In his book about the *Tractatus* Eric Stenius has coined the term "syntactical metaphor" for this phenomenon that he described as a discrepancy between the content to be discussed and the best syntax he was able to propose for formulating this content. The term "syntactical metaphor" expresses that not only words and phrases can be used metaphorically so that a hearer of a metaphorical utterance must grasp the difference between the usual and the new meaning like in the expressions "a sweet apple" and "a sweet little dog." But also the structural devices of language, the means of building sentences, are used in such a "transposed" fashion, so that here too the hearer must grasp the difference between the meanings that such a device can have in different contexts. For example the form "a is no P" in the (false) sentence "the city of Berlin is no city" is used with a transposed meaning in Frege's famous (true) sentence "the concept *horse* is not a concept."[24] In general Stenius characterizes sentences of the second kind by saying: "Its sense does not have the form suggested by its logical syntax, but nevertheless this syntax seems to be the best syntax we can give it."[25] In light of our discussion this means that the intended unity of the respective sentence is not that which is signalled by the original use of the form, but it means at the same time that we have no linguistic means by which to give the "correct" form. The very idea of a logically correct language that would mirror the forms of all contents in an explicit and unequivocal (non-ambiguous) fashion is misguided. Indeed, we can see that, if Wittgenstein is right, it makes no sense to speak of "a correct form" in the first place.

In Wittgenstein's words here we encounter the difference between "surface grammar" and "depth grammar" (PI 664). Mathematical objects like numbers, for example, are objects in the sense of surface grammar. We can refer to them with the help of sentences that sound like sentences about stones. But in fact they are not objects in the sense that stones are, and this is revealed when we describe the function they have in language games, when we describe their depth grammar.

It has been noted above that among the omissions of traditional theories of meaning (i.e., of theories that are inspired by Frege) Taylor mentions the articulation of something new and the constitution or disclosure of characteristic human concerns. It is a special and difficult family of questions when we ask in which of these areas we would want to say that language opens a path to or discloses something that already existed but has so far remained unnoticed, and in which cases we would rather say that the activity of speaking has a constitutive character, i.e., that the activity itself brings something into existence that has in no sense existed before. Arithmetic, for some contemporary philosophers and mathematicians, is an example for the constitutive role of language: our forebears have "invented" the activity of counting things, and in this way have invented the numbers. We humans had set up certain rules for certain of our activities a long time ago, and now we are still busy expanding and modifying them and exploring the logical consequences of such steps.

A related question in the philosophy of religion is even more difficult to answer: On the one hand we want to say that religions respond to "something"; not to an object, in important cases, not to a "state of affairs" in the sense of a complex of things like buildings, not (or not only) to historical happenings, but to the "human condition," i.e., to something that certainly is not of our own making. And they articulate and recommend a kind of experiencing this condition. On the other hand, it seems legitimate to say that the particular linguistic means belonging to a particular religious tradition (like the particular analogies and similes it employs) are "man-made" in much the same way as numerals are. So one could say that in religion the linguistic entities (like the stories told) are "constructed" by language, although what they respond to is not; it is disclosed.[26]

Can There Be a Theory of Meaning?

There has been an *old* debate about this subject in Oxford in the 1980s. In these days, Gordon Baker and Peter Hacker had tried to show that no axiomatic-deductive theory of language of the kind Michael Dummett had envisaged is possible for natural languages.[27] We can see now that they were right in this: calculating the meaning of a sentence along the lines of truth-conditional semantics will not reach the level of depth grammar and this means for many sentences: it will not reach the level of meaning. The main reason for this is that in the case of a natural language such a "calculation" involves the speaker's competence to "decipher" syntactic and semantic metaphors. When we move in natural languages, we constantly have to build bridges to meanings in a way that cannot be accomplished by understanding forms alone, be they grammatical or logical forms. Sure enough, we have to *understand the surface structure*, for example, of the sentence "two is even": two is an object and it has the property of being even. But we have to understand also that this evenness is not the one we know from material objects (semantic metaphor) and that to be an object here is not the same as being an item among the "middle size dry goods"[28] (syntactic metaphor). So "calculating the sense of a sentence from its elements and the kind of their composition" will not go far enough if it stays on the level of forms; it would be a case of "assimilating the descriptions" (*PI* 10, 14).

Paradoxically, today Hacker finds himself attacked by the so-called "resolute" readers of Wittgenstein (mainly, Cora Diamond and James Conant)[29] in much the same way in which he himself had attacked Dummett. Their accusation is that traditional readers of Wittgenstein, including Hacker, are clinging to a picture of language that is still too close to the conception of Frege, a picture like Rudolf Carnap's, who thought (as we have noted) that by making explicit the rules of a so called "logical syntax" it would be possible to exclude nonsense, as he said, "automatically." Against this, the resolute readers insist that no such implicit rules exist and that therefore we cannot rely on them when we try to decide whether a given utterance makes sense or not.

At this point the resolute readers are right: for natural or "living" languages it is not possible to draw a sharp line between sense and nonsense. Instead, we can appeal to the common usage our respective language community has made of linguistic expressions so far, but such an appeal does not necessarily render deviant uses nonsensical. What is missing in the resolute readers' account, however, is again a discussion of language structure, whether we want to call such an account a "theory" or not.

Often we manage to make use of our (from the logical point of view "inadequate") linguistic forms without being misled by them. This discloses a trait of our language competence that is indeed of great importance for understanding ourselves as human agents, not as imperfect machines. It might be here, where at least some of what Taylor has referred to as the mysterious side of language resides.[30] We can "misuse" old forms (and old lexical items) to say something new and to explore new cultural territories; and in many cases we are understood.

Conclusion: The Strengths and Limits of Taylor's Expressivist Position

I conclude this paper with a personal story. It was on occasion of a seminar on theories of meaning at the University of Konstanz in the summer of 1981 that a bright young linguist, a formalist who all the same was quite impressed by Taylor's exposition of the "triple H theories," asked in the discussion period how these theories would account for linguistic structure. Taylor stopped to think about it and then replied that he as yet had no answer to this question. But if this were the last word on the matter the triple H approach would give no more than an account of one-word sentences. It could for this reason not be called a theory of meaning for natural languages. In these the meanings of the sentences depend on the meanings of their constituent words and the ways they are put together. So we do need an account of our ways of putting words together in order to produce semantically unified sentential wholes.

For me, at this time an attentive reader with strong sympathies to Frege as well as to Wittgenstein, this lacuna in Taylor's in all other respects fascinating and convincing account of natural language was a great challenge. My attempt to fill it resulted in my 1992 book *Phantasie und Kalkül*. Over the years Taylor found time to read it and when, not without his encouragement, a partial English translation was prepared he contributed a foreword.[31]

The results of our respective work on language fit together perfectly well. Indeed, in his latest book, in which he offers a comprehensive account of his expressivist perspective on language, he explicitly endorses my reading of Wittgenstein.[32] To the systematic consequences he draws there I can fully agree: "On this reading of Wittgenstein he is not simply a negator of all attempts at systematicity. On the contrary, he sees how different uses are linked. But these links involve projective steps of a metaphorical type (understanding A through B); and these are not in the repertory of analytic philosophers seeking the kind of semantic relations which Brandom examines."[33]

In order to understand ourselves as human agents and speakers in an adequate way it is necessary not to leave the understanding of linguistic structure to the logicians or to the formal linguists, who are too much in the grip of the calculus-picture as developed by Frege for his logical and mathematical purposes. He himself needed an instrument to guarantee that his proofs do not make use of unrecognized premises. This instrument was the logical calculus. But with help of "honorary triple H author" Wittgenstein, we are able to understand the quite different role structure has in natural languages: how it can originate, in which respects it can be compared with a calculus, and in which respect it is fundamentally different. Structures of natural languages involve links that work like metaphors. As human speakers we can arrive at sentence meanings via understanding their parts and the ways they are composed. But the way in which we achieve this result in many cases is not the way of calculation. What is needed is to make and to understand creative steps. Only in this way the most important of the human concerns can be articulated.

3

Taylor's Engaged Pluralism

RICHARD J. BERNSTEIN

When thinking about this paper on Charles Taylor, a passage from Hannah Arendt kept intruding itself. She wrote:

> I have always believed that, no matter how abstract our theories may sound or how consistent our arguments may appear, there are incidents and stories behind them which, at least for ourselves, contain in a nutshell the full meaning of whatever we have to say. Thought itself – to the extent that is more than a technical, logical operation which electronic machines may be better equipped to perform than the human brain – arises out of the actuality of incidents, and incidents of living experience must remain its guideposts by which it takes its bearings if it is not to lose itself in the heights to which thinking soars, or in the depths to which it must descend.[1]

Taylor might well have written this passage, since it perfectly characterizes how his thinking is grounded in his experience. It makes perfect sense that this celebration of his life and work takes place in Montreal. For despite his intellectual journeys and travels throughout the world – despite the heights to which his thinking has soared and the depths to which it has descended – this is the home to which he has always returned. Taylor is the ideal type of the rooted cosmopolitan, and his roots are here in Quebec.

I have been in dialogue with Charles ever since he published his first book *The Explanation of Behaviour* (1964), and in rereading his work for this conference, I was struck by a theme that runs through all of his writings – what I call "engaged fallibilistic pluralism." Let me explain what I mean. Much of our thinking not only in the social and humanistic disciplines, but also in politics and morals, and in everyday life, tends to move between extremes. There are those who are drawn to the ideal of universality and objectivity. In science, politics, and morality there has been a stubborn conviction that unless we can establish that there really are universal principles and a neutral "objective" perspective, we are threatened by a self-defeating relativism. And despite what the defenders of relativism claim, they cannot avoid what Karl Popper once called the "myth of the framework." This is the myth that "we are prisoners caught in the framework of our theories, our expectations; our past experiences; our language" and that we are so encased in these that there is really no common language that we share with those enclosed in radically different frameworks.[2] Carried to its extreme, this relativism calls into question not only universality, but also truth and objectivity. Of course, this is not simply a temptation and worry of philosophers; it arises in many concrete discussions of multiculturalism and practical politics. The opposing stances here may take different forms. Sometimes they are characterized as universalism versus relativism, sometimes as objectivism versus subjectivism, sometimes as modernity versus postmodernity. But despite these variations, there is an underlying structural logic. We are ultimately left with two – and only two – alternatives. As Taylor says in another context, "in the polemics around modernity, more nuanced understandings tend to get driven to the wall, and these two slug it out."[3]

We can read Taylor's work as criticizing the modes of thinking and acting that keep spinning around opposing extremes. One of the deepest motivations for his critique is that the oscillation between these unsatisfactory extremes distorts and obscures the real social, political, and personal problems that we confront. Frequently, those who defend versions of the myth of the framework speak about incommensurability as if this were a fixed epistemological and/or metaphysical barrier. As I read Taylor, he is affirming that there are real incommensurabilities in our cultures, religions, politics, and morals, but he does *not* think that they are rigid epistemological or metaphysical barriers. These incommensurabilities present us with *practical* challenges that can be difficult and painful to confront. Nevertheless, we can achieve a more subtle and sensitive understanding of what is radically different from ourselves and, at the same time, gain a deeper understanding of ourselves. Engaged fallibilistic pluralism requires both the recognition of what Levinas once called "the otherness of the other" and, at the same time, an enlargement our own horizons (to use Gadamer's expression). Although I think that this orientation pervades all of Taylor's work, I want to focus on three different contexts in which it is central: first, his reflections on multiculturism, especially with reference to Quebec; second, his appropriation of the hermeneutical idea of a "fusion of horizons"; and third, his understanding of what is distinctive about a secular age.

First, Taylor is a Quebecker with a fierce loyalty to both his English and his French heritage. And the tensions and cross-pressures of this dual loyalty have shaped much of his practical and political life and thinking. Sometimes Taylor has been classified as a communitarian who presumably stands opposed to liberalism. However, this alleged dichotomy distorts Taylor's orientation. I do not think the issue for him has ever been the disjunction between liberalism and communitarianism. His primary concern has been what *kind* of liberalism should be endorsed. Quebec has always been his test case. Why? Not simply because Taylor has experienced the tensions and opposing pulls in his everyday life, but because it serves as a paradigm of what it means to face up to *practical* problems about incommensurability and identity. Taylor challenges the type of liberalism that he calls "proceduralist liberalism." This is the type of liberalism that – as Michael Walzer phrases it – "is committed in the strongest possible way to individual rights, and, almost as a deduction from this, to a rigorously neutral state, that is a state without cultural or religious projects or, indeed, any sort of collective goals beyond the personal freedom and physical security, welfare, and safety of its citizens."[4] Taylor is certainly committed to the idea that there are individual rights – indeed individual rights that any democratic state ought to protect. But the problem for Canadians is how to reconcile the protection of individual rights of *all* citizens with the survival and flourishing of French culture in Quebec, as well as other cultures. Taylor is calling for an enlarged, revised, more nuanced liberalism – not the abandonment of liberalism in favour of protecting and reifying some special community: "A society with strong collective goals can be liberal, on this view, provided it is also capable of respecting diversity, especially when dealing with those who do not share its common goals; and provided it can offer adequate safeguards for fundamental rights."[5]

But what does this mean in practical terms? Does it mean that Quebec has the right to require that all commercial signs be written in French? Is it legitimate for the province to specify who can and who cannot attend

English-speaking public schools? The honest answer – and I think it is Taylor's answer – is that there is no abstract way to establish once and for all what is and is not permissible to do in order to the facilitate the survival and flourishing of French culture in Quebec. These are issues that can be resolved only in *concrete* practical political debate that is sensitive to specific contexts. But what can be philosophically defended is the idea of an *enlarged* liberalism – a liberalism that acknowledges cultural diversity. The models of liberalism that Taylor favours are those that are "willing to weigh the importance of certain forms of uniform treatment against the importance of cultural survival, and opt *sometimes* in favour of the latter. They are thus in the end not procedural models of liberalism, but are grounded very much on *judgments* about what makes a good life – judgments in which the integrity of cultures has an important place."[6]

Consider how participants who take one of the extreme positions view each other. For those who believe in an uncompromising commitment to individual rights, it is deeply offensive to be told that any Canadian province has the "right" to dictate the language of commercial signs or to specify who may attend English or French public schools. For them, this is clearly a violation of the individual rights that should be guaranteed for all citizens. Many Canadian citizens vehemently objected to the ill-fated Meech Lake agreement, which proposed to recognize Quebec as a "distinct society." However, their opponents feel just as deeply that such an uncompromising commitment to "individual rights" exposes the sheer hypocrisy of claims about a neutral state. It is not neutral at all but will inevitably destroy the integrity of French culture in Quebec. Some have argued that the only way to resolve this incommensurability is to call for political separation. Each side is "driven to the wall." Taylor has dedicated a good deal of his life and thinking to undercutting these extremes – to showing how we might face up to this incommensurabilty in a reasonable manner. We can elaborate a more "hospitable variant" of liberal democracy, one that accommodates cultural difference without giving up on the idea that there are fundamental individual rights that must be protected. To the extent that such an alternative is concretely realized, there will be a new sense of shared identity among those who initially radically opposed each other. But how does one decide what individual rights are fundamental and should be guaranteed to all citizens? And where and when should there be an accommodation to cultural differences? This is an issue that can only be resolved in political democratic debate; it demands sensitivity to context, deliberation, and judgment. And of course, these judgments are (or should be) open to public criticism. This is why Taylor's reflections on Quebec and Canada have important consequences for debates about multiculturalism throughout the world. As territorial borders become more porous, as immigration (legal and illegal) increases, there has been an ugly digging in of extreme positions – e.g., what is required to be a "true American," a "true Frenchman, a "true German," a "true Quebecker." However, if one takes a more flexible and pluralistic approach to liberal democracy, if one is hospitable to cultural differences (which are always changing), then there are practical ways of achieving a politics of mutual recognition where individuals and groups enlarge their horizons and share a new identity.

Second, if we reflect on the type of pluralism that Taylor defends with regard to the tangled issues of multiculturalism, we can introduce the second context for witnessing Taylor's engaged fallibilistic pluralism. This is already implicit in his explication of a liberalism that is more hospitable to cultural difference. Taylor is basically calling for "a fusion of horizons" (Gadamer) between those who are initially wedded to a rigid conception of individual rights and those who are concerned to see that their cultural identity is sustained and allowed to flourish. Taylor rightly declares: "The great challenge of this century, both for politics and for social science, is that of understanding the other."[7]

From his earliest writings until the present, Taylor has been a persistent critic of all forms of scientism and reductive naturalism that claim that we can completely understand and explain human life in terms of concepts and theories characteristic of the natural sciences. When Taylor started his career, behaviourism in the social sciences was the rage. Nobody today defends classical behaviourism, but there are those who think that sociobiology, evolutionary psychology, rational choice theory, and the "breakthroughs" in the neurosciences are *all* we need to understand and explain human beings.

Taylor's classic article "Interpretation and the Sciences of Man" (1971)[8] was written at a time when many social scientists were convinced that the social sciences were to be modelled on what they *took* to be the character of the natural sciences. In this article Taylor argued that such a view is not only mistaken but perverse. Drawing upon phenomenological insights, he suggested that a proper science of human beings must be hermeneutical. This is how he characterizes a hermeneutical science of politics:

It would not be founded on brute data; its most primitive data would be readings of meanings, and its object would have the [following] properties ... the meanings are for a subject in a field or fields; they are, moreover, meanings which are partially constituted by self-definitions, which are in this sense already interpretations, and which can thus be reexpressed or made explicit by a science of politics. In our case, the subject may be a society or community; but the intersubjective meanings ... embody a certain self-definition, a vision of the agent and his society, which is that of the society or community.[9]

Such a science

cannot but move in a hermeneutical circle. A given reading of the intersubjective meanings of a society, or of a given institutions or practices, may seem well founded, because it makes sense of these practices or the development of that society. But the conviction that it does make sense of this history itself is founded on further related readings.[10]

Taylor knew that he was criticizing what had become – and still is in many places – a modern orthodoxy. He concludes this article by telling us

There are thus good grounds both in epistemological arguments and in their fruitfulness for opting for hermeneutical sciences of man. But we cannot hide from ourselves how greatly this option breaks with certain commonly held notions about our scientific tradition. We cannot measure such sciences against the requirements of a science of verification: we cannot judge them by their predictive capacity ... These sciences cannot be *wertfrei*; they are moral sciences in a more radical sense than the eighteenth century understood. Finally, their successful prosecution requires a high degree of self-knowledge, a freedom from illusion, in the sense of error which is rooted and expressed in one's way of life; for our incapacity to understand is rooted in our own self-definitions, hence in what we are. To say this is not to say anything new: Aristotle makes a similar point in Book I of the *Ethics*. But it is still radically shocking and inassimilable to the mainstream of modern science.[11]

This is a fighting creed. Many of Taylor's work since the 1971 article – including *Sources of the Self* and *Modern Social Imaginaries* – elaborate and develop this hermeneutical orientation.

But how does this relate to what I have called Taylor's "engaged fallibilistic pluralism"? I can answer this by focusing on his discussion of Gadamer's conception of horizon. For what Taylor says about Gadamer is just as applicable to his own orientation. Gadamer, Taylor tells us, "shows how understanding a text or an event that comes from our history has to be construed not on the model of the 'scientific' grasp of object but rather on that of speech partners who come to an understanding."[12] Although in *Truth and Method* Gadamer was primarily concerned with understanding tradition and how it shapes us, his model of dialogue or conversation is applicable to all the human sciences. The dialogical model is just as fundamental for a contemporary understanding what initially appear to be incommensurable cultures, religions, politics, and morals. "There are three features of understandings – they are bilateral, they are party-dependent, they involve revising goals."[13] To say that they are bilateral is to underscore that a conversation involves different parties. We are not exclusively trying to gain a unilateral grasp of an object. Such an understanding is party dependent in a radical sense: "The terms of our best account will vary not only with the people studied but also with the students. Our account of the decline of the Roman Empire will not and cannot be the same as that put forward in eighteenth-century England, or those that will be offered in twenty-fifth-century China, or twenty-second-century Brazil."[14]

Understanding always presupposes prejudgments – background implicit knowledge – that we can never make *fully* explicit. This background knowledge changes over time and is shaped by our histories. Initially, there is a temptation to project our prejudgments and prejudices on what we take to be other than us. But if there is openness and a willingness to question our own entrenched prejudgments, we can learn to listen and respond to what initially appears as radical other than us. Unlike the case of natural scientific knowledge of an object, "coming to an understanding may require that I give some grounds in my objectives. The end of the operation is not control, or else I am engaging in a sham designed to manipulate my partner while pretending to negotiate. The end is being able in some way to function together with a partner, and this means listening as well as talking, and hence may require that I redefine what I am aiming at."[15] Of course, there are significant differences between understanding a classic text or a different historical period and understanding a partner that can *literally* speak back to us, but the dialogical model applies to both. If, for example, I really want to understand the social imaginary of those who once lived in an enchanted cosmos, then I must have the imagination to break out of the categories and concepts that seem so natural and even self-evident in a disenchanted world. But this doesn't mean that I can simply jump out of my own perspective, my background knowledge and prejudgments. A dialogue that takes place between partners is not from some third-person, neutral perspective. We must allow ourselves to be challenged by what is genuinely different. "We will see our peculiarity for the first time, as a formulated fact about us and not simply a taken-for-granted feature of the human condition as such; and at the same time, we will perceive the corresponding feature of their life-form undistorted. These two changes are indissolubly linked; you cannot have one without the other."[16] It is in and through the encounter with what is *other* that we come to a deeper understanding of ourselves.

Unlike the "myth of the framework," Taylor is not presupposing that frameworks, languages, cultures, religions are self-contained monads. We are not prisoners locked into our own identities. We can always enlarge our frameworks, our languages, our horizons and at the same time achieve a more critical judgment of ourselves. Taylor is certainly not a relativist. This becomes clear when he states:

Gadamer's concept of 'horizon' has an inner complexity that is essential to it. On one hand, horizons can be identified and distinguished; it is through such distinctions that we can come to grasp what is distorting understanding and impeding communication. But on the other hand, horizons evolve, change. There is no such thing as a fixed horizon ... A horizon with unchanging contours is an abstraction. Horizons identified by the agents whose worlds they circumscribe are always in movement. The horizons of A and B may thus be distinct at time t and their mutual understanding imperfect. But A and B by living together may come to have a single common horizon at $t+n$.[17]

There is a tendency in all of us to think that our way of thinking is so basic, natural, and "enlightened" that we read, judge, and evaluate others according to our own accepted norms and standards. This type of ethnocentrism is not innocent; it is exemplified in imperialism, colonialism, and Eurocentrism. It is also exemplified today when a majority group demands that an "alien" minority must conform to its language, values, standards, and norms in order to be accepted as citizens. But we should not delude ourselves into thinking that there is some easy way to achieve a fusion of horizons. Despite our best efforts, we have to be prepared for failure. What is far more common in the modern world is the breakdown of communication – misunderstanding and fragmentation. Taylor speaks of the malaises of modernity. His hermeneutical orientation and his critical engaged fallibilistic pluralism are intended to help us to overcome these malaises.

Before passing on to the third context in which we witness Taylor's engaged pluralism – his analysis of a secular age – I want to bring out another basic dimension of his thinking. Much of Taylor's work during the past few decades has been concerned with developing a more nuanced and subtle understanding of modern social imaginaries. The plural "imaginaries" is crucial. Against a prevailing view that there is (or can be) a single all-inclusive abstract theory of modernity, Taylor argues that there are multiple alternative modern social imaginaries. A social imaginary is not to be confused with a *theory* of social reality. It consists of the ways in which ordinary people imagine their social existence, how they fit together with others, how things go on between them and their fellows, how their expectations are normally met. It also consists of the deeper normative notions and images that underlie these expectations. Understanding a social imaginary means not only probing its historical sources and the various strands that constitute it, but also exposing its internal conflicts, tensions, and contradictions. A good example of such nuanced understanding is what Taylor takes to be the dilemma of modern democracy.

Democracy is at once "a great philosophy of inclusion," but it is also based on exclusion. Democracy is inclusive in the sense that it is commitment to "government of *all* the people" – government of the people, by the people, for the people. But at the same time, "democratic states need something like a common identity" – cohesion that is more than an aggregate of isolated random individuals. This demand for cohesion leads to a variety of forms of exclusion, which can range from violent ethnic cleansing to a type of exclusion that takes the form of forced integration into a dominant culture:

Democracies are in a standing dilemma. They need strong cohesion around a political identity, and precisely this provides a strong temptation to exclude those who can't or won't fit easily into the identity which the majority feels comfortable with, or believes alone can hold them together. And yet exclusion, besides being profoundly morally objectionable, also goes against the legitimacy of the idea of popular sovereignty, which is to realize the government of *all* the people. The need to form a people as a collective agent runs against the demand for inclusion of all who legitimately have a claim on citizenship.[18]

Taylor is sharply critical of those who think that some form of "procedural liberalism" allows us to solve this dilemma. He argues that the "key to facing the dilemma of exclusion creatively" is the "idea of sharing identity space."[19] Taylor doesn't really spell out what this means, in part because he tells us that "solutions have to be tailored to particular situations."[20] Whatever we may think of Taylor's idea of a shared identity, I want to emphasize that Taylor's deep pluralism enables us to perceive the real dilemmas, tensions, and incommensurabilities that we need to confront and negotiate in our everyday lives.

Finally, I want to turn to how pluralism manifests itself in Taylor's more recent writings about religion. *A Secular Age* is an enormously complex book that weaves together many different strands. Some have read it as an extended apologia for Taylor's Christian faith – a defence of his belief in a transcendent God. Others emphasize how the book presents a sustained critique of what he calls "exclusive humanism" and the "subtraction thesis" of secularization. Still others admire (or criticize) Taylor's historical narrative of the transformations of Latin Christianity from the Middle Ages until the present. But few have commented on how it contributes to his hermeneutic pluralistic orientation. Taylor is certainly up front about his own Christian commitment. Too few have taken seriously what he announces as his primary objective: "The change I want to define and trace is one which takes us from a society in which it was virtually impossible not to believe in God, to one in which faith, even for the staunchest believer, is *one human possibility among others*. I may find it inconceivable that I would abandon my faith, but there are others, including possibly some very close to me, whose way of living I cannot in all honesty just dismiss as depraved, or blind, or unworthy, who have no faith (at least not in God, or the transcendent). Belief in God is no longer axiomatic. *There are alternatives.*"[21]

I take Taylor seriously when he says that faith in a transcendent God is "one human possibility among others" and that there are alternatives. This is what he means by a secular age. A secular age is *not* one in which a belief in a transcendent God is totally rejected or considered passé. On the contrary, a secular age is one in which such a faith is a genuine possibility, but one that competes vigorously with other alternatives. It is an age in which the conditions of belief have changed dramatically, such that "the shift to secularity in this sense consists, among other things, of a move from a society where belief in God is unchallenged and indeed, unproblematic, to one in which it is understood to be one option among others, and frequently not the easiest to embrace."[22] Taylor's frequent use of the term "options" can be misleading because it makes it sound as if deciding whether or not to believe in a transcendent God is exclusively a matter of personal free choice. His account of the emergence of the "buffered" self may lead us to think that choosing to believe in a transcendent God is like choosing a style of dress. But I take it that this is just what Taylor rejects. "Secularity," Taylor tells us, is "a condition in which our experience of and search for fullness occurs; and *this is something we all share, believers and unbelievers alike.*"[23] Some critics have argued that the alternatives to belief in God always existed, but this misses Taylor's main point. The background conditions of belief in which alternatives present themselves in the contemporary world have changed radically over the past several centuries.

There is a tension that runs through *A Secular Age*, but I think it is a creative tension. Taylor criticizes those who think that religious faith and serious belief in God is no longer (or ought not to be) a serious possibility. His strategy in critiquing this conviction is multifaceted. He sharply criticizes "self-sufficient exclusive humanism." This is a version of humanism that actually emerged from Christianity itself. At first, it was a theoretical orientation limited to an elite, but gradually it became a widespread background conviction of ordinary people. Taylor's thesis is that the distinctive sense of secularity that characterizes our times arises with the emergence of exclusive humanism: "The coming of modern secularity in my sense has been coterminous with the rise of a society in which for the first time in history a purely self-sufficient humanism came to be a widely available option. I mean by this a humanism accepting no final goals beyond human flourishing, nor any allegiance to anything else beyond this flourishing. Of no previous society was this true."[24] For Taylor, this is the heart of the matter. The key issue is whether there is something "beyond" this goal of human flourishing. Throughout he seeks to elicit for us those profound experiences that indicate that there is indeed something more than human flourishing. A faith in a personal and loving God can be a source of a deeper, more intense spiritual life, and can provide a richer sense of "fullness" than those who remain skeptical or agnostic about the existence of such a transcendent being. He tells us: "This whole book is an attempt to study the fate in the modern West of religious faith in a strong sense. This strong sense I define, to repeat, by a double criterion: the belief in transcendent reality, on the one hand, and the connected aspiration to a transformation goes beyond ordinary flourishing on the other."[25] But despite his passionate affirmation of his Christian faith, Taylor knows there are alternatives – that there are those who live rich human lives *without* believing that there is anything beyond human flourishing.

Some of Taylor's sharpest prose is expressed in his critique of what he labels CWS – "closed world structures." These consist of those orientations that categorically deny the existence of anything that is transcendent. He also argues that exclusive humanism is an unstable position that contains its own dilemmas and even generates the varieties of anti-humanism that have become fashionable in a post-Nietzschean world. For Taylor, persons living in secular societies live in a disenchanted immanent frame. This is true for both believers and nonbelievers. But there is nothing about this world that *necessarily* excludes transcendence. This is a pluralist world where many forms of belief and unbelief jostle.

At times, there is a disparity between Taylor's rhetorical stance and his argument. His *polemic* is directed against those who think that there is something about the modern secular world that necessarily excludes a faith in a transcendent God. But his *argument* is actually much more modest, namely, that there is the nothing in a modern secular world that rules out the viability of such a committed faith. It remains a viable option. I don't think Taylor does justice to the many varieties of *nonexclusive* humanism that exist today – particularly to those that do *not* want to rule out the *possibility* of the type of belief that Taylor defends but nevertheless are skeptical or agnostic about ontological transcendence.[26] They are not convinced that religious believers experience a sense of fullness and spirituality that is deeper and more meaningful than what nonbelievers experience. Militant atheism and exclusive secular humanism are not the stances that characterize most of those who are skeptical or agnostic about strong religious claims about transcendence. Taylor knows this. That is why I call his *argument* a modest one, because regardless of his own personal beliefs, he does not want to deny that nonbelievers can lead rich, meaningful, fulfilled lives. Recall what I quoted earlier: "I may find it inconceivable that I would abandon my faith, but there are others, including possibly some very close to me, whose way of living I cannot in all honesty just dismiss as depraved, or blind, or unworthy, who have no faith (at least not in God, or the transcendent)."[27] In a secular age there are a plurality of alternatives; that is precisely what defines it.

An engaged fallibilistic pluralist will always try to show – by arguing, by appealing to lived experience, by telling stories and constructing narratives – why the alternative that he favours is more attractive, more adequate, richer, more illuminating than those that he rejects. But he also acknowledges his own fallibility and recognizes that reasonable people can *disagree* about fundamental issues. Meaningful disagreement is what keeps dialogue and conversation alive. There is no incompatibility between passionately defending one's basic convictions and recognizing that there are alternatives. Taylor, who has always been passionate about his convictions, has also exhibited the all-too-rare virtue of listening to others. He acknowledges the strengths (as well as the weaknesses) of what he opposes, and has sought to achieve a "fusion of horizons."

Several years ago, in another context, I characterized what I mean by "engaged fallibilistic pluralism": "Such a pluralistic *ethos* places new responsibilities on each of us. For it means taking our own fallibility seriously – resolving that however much we are committed to our own styles of thinking, we are willing to listen to others without denying or suppressing the otherness of the other. It means being vigilant against the dual temptations of simply dismissing what others are saying by falling back on one of those defensive ploys where we condemn it as obscure, woolly, or trivial, or thinking we can always easily translate what is alien into our own entrenched vocabularies."[28]

Taylor, in a spirited defence of what he was trying to do in *A Secular Age*, affirms this pluralism:

> I think what we badly need is a conversation between a host of different positions, religious, nonreligious, antireligious, humanistic,

antihumanistic, and so on, in which we eschew mutual caricature and try to understand what 'fullness' means for the other ... There are many things to be said in favour of such a conversation. But the one that I think is of paramount importance is that it is an antidote to the tendency of some people in all positions to project evil onto other positions and call for their elimination for the sake of mankind. This tendency has risen to world-threatening force in many milieus, and it is all too easy for this total, potentially violent rejection to call forth equal and opposite modes of rejection from the positions it targets.[29]

This is the spirit that pervades all of Taylor's work. It is not just a theoretical stance but also has the utmost practical significance. There are powerful tendencies blocking and distorting the sort of conversation that presupposes a serious, imaginative, respectful, and agonistic encounter among a plurality of positions. In my judgment, Charles Taylor has been an exemplar of the passionate engaged pluralist for our time. Of course, this doesn't exclude or eliminate sharp disagreement with him on specific issues. However, when one disagrees with him then one should argue with him in the same generous hermeneutical spirit that Taylor exemplifies and practices. In a genuine dialogue or conversation – as Gadamer tells us – no one has the final word.

PART TWO

Religion and Modernity

4

State-Religion Connections and Multicultural Citizenship

TARIQ MODOOD

While many liberals believe that the state should be neutral on matters of the good and culture, and above all on religion, multiculturalists hold that the state should not be blind to difference.[1] Indeed, it should actively play a role in constructing and promoting a multicultural polity and national identity in which minority identities are respectfully included. This first tension can lead to a second one. For, if multicultural recognition, respectful inclusion, and the multiculturalizing of the public space and national identity were to include minority religious identities, then this can clash with those forms of secularism based on the radical interpretation that religion should play no or a highly restricted role in politics, or at least law and governance.[2]

This may seem to pit multiculturalists against secularism. This, however, is not the case where radical secularism is not the dominant mode of political secularism, such as in Western Europe, where all states support one or more version of Christianity. Some secularists, including prominent academics, do indeed speak of a "crisis of secularism" but that is because they have an exaggerated view of the requirements of secularism or are mistaken about the kind of secularism practiced by Western European states.[3] This gap between theories of secularism and actual secular states reminds me of one of the pioneering moments of multiculturalism. Will Kymlicka has rightly pointed out that while liberal political theorists were arguing that liberalism has no truck with group rights, several liberal states had by the 1980s begun to implement policies using notions of group identities and group rights. Kymlicka argued that the practice of the liberal state was superior to the theories of academics and so we needed to get theory to catch up with practice.[4] Similarly, I think it became apparent in the 1990s that some of the practices of some liberal states were, in respect of secularism, superior to the theories of academics and we need to catch up with practice. (A small irony here is that Kymlicka himself is a secularist that has no truck with the kind of Western European state practice that I shall suggest is a resource for multiculturalism).[5]

My way out of the tensions between multiculturalism and liberalism and between multiculturalism and secularism is to argue that the presence of state-religion connexions (SRCs) is not normatively problematic in itself. They can be consistent with liberal democratic constitutionalism and may be a means of including ethno-religious minorities within a multicultural citizenship. I do not here discuss the multiculturalizing of existing SRCs but seek to establish that in principle they are integral to a historical and reasonable version of secularism and do not constitute an indefensible privileging of religion.

Political Secularism and State-Religion Connections

I am committed to political secularism in general, which I take to be the view that political authority does not rest on religious authority, and that the latter does not dominate political authority. Each form of authority has considerable – though not absolute – autonomy. I believe this is the generic idea common to all versions of liberal democratic states. Note that it does not say anything about whether states may have an "established" religion or whether there has to be "a wall of separation" between organized religion and the institutions and resources of the state. It is part of my argument that some versions of "establishment" as a subset of SRCs are compatible with some versions of political secularism. I take these versions of political secularism as part of a broad historical movement within Western Europe (with France being a notable if partial exception), which I refer to as "moderate secularism" (not a narrow status quo in a specific country at a specific time).[6] The key feature of moderate secularism is that it sees organized religion as not just a private benefit but as a potential public good or national resource, and which the state can in some circumstances assist to realize – even through an "established" church. These public benefits can be direct, such as a contribution to education and social care through autonomous church-based organizations funded by the taxpayer, or indirect, such as the production of attitudes that create economic hope or family stability. National identity, cultural heritage, ethical voice, and national ceremonies may also be involved. Note that the public good of religion, and therefore possible SRCs, in moderate secularism is not confined to the organized delivery of public services but includes identity and recognition within its possible ambit. Of course religion can also be a "public bad" – it can for example in some circumstances be a basis for prejudice, discrimination, intolerance, sectarianism, and so on – and so the state has a responsibility to check the bad as well as enhance the good.[7] Moreover, if religious organizations are supported with public funds or tasked by the state to carry out some educational or welfare duties then they must be subject to certain requirements – such as equal access or non-discrimination.

It is clear then that in moderate secularism the state-religion entanglements do not just flow one way, can have various aspects, and are highly context dependent, not least on what kind of religion or religions are present. Moderate secularism is nevertheless consistent with my minimalist definition of political secularism as relatively autonomous forms of authority without an entailment of absolute institutional separation though many political theorists would not accept that it is a form of secularism.[8] While I argue that a formal or legal or constitutional connection is characteristic of north western European secularism, it being the historical form that secular states have taken, an alternative view of secularism is encapsulated in Rajeev Bhargava's claim that "in a secular state, a formal or legal union or alliance between state and religion is impermissible."[9] Bhargava is best known for his view that the Indian polity has something to teach the West, namely that it is possible for a secular state to have principled, secularist reasons for rejecting strict separationism. He argues that while India is one of the few states in the world to be defined as "secular" by its constitution it has an active policy of supporting and interfering with the religions of India. He holds that such policy behaviour is consistent with secularism. His explanation is based on dividing the idea of a secular state into three levels: ends, institutions, and laws/policies. At the third level the normative ideal is "principled distance," namely that the state is bound to interact with religions but must do so without favouring any or some religions relative to others. These interactions should be governed not by religious principles but by the principles and policies that the state is independently committed to. So, if the state is committed to pursuing affirmative action to help disadvantaged and stigmatized minorities then the state may choose to invest (disproportionate) resources in improving the educational standards of a disadvantaged religious minority if there is a sound analysis that doing so will help to meet its overall goal. This is not, Bhargava argues, to favour a religion; it just so happens that principled state policies and the state benefiting a religious group (temporarily) co-incide. Hence, he is insistent that to rule out such policies in the name of secularism is dogmatic and mistaken. His argument that at this third level of policy the state may be flexible, pragmatic, and religion-friendly (as long as not biased in favour of any religion beyond where policy requires) is well made and convincing. My disagreement with Bhargava is in rela-tion to his analysis of secularism in relation to the other two levels, those of ends and, in particular at the level of state structure. There he allows no flexibility and works with dichotomous distinctions: he forces, for in-stance, a choice between "establishment" or secular as he argues that there can be no overlap or duality of function between state and religious per-sonnel.[10] I think however that at this level too we need elasticity and this is what a number of European states have done historically, and indeed continue to do even in the absence of formal establishment – for example through corporatist state-church partnerships in relation to education and welfare, as in Germany, or a state-level consultative council of religions, as in Belgium. Such European states certainly have the policy-level connec-tions with organized religions (principally churches) but the connection is not confined to that, and even the latter has a long-term character such that it is more a part of the state structure (e.g., of the tax-funded educa-tion system) rather than of policies that change with governments or new programmes of action. To think of such long-term state-religion "alliances" simply as a set of policies is to considerably understate them as they over-lap with structures of governance and state agencies. With state-religion connections present at more than one level we have a more substantial connection than Bhargava's and related theories can include within their conception of legitimate secular states.

Interestingly, Bhargava allows that "weak establishment" of the kind that exists in England (and "weaker" still in Scotland, with the Presbyter-ian Church recognized as a "national" church) is more or less a secular state. That is politically sound but it is not clear how he can make this move within his theory; it seems to lack a theoretical rationale.[11] Cécile Laborde offers one rationale when she says there are liberal forms of establishment – which are such either because they are "multi-faith," or because they are only purely symbolic and do not confer any substantive advantage on the publicly recognised religion."[12] For Laborde, the US seems to be an example of a "modest separation," while Europe is mainly versions of "modest establishment." She gets some of her terminology from Ronald Dworkin, who thinks that there is some truth to the conservative reading of US history, viz., that it was founded as a tolerant religious nation (tolerant of unbelief) but in the second half of the twentieth century unelected judges made it a tolerant secular nation (tolerant of belief).[13] He also thinks that while somewhat complex, Britain too is a secular nation that tolerates religion as "its established church owes more to its love of tradition and ceremony, I think, than to any genuine shared national religious commitment."[14] Dworkin is right that the British state and politics is a form of secularism[15] but I think the language of "separation" is quite misleading, as is seeing departures from absolute separation as departures from political secularism. In any case, I want to defend the possibility of state-religion connections (of which certain kinds of establishment may be one version) that go beyond what Bhargava and Laborde believe are consistent with liberal and/or secular principles.

My understanding of a SRC is: some kind of relationship with the state such that a religious organization participates in the functions of the state or is a partner in governance, helping the state to discharge some of its duties and implementation of policies, or it is continuously supported by public funds, or it is part of the symbolism of the state in a clearly non-neutralist way; some form of "formal or legal union or alliance between state and religion" to use Bhargava's disapproving vocabulary. The example that I am most familiar with and exercised by is the Church of England's relationship with the Head of State (the monarch is the Supreme Governor of the Church, and only assumes the throne after being anointed in oil by bishops); its position in the House of Lords (twenty-six bishops sit in the upper house of the legislature by right and have full voting rights); its role in the national system of education (several thousand church schools are nearly wholly dependent on state funding); and recently it has come to see itself, and to be seen by government, as having a responsibility to promote multi-faith harmony.[16] Whilst some aspects of this relationship are symbolic, it is evident that it goes beyond the symbolic. On the other hand, there is no pretending that the church has a lot of power within the state and hence I think it may be characterized as a form of "weak establishment"; and my argument is that such an arrangement is consistent with political secularism.[17]

The Church of England is not the only example I have in mind in relation to SRCs. The term is capacious enough to include the status of Catholic and Protestant churches as legal corporations with various rights and entitlements, including having the state collect a voluntary tithe through the tax system and receive large amounts of public funding in order to carry out various welfare functions autonomously or semi-autonomously; an arrangement that has been referred to as "multiple establishments."[18] It also includes the presence of an established church together with other, lesser and varied forms of recognition of other churches and faiths by the state as in Denmark.[19] It includes also the Belgian state's recognition of several religions as national religions and the French state relationship with Catholics, Protestants, Jews, and Muslims at the highest level of the executive.[20] Moreover, it should be clear that when I include "weak establishment" within the category "State-Religion Connexions" (SRC) that I believe are consistent with, indeed a part of Western European moderate secularisms, I am not including what may be called "full establishment" or a confessional state – Western European states may have been like this once but they ceased to be some time ago, and are not so today. Nevertheless I do mean much more than what Laborde calls "symbolic" establishment,"[21] and also more than what some people mean by the "post-secular," namely the allowing of the presence of religious views in political debate[22] as long as those views or those religions are never identified with the state.[23] Veit Bader has a helpful definition of weak establishment as "constitutional or legal establishment of one State-Church, and de jure and de facto religious freedom and pluralism."[24]

There is a view that while there may be something like moderate secularism present in Western Europe and elsewhere, in the twentieth century it has continually given way and become weaker – perhaps even that there is a historical process at work that will ultimately lead to the disappearance of SRCs and the triumph of full secularism. Actually, there are certain substantive policy areas where SRCs have grown. Moreover, this is not just in the last decade or so, that is to say, in the period identified as "post-secular." One of the biggest growths in SRCs in England and France has been in the area of education and took place around the middle of the twentieth century. The 1944 Education Act meant a big growth in state funding of church schools (mainly Anglican and Catholics but in due course extended to some others too) such that by the end of the twentieth century about a quarter to a third of pupils in England and Wales were in state-funded church schools. Similarly, and somewhat unexpectedly, given how French *laïcité* is standardly and comprehensively contrasted with England, the "Debré Law" of 1959 enabled church schools (nearly all Catholic) in France to be nearly wholly subsidised by the state (17 per cent of all pupils in 2011–12).[25] Despite the emergence of a new, hardened *laïcité* in response to Muslims in the last few decades, this state-Catholic arrangement has not been reversed nor properly extended to Muslim people.[26] Moreover, in the last couple of decades SRCs have formed in relation to "community relations" or "interfaith relations" (in relation to England, see endnote 18) and currently several states are exploring and enacting the transfer of the delivery of some welfare services from the state to civil society, including religious organizations.[27] So, whether we look at the matter in terms of the last century or just the last couple of decades, SRCs have both declined and have grown under various liberal democratic regimes.

Formal "weak" establishment, informal establishment, and SRCs in general, then, are not a primary issue of secularism but a secondary one to do with context, time, and place, including no doubt the political as well as the economic costs and benefits of, for example, moving from one set of arrangements to another.[28] I acknowledge that the historical movement has been generally for SRCs to be thinned down, to be marginalized, and to be pluralized, despite some of the strong counter-examples I have just offered. It does not mean, however, that we have to take the thinning down to its nth point if there is a good reason to slow down, halt, or even reverse the process, and it is interesting that in few states, if any, have many legislators or publics considered doing so. I suggest that egalitarians accommodate new, marginal, and stigmatized groups – most notably, Muslims in Western Europe – in a spirit of multicultural citizenship.

Multiculturalism, Liberalism and State-Religions Connections

As I have stated my view of multicultural citizenship in a number of places and space here is limited, I will restate it very briefly and concentrating on what is absolutely necessary for my argument here.[29] Our most fundamental concept of equal citizenship is that all citizens have the same rights and duties, are treated the same by the state and by each other qua citizens and there is no discrimination on grounds such as gender, ethnicity, race, religion, sexuality, and so on. However, we also understand that these social dimensions are also bases of identity that are important to some of their bearers and who seek respect and "recognition" from fellow citizens and the state, especially in conditions where these identities have been stigmatized or marginalized.[30] These identities are not straightforwardly chosen, people do not choose to be born male or female, black or white, though there are elements of choice and the meaning of these identities is contextual. In any case, there is some room for individuals to choose what kind of and how much of an identity to project publicly and to have others publicize. For example, some black people do not want their blackness to be noticed politically; others insist on it and demand for example the right to autonomous organizations within political parties and trades unions and for special rights of representation (e.g., a number of reserved places on a national committee). If a polity gives expression to respect for group identities and group representation, or even simply group equality of opportunity, then the principle of treating everybody the same – "colour-blindness," and so on – has to be modified. Some people, including some multiculturalists, believe that while what I have described holds for all the other bases of identity that I have mentioned, religion is an exception as it is something chosen, whilst all the others are largely "given." This, however, is a false distinction. One does not choose to be born a Muslim but being of a Muslim background or being perceived as such can be the basis for a diminished citizenship in just the same way as other bases of identity. Of course, some Muslims may not want to project a religious identity and may believe that religion is a private matter. But other Muslims may not. This is the same point as I was making about blackness and it also applies to gender and sexuality: multicultural identities have an element of "givenness," which is not only biological but is socially constructed and ascribed. There is also an element of choice in self-designated identity, in particular in relation to issues of privacy and publicity. However, there is one important implication for religion that should be highlighted. Multiculturalist accommodation of groups is primarily as identity or community based on descent and only secondarily about faith; it is based on recognition and inclusivity, not the truth of doctrines. In so far as doctrine comes in, it does so indirectly, for example, protecting Jewish people from incitement to hatred may mean protecting them from certain insults to their religion (e.g., that they are Christ-killers or their rituals involve the sacrifice of Christian babies), or allowing the community to transmit its identity over generations may require public support for Jewish schools in which Judaism is taught and not just or in addition to the national religion or non-religious ethics.

The first and most basic argument, then, for including religious identities, and specifically for the multiculturalist accommodation of a religious minority is not by a comparative reference to Christians but by reference to equal respect; in so far as there is a comparative reference, the initial comparative reference is to the egalitarian accommodation of women, black people, queer people, etc. Perhaps the most immediate implication for political secularism is that any political norm that excludes religious identities from the public space, from schools and universities, from politics and nationhood – what I call "radical secularism," which tries to privatize religion, is incompatible with multicultural citizenship; and if religious identities face this kind of exclusion but not identities based on race, ethnicity, gender, and so on, then there is a bias against religious identity and a failure to practice equality between identities or identity groups. When groups protest against such forms of exclusion, as Muslims have been doing, we should identify what they are asking for and consider whether it is reasonable, and here the argument has to soon become contextual. Do we normally grant such things? If we do, is there a reason to not continue to do so or to not pluralize it? Conversely, if we do not normally grant such things, is there a good reason to do so now? This is not merely about precedent or status quo – it is looking at precedents, the status quo and considerations about what will work and runs with the grain of familiar norms and practices from the point of view of multicultural inclusion.[31] Inclusion may be possible without using SRCs but using SRCs may be one way or part of a way to achieve inclusion.

I will consider two important objections to the SRCs that I am saying may be justifiable and may be of value in relation to the accommodation of minorities. The first objection is one of principle, while the second is more contingent. The first objection is that I am in breach of the liberal requirement of state neutrality, that the state should not be seen to be associating itself with a conception of the good and especially not a religion. I have a number of responses, the first of which is that if "neutral" means a state with no cultural or religious character, then that is an impossible condition to fulfil. There is no such thing as a culturally contentless state or public space. The state will always have some historical-cultural character. For example, there will be an official language(s) in which the business

of the state is conducted in and which provides the rhetoric, the collective memories, and the cultural texture through which civic communication is achieved. Similarly, any state will draw on a specific set of ethical,
political, and legal traditions, and while they will have some element of
universality, they will always have some particularity too. Moreover, this
particularity extends to the ways in which the state-religion connection is
expressed. This will be true of its substantial aspects such as the presence
of the bishops in the House of Lords as well as of its symbolic aspects
such as the ways in which prayers are part of the parliamentary calendar
in the UK or a large cross dominates the chamber of the Quebec provincial
assembly. While it is true that language is essential to the functioning of a
state whereas religion is not, the state-religion question is not optional. In
any case, in respect of being optional, religion is on a par with many things
that are unproblematically supported by states. For example, the state supports non-essential but valued activities such as the motor industry or the
Olympics. While in each case state funding has its critics, few people hold
the view that state support should be confined to only those activities essential to the existence of a state.

If by "neutrality" is meant not cultural contentlessness but that the basic
structure of the state and its laws and policies must not be derived from
or can only be justified by reference to a religion because, say, such justifications must be consistent with what Rawls called a "political conception
of justice." Bearing in mind that Rawls was ruling out not just appeals to
religion but to all "comprehensive doctrines"[32] then SRCs can be consistent
with this understanding of neutrality albeit with two qualifications. Firstly,
we must not assume that political justice in this basic sense is cut and
dried, that the principles are only consistent with a small set of comprehensive doctrines and susceptible to a narrow set of meanings. Charles Taylor
usefully offers a capacious understanding of "overlapping consensus,"
namely a flexible and dialogical way of (re)interpreting the core principles
of political justice and of how they may be implemented.[33] We can take
this one step further by not thinking of "overlapping consensus" as simply
an overlapping set of derivations from discrete comprehensive doctrines
evaluated against an independent a priori standard of justice, but rather
as an interactive, dynamic process of persuasion and mutual learning,
which is always a work in progress and we might better express by calling
it "consensus building."[34] Rawls's political conception of justice is in effect,
as Bader points out, best understood not as an epistemological filter of

"reasonableness" but politically as adherence to Liberal Democratic Constitutionalism (LDC) – which of course has a substantive political content and so is far from politically neutral in the normal meaning of the term.[35]

Secondly, if we assume LDC as a baseline or a core that we want all politics and political institutions to work from, including SRCs, it means that the state cannot subtract from LDC, it cannot be less than LDC. It does not mean that the just state cannot build on LDC; indeed, that is exactly what it must do. On this understanding of "neutrality," the state can pursue socio-political projects such as, say, elimination of poverty, or to put a man on the moon, or to enhance inter-faith understanding amongst citizens or in the world generally; it can even identify with one or more comprehensive doctrines, socialism, or liberal perfectionism – as long as and to the extent that such state identification or projects remain within the limits of LDC. A state can identify with a philosophical or religious doctrine, but it cannot make citizens conform to this doctrine in ways that violate the norms of LDC. It can in principle declare "In God We Trust" or "Islam Is the Solution," but all entailments must be acted upon in ways consistent with liberal democratic constitutional rights and processes. Moreover, there are limits to what we can hope for from the state. For example, religious truth can't come from the state/politics (as Locke pointed out) – no more than scientific truth can come from the state/politics, or indeed art, or healthy living. Yet that does not mean that the state cannot promote religion any more than it means that the state cannot fund science or art or health care.[36] It is true that the state cannot require any citizen to believe in the truth of any religious doctrine, but no more can it require a belief in any comprehensive or political doctrine. The state may fund science at universities or may fund church-run schools without requiring any citizens to believe in any scientific hypothesis or religious doctrine.

It may sound like I am saying that it is consistent with LDC (what others may choose to call the liberal neutral state) to privilege religion. Yes, a kind of "privileging" of religion is permissible. For example, a particular state may fund church schools teaching the national curriculum but not schools organized around atheism or "race." Such funding is a kind of privileging of religion, but in a multiplex way. "Multiplex" is a word that conjoins "multiple" and "complex." The Oxford English Dictionary defines it as an adjective describing the "involving or consisting of many elements in a complex relationship." The state typically engages in not merely multiple cases of privileging but moreover this privileging is not all of one basic kind. The state may legitimately choose to give funding and prestige to banking, to opera, to the Olympics, and to "blue skies" scientific research – but without using the same arguments or the same metrics of calculation. So similarly, within a state regulated system of schooling the state funding of faith schools cannot simply be ruled out because it is a form of privileging.

The liberal state may recognize that religion is special[37] and may honour and support it in special ways but this is not necessarily equivalent to simple "privileging." So you could say that there is a multiplex privileging or a multiplicity of privileging and that there is no special or unique privileging of religion. What this shows is that the concept of "neutrality" is not very helpful over and beyond a requirement not to subtract from LDC.

So far, I hope I have shown that the "privileging" of religion is not in principle inconsistent with LDC. This leaves unresolved many questions about what shape this privileging should take. I cannot resolve them, but I would like to identify some of them and offer a couple of comments. There are in fact three separate issues of "privileging":

i) Religion relative to non-religion, e.g., ethnicity, nation, or economics. The multiculturalist view should be that no one type of identity or social dimension (e.g., religion, ethnicity, gender, class) should be privileged at the expense of the others. Moreover, there is no single measure of importance and so a variable geometry is inevitable: how a state will promote the Olympics will be different from how it will promote religion.

ii) Religion relative to no religion: this is the most difficult issue but not specific to this case, the same applies to sport and no-sport, for just as there are people who think that religion should not be privileged and paid for out of taxes, so people hold the same view about sport. Hence, I suggest "multiplex privileging" may not be a kind of second best – there may be no other way of resolving a "bias."

iii) One religion relative to another. This is not easy either, and I do not have a fully worked out view on this; but I do offer some important considerations. We should equalize upwards not downwards.[38] That is to say, the presumption is that if there is a benefit that one party has and the other does not (to the same extent), then the party with the lesser benefit or without the benefit, should be brought closer to the level of the other party, rather than the other way round. We should not for example ask schools or other public institutions to stop celebrating Christmas because of the presence of Muslims or Hindus; rather, we should extend the public cele-brations to include Eid and Diwali.[39] All the evidence suggests that this is what most minorities, especially Muslims, want – certainly in Britain. It is not the case that "accommodating Muslims in the political sphere, certainly requires abandoning a commitment to the Christian norms that have, historically, defined European states."[40] The challenge is not how to fully de-Christianize our states, but rather how to appropriately add the new faiths alongside older ones. This indeed is what is happening across much of Western Europe. What is interesting is that those most uncomfortable with this are not Christians or Churches but ideological secularists.

It may be useful for readers, especially for American readers, to see how distant my views are from First Amendment disputations in the US. So let me very briefly say what the position I am arguing for implies for the five-part *Private Choice Test*. I am referring to the test developed by the US Supreme Court to determine whether an educational voucher programme that benefits religious schools is constitutional[41]:

1. The program must have a valid secular purpose (Private Choice Test).

    Yes; but it may also have some sort of religious purpose or endorsement (Modood).

2. Aid must go to parents and not to the schools (Private Choice Test).
    In Western Europe nearly all states subsidise faith schools and this is part of my understanding of moderate secularism (Modood).

3. A broad class of beneficiaries must be covered (Private Choice Test).
    Not necessarily, sometimes religious groups may be targeted in an affirmative action manner if multicultural equality is best promoted that way in the specific circumstances (Modood).

4. The program must be neutral with respect to religion (Private Choice Test).
    I offer an understanding of "neutrality" based on LDC and multiplex privileging (Modood).

5. There must be adequate nonreligious options (Private Choice Test). Yes, where this is applicable, e.g., in relation to schools, health services etc. (Modood).

My response, then, to the objection that SRCs are a violation of liberal neutrality is that if we mean cultural neutrality, that is a condition impossible to satisfy; if we mean something like LDC, that is consistent with what I call multiplex privileging and which I suggest can take many forms, of which SRCs are one. While SRCs like the current Anglican "establishment" are unsatisfactory in terms of multicultural citizenship, it may be the case that, in a pluralized form, they offer a basis for the multicultural inclusion of religion, which would be blocked if they were to be abolished without alternative SRCs to be put in their place. It has, however, been argued that the Anglican establishment (and similar SRCs in other countries) alienates those who are outside the established Church[42] in contrast to the inclusionary effects of a "separation" regime, namely US denominationalism.[43] This indeed is the second, more contingent objection.

"Establishment" and the Alienation of Muslims

Bhargava has argued that what I call moderate secularism, is "irretrievably flawed" and while it has accommodated Christians it will not be able to accommodate Muslims.[44] While Bhargava's view of the "irretrievably flawed" nature of European secularisms or church-state relations is based on a contrast with India, others take a similar view by comparing Western Europe to the United States. Kymlicka, for example, has argued that "American denominationalism ... has been successful precisely in relation to ... religious groups composed primarily of recent immigrants, and Muslims in particular," who are more likely than European Muslims "to express the feeling that their religion and religious freedoms are fully respected, and that they are accepted as citizens."[45] Similarly, it has been said of the US in explicit contrast to certain European countries (e.g., Britain) that "without the separation of church and state, we believe, the religions imported by past immigration streams could not have achieved parity with Protestant versions of Christianity."[46] The claim that "weak establishment" or "moderate secularism" of Britain alienates the majority of Muslims is of course an empirical claim and as such it ignores the evidence about the strong sense of British identification and national pride amongst Muslims in

Britain. For example, an analysis of two national Citizenship Surveys concluded: "We find no evidence that Muslims or people of Pakistani heritage were in general less attached to Britain than were other religions or ethnic groups."[47] This has in fact been the finding of many surveys – including a recent one, which concluded that overall British Muslims are more likely to be both patriotic and optimistic about Britain than are the white British community.[48]

Equally, we know that British Muslims include many vociferous political groups and between them they have mounted many arguments, not to mention campaigns, in relation to socio-economic deprivation, religious discrimination, incitement to religious hatred, various foreign policies, anti-terrorist policies, and so on.[49] So Muslims in Britain do seem to feel excluded and alienated by some aspects of British and indeed European society. Yet there is no record of any criticism by a Muslim group in relation to the establishment. On the other hand, many Muslims complain that Britain is too unreligious and anti-religious, too hedonistic, consumerist, materialist, and so on. Muslims protest much more about secularist bans on modest female dress, such as the headscarf (banned in French state schools since 2004) and the face veil (banned in public places first in France, followed by a number of other European countries) than they do about "establishment" or Christian privileges. Muslims and other religious minorities appreciate that establishment is a recognition by the state of the public and national significance of religion, and so holds out the prospect of a "multi-establishment," which disestablishment would foreclose without conferring any advantage to the religious minorities. This appreciation is partly the result of the fact that the Church of England takes its mission to serve the country seriously, including wanting to incorporate new minority faith communities in its vision of the country and its sense of responsibilities.[50] When, at Christmas 2011, David Cameron said we should assert that Britain is "a Christian country" – the first time a British prime minister had spoken like that for a long time – it was welcomed by Ibrahim Mogra, the then chairman of the Mosque Committee of the Muslim Council of Britain and later the assistant general secretary. This does indeed suggest that Britain's difficulty integrating Muslims has more to do with what Casanova himself identifies as the more important factor – namely, what he calls "recent trends towards drastic secularisation."[51] Hence if the US is better at integrating post-immigration religious minorities it may be not to do with its non-establishment but the greater presence of religion and in particular the greater social status of religion and its closeness to the mainstream of society.[52] In this respect, it is important to note that while the US may be more of a secular state than Britain, the latter is more of a secular society and has a much more secularist political culture. The "there shall be no establishment" constitutional clause may work well for the US in certain respects, but it is far from stress-free as evidenced by the rise of an embittered Christian Right, including its support for aggressive foreign policies and Islamophobic politics as extreme as those in Europe, and more conspicuously led by Christians.[53] Indeed, some of the luminaries of the US Right were a source of nourishment for the Norwegian mass murderer, Anders Breivik.[54]

An alternative understanding of alienation to the one I have been discussing might not be simply about experience but might be understood as "objective alienation."[55] This is something that might be said to exist even if the sufferers were not aware of it. I suppose the idea would parallel something like what Marx says about alienation, namely that it is not simply an experience but a degraded condition of humanity where labour has no possibility of creativity or self-expression.[56] The danger – not at all hypothetical – with a concept of objective alienation is that it will be used to deny the need for evidence in the way that, say, French republicans and others regard girls and women wearing the headscarf as oppressed and dominated even when the females themselves insist they are not and no evidence can be found to suggest that coercion or intimidation is taking place. In practice it is views such as these that are the basis for some of the domination of Muslims through "state paternalism" or at least "educational paternalism."[57] A satisfactory account of objective alienation would need to relate how it handles evidence and in particular counter-evidence and this is not present in the accounts I have been examining.

The disestablishmentarian's argument, then, that contemporary Christian SRCs alienate groups such as Muslims is based on certain secularist assumptions, not evidence. Secularists concerned with minimizing the alienation would do well to first focus on how their secularism alienates. Moreover, if I am right in suggesting that Muslims and other religious minorities are seeking equality through levelling up, not levelling down – accommodation within something resembling the status quo in Europe, not a dispossession of Christians churches – then what we have is an additive not a subtractive view of inclusivity. Typically, recognition or accommodation implies making a particular social dimension more (not less) politically significant. Equality movements do not usually seek less political importance for their organizing social category. This is the case with race, gender, minority nationalities, sexual orientation, class, and so on. It is difficult to see why religion is to be treated differently. Hence the challenge, as I said earlier, is not how to de-Christianize Western states but rather how to appropriately add the new faiths alongside the older ones.

I believe that multicultural equality needs to include groups centred around a religious identity. An implication of this is some kind of public multi-faithism in an SRC way but the institutional form this may take can vary and I am not committed to one form. In relation to Britain, for example, it does not have to be within an Anglican establishment, nor its equivalent in other countries; but that it, pluralized in some way, does offer one way forward and we should consider it as a practical proposition. It may be that it is the least disruptive and may allow those for whom establishment is important, or who are uncomfortable with multiculturalism, a relatively unthreatening way forward. At least I hope I have raised the challenge of how we are to give appropriate recognition to ethno-religious groups if it is not in part by pluralizing existing SRCs.[58] By "existing SRCs" I mean the context of moderate secularism within LDC, where religious authority does not dominate political authority, where when religious organizations are publicly funded to deliver social services, citizens have options to receive the same services by non-religious organizations, and where, more generally, there is multiplex privileging and religion is not privileged in a unique and special way. Instead, a wide range of non-religious activities are also privileged.

5

Taylor, Rawls, and Secularism

RONALD BEINER

I'll begin with a brief account of my views about secularism; then offer a quick discussion of Charles Taylor's (not dissimilar) account; and then try to trace what's the same and what's different in those two accounts. There are differences between us, but they are pitched more at the level of rhetoric than of substance. Still, rhetoric matters.

It strikes me that the ideas that really matter in the area of religion and politics are rather simple and prosaic ones – namely, why we in the West live in a fundamentally secular society, and why we should be deeply fearful about living in a society that is anything other than fundamentally secular. Above all, we need reminders about easy-to-take-for-granted facts about contemporary political life. We wouldn't want to have barred Mitt Romney from seeking the US presidency on account of his religious beliefs, but neither would we want those religious beliefs to have had any special authority should he have become president. Why? First of all, because political association is a community of citizens, not a community of believers. To borrow a formulation of Will Kymlicka's that for me articulates a foundational principle: "The boundaries of state and nation rarely if ever coincide perfectly, and so viewing the state as the possession of a particular national group can only alienate minority groups. The state must be seen as belonging equally to all people who are governed by it, regardless of their nationality."[1] The principle is just the same (and just as valid) if we substitute "religion" and "religious" for "nation" and "national" (and the principle obviously has no less force in cases where a minority religion rather than the majority religion holds the seat of power). For the

Church of Latter-Day Saints to have any special authority vis-à-vis other denominations or other religions would mean that the state would be "owned" by Mormons – or owned by them to a greater extent than it is owned by other citizens. This would be, to put it fairly mildly, normatively problematical.

In the contemporary United States, there is no shortage of theocratic political actors who believe, as the Reverend Jerry Falwell memorably put it in his Independence Day sermon of 1976, that "the idea that religion and politics don't mix was invented by the Devil to keep Christians from running their own country."[2] The number one desideratum in thinking about secularism is to be able to explain to these people why theirs is not a legitimate kind of politics. (One of the reviewers of my book on *Civil Religion* wrote that he couldn't understand why I opposed secularism to theocracy rather than opposing secularism to religion. The answer is simple. Theocracy is the *politicization* of religion. There's no necessary contradiction between religion and secularism, but there *is* a necessary contradiction between *theocracy* and secularism.)

Theocracy is neither an abstract theoretical possibility nor the memory of a long-banished past; it is a real part of the political present. Even years after a freely elected Islamist government in Egypt was overthrown by the Egyptian military, polls continue to show that the majority of people in Egypt believe that Sharia should be the law of the land and that Egypt should be a theocratic state. And even in a secular republic like the United States, explicitly erected on Enlightenment principles by its founders, it's clear that Donald Trump would have won neither the Republican nomination nor the presidency without the committed support of countless right-wing evangelicals voting for him on the basis of their own theocratic agenda. Trump's vice-president, Mike Pence, is politically a theocrat in the sense that he too believes that national policy should be at the service of (his own) faith. An essay from *The Atlantic* in 2017 cites a Public Policy Polling study according to which Republicans, by an utterly astonishing two-to-one majority, "support establishing Christianity as the national religion."[3] All of this suggests that theocratic politics is alive and well in the contemporary United States, notwithstanding the firm commitment of its founders to Lockean secularism.

In certain circles it has become fashionable to speak of "post-secularism," as if secularism had now in some sense become outdated (in need of a cultural sequel, just as "modernism" had to be succeeded by

"postmodernism"), rather than something that has to be perennially struggled for and defended. In contrast to that, we need to keep focused on
an understanding of secularism cast in directly political terms. A secular
regime is one where members of the society are given sufficient breathing
space vis-à-vis religion that the political agenda is not subject to compul-
sory dictation on the part of religious authorities, and citizens can conduct
their deliberations about political matters in a distinctively political (citizen-to-citizen) idiom.

None of us knows where the universe comes from or why it exists. Theists don't know. Atheists don't know. Agnostics don't know. None of us
knows. So for any group of people to come forward and say, not only do
they have privileged access to the source of the universe, but they know
what rituals it wants performed and what moral codes it wants to see prevail – well, that's both a colossal presumption, morally and intellectually
speaking, and also a colossal (and potentially dangerous) claim to power
and authority. It must be resisted when asserted as a basis of civic privilege.
On the other hand, we also have a duty (a civic duty, not a moral duty) not
to express contempt for the sincerely held beliefs of our fellow citizens.[4]
We have no choice but to take our fellow citizens as we find them, and
give them civic space to communicate their political opinions in a manner
corresponding to their actual beliefs. I'm aware that there is something of
a tension between the two sides of the issue I've tried to articulate: letting
people give expression to their actual beliefs, but not allowing those beliefs to be leveraged on behalf of indefensible power and authority. Bridging this tension is something we're able to pull off politically through the
kinds of compromises that we're familiar with in liberal democracies. We
don't bar Mitt Romney from the political arena just because he is a former
bishop of the Mormon Church,[5] and may have strange ideas of how God
revealed Himself and what He expects of us. But neither do we tolerate the
idea of a Mormon bishop becoming US president as a prelude to instituting a Mormon theocracy. That's the liberal compromise.

One view of the relationship between religion and citizenship is that
religionists should be disciplined to express themselves in ways that steer
clear of philosophically controversial "comprehensive doctrines." That's
familiar to everyone as the Rawlsian idea of "political liberalism" in its
simplest form. (Rawls himself was forced to develop increasingly con-
voluted versions of this doctrine on account of the outrage and indigna-
tion aroused, understandably, by his initial formulations.) Rawls wants a

political domestication of religion. But he doesn't want to present it *as* a domestication of religion, or present it in a way that suggests any kind of singling-out of religion for special treatment. So he hits on the idea of a proscription of *all* "comprehensive doctrines," whether secular or religious. From his point of view, all comprehensive doctrines, whether religious or philosophical, are in principle "sectarian" and therefore cannot be appealed to in underwriting a properly liberal regime. Hence (despite the paradox), it is illegitimate to appeal to a liberal philosophy of life in founding a liberal polity. If Catholics cannot legitimately found the state on a Catholic view of life (because its laws and policies will also apply to Protestant co-citizens), and if Protestants cannot found the state on a Protestant view of life (because its laws and policies will apply to Catholic co-citizens), then the conclusion might seem equally compelling that one also cannot found the state on a liberal-secular philosophy of life, because (again) those who do not subscribe to this philosophy of life will be bound by its laws and policies. Political liberalism claims to solve this problem by subjecting all comprehensive doctrines, whether religious or secular, to the test of public reason.[6] I reject that Rawlsian view. Again, one has to take fellow citizens as one finds them, and allow them to articulate themselves politically in a way that actually expresses who they conceive themselves to be. Rawls's ban, or partial ban, on comprehensive doctrines in the political sphere is misguided, not just because it will be applied in ways that are necessarily non-neutral (hence defeating what Rawls intended with his idea of public reason), but also because no one can properly be expected to leave their existential commitments at the doorstep when they enter the sphere of civic life. How can we not find very odd a political philosophy that demands that we drive a wedge between our identity as human beings and our identity as citizens? My own view is that the illegitimacy of theocratic politics is an entailment of a strong doctrine of citizenship. There's a sense in which Rawls is saying something quite similar to this; but Rawls's ban on comprehensive doctrines within the sphere of public reason makes it harder to affirm philosophically the primacy of citizenship in relation to other aspects of human identity, even if that is in fact an underlying Rawlsian theoretical commitment.[7] (Rawls objects to this because it commits the great anti-liberal sin of telling people how to be human, which all versions of perfectionism do in one way or another.)

Charles Taylor's reflections on the nature of modern secularism are so far-reaching in their scope, and so intimidating in their scale, that it would be folly for me, within such a short discussion, to attempt anything more than a very circumscribed response. Hence I'll restrict myself to a couple of Taylor's contributions on this topic: his essay "Why We Need a Radical Redefinition of Secularism,"[8] and his book with Jocelyn Maclure, *Secularism and Freedom of Conscience.*

Let's start with the "Radical Redefinition" essay. What defines a secular regime, on Taylor's account, is (1) the right not to be coerced in one's religious beliefs or lack of such beliefs; (2) the equality of citizens, irrespective of their beliefs or non-beliefs; and (3) the assurance that all voices will be heard and respected. Taylor emphasizes that it is especially important that we exert ourselves "to maintain harmony and comity between the supporters of different religions and Weltanschauungen."[9] If we need a "radical redefinition" of secularism, what is the reigning conception of secularism that is in need of being "radically redefined"? It would seem that Taylor has two targets primarily in mind – Atatürk's Turkey,[10] and contemporary French republicanism. The latter continues to be animated by the "Jacobin" impulse (inspired by Rousseau) that there must be a more unitary foundation for peoplehood than can actually be squared with the realities of life in a radically multiculturalized world.[11] Taylor rightly acknowledges the historical fact that "in the French case, *laïcité* came about in a struggle *against* a powerful church."[12] But for Taylor, this historical background does not fully absolve the excesses of Jacobinism.

Taylor, I think, makes out his "new" conception of secularism to be more novel and more controversial than it really is. What he offers, in my view, is the standard understanding of a secular regime, accompanied by a more emphatic determination to be welcoming of religious and culturally marginal voices in the civic conversation. If one takes Taylor's two miscreant regimes – Atatürk's Turkey and "hyper-republican" France – as somehow defining a kind of *archetype* of the properly secularist regime, then I suppose it might be possible to speak of a need for "redefining" secularism in light of the challenges of addressing contemporary multicultural realities. But of course there is no reason for regarding *those* two regimes as archetypically secularist, relative to, say, the founding of the American republic. More broadly, I agree with Taylor that there is no need to posit one uniform institutional template for defining the separation of church and state, hence making allowance for the pluralism that is so important to Taylor.[13]

Let's turn now to the book that Taylor co-authored with Jocelyn Maclure, *Secularism and Freedom of Conscience*. Here is the passage in the Taylor/Maclure book that expresses the normative core of Taylorian secularism: "In a society where there is no consensus about religious and philosophical outlooks ... the state must avoid hierarchizing the conceptions of the good life that form the basis of citizens' adherence to the basic principles of their political association. In the realm of core beliefs and commitments, the state, to be truly everyone's state, must remain 'neutral.' This implies that the state should adopt a position of neutrality not only toward religions but also toward the different philosophical conceptions that stand as the secular equivalents of religion."[14]

Taylor's appeal to the idea of the state being "truly everyone's state"[15] is highly reminiscent of the Kymlickian principle I quoted at the beginning of this chapter – which is why I said that in substance our views are quite similar. But this principle of the state belonging to all of its citizens, and therefore being prohibited from articulating a state philosophy founded on a sectarian basis, is enveloped by Taylor/Maclure in a Rawlsian vocabulary that needs some unpacking. We can call it Taylor's "Rawlsian turn." (Taylor's reference to "philosophical conceptions that stand as the secular equivalents of religion" is obviously an allusion to the Rawlsian conception of "comprehensive doctrines."[16]) This reliance on Rawlsian categories is, I have to say, a bit jarring for someone like me, schooled in the debates of the 1980s.[17]

Let's start with the idea of "the neutral state." What the "state neutrality" idea is intended to convey is not only that theocracies of all descriptions are illegitimate but also that the liberal state should not use the idea of secularism as a rationale for pursuing a war against religion (as has arguably been the case with some of the secularist regimes that most trouble Taylor). I have no disagreements here. But the appeal to "neutrality" is nonetheless problematic, for as Taylor himself has helped to teach us, nothing in life is neutral.

It is fairly easy to see what is driving Taylor towards Rawlsianism. Clearly, it is the worry that if we concede that there is a comprehensive doctrine (a view of life) embodied in the liberal state, that will provide a mandate for (what Taylor sees as) the "bad" versions of secularism such as the one we see in France, which leans on Muslim schoolgirls to shed their hijabs, and requires both them and their parents to profess an allegiance to a French-republican "civil religion" of robust *laïcité*.[18] In short, it is Taylor's multiculturalism that is pushing him towards Rawlsianism. But putting to one side this more militant French version of secularism (now embraced also by Quebec!), surely even the "good" secularism that Taylor prefers embodies non-neutral conceptions of the good. If our state is founded on notions of liberty, equality, and upholding the common dignity of all citizens, then there are definite conceptions of the good instantiated in the liberal state. (Taylor, following William Galston, calls this a "minimal perfectionism."[19] But a minimal perfectionism is still perfectionism, not neutralism.) It may be "neutral" between Christian liberals, Muslim liberals, and agnostic liberals; but it is certainly not neutral between a liberal vision of life (including civic life) and various non-liberal visions of life (including civic life).[20] And if it is not neutral in the latter sense, it is not neutral, *period*. (Imagine trying to persuade Nietzsche or Marx or Heidegger that the Taylorian/Rawlsian conception of liberal citizenship does not embody comprehensive doctrines, that it is "neutral" between rival visions of human life.) The notion of more neutrality or less neutrality makes little sense. "The neutral state" either is or isn't neutral. It isn't.

Reading this 2011 book, one cannot help wondering whatever happened to the famous liberal-communitarian debate of the 1980s. That debate was substantially defined by Rawls's commitment to "the priority of the right to the good," and the largely Taylor-inspired insistence that conceptions of the good are never absent, and never lose their ultimacy.[21] This (along with much else) is one of the things that I learned from Taylor in my youth. Rawlsian neutralism never went away – in important ways, that neutralism became more radical.[22] But Taylor's commitment to a style of theorizing oriented to ambitious conceptions of the good and their centrality to moral life (at least in their *political* relevance) seems to have weakened. Or at least that's what his rapprochement with Rawls suggests to me (judging by the texts I'm looking at in this chapter). The unmistakable implication of chapters 1 and 2 of *Secularism and Freedom of Conscience* seems to be that Rawlsian political liberalism gives a better account of Taylor's multicultural commitments than does the doctrine of the ultimate primacy of conceptions of the good. If Taylor (or Taylor/Maclure) has been drawn to a Rawlsian self-understanding, I want to urge a return to Taylor's erstwhile commitment to a conception of political philosophy fundamentally oriented to conceptions of the good. To borrow a formulation suggested to me by Cécile Laborde, one might speak of a Rawlsian "temptation" that needs to be resisted.

Here's an example. If a liberal civic community takes its stand on the principle of full civic equality, it is hard to see how it can resist the claim to equality instantiated in gay marriage – and indeed changes to marriage laws in liberal societies such as Canada and the US have moved dramatically in the direction of gay civic equality in recent years. Abiding by Rawlsian strictures, we declare that this change in civic norms is "philosophically neutral," related neither to a religious vision of life nor to a non-religious vision of life. It is, so to speak, metaphysically and existentially agnostic. It is simply the playing-out of the freestanding political commitments of citizens of a liberal polity. But how would, say, an evangelical Christian or arch-conservative Catholic react to this claim of neutrality? And wouldn't the evangelical Christian or conservative Catholic be right to react with incredulity? Surely there's *some* vision of life at play in affirming a robust conception of gays as citizens among citizens. As I have made the point elsewhere,[23] we cannot expect a comprehensive doctrine to be trumped by something that is less than a comprehensive doctrine. My alternative to Rawlsian philosophical neutralism is what I've called citizenship – or civicism – as a comprehensive doctrine[24] (namely, an existential commitment to a life of equal citizenship), and secularism both as I define it and as Taylor defines it is part and parcel of this comprehensive doctrine. I am not convinced that appeal to a mere "overlapping consensus" would ever have gotten us to an acknowledgment of the justice of gay marriage. But I am convinced that such an acknowledgment is required by a robust conception of shared citizenship. This example suggests to me that we are not likely to do full justice to the relationship between citizenship and secularism within Rawlsian parameters.

Let me make three further points. First, I've undergone my own process of "Rawlsianisation" over the last twenty years or so (who hasn't?); so I shouldn't get too cocky. Second, this business about neutralism may seem like just a "quibble" over language. But for philosophers these sorts of quibbles matter a lot. Third, and most important, Taylor in the texts I've been responding to radically understates problems of philosophical coherence in Rawlsian political philosophy. Why is Rawlsianism not coherent? If I spontaneously privilege the idea of ecumenical citizenship – of being fair to all citizens just in their capacity of being fellow citizens – then *liberalism* is my comprehensive doctrine. If there are non-liberal aspects to my view of life or to my view of the good, and I subordinate these to the imperatives of shared citizenship, then the idea of shared citizenship has trumping power within my philosophy of life. Hence the idea of citizenship as a comprehensive doctrine, that is, as a privileged existential commitment. Either way, there is no philosophical neutrality.

What matters is not just that prior to "The Idea of Public Reason Revisited" Rawls wanted to shut up religious believers, and subsequent to "The Idea of Public Reason Revisited" he became willing to let them speak and contribute as citizens – which is unquestionably the main issue for Taylor. For me, by contrast, the much larger concern about Rawls is that the idea of neutralism – of not politically privileging conceptions of the good – is at the heart of the very *conception* of political liberalism. What "political liberalism" fundamentally means is that grand reflection on the ends of life is redundant – because the sociological coming-to-be of a liberal society provides the overlapping consensus needed to sustain a liberal society.[25] In fact, such reflection is potentially subversive of a liberal society because, insofar as it encourages people to focus on the philosophically deep commitments that divide them, it may actually *disrupt* the overlapping consensus that has already been achieved. Hence the philosopher reins in their natural inclination to pursue and debate these deep questions, and instead invents a new way of doing political philosophy (viz., political liberalism) that circumvents or steers clear of the philosophically deep commitments that threaten to reawaken existential conflicts between citizens of a liberal society. It strikes me that forgoing this whole dimension of ambitious reflection on the ends of life – an exercise in self-reflection that helps to constitute our humanity, after all – is a very large price to pay for the embrace of Rawlsian liberalism. In any case, the idea that one could affirm a vision of politics without endorsing any particular conception of ultimate human flourishing is chimerical. A society centred on liberal-egalitarian ideas of decency and mutual respect is obviously very different from societies fundamentally geared towards warrior honour, or Sparta-like republican virtue, or piety, or contemplative communing with nature, or other non-liberal views of the human good. So non-neutral conceptions of the good are inscribed in the liberal experience of life, whether Rawlsians want to acknowledge this or not.

There is one other big issue where I'd like to take issue with Taylor. At the end of *Secularism and Freedom of Conscience*, Taylor and Maclure say that they would want a liberal society to censor neither Salman Rushdie nor Richard Dawkins and Christopher Hitchens. But there is a consistent suggestion throughout Taylor's work that we would all be better off if "hard-line secularists" toned down their aggressive challenges to religion.[26] Here is my response: far from seeing Dawkins and Hitchens as doing something wrong, isn't that what we're supposed to be doing in a liberal society? Engaging in a vigorous debate of ideas? And how are we supposed to do that if the people on one side of the debate are supposed to muzzle themselves, and be so respectful of the other side that their critical challenges are not really challenges at all?

There are all kinds of banal rubbish associated with life in a modern liberal society (consumerism, a moronic mass culture, bureaucracy, technocracy, etc.). But one of the things that certainly is *not* banal rubbish is the unbounded exercise of free thought and free speech. The vigorous exercise of this prerogative of free expression began with the Enlightenment, deploying the full critical repertoire of argument, irony, and satire. Without that, we would probably all still be subject to the oppressive reign of clerical authority – of what the great heretics of the seventeenth century rightly called "priestcraft" – as we had been for centuries and centuries before the Enlightenment. And there are today many millions of people in the world still subject to that kind of suffocating oppression.[27] This is actually a fairly large question of political philosophy (and politics too!): living within the space of liberty created by a basically secular regime, do we put our intellectual energies into forging solidarity with secularists in religiously dominated societies who are still struggling for the space of liberty that we are lucky enough to enjoy? Or do we put our energy into protesting against the supposed marginalization of religious believers in a society like ours, fundamentally geared to secular ends? And even if we basically side with secularism (as Taylor does), another fairly large philosophical question concerns the rhetoric by which one expresses one's endorsement of secularism.

There is a larger issue here, namely whether it's appropriate for us to look for normative anchors – and also, the issue of whether political philosophy is the discipline tasked with locating and articulating these normative anchors.[28] Or is it the case that respect for cultural and religious pluralism is the primary – one could say, the overriding – normative concern? I think that Taylor's philosophical inclinations – akin to those of his teacher, Isaiah Berlin – lean towards this latter view. By contrast, I'm of the view that the upholding of secularism as a political ideal ties into firm normative principles, and as such traces a limit to normative pluralism.[29] It also has to be said that the appreciation of cultural diversity does not help very much in addressing the ongoing conflict between secularists and anti-secularists in various societies, such as those in the Middle East, where theocratic political movements continue to attract much support. *Either* one thinks that the secularists represent the cause of civic sanity and justice (which is the view of all Western liberals) *or* one thinks that this is another case of Western imperialism imposing its own ethnocentric preferences, and hence denies any normative privilege accorded to secularism. This is a pretty unyielding either/or, normatively speaking, and is unlikely to bow to considerations of cultural pluralism. (The secularist ideal was encapsulated nicely by Theodor Herzl when he wrote that priests need to be confined to their temples just as an army needs to be confined to its barracks.)

Politically speaking, a secular society is one where religious authorities have no special clout, and insofar as they participate in political debate (which is legitimate), it is on a citizen-to-citizen rather than minister-to-those-who-are-ministered-to or pastor-to-recipients-of-pastoral-care (that is, shepherd-to-sheep) basis. That's become the norm in Western liberal societies, and we should not allow ourselves to become so fearful of appearing Eurocentric that we hesitate to affirm that norm as normatively justified.[30]

PART THREE

Moral Agency and the Self I

6

What If Anything Is Wrong with Positive Liberty?

THE STRUGGLES OF AGENCY IN A NON-IDEAL WORLD

JOHN CHRISTMAN

The idea of freedom plays such a complex and powerful role in political discourse that it is no surprise that philosophical controversies about its meaning have been so seemingly endless. As an essentially contested concept, the idea of freedom (or liberty) has functioned as a centrepiece for countless deep and abiding theoretical debates and social struggles. Charles Taylor's trenchant critique of the purely negative concept of liberty still resonates with those of us who search for an understanding of self-determining agency that will not run afoul of an avowed commitment to pluralism and respect for difference.[1] Indeed, despite Taylor's arguments, theorists recently have continued with attempts to carve out a purely negative sense of liberty that avoids what they see as the pitfalls of its positive cousin but still names the condition of human social and political life that is central both to ideals of justice and struggles against oppression.

Yet these recent accounts have failed, I think, to properly understand the deepest motivations behind calls for a positive understanding of agency, ones where the exercise of self-government is crucial but which nonetheless operates in a social field of broad pluralism of identities and value commitments and which takes fully into account the social nature of the self. Such an "exercise concept" of freedom, as Taylor labeled it, must also account for the ways that complex dynamics of power serve to shape both the external landscape of action and the internal structure of agency itself. Conceptualizing freedom in ways that are sensitive to these factors but go beyond the pure opportunity concept of traditional (and current) versions of liberty remains a daunting challenge.

The complex amalgam of controversies surrounding notions of freedom is surely too vast to cover comprehensively here, but I want to look closely at some selective aspects of these recent attempts to resuscitate a purely negative model of freedom and specifically to examine the reasons these theorists give for rejecting a positive alternative. After discussing those attempts to develop a negative idea of freedom and noting their pitfalls, I will sketch the broad contours of a positive view, one very much inspired by Taylor's thought but developed along independent lines. In so doing, however, I will bring to the fore new challenges that current conditions pose to such a view.

One last preliminary: much recent political philosophy has highlighted the ways that theorizing about fundamental concepts and principles should proceed in light of non-ideal conditions of the social landscape.[2] Doing so underscores the way in which *perspective* matters a great deal in making intuitive judgments about the meaning and implications of concepts. In this case, it will be important to reflect on the meaning of freedom both from the viewpoint of those enjoying its protections as well as from those struggling to attain it. As we will see, that is of no small consequence in sorting through these complex and trenchant debates, especially when many points turn on the alleged intuitive superiority of this or that aspect of a concept.

I. The New Negative Liberty and What Is Still Wrong with It

Various thinkers have responded to critiques of negative liberty such as Taylor's by developing what they take to be a conceptually defensible idea of freedom that also can serve as a fundamental value category in liberal political principles.[3] That is, they develop allegedly value neutral, empirically measurable models of freedom that can function in this manner. In doing so, they hope to avoid the various pitfalls of rival notions that, for example, see freedom as a moralized idea, or understand liberty as defined with reference to desires, or do not give a properly restricted notion of what counts as a constraint. The motivation in general is to develop this idea squarely within the confines of a liberal empiricism, where value neutrality and measurability are desiderata.

The main idea of these views is that in order for the idea of freedom to function the way it does in theoretical discourse, it should be seen as referring purely to opportunities to act – so that freedom refers to the absence of physical barriers to actions that agents are able to perform but which are blocked by the actions of other human beings.[4] On Mathew Kramer's view, for example, a person is free to do x if and only if she is able to do x, and she is unfree to do x if and only if she would be able to do so in the absence of being directly or indirectly prevented from so doing by the actions or dispositions of other persons.[5] Others have echoed this approach, stressing that freedom is a function of external barriers to action independent of whether such actions are desired by the agent, virtuous, valuable, or morally permissible.[6]

Below I will discuss positive freedom in some detail, but what can be noted here is the way that these negative opportunity conceptions of liberty avoid the key aspect of those positive ideas – namely that any aspects of the *agency* of the subject of freedom is relevant to her being free. All that matters are the barriers to her action, not her relation to that action, the effectiveness with which she might be able to perform it, or whether such action in any way reflects her authentic value perspective. In this way, these negative accounts attempt to capture the value neutrality and empirical observability of freedom as that idea functions in (for example) liberal democratic political theory.

One characteristic motivation behind these negative views is the contention that only such an austere view of freedom gives us an adequate understanding of what it is to be constrained. On the one hand, they claim to avoid what they see as the fatal pitfalls of any view of freedom that ties the understanding of a constraint to the desires of the (free) agent, and on the other they argue that only constraints placed in our path by other human beings count as such.

Both Carter and Kramer reiterate Isaiah Berlin's objection that positive conceptions of freedom posit untoward references to the agent's desires in understanding both her liberty and, correspondingly, the constraints we describe her as facing. Reference to the internal states of the agent in calculating her freedom, they argue, implies the paradoxical idea that we can be made more free not by changing the world but by changing ourselves. Even worse, adaptation to constrained circumstance where we simply stop wanting to perform the actions we are prevented from performing, makes us more free. As Berlin famously puts it: "It is as if I were to say: 'I have a wounded leg. There are two methods of freeing myself from pain. One is to heal the wound ... But ... [the other is to] get rid of the wound by cutting off my leg.'"[7] This strikes us as counterintuitive, it is claimed, but also runs against the quest to make liberty a phenomenon that is observable and measurable externally.

This is a much-discussed objection. To consider its power, we should ponder whether the implication concerning freedom's being increased due to facts about the agent herself rather than her surroundings is all that paradoxical, at least when considered carefully. Clearly, for example, various aspects of our physical surroundings that constrain our actions (and which were put in place by others) do not even occur to us affecting our freedom, exactly *because* the movements they prevent are not on our practical evaluative radar.

Unless, of course, they are, or become so: it would never occur to me to think that a few sharp objects strewn on the sidewalk count as a constraint on my freedom, as I blithely step past them in the normal course of events. But were I to develop a devotion to a religious practice whose rituals required me to lay prone in supplication on the very path where such objects lay, suddenly I *would be* constrained. What's different? In one case the actions that the objects prevent don't even occur to me as one's that I would value doing or which I could not easily work around to achieve my everyday goals. But in the second case, the actions prevented by the objects are fundamentally important to me, and so calling them constraints seems apt. The difference in the two scenarios is not in the world, it is in *me*. But that seems exactly right.

To be clear, however, the driving force behind the objection to desire-sensitive accounts of freedom (or of constraints) is that in many cases adaptation to a constrained environment is undertaken as a fearful response to the constraints *themselves*. In such cases it is understandably claimed that changing one's character in reaction to barriers in fact merely internalizes one's oppression rather than expands one's options. But that worry has more to do with nefarious processes of preference change than with the general issue of whether the definition of a constraint must be desire-independent. As I and others have argued, one merely needs an account of "autonomous" preference change to supplement the account of a constraint to avoid these untoward Stoicist implication.[8]

More importantly, the conception of a constraint as desire-dependent focuses overly narrowly simply on *desires*; as I will discuss below, one can define constraints in terms of the broad value perspective that motivates agency and orients moral judgment rather than simply what a person desires at a time. That is, we should not simply ask what prevents a person from doing what she wants, but rather what aspects of her social space restrict her pursuit of projects she values from the perspective of her practical identity more broadly. In this way, counterexamples of the sort typically generated would have to involve persons shifting their value frameworks *as a whole* and thereby increasing their freedom. But – as I will explain further in a moment – a plausible account of a person's practical identity will be *diachronic* and hence will include conditions about preference change and adaptation. Thus our fears that such a model of freedom commits us to endorsing an Epictetan program of slavish self-denial will be obviated.

Finally, it is not at all clear that models of negative freedom themselves can avoid a conception of a constraint that is devoid of reference to the internal states of the agent, even to states the agent may control. This charge has been much debated.[9] The basic accusation is that negative accounts see freedom as a function of the absence of barriers to what a person is able to do. However, what a person is able to do can be altered by her own acts of will. Imagine that a person has an ability to perform some activity even when facing a minor barrier, say when hurdles have been placed on a track ahead of her but she can easily jump over them and run down the track. Due to her lack of practice (stemming from her change in desires), the hurdles then become a prohibitive barrier. She has then become less free by changing herself rather than the world changing around her. Insofar as constraints are a function of a person's ability and abilities are dependent on desires, then freedom (on standard accounts like Kramer's) are a function of desires.[10]

But as I mentioned, this is not problematic in any case, as long as the sensitivity to the (free) agent's perspective is characterized in the right manner. More generally, views of liberty that see it as pure opportunity for action have greatest trouble accounting for the individuation of opportunities in ways that make sense of the value of having such opportunities without themselves relying on a positive account of freedom. Charles Taylor famously raised this issue by considering two societies, one with neither traffic lights nor freedom of religion and the other with religious freedom and many traffic lights. The latter is clearly, he argues, the freer society even if it turns out that traffic lights constrain far more numerous actions than religious restrictions do, measured simply by neutral counting. But religious activity is far more valuable than driving without stopping, so the judgment of greater freedom must rest on the greater importance religious activity has.[11]

Recent theorists have responded to Taylor's claim along various lines. Carter's general worry about what he calls "value-based" conceptions (and he thinks all relevant positive accounts are value based in this way) is that they cannot account for freedom's non-specific value, its value independent of the value of the particular pursuits it makes possible.[12] And seeing freedom as valuable only by way of its connection to these pursuits makes it redundant in the political evaluation of social conditions. If freedom amounts to being unobstructed in doing what one values, then freedom's importance is simply a function of the value of those pursuits. Indeed, since we already have terminology that refers well enough to that value (accomplishing one's goals, getting what one desires, etc.), the language of freedom would then be otiose. Moreover, tying freedom to value makes the measurement of overall freedom either incoherent or similarly redundant on the measure of a person's abilities to pursue specific valued ends.

Defenders of an opportunity conception of liberty disagree among themselves about whether value considerations should be brought into the conceptualization of freedom, either concerning particular acts or overall freedom.[13] Be that as it may, defenders of such accounts must make some case for the overall (and profound) value that freedom is thought to have. And although they attempt this in various ways,[14] it remains unclear how viewing freedom as neutrally counted constraints will capture its value without specifying how the absence of those constraints relates to the perspective of agents.

Indeed, this was precisely the lesson from earlier critiques of negative liberty such as Taylor's: not only does seeing freedom as mere opportunity rob that condition of its obvious value, it also undercuts our ability to meaningfully count constraints and opportunities at all. Seeing freedom, as Carter does, as purely a function of the physical space one is able to occupy (as determined by the actions of other persons) implies that freedom is enlarged or contracted whenever a trivial change in my physical environment occurs. Any object whatever, on this view, counts as a constraint to an action that involves occupying the space where that object sits.

Kramer accepts this implication explicitly, and in fact argues that my freedom is enhanced whenever a person is born in the world, since this adds to the total conceivable actions now available to me (that is, those involving that person). He then adds "value multipliers" to the calculation of how much overall freedom this new option adds, which he admits is vanishingly small in a single instance.[15] But do we really want to go down this path? My own intuitive response is that this renders the notion of (increased) freedom meaningless, and while it is certainly coherent to claim that freedom is merely the possibility of unimpeded action, such a view fails to capture why (greater) freedom is worth struggling for and how particular forms of liberation provide profound degrees of it.

What has gone wrong is attempting to see freedom solely in terms of neutral counting of opportunities without reference to agents' value perspectives. What matters first are the purposes and values that give meaning to our plans and projects, so that the idea of freedom can be built from that vantage point – rather than simply enumerating open avenues to movement.[16]

II. The Alternative: Freedom as Effective Agency

These comments on negative accounts of freedom are meant merely as a variation of worries that Taylor and others have raised about viewing liberty in a manner that assumes an overly narrow view of human social existence, action, and identity. For the subjects of freedom exercise that trait while embedded in complex and shifting webs of social identity, projects and plans, and modes of recognition and status; all of this gives meaning to the freedom they enjoy. Ignoring these social and historical aspects of agency, indeed ignoring factors concerning the quality of agency generally in fashioning a concept of freedom, threatens to denude that idea of its social and political power.

The alternative we will now consider in no way arises simply from the objections raised about negative views, as versions of positive freedom are motivated by any number of additional premises about agency and social life. Specifically, a richer conception of the agent as the subject of liberty is introduced along with an explication of freedom. This conception is one in which, for example, free actions are seen as arising from values authentically held by the person – and not the result of surreptitious or manipulative external forces – and the options she faces (which freedom measures) are understood in relation to her evaluative perspective and not merely listed neutrally as objects in her path. This broader conception of agency, in both its power and its dangers, is explored in what follows.

However, seeing freedom as conceptually connected to the values of agents, or indeed to values per se, has long raised questions from liberal corners about the ways such an approach will run afoul of the requisite value neutrality required of liberalism, so we should tend to those worries before proceeding further. For Carter, seeing freedom as Taylor does as a function of what is valuable in life over and above our first-level motivations fails as the basis of a measure of *overall freedom* since there is no plausible way of distinguishing, weighing, and comparing such valuations in an unproblematic (and liberal) manner.[17]

What is required is indeed an argument for the value of positive liberty that is not overly specific so as to collapse into other concepts in a way that make reference to liberty per se otiose or attaches it to specific pursuits the value of which is reasonably contestable. This last worry is, of course, the source of the alarm sounded by Berlin. However, many have attempted to work out a conception of freedom as effective agency that does not run afoul of the commitment to diversity, tolerance, and value neutrality characteristic of liberal theory. Liberty would then need to be defined in ways that reflect the perspective of the complex, socially embedded agents who value having (or struggling for) that trait in a way that does not link freedom to contestable social values. As we noted, Taylor has laid the groundwork for such a view, and others have taken different routes to examine and develop similar ideas.[18] While it not possible to spell out such a view in adequate detail here, the broad contours of the approach should be sketched to show that critiques energized by these newer defenses of negative freedom can be obviated but also to set the stage for the remaining challenges I want to discuss.

Freedom in the positive sense I refer to here contains conditions of "effective agency" and "authenticity." The first includes basic capabilities for reflection, choice, and action that can be seen as roughly parallel to Amartya Sen's requirements of agency freedom – the enjoyment of basic capabilities for formulating and pursuing valued functionings.[19] These include, for example, the absence of certain disabling conditions as well as access to various resources and social conditions that make decision and choice feasible. (I am sensitive to the charge that any such list of basic capabilities or corresponding disabilities threatens to disenfranchise the agency of the oppressed, so such an account must be complex and subtle.)

Now some have raised objections to the capability approach that Sen advances, in particular the concomitant view that "agency freedom" has intrinsic value. Sen supports this idea with examples such as contrasting fasting with starving: both involve not eating but the latter is a terrible imposition while the former is a (perhaps heroic) expression of agency. But Carter argues for instance that such examples show not that agency freedom has value as such but rather that it has value as a necessary condition of the activities that are themselves valuable. But attaching the value of freedom to the value of activities has implications that run against the broad value neutrality of liberal political theory (to which Sen and others are on record as being committed).[20]

However, Sen defines capacities in ways that range over various valued functionings, so that a person with the capacity to form intentions, move in physical space, interact with others, join or maintain membership in a social group, and on up the ladder of more and more complex pursuits, enjoys a kind of capacity whose value does not reduce to any one of those pursuits. Capabilities include the ability to change and move within social options, deliberate about one's choices, and (under optimal conditions) turn intentions into actions. Seeing freedom as a function of such capacities does not reduce the value of having that freedom simply to the value of any one such activity.

But in addition to having capacities of this sort, some have urged that freedom involves acting on one's *own* values and aspirations, and not ones we are manipulated into adopting or that result from addictions or compulsions. What is sought after in such a condition are the requirements of "authenticity," though one must be careful to avoid implying with the use of that term that freedom is only the expression of some ideal true self, independently of what the actual agent values.[21]

Authenticity conditions, as we intend use the term here, relate to a person's ability to reflectively accept her basic motives in light of a conception of herself that is social as well as historical, embodied, and structured by a complex matrix of interpersonal and social dynamics. This idea of what we could call the person's "diachronic practical identity" is meant to capture the basic evaluative orientation that both makes sense of past choices as well as guides current decisions and future plans. It need not be fully transparent to us, settled, nor articulable; and it is not simply a set of propositions about what is valuable, sacred, or ideal for us. It is an orienting structure with cognitive and affective elements that shapes moral perceptions as well as forms the basis of choice.

My own view is that the positively free person is able to accept her basic motives (amidst her social condition) from the perspective of this practical identity upon reflection in light of her past and ongoing social self-development; moreover I propose that she is able to do so without deep alienation. This is a procedural model of self-government in that it makes no substantive reference to particular values in setting out these conditions, and so in this way attempts to side-step charges of insensitivity to pluralism and difference. Though some "weakly substantive" commitments in this model may be necessary for it to play the role in social evaluation that we ask attributions of freedom and autonomy to play.

In this way, such a model can be seen as an attempt to steer around the sorts of objections raised about positive liberty just referenced, for it is to adopt a conception of freedom that is, if not value-neutral, at least value invariant across a wide array of reasonably contestable moral and ethical orientations. That is, one could adopt a procedural conception of authentic values relative to which one has the capacity to act and hence enjoy freedom in this positive sense.[22]

Now some have claimed that views of authenticity of this sort which require any sort of self-reflection as partially constitutive of (free) agency face the threat of a regress, as one must ask how those acts of reflection can be designated as themselves authentic, without positing ever more levels of introspective evaluation.[23] The reply to this objection is to require that the acts of authenticity-establishing reflection in fact "speak for the agent" and do not require ever-further acts of reflective endorsement. Harry Frankfurt's attempt to do this involves reference to one's "deepest cares," which do not need further authentication because this just is the agent's motivational voice, so to speak. Charles Taylor's version of this attempt is to posit strong evaluations or foundational commitments as the anchoring element of the self, though a value-neutral conception of freedom would want to avoid this reference if such valuations are viewed in any non-perspectival manner.[24] In my own case, I have referred to diachronic practical identities and have added conditions describing the basic ability to introspect and evaluate oneself. Given such theoretical attempts, which have of course faced ongoing objections but which are not obviously untenable, it cannot be claimed that conceptions of positive freedom that include conditions of self-reflective authenticity are meaningless or incompatible with value neutrality and social difference.

All that said, we have approached the issue of freedom by way of a rhetoric that leaves us open to a perennial complaint that such articulations inherit the hyper-individualism of classic liberal ideals. As we mentioned earlier, adequate accounts of freedom must pay due homage to the social elements of identity. Let us now briefly consider recent attempts to respond to that demand.

III. Freedom and Social Relations

Another apparent contrast between negative and positive accounts of liberty, at least as those ideas have developed in the last few decades, is that the former is seen as maintaining a closer connection with liberal individualism than the latter. That is, negative liberty attaches to individuals alone – indeed one can be free in that sense by being left entirely alone it seems – while positive freedom requires particular kinds of relations with others, ones of collective self-determination, mutual recognition, and so on.[25]

In some ways, however, this contrast is somewhat overdrawn, in that even negative accounts have virtually all included conditions that include non-derivative reference to social relations themselves. That is, one aspect of opportunity accounts of freedom is the generally shared insistence that the only barriers to action that officially count as limitations on liberty are those put in place by the actions of other human beings.[26] From one perspective this seems puzzling, in that the experience of a person facing barriers to movement will have the character it has independently of how that movement came to be circumscribed. But defenders of this view insist that those barriers to movement put in place by others have a "special significance" in relation to measuring freedom.[27] We could call this the "human source restriction" and it is worth pondering a moment because of the way it highlights the question of individualism in models of freedom.

Defenders of the human source restriction give various reasons for this designation, many repeating the claim that since theoretical accounts of freedom are a part of social and political philosophy, and such philosophy concerns human relations and not natural phenomena, we should define freedom as only a function of human-sourced restrictions. But this is perplexing, since social and political philosophy does and should deal with any number of phenomena that arise from non-human sources, such as disease, disability, natural disaster, and so on. Virtually all human conditions, whether caused by others or not, can be attended to by human efforts, so insofar as social philosophy determines how we should expend those efforts, nothing should be out of bounds I would say.[28]

Matthew Kramer admits that there is no non-circular way to explain why only human-sourced restraints count for negative theories, though he maintains that such constraints present this "special significance" in endeavours to define and measure freedom.[29] But defenders of negative accounts face a peculiar challenge here, for in their drive toward ensuring the value-neutrality (and the empirical observability) of liberty they have fewer resources from which to draw to account for why restrictions that are caused by others count in a *unique* way in our appraisal of overall freedom. What this reveals is that even these negative accounts really involve a view about interpersonal relations, where being forced to do something as a result of another's will victimizes me while being constrained by the lifeless physicality of my environment does not. But the only reason I can see for thinking the former is a limitation of freedom but the latter merely a fact of life is that one is concerned to guarantee certain kinds of social relations in one's picture of the ideally free society.

Positive approaches to freedom allow us to look further into the dynamics of agency, taking account of how self-government can fail when any of the multiform requirements of socially situated action are lacking. External restrictions take on special character (as restraints) when they function to prevent valued pursuits by socially structured agents. This reference to the social constituents of the self can motivate the conceptual attention to certain barriers and not others in counting constraints, but it also allows notions of freedom to capture forms of enslavement whose structure is independent of simply the number of physical options one enjoys.

In a striking passage from Frederick Douglass's autobiography, he writes that "if any one thing in my experience, more than another, served to deepen my conviction of the infernal character of slavery, and to fill me with unutterable loathing of slaveholders, it was their base ingratitude to my poor old grandmother."[30] What the slave owners did to this poor woman was not to subject her to beatings or to force more gruelling work on her, but to give her her own small hut to live in, alone and completely without interference or further duties. Douglass, however, describes it this way: "And, to cap the climax of their base ingratitude and fiendish bar-barity ... they took her to the woods, built her a little hut, put up a little mud-chimney, and then made her welcome to the privilege of supporting herself there in perfect loneliness; thus virtually turning her out to die! If my poor old grandmother now lives, she lives to suffer in utter loneliness; she lives to remember and mourn over the loss of children, the loss of grandchildren, and the loss of great-grandchildren."[31] What is remarkable about this passage is that in the chronicle of countless acts of violence, murder, rape, and forced labour that constitutes slavery, Douglass chooses an act of *separation* as one that "more than another, served to deepen my conviction of the infernal character of slavery." The source of the oppres-sive restrictions is the same whether slave-masters are forcing Douglass's grandmother to work or to fend for herself; but the severing of her ties with her children fractured more profoundly her social self-understanding. Only accounts of freedom that take social relations properly into account can reflect this difference.[32]

Attempts to capture the fundamentally relational nature of agency (and hence of freedom) have taken numerous forms, many of which are parallel to, if not inspired by, Taylor's rich account. In particular, Taylor's insist-ence on the dialogical nature of self-understanding, as well as the need for social recognition as a central component of that dialogical process, has reverberated in various other accounts of social self-government, many of which are worked out under the rubric of "autonomy."[33]

In many of these views, what is required for self-governing (autono-mous) agency is external recognition of one's "normative authority" as Catriona Mackenzie puts it.[34] Or, in Phillip Pettit's account of freedom as discursive control, a free self must be able to identify with her motiva-tional states in a way that is avowed and honoured by others in discursive exchange.[35] In particular, freedom requires that others who are engaged in dynamic interaction with the agent treat them as "worthy of address."[36]

Many other such views emphasize the role of social recognition in char-acterizing autonomy or freedom. Axel Honneth, for example, has under-scored the importance and complexity of recognition in conceptions of the subject in critical political theory. Drawing on this work, Honneth and Joel Anderson have sketched a conception of autonomy that includes such rec-ognitional elements. They argue that personal autonomy involves recogni-tion in ways that are stronger than merely a contingent connection, that in at least three spheres of recognition relations – self-respect, self-trust, and self-esteem – the vulnerabilities to which individuals in the current age are subject (and against which autonomy is meant to protect them) require that particular relations of recognition are conceptually required for autonomy in a full sense. As they put it, proper relations of self-respect, trust, and esteem are needed so that "full autonomy – the real and effective capacity to develop and pursue one's own conception of a worthwhile life – is facilitated by relations-to-self (self-respect, self-trust, and self-esteem) that are themselves bound up with webs of social recognition."[37]

So the view that emerges from this work sees freedom as not only reflective self-acceptance in light of one's socio-historical nature (as I put it earlier in my own account) but also that modes of social recognition be required to secure one's status as a participant in a discursive process of social self-construction. In these ways, positive models provide more robust conceptual resources by which to account for the reasons that some interferences – for example those emanating from other human beings – serve to limit liberty while floors and ceilings and stop-lights (under most conditions) do not, or do not significantly.

It is important to note three things about the conceptualization of freedom I am sketching here, all of which contrast in some way with other similar accounts, including Taylor's. First, although freedom is understood relative to valued pursuits (via reference to the agent's practical identity), such values are not defined objectively, so the charge that freedom will be consistent with the imposition of contestable values is avoided. Second, the relations of recognition and respect for the person's normative authority that such a view requires are not specified as a priori requirements for freedom as such; rather it is maintained that self-government will require such recognition as a general psychological necessity whose importance is contingent on that agent's needs for self-affirmation in order to act competently and effectively. In other words, relations with others are not conceptual conditions of agency as such but causal requirements whose contours vary with the case in question.[38] Finally, and relatedly, such socio-relational conditions of agency are required because of the social nature of *selves*. Insofar as selves are constituted by certain social relationships, maintenance and support for those relationships will be necessary for self-government – but the "insofar" in that phrase cannot be overemphasized, for models of positive liberty that exclude such flexibility and contingency yield untoward judgments about both the value of freedom and the requirements for attaining it.

In this light, I want to close with a discussion of how these requirements of social recognition in models of freedom run up against new and particular challenges that arise from current global conditions. Specifically, these conditions are ones where mobility and the need to renegotiate one's social self-understanding arise because of one's changed social location. These factors carry with them new vulnerabilities and modes of oppression relevant to our understanding of freedom. In many current settings, settled identities, stable life situations, or fixed geo-political locations cannot be assumed for the agents in question. Properly confronting such conditions will force us to think further about the implications and presuppositions of accounts of freedom that tie that concept to relational dynamics of social recognition of settled identities.

IV. New Modes of Global Oppression and Their Challenges to Freedom

Globalization in general and labour migration specifically has produced unprecedented numbers of people who live in communities separate from their geographical and cultural "homes." It is estimated that over 185 million people live outside of their country of birth, 2.9 per cent of the global population. Of this number, more than seventeen million are refugees and twenty-two million are internally displaced people.[39] Of particular relevance here are the huge numbers of individuals who are dislocated either from human trafficking, labour smuggling, or refugee status. In these latter categories are individuals who find themselves in conditions of social dislocation as well as disorientation and distress as a result of coercion, fraud, violence, and need. Of course, social relocation is nothing new – indeed the trans-Atlantic slave trade offers a striking and momentous example of it – though migration to foreign social settings either under duress or the pressure of material circumstance has become an increasing and systemic aspect of the contemporary landscape.

The phenomenon of migration carries with it challenges concerning agential capacities, social recognition, and the precarious connection to community that positive models of freedom stress. For the new immigrant, however, it may be unclear what social resources there are to exercise capacities for meaningful work and leisure, the negotiation of a social identity in a foreign setting, often one with pronounced patterns of discrimination and opprobrium towards the (majority's dominant understanding of) the identities in question. The claim that freedom requires effective agency along with relations of recognition and support must grapple with the ways that the *terms* in which such support must be provided are very much a matter of contestation and subject to the happenstance of prejudice and power dynamics.

Consider, for example, the case of refugees or trafficked labourers. Ones who manage to escape the immediate coercive conditions of a camp or forced labour will still have a long way to go to achieve freedom in a meaningful sense. They must attempt to find a way of life in a new location as an immigrant or internally displaced person, and they may also not have realistic opportunities (in the short run) to return to their homeland. It is these types of individuals that questions of self-trust and social recognition become most complicated and poignant. Most often the person is a foreigner (typically without a passport), which may mean also that (a) she has little or no local language ability, (b) she faces deportation as an illegal immigrant (unless, and only in some jurisdictions, she can show she faces violence if returned home), but (c), for formerly trafficked sex workers for example, she cannot return to a home environment without facing shame and social retribution, as well as the economic deprivation that this entails.

What this means is that the process of ending the enslavement of those experiencing such social dislocation involves more than that removal of restrictions; clearly the process also involves the actual provision of material, social, and cultural resources that would allow the person to reformulate a life plan that she can embrace at some level. This may mean speaking to her in her own language, finding locales (perhaps also émigré communities) where she can find cultural camaraderie and social support, and providing other tools necessary for her to formulate, restructure, and pursue an adapted practical identity. But it may also involve providing means of assimilation into the host locale. The contingencies are numerous, and conceptions of the self as a social being that underwrites positive conceptions of freedom must be vigilant in avoiding the imposition of pre-established social identity structures when such identities are in the process of re-negotiation and change.

Several important lessons relevant to our understanding of freedom and autonomy can be gleaned from these considerations. The first is that restoring (or establishing) agential competence – including self-trust – is required for meaningful freedom, since those who escape one type of violent bondage may well face another, internal slavery in the form of addiction, sickness, illiteracy, and other forms of deprivation.

Moreover, those in the process of renegotiating a social identity in the midst of a new and perhaps hostile environment will be ill served by a conception of freedom that relies on or reinforces sedentary and perhaps oppressive identity labels in the dynamics of recognition and cultural naming. When aid workers or surrounding community members rely on over-simplified or preconceived ideas of what it means to be from a certain region of the world, and the person attempting to overcome the social disorientation of her new environment experiences ambivalence about that previous identity as well as possible new ones, conceptions of freedom that require the expression of social recognition (using these over simplified identity categories) can be actually dangerous. Only if the object of recognition is the aspect of agency that involves the struggle for, as well as the protection *of,* the person's social self-understanding will such dangers be avoided.

I mentioned earlier those who claim that proper expressions of recognition of the practical capacities of agents are conceptually required for freedom (and not merely important facilitators of the development of freedom). The worry I am expressing here is that recognition of one's ability to pursue plans grounded in one's practical identity may assume that the object of that recognition – the type of person one is and the shape of that practical identity – is somehow fixed in place and knowable by others. I cannot recognize you as an exemplar of a value scheme unless I know, or presume to know, the value scheme by which you define yourself.

However, the socially displaced individuals I am discussing are often in a disorientingly fluid position relative to their practical identities. The cultural settings that gave meaning to those identities, which quite literally provided the language in which it is expressed, is not (or may not be) currently available.

Often in the case of unwilling trafficked sex workers, a traumatic disconnect has typically occurred between their earlier practical identities and the ones now available to them. After enduring the conditions of forced (sexual) labour, for example, such persons have already egregiously violated (been forced to violate) various fundamental religious and ethical commitments that defined their moral perspective and social world, and it is often the case that they are barred physically and materially from returning to the families and locations that gave support and meaning to those commitments. They must, then, renegotiate a value frame that picks up on the remnants of those earlier values but provides non-alienating motivational schemes for their life after liberation. In such cases, it is surely the case that previous commitments are not completely destroyed or unavailable – the young woman might continue to see herself as a Muslim or Catholic despite her experiences – but the strains of those earlier perspectives must be refashioned in light of new possibilities (in a new country, in a different language, and among different compatriots).[40]

More importantly, however, both theorists of autonomy/freedom and those in a position to help facilitate this process of transition must determine how the complex experimentation and social striving that these sorts of relocations involve are aimed at re-establishing a diachronic value framework, a practical identity that can meaningfully sustain judgments about further actions and decisions in the person's future. Admittedly, the standards of intelligibility and stability that such value frames must exhibit for autonomous agency to be re-established are under-theorized here, but my point in this analysis is to underscore the provisional nature of the process rather than the clear and fixed endpoint at which it aims.

Of course theorists in this vein have mentioned the need to communicate our identities in new and foreign settings in order to enjoy the recognition required for freedom. Taylor, for example, discusses such cross-border encounters but insists that there must be a "fusion of horizons" in the encounter between individuals (or groups) across cultural lines.[41] Indeed, in discussing the ways that internalized dialogue structures the identities that are the cite of social recognition, Taylor emphasizes the way that such identities are not given a priori but must be "won" by way of social exchange.[42] My point here is to emphasize this insight but to also point out that tying conceptions of freedom to requirements of recognition carry the danger that such a picture may assume an overly fixed and settled self-understanding on the parts of the people involved, where the reality is more often closer to a search for a new version of oneself rather than a settled stranger in a strange land.

It is in consideration of these kinds of cases that I have insisted that positive models of freedom must require social recognition of one's practical identity as a contingent and flexible requirement, one that does not assume that such an identity is fully formed and fixed. It must be possible to pursue a path to freedom of this sort while at the same time renegotiating that social practical identity, perhaps in confrontation (though hopefully in supportive interaction) with surrounding others.

Conclusion

As I noted when we began, the contours of a political value like freedom will turn on the perspective from which that ideal is approached. In the conditions of new forms of oppression and vulnerability we find in the current global landscape, the perspective of those struggling for liberty brings to light unique aspects of that concept. Political philosophy must do more to include such perspectives, as much as speaking for others (not to mention the subaltern among us) is possible, in the ongoing and complex social commentaries we embark upon.

What I have tried to do here, if only provisionally, is to mark out some of the paths that theorists have taken in developing accounts of freedom and to distinguish more productive ones from those less promising. I have attempted this by suggesting that the recent conceptions of negative freedom developed by liberal theorists are still open to some version of the critique Charles Taylor made famous some time ago. In addition, and in a way independent of those replies, I attempted to sketch an outline of a positive conception of freedom that avoids many of the standard worries about such notions but captures the richer understanding of socially and historically embedded agency, an understanding that arises from Taylor's work. I ended, however, with a discussion of some of the dangers of certain aspects of that idea of liberty in a world of fluid (and threatened) identities, mobile and vulnerable populations, and struggles for renegotiated social self-understandings. In so doing, I hope to have shown yet again the inestimable value of Charles Taylor's contributions to these conversations across the many decades that we have been studying his invaluable work.[43]

7

What's Right with Positive Liberty

AGENCY, AUTONOMY, AND THE OTHER

NANCY J. HIRSCHMAN

As one of the few, if not only, contributors to this volume who has been to Albania, I always feel a special affinity for Charles Taylor's famous essay "What's Wrong with Negative Liberty?"[1] In that essay, Taylor invokes Albania's extremely few traffic lights as an example of how the absence of external impediments by itself is insufficient to establish whether I am free or not: the quality of the actions I am being prevented from doing, as well as their importance to my sense of self, my plan of life, my goals and intentions, are much more significant, to begin with. In the capital of Tirana, when I was there in the early 1990s, there were three traffic lights and they were frequently out of order, as electricity was rather spotty at the time; so one would be free to drive unimpeded by traffic lights, as opposed to, say, downtown Manhattan. But of course one would be restricted in other activities when Taylor wrote his essay in the 1970s, such as criticizing the government, publishing one's opinions ... or buying a car.

Or, for that matter, activities such as learning widely about the history of political thought. I went to Albania in the autumn of 1993 as part of a project sponsored by the Conference for the Study of Political Thought (CSPT) and funded by the International Research Exchanges Board (IREX), to connect with colleagues in the newly accessible countries of eastern Europe. We spent about two weeks in Albania, running faculty seminars – including one on "What's Wrong with Negative Liberty?" – conducting pedagogy workshops, teaching classes, and holding a public roundtable on the topic of "tolerance," which were featured on television news. Since Albania had only one television station at the time, and not much programming, we were on TV a lot. To add to the surreal quality, the other major story on the news was Boris Yeltsin's use of Russian tanks to shell parliament.

But with Charles Taylor's "What's Wrong with Negative Liberty?" ever on my mind – as it has been since I read it as a first-year graduate student – I did notice the very few traffic lights in the city, and relatively few cars. This was lucky indeed for the sheep that grazed in public parks and wandered through town – and perhaps also for us. Dependent on a variety of Albanian drivers who were not very skilled, to take us through the country and around the city in cars that lacked even seat belts, I was grateful for the absence of other automobiles with which we might otherwise collide. But of course the point that Taylor was making with the traffic lights was what was so potently observable: the university, still recovering from the riots that resulted in the deposing of the dictator Enver Hoxha, had no electricity; the windows had many broken panes; the walls were pitted; there was no functioning library, in fact there were no books. The faculty were poorly educated, they worked from very old lecture notes without much access to contemporary secondary sources, and much of the political theory they had been taught was bad Marxism. The students were eager, bright, intellectually starved; the best of them were destined to leave the country. The quality of the freedom they had in Albania, before the wall came down, was quite impoverished; but even after the wall came down the freedom of the people was limited at best.

Certainly, such freedom was relished nonetheless. Nobody, and certainly not Charles Taylor, would deny that negative liberties are vital to human happiness; what the Albanians relished were the *possibilities* that lay ahead. As Taylor puts it in *Sources of the Self*, "the issue for us has to be not only where we are, but where we're going."[2] And as Taylor also wisely says, negative liberty cannot make sense, it cannot flourish, without positive liberty. However, in this book Taylor pushes further on the key themes of "What's Wrong with Negative Liberty?" For what makes us human – and not just free – is our ability to realize our higher order desires, and to discriminate among our desires. Hence positive liberty is not just "another" model of freedom: it is the essential notion of freedom. We cannot be fully human without positive liberty.

And so, upon a second trip the following summer, we encountered some radical changes. The university not only had electricity, but a few computers, compliments of George Soros, to whose attention we had brought the philosophy faculty on our earlier visit. American Christian evangelicals had painted the classrooms and provided some classroom furniture, leaving without many converts. The books we had brought on our previous visit, in French and English primarily – including *The Idea of Freedom* – had been catalogued and shelved in a miniature library, with plans for expansion underway as texts began to be translated into Albanian. Many of the faculty had been able to study at various universities in France and Italy and brought enhanced abilities to their classrooms.

So Albania is an even better illustration of the limitations of negative liberty, and the importance of positive liberty, than perhaps Taylor first realized. The most important contribution of Taylor's essay, of course, was to rescue positive liberty from the two-dimensional caricatures to which it is often consigned. As he notes in that essay, most negative liberty theorists dichotomize the two models, reducing both: positive liberty is collapsed into communist totalitarianism, while negative liberty retreats behind the "Maginot Line mentality" of defining freedom as the absence of external constraints, à la Thomas Hobbes. Much of this is due to Berlin's formulation itself, and Berlin clearly had political motivations for his categories, wanting to ally positive liberty with bad-guy communist dictatorships and negative liberty with good-guy Western democracies. But it had a great deal of philosophical weight and influence. Many illustrious philosophers and political theorists, such as George Kateb and Richard Flathman, have passionately held onto a quasi-Hobbesian understanding of strict negative liberty as the only plausible and defensible conception of freedom.[3]

But there are primarily three enhancements positive liberty makes to negative liberty, two of which Charles Taylor overtly sees, one of which I believe he does not see, although I believe that his view of positive liberty makes it possible for us to see. The first is that positive liberty concerns itself with the "positive" provision of the conditions necessary to take advantage of negative liberties, such as providing wheelchair access to buildings or scholarships for education. It is this aspect that my Albanian experience illustrates most clearly: by obtaining new resources the Albanians were able to improve their educations and the educations of their students, thereby opening up further options that they had not imagined before. The definition of barriers as external impediments is too narrow, as Taylor persuasively argues; for instance, freedom of education is rather hollow if you cannot afford tuition or get into the building where instruction is offered because you use a wheelchair – or if the building has no lights, no textbooks, no qualified instructors. Adopting a more social notion of the self, positive liberty is able to view individual conditions such as disability, as well as social conditions such as poverty, or an undeveloped economy, or the disorientation of political upheaval, as barriers to freedom that can be overcome by positive action, or the provision of conditions the individual cannot create on her own.

Taylor does not spend a lot of time and attention on this aspect because, as he suggests, various negative liberty theorists have endorsed different versions of this idea and incorporated it into their own conceptions of negative liberty. But it sets the stage for the remaining two major contributions that positive liberty makes.

The second contribution is the focus on "internal barriers." This is the key focus of "What's Wrong with Negative Liberty?," Taylor spends a great deal of the article analyzing it. According to Taylor, and building on Harry Frankfurt's theory of free will, we can have "second order desires," or "desires about desires." Taylor's argument, to summarize it quickly, is that if we have conflicts of desires, which are "qualitatively discriminated," then it is not enough to experience an absence of external restraints, because the immediate desires I have may frustrate my true will. Taylor most famously offers the example of "spiteful feelings and reactions which I almost cannot inhibit are undermining a relationship which is terribly important to me ... I long to be able not to feel this spite. As long as I feel it, even control is not an option, because it just builds up inside until it ... bursts out."[4] Positive liberty theory, on Taylor's account, says that when he gives in to spite, he is not just weak willed but unfree, because he is violating his true desire, on which he has reflected at some length.

But of course it follows from the notion of internal barriers that others may know my true will better than I, particularly when I am in the grip of these self-destructive desires: Taylor calls this the "second guessing" problem, because others claim to know what you want better than you do yourself. It is the most troubling aspect of positive liberty: determination of the will by others, and specifically by the state. This is the nightmare that Berlin particularly argued against in "Two Concepts of Liberty," with good reason.

But what Berlin and other negative liberty advocates seriously underplay, and what Taylor brings out so brilliantly, is the idea of an individual having conflicting desires and a divided will. Consider the smoker trying to quit, but a stressful situation makes him want a cigarette. If I were to snatch the cigarette from his lips, we could certainly argue that I interfere with his freedom, in the negative liberty vein; but we could equally clearly argue that I am helping him realize his higher or true desire, to quit.

Of course, as Taylor explains, in these examples we could argue that we don't "identify" with the "lower order" desire, such as the smoking, or the spite, so he then goes on to wrestle with conflicts where I seem to identify equally with both desires – such as staying with my dying mother versus joining the French resistance. But even addiction is less clear-cut than we commonly imagine; if you ask any smoker, even one who wants to quit, she will identify the smoking as a desire that is clearly part of her. Many former smokers continue to miss smoking, even though they know quitting was the wisest choice. And this fits with recent studies showing that addiction is *not* an enslavement driven by the inability to withdraw, but rather is driven by pleasure: we do the things to which we are addicted because we enjoy them, suggesting more (though far from complete) autonomous control than is commonly thought.[5] So we should not be distracted by our assumptions about "addiction" or "compulsion," as freedom theorists often are – and this means that Taylor's case is even stronger.

At the same time, feminist insight into the concept of "difference" suggests that it is problematic for political philosophers to make assumptions about what a particular subject "really" wants, or what "the reasonable person" or the "normal person" should want. For instance, even if women and men occupy opposing interest positions in contexts such as domestic violence, the implication that the term "women" constitutes a unified category, and that "women" thereby all want the same things, is problematic; when intersected with other categories like sexuality, race, class, ethnicity, religion, and culture it becomes quite untenable for philosophers to assume what individuals want, or to say that what we would want must be what we imagine they should want. Recent work on disability studies in particular brings out the stark failure of imagination of political philosophers in understanding bodily difference and how such difference may introduce a range of desires completely unimaginable to others different from them: many advocates for Deaf culture, for instance, see deafness as a good, a quality that they value, in strong contrast to the dominant view that deafness is intrinsically disabling and undesirable. So the standard assumptions that are made about what any "rational" person should want must be called into question.

That is what leads to the third way that positive liberty challenges negative liberty. It is an aspect that most theorists of freedom do not recognize – including, I think, Taylor. Nevertheless I do believe that his version of positive liberty deploys the "social construction" of the choosing subject of liberty, of the person who has desires and makes choices. If it is possible to say that we can have conflicting desires, and if it is possible to rank these desires as better or worse, more and less valuable, then the issue of who I am comes inevitably into play: how is it that I have the desires I have? Why do I make the choices I do? Such questions invite us to consider the social construction of the choosing subject, of the individual agent who has desires and makes choices within specific social, historical, and institutional contexts.

The idea of social construction maintains that human beings and their world are in no sense given or natural, but the product of historical configurations of relationships. Our desires, preferences, beliefs, values – indeed the way in which we see the world and define reality – are all shaped by the particular constellation of personal and institutional social relationships that constitute our individual and collective identities. Understanding them requires us to place them in their historical, social, and political contexts. Such contexts are what makes meaning possible; and meaning makes "reality."

Certainly there are varying degrees of the "social construction thesis," and what I have articulated here may seem to be a more "radical" version – that any possible empirical existence must be translated into language and thought be turned into "reality," which is always already an interpretation. Taylor does not go as far as this, of course, but rather tries to reconcile the fact that we become who we are through language, practice, and culture with a strong conception of agency. This reconciliation attempt most often leans toward the liberal side rather than the social constructivist side; but I believe that a strong social constructivist understanding of positive liberty comes out of Taylor's insights about internal barriers to liberty and the unavoidability of second guessing.

The case for my interpretation is hardly straightforward; moreover it is complicated by a variety of positions that Taylor takes. Indeed his account of Foucault in *Political Theory*, as well as his exchange with William Connolly, suggests that he might not agree with it at all. For it does not cohere with Taylor's very strong and rich conception of agency.[6] Taylor develops a conception of the self as agent who, in order to be considered free, has to be capable of self-reflection, of judgment, of "choice" in a meaningful sense. It is a rich and robust notion of the choosing subject, the free agent. In order to appreciate this, the importance of internal barriers to freedom has to be understood and appreciated. In his essay "What Is Human

Agency?" Taylor pays a great deal of attention to "strong evaluation," suggesting that agency is tied with what we normally might call "autonomy," entailing reflection and deliberation over my choices, and over my desires, particularly my second-order desires.[7]

But I think this somewhat runs against Taylor's own conception of positive liberty. For instance, returning to Taylor's spite example, he describes the feeling as emerging spontaneously from within himself, the highly individuated subject, without any attention to the context within which it has developed or exists: where does the spite come from? Why does he feel it? When he says he "almost can't inhibit" it, what lies in that space between the "almost" and the "can't"? What is the history of this relationship – or indeed of other relationships and events in his life – that have led him to this sort of reaction? Why does he feel spite rather than, say, withdrawal or self-pity or sadness? Moreover, what are the criteria for determining the "importance" of the relationship? How does he know that this relationship is important to him or good for him? For instance, perhaps the relationship isn't really "good" for him, not in accord with his "true" interests, and spite is his subconscious way of communicating this to himself.

It is important to note that this issue of internal barriers is more than a psychological question, however, because such barriers are experienced within historical and social contexts, and a particular framework of understanding that defines and shapes our understanding of who we are, what we want, and how our actions can be interpreted. Taylor gestures toward this idea by acknowledging that second guessing is unavoidable when we confront such situations. But in Taylor's exchange with Connolly on Foucault, I think this is an idea he somewhat resists; though I think I agree with Connolly that Taylor does himself a disservice, because this process clearly involves others' interlocution. As Taylor says in "The Politics of Recognition," we are formed dialogically. The robust agent that Taylor envisions, as he acknowledged, is situated within larger material and symbolic contexts – such as language – that are not of our making or choosing: "We become full human agents, capable of understanding ourselves, and hence of defining our identity, through our acquisition of rich human languages of expression."[8] So logically, just as Taylor sees that the relationship is important to him and wants to stop his spiteful behaviour, so could we then identify the spite as in fact protecting him from the relationship, which perhaps isn't a truly "good" or "healthy" one. But of course then what's to stop us from saying that such justification of spite is simply a more sophisticated way to rationalize his fear of commitment? And so on, in an endless stream of second-guessing.

This is not to reject second-guessing at all; and I realize that Taylor's goal in this discussion is simply to get us to understand that the existence of "internal barriers" does not automatically entail "second-guessing," just as we cannot ever completely rule it out. It is possible that Taylor's views changed over time to include a stronger social constructivist view. But by not incorporating such factors into his example, he invites us to explore further what it suggests about his view of the free individual, and the unspoken assumptions that underlie that view. And I suggest that that view is a complicated one that somewhat ambiguates between strong agency and a strong social constructivism.

What social constructivism tells us is that figuring out what an individual person "really" wants demands a working through of history, relationship, and context – all of which requires the deep interrogation of the self and the social context in which that self is situated. I believe Taylor recognizes this, particularly in his critique of atomism, which certainly demonstrates his appreciation of the limits of individual agency. In his view, understanding the self is a social process. It presupposes language, a conceptual vocabulary, as Taylor notes in the various chapters of *Human Agency and Language* and other writings; a system of signs with which to formulate and represent my own experience to myself as well as to others; and it requires others with whom I can be in conversation, to analyze and determine what desires are really mine, and really better for me.

But this, in turn, raises the question of where to draw the line between the internal self and the external world, because our self-understandings, our desires and choices, as well as the barriers we experience, always need to be understood in context, as Taylor notes. If individuals exist in contexts, then they – their feelings, desires, thoughts, wills, preferences – cannot be understood outside of those contexts, as abstract and self-contained units. Without such specificity of context, the individual too is unspecified, an abstraction.

In his rejection of the "monological ideal," Taylor indicates that this influence and social embeddedness is ongoing, much as I am arguing social constructivism requires; but he focuses on "people we love" and "significant others," consistent with his very strong conception of agency.[9] This does not acknowledge how impersonal a great deal of social construction is, how deeply subject to these forces we are, and how in the process free agency and free will become diminished from the ideal which we have developed in modern political thought. Most of the "others" from whom, or with whom, we are dialogically formed are themselves shaped and formed by others. And these others in turn are formed by still others, on and on through the course of history. So this involves many, many, people we do not know and often do not even actively encounter. Moreover, none of those people live in social vacuums, but express the societies and social relationships in which they live. And those relationships and societies may be oppressive, they may be liberating, they may reflect privilege or express domination, all of which becomes incorporated into our self-understandings, our subjectivities as agents. And of course many of the most important relationships that do this forming are not directly with people themselves, but through and via institutions, practices, cultures, and social structures that overwhelm and escape the intentionality of the people participating in them. These shape us as people, and also the parameters of our interactions, the character of our relationships, and the possibilities for the person that I can become.

So social constructivism deploys a conception of agency that is somewhat looser than the one Taylor develops, and this is where I wonder about the degree to which my argument departs from his or whether he really has shown me the way to it. It employs a conception of the self that is related to, linked to, even mutually constitutive of, the other. As I read him, I think that even given his deep attention to sociality, Taylor assumes a particular notion of the self that is relatively self-contained. Even his account of the "divided self" in "What's Wrong with Negative Liberty?" sometimes comes across as somewhat too individualistic: it implies not only that I can but perhaps even that I must be able to identify higher desires as mine and I must reject the lower desires as alien. I think there is some unavoidable logic to this – after all, how can I know a desire is mine unless I know it? – but it also reduces the complexity of the case he is making, and thereby ironically risks oversimplifying positive liberty.

For it leads to a view of the other as clearly outside the self. In "Politics of Recognition," for instance, Taylor defines the other in terms of different cultures about which we can only ever have incomplete understandings, as outsiders, precisely because that is the meaning of "the other": divorced from self. Certainly, *respect* for the other is key in his work, as is recognition; Taylor says that "Misrecognition shows not just a lack of due respect. It can inflict a grievous wound."[10] And as Richard Bernstein notes in his chapter, *understanding* the other is an important project for Taylor. But my point is a little different; it is about how the other is *conceptualized*. And in this regard, I believe that the other is fairly clearly demarcated from the self in Taylor's presentation of positive liberty – perhaps even incommensurable.

The social constructivist variation of positive liberty, by contrast, allows the notion that the other is a function of the self, a product of the self, even a projection of the self. This was Beauvoir's brilliant insight in *The Second Sex*. To say that woman are "other" could, and to a significant extent does, mean that women are fundamentally different from men; perhaps they are emotional to men's rational, they live in their bodies rather than their minds, and so forth.[11] Feminists even before Beauvoir – Mary Wollstone-craft, for instance – have argued that such dualities are false; and yet they are also true, in Marx's sense of the standpoint of the proletariat. They are false in that women live in their minds just as much as men do, and men live in their bodies as much as women do; women deploy all kinds of rationality, and men feel all sorts of emotions. That is, such dualities do not reflect the materiality of the experiences of living women and men. Yet the ideological constructs of gender produce those very realities it claims; men may feel emotions, but they are socialized to repress them while women are free to express them, just as women are taught to obsess about their bodies and their appearance in ways that men are discouraged from doing. This what the terms "woman" and "man" come to mean, at least in the West. That is, women are socially constructed *to be* the other; it is not just that women *are* different from men, so men have to work really hard to understand them. Women are not that different, Beauvoir argues, and what men have to learn to understand is how they are forced to trans-late the relatively small differences between men and women in grossly exaggerated ways that become the basis for all sorts of social inequalities. Difference, otherness, is a social product – something that humans create, not simply a reflection of a pre-existing reality. So it is not so much that we need to work to tear down walls between us so much as that we need to stop spending so much energy erecting them and shoring them up.

By suggesting that people are *produced through* social formations, and not simply *limited by* them, social constructivism thereby calls into question the assumption of what is genuine or true to the self, and what is false; of what is self, and what is other. As Kathy Ferguson puts it, "It is not simply that [we are] being socialized; rather, a subject on whom so-cialization can do its work is being produced."[12] That is, we need to pay attention to the otherness within. If social construction characterizes our entire social identity and being, if everyone is always and unavoidably socially constructed, then not only our restrictions, but our powers as well must have been produced by this very same process. Who we are – the "choosing subject" – exists within and is formed by particular contexts. The contexts in which we live produce our agency. Yet, while they make our agency possible, they often simultaneously put restraints on freedom. This duality of social construction permits, even requires, a more complicated engagement of the question of freedom. For indeed, social construction suggests that the dichotomy between negative and positive liberty, and between internal and external restraint, is itself a construction; we must see the self as socially constituted in this very deep way.

Social constructivism thus adds an important dimension to positive liberty by showing us that a focus on external barriers will be weakened without attention to the internal ones, as well as to the larger social, institutional, and cultural contexts in which such barriers are created and operate. I think this is what Taylor's argument shows us as well: the inherently social dimension of internal barriers and the relationship between internality and externality. That is, it is Taylor's argument that makes this insight possible, at least as I read him. I believe Taylor's positive liberty leads us to the insight that we must acknowledge the *interaction* of "inner" and "outer," to see them as interdependent in meaning and in practice, in order to interrogate the social construction of the choosing subject, the subject of liberty. This interaction does not result in determinism – the view that since there is no way not to be socially constructed, there is no way to change ourselves because humans cannot control these large social formations – but rather provides the means for identifying not only the ways in which power relations are structured, but why it is so difficult to see those relations and that structure.

In my view, the possibilities of social construction, and the focus on the internal aspects of liberty – desire, will, identity, and how they both facilitate and block freedom – is the most important contribution of Taylor's reconstruction of Berlin's typology. Charles Taylor has written so many wonderful, eloquent, books, much grander in scope than this one article, and other essays in this volume expound on the virtues of these grand, important, even momentous works. But I believe they all address issues this article originally raised. For me, this article is the most important thing he ever did; it shaped my intellectual and professional life, charting a path for me throughout my career. Thank you, Charles Taylor, for writing it, and for all your marvellous contributions to political theory and philosophy.

PART FOUR

The Interpretation of Modernity

8

Whatever Happened to the Ontic Logos?

GERMAN IDEALISM AND THE LEGITIMACY OF MODERNITY

MICHAEL ROSEN

I

Charles Taylor's unique voice – intense, acute, challenging, profound, but never pompous or pretentious – has enriched the conversation between philosophy and politics for more than fifty years. His work is an inspiration and ideal, even to those of us who respectfully dissent from some of the positions he advances. In this paper I am going to register both agreement and disagreement.

Let me start, very briefly, with what I take to be a profound methodological agreement. I too am happy to shroud myself within what, in *A Secular Age*, Taylor light-heartedly calls "the spectre of idealism,"[1] by which I take him to mean that the best way to connect philosophy and society is to understand that ideas – ways of seeing and understanding the world – are not mere by-products of material or economic processes. The mistake (my language, not his) is to imagine that idealism must be simply the inversion of materialism: that the idealist perspective understands society as ultimately determined by a set of independently developing ideal processes in the same way that the Marxists imagined it was by independently developing economic processes.[2] But that is not the way in which idealism should best be understood.

Moreover, Taylor is also absolutely right, in my opinion, to think that what is at issue in the human sciences is not "mechanistic materialism" so much as "motivational materialism"[3] – and that motivational materialism is something that we should be very reluctant to accept. Human beings are essentially normative agents and any reductive attempt to give an account of their activity in prudential or instrumental terms – as maximising some non-normative value – needs to have a very good reason to undercut what is so salient in any sane person's observation of politics and society: that values and ideals are central to political practice. It would take far more than a vague, generic commitment to "materialism" or the idea of scientific method to make such radical revisionism plausible.

I move now to disagreement. I do so not because I wish to dwell on those disagreements but because I want to use the picture that I shall develop in contrast to Taylor's as a background against which to depict what seem to me to be crucial aspects of a period of thought to which Taylor himself has given the deepest study, but which has receded in prominence in *A Secular Age* – German Idealism. I shall argue that German Idealism represents a seminal moment in the long, drawn-out process of secularization, one that initiates a distinctively modern conception of self-transcendence through community.

To start, here are two pictures of (Latin) Christianity. According to the first, when Christianity was in its heyday – from, shall we say, around the time of the fall of Rome until about 1500 – human beings lived in what was, effectively, a different world. The natural world was a cosmos, an embodiment of divine order and agency. The social world was an integral part of that cosmos, deriving its legitimacy through its relationship to a transcendent source. Furthermore, human beings themselves were different, finding expressive identity within ways of life and political structures whose validity was not a matter for challenge or question. Succinctly put, this was a world "in which spiritual forces impinged on porous agents, in which the social was grounded in the sacred and secular time in higher times, a society moreover in which the play of structure and anti-structure was held in equilibrium; and this human drama unfolded within a cosmos."[4]

Here, in contrast, is a different picture. Human beings seek reconciliation – that is, they need to find ways of understanding the world that enable them to live lives they find acceptable in the face of the inescapable human facts of death and suffering. Appreciating this need must frame our understanding of religions as well as of other systems of belief and practice that may not count as religious, if, by "religion," we understand something that makes reference to a reality that transcends the world as mortal human beings experience it.

Christianity and its monotheistic sister religions, Judaism and Islam, respond to the need for reconciliation in a distinctive way. They are both monistic and, essentially, rationalistic. That is to say, they represent views of reality within which everything can ultimately be explained in relation to the agency of a single omnipotent, omniscient, and benevolent creator-God.

Yet this monistic rationalism brings with it severe tensions, tensions which express themselves particularly acutely when it comes to reconciling human beings with evil, particularly those evils that are not (at least, are not obviously) the result of human agency: death and physical suffering.[5] So much so that Christianity is haunted by, as Blumenberg puts it, the "threat of gnosticism." Evil always threatens to become independent in some way, whether personified in the form of Satan and his fellow "rebel angels" or, more subtly, in compromising the full scope of each of the divine characteristics I mentioned earlier.

Here is Taylor's own, obviously heartfelt, response to this problem:

Someone close to you dies. You may want to hang on to the love of God, to the faith that they and you are still with God, that love will conquer death, even though you don't understand how. What do you say to the challenge of theodicy? One answer could be: that in a sense, God is powerless; that is, he cannot just undo this process without abolishing our condition, and hence our coming to him from out or through of this bodily condition – although occasionally the spark of our coming to him lights up, and there can be surprising cures.[6]

Note three things about this passage. First, there is the acceptance of a limitation on divine omnipotence. Evil is the price to be paid for good, even by God – in this case, the good of human, physical embodiment.[7] But then why should a just God allow this price to be paid by the innocent? At this point, we need to think of an afterlife ("love will conquer death, even though you don't understand how"). Finally, the door is not closed on the miraculous ("there can be surprising cures"), modern science notwithstanding.

II

My point in putting the problem of theodicy at the centre of our understanding is not to belabour the internal difficulties of Christianity but to bring out the way that this leads to an, as it seems to me, important contrast with the picture of Christianity taken from Taylor that I sketched earlier. If we accept that first picture, the transition away from the embedded world of social meaning of Christianity in its heyday must be puzzling. Why should human beings have chosen the modern world with its coldness, isolation, and disorientation over its rich, meaningful predecessor? Western Europeans appear to have sacrificed their birthright of experiential plenitude for a mess of instrumental knowledge and control. On the second picture, by contrast, a central part of the story of the transformation of Christianity is that it is endogenous; changes came about as human beings responded to problems internal to Christianity that can be connected back to its origins. Given the tensions endemic in the monotheistic project, it is no surprise that no single set of solutions should have proved enduringly stable.

For Augustinian Christianity, the world is *not* good. Fallen humanity has been cut off from divine goodness by Original Sin (although, thanks to the redemptive sacrifice of Jesus Christ, not from divine grace) and our life in this world gives constant testimony to this fact – our suffering here serving to point to the central truth that the kingdom of Christ is "not of this world." Yet this biblical/Pauline/Augustinian narrative of Original Sin is in obvious tension with God's goodness. If God is good, then he is just, and, if God is just, then, even if it was right for him to punish Adam and Eve a few thousand years ago, how can it be just for him to continue to punish us, their presumed descendants? (This is one of the arguments that added to the agony of Pascal.)

From this perspective, the great watershed of Christianity is not the Protestant Reformation (Luther and Calvin continue the Augustinian tradition, albeit with very different accounts of divine grace) but the early modern assertion of the goodness of the world – an assertion associated with (but not confined to) Deism. The world is good because it has been ordered to further human well-being; the great law of nature is that everything is to be preserved (to use Locke's phrase) "as much as may be."[8] The assertion of the goodness of the world proved fragile, however. Belief in it is widely assumed to have been destroyed by some combination of the Lisbon earthquake and Voltaire's *Candide*. The problem lies not just in the continuing fact of suffering, which appears to compromise divine omnipotence (why must God "pay the price" of evil for the achievement of the greater good of an overall order?) but also in its uneven distribution, which appears to conflict with divine goodness (how can it be just for some to bear the necessary costs, even if others benefit?). An afterlife, of course, might square accounts, but then there would be no fundamental difference between this view and its Augustinian predecessors – this world is morally incomplete without another one to point to.

III

It may be surprising when I say that Kant – the author of an essay "On the Failure of All Previous Attempts in Theodicy" – should have an answer to the problem of theodicy at all. But he does, I shall argue. Kant's radical solution serves to highlight monotheism's difficulties. But, at the same time, he opens the way to a very different strategy of achieving reconciliation, one that is, I shall argue, transformed and extended by his Idealist successors, and that, after them, becomes a potent ingredient in the self-understanding of our "secular age."

The early modern assertion of the goodness of the world takes an important premise for granted. If the problem lies in death and suffering, then it would seem to be assumed that the goodness of the world lies in – what? – life and happiness. In other words, the problem is posed in what are, broadly speaking, eudaemonist terms. It is this premise that Kant rejects. God's goodness does not consist in his having placed us in a world created for our well-being (in the sense of happiness) but in his gift to us of moral agency – agency in the full, radical sense, so that we are each individually capable of being held responsible for our actions by an impartially just God. For this to be the case, we must be free, informed, and so on.

From this perspective, aspects of Kant's moral philosophy – his doctrine of noumenal freedom, his insistence on the purity of moral motivation and his assertion of the intrinsic value of punishment, to name three of the most salient – that his modern, secular admirers downplay emerge as consistent – indeed fundamental – elements in his enterprise. If I am right – and I think that I am – Kant is not the half-hearted secularist that readers since Heinrich Heine (*"Der alte Lampe muss einen Gott haben"*) have supposed but someone with a strong, if highly unorthodox, religious position – one that comes very close, so far as I can tell, to Socinianism.

But I have no time to explore this here. What is important for my argument is that, for Kant, the central issue of theodicy becomes not happiness but justice – "the bad state which the disproportion between the impunity of the depraved and their crimes seems to indicate in the world."[9] What matters, says Kant, is not the sufferings of the righteous, but the fact that evil goes unpunished: "the lament over the lack of justice shown in the wrongs which are the lot of human beings here on earth is directed not at the well-being that does not befall the good, but at the ill that does not befall the evil (although if well-being occurs to the evil then the contrast makes the offence all the greater). For under divine rule even the best of human beings cannot found his wish to fare well on God's beneficence, for one who only does what he owes can have no rightful claim on God's benevolence."[10] It is this – and not the need to compensate unhappy yet morally worthy individuals by offering them happiness in a future life – that makes belief in immortality compelling. "It is from the necessity of punishment that the inference to a future life is drawn,"[11] Kant writes in a footnote at the end of the *Metaphysics of Morals* that seems, you may not be surprised to hear, largely to have escaped the notice of Kant's modern advocates.

Now perhaps this reading makes certain of Kant's less plausible doctrines consistent, you might say, but if that is the position one ends up with then Kant's answer to the theodicy problem is hardly an improvement over its predecessors. Be that as it may, the transition from happiness to justice has an extraordinarily important consequence. If the reconciliation of human beings with their condition requires the abolition of death and suffering then it is clear that that is a project that only a divine agent, capable of action that transcends the laws of nature as we know them, can achieve. But Kant's change of theological perspective creates a secular historical *telos* for the goodness of the world: justice – the coincidence between agency and outcome – is a human project, something that we can bring about together in this life. As he says in his *Lectures on Ethics*:

The final destiny of the human race is moral perfection, so far as
it is accomplished through freedom, whereby man, in that case, is
capable of the greatest human happiness. God might already have
made men perfect in this fashion, and allotted to each his share of

happiness, but in that case it would not have sprung from the inner *principium* of the world. But that inner principle is freedom. The destiny of man is therefore to gain his greatest perfection by means of his freedom. God does not simply will that we should be happy, but rather that we should make ourselves happy, and that is the true morality. The universal end of mankind is the highest moral perfection; if only everyone were so to behave that their conduct would coincide with the universal end, the highest perfection would be thereby attained. Every individual must endeavour to order his conduct in accordance with this end, whereby he makes his contribution such that, if everyone does likewise, perfection is attained.[12]

To put it briefly, we are dependent on one another for justice. The "highest human happiness" *is* attainable. But to achieve it is a collective endeavour that requires human beings to work together. In a world in which murderers lurk at the door, following our individual duty of truth-telling may lead to horrifying results. It is not enough for one or a few of us to do our duty; every individual must make his contribution – the free riders must pay their fares or get off the bus! Kant's conception of the highest good brings religion and politics together in the idea of an ethical community. However remote the achievement of justice may be, it remains a viable political ideal: "this highest moral good will not be brought about solely through the striving of one individual person for his own moral perfection but requires rather a union of such persons into a whole ... toward a system of well-disposed human beings ... a universal republic based on the laws of virtue." It is entirely appropriate that Kant raises this idea in his writing on religion, for, as he recognizes, the idea is exactly that of a church – a church whose members are united in the common enterprise of the realization of a virtuous community. Yet it brings the idea of a church down to earth – the attainment of justice is a collective human project, one in which we should see ourselves as engaged through history.

IV

If Kant's account of the goodness of the world in terms of justice, not happiness, set the frame for what followed, later German Idealism represented a rejection of two of its basic elements. The first (and best-known) is the rejection of the Kantian framework of morality as a matter of law, duty, choice, desert, punishment, and justice – a framework that is, I have claimed, essentially connected in Kant to the idea of the individual as apt to face the judicial verdict of a just God. The rejection of this conceptual network – *Moralität* – is especially clear in Hegel's early, theological (or theologico-political) writings. Since it is very well known, however, I shall not dwell on it here, except to assert as strongly as I can that the critique of Moralität by no means represents a restoration of the kind of connection between morality and happiness that Kant so austerely rejected.

Less obvious, but vital, in my opinion, is the abandonment by the later German Idealists of the doctrine of personal immortality. This, of course, was not something to be asserted bluntly and directly at that time, especially not by men seeking employment in state-controlled universities. Yet it is apparent enough in that least diplomatic of the German philosophers of the late eighteenth and early nineteenth centuries, Fichte. Fichte, you will recall, lost his professorship at Jena over what came to be known as the "Atheism Dispute." Complicated and tangled as that story is, it is worth remembering that its origin lies in the publication by Fichte in his *Philosophisches Journal* of an essay by Friedrich Karl Forberg, one of whose main contentions was to deny belief in an afterlife as necessary to a "moral religion."

Yet take away the belief in personal immortality and we do not fall back (as was alleged) into "nihilism" – the acceptance of human existence as no more than a limited concatenation of experiences, pleasurable or otherwise. On the contrary, as Hegel documents with brilliance and (perhaps deliberate) obscurity in the *Phänomenologie des Geistes*, there are other, potent ways of seeking reconciliation through self-transcendence, even when individualistic beliefs in reward and punishment through personal immortality have lost their hold.

Belief in personal immortality offered the hope of self-transcendence through the preservation of personal identity, despite physical destruction. In its place, German Idealism initiates the exploration of self-transcendence through – to use an anachronistic but still, I think, apt term – *identification*.

To get a flavour of what is involved, we can do no better than consider this quotation from Fichte's *Bestimmung des Gelehrten*. Our spirits are exalted, says Fichte, when we see the way in which human beings have co-operated in a community so that "the successful progress of any member is the successful progress of them all" and all the more so, when we think of it from our own perspective:

Our sense of our own dignity and power increases when we say to ourselves what every one of us can say: My existence is not in vain and without any purpose. I am a necessary link in that great chain which began at that moment when man first became fully conscious of his own existence and stretches into eternity. All these people have laboured for my sake. All that were ever great, wise or noble – those benefactors of the human race whose names I find recorded in world history, as well as the many more whose services have survived their names: I have reaped their harvest. Upon the earth on which they lived I tread in the footsteps of those who bring blessings upon all who follow them. Whenever I wish, I can assume that lofty task which they had set for themselves: the task of making our fellow men ever wiser and happier. Where they had to stop, I can build further. I can bring nearer to completion that noble temple that they had to leave unfinished.

'But,' someone may say, 'I will have to stop too, just like they did.' Yes! And this is the loftiest thought of all: Once I assume this lofty task I will never complete it. Therefore, just as surely as it is my vocation to assume this task, I can never cease to *act* and thus I can never cease *to be*. That which is called 'death' cannot interrupt my work; for my work must be completed, and it can never be completed in any amount of time. Consequently, my existence has no temporal limits: I am eternal. When I assumed this great task I laid hold of eternity at the same time. I lift my head boldly to the threatening stony heights, to the roaring cataract, and to the crashing clouds in their fire-red sea. 'I am eternal!' I shout to them. 'I defy your power! Rain everything down upon me! You earth, and you, heaven, mingle all of our elements in wild tumult. Foam and roar, and in savage combat pulverize the last dust mote of that body which I call my own. Along with its own unyielding project, my will shall hover boldly and indifferently over the wreckage of the universe. For I have seized my vocation and it is more permanent than you. It is eternal, and so too am I!'[13]

Listening to Fichte, we can quite plainly hear (for the first time?) the voice of that distinctive figure of the nineteenth and twentieth centuries, the secular revolutionary, eager to sublimate his identity into the collective progress of mankind. "The revolutionary," as Nechayev puts it in his "Revolutionary Catechism," "is a doomed man. He has no personal interests, no business affairs, no emotions, no attachments, no property, and no name. Everything in him is wholly absorbed in the single thought and the single passion for revolution."[14]

Identification with the progressive transformation of society is not the only way for individuals to seek transcendence in community, however. It may equally take a conservative form. It is striking, is it not, how far the rhetoric of modern, romantic conservatism – the submissive self-identification of the individual with the transcendent, organic power of tradition – came on the scene at exactly the same time as Fichte's radicalization of Kantianism – above all in that "revolutionary book against the Revolution" (Novalis), Edmund Burke's *Reflections*.

V

What does all of this tell us about the "legitimacy of modernity"? It is common enough for those who criticize our secular age from a commitment to traditional religion to depict the modern world as under the dominance of rationalism, individualism, and voluntarism. Yet to do so ignores how far the nineteenth and twentieth centuries were – for better or for worse – centuries of collectivism, community, and commitment. This is self-transcendence, however, within what is, to use Taylor's terminology, an "immanent frame." Such visions of collective self-realization make no claim to overcome the existing laws of nature, entail no belief in an afterlife. They involve forms of identification of new kinds, not mere hangovers of earlier structures in which an omnipotent creator-God stood at the centre.

Indeed, this turn to the search for self-transcendence through the identification of the self in community has come to inhabit modern theism itself. Rationalistic religion having foundered on the rocks of the theodicy problem, God is no longer the cognitive foundation he was in the heyday of Latin Christianity, confidently issuing dogmatic pronouncements on belief and conduct to be enforced coercively against heretics and unbelievers by his institutional representatives. So what is left? There are, of course, anti-rationalist escape routes – the ostrich strategy of fundamentalism, that accepts "on faith" accounts of the nature of reality that blatantly conflict with everything that we know from science and history; and the desperate, Kierkegaardian/Wittgensteinian fideism that seeks to place religion outside the realm of the factual entirely. For the most part, however, religion, it seems, has itself become part of the post-Romantic project. God has retreated until he is no more than an elusive and ambiguous horizon at the edge of the search for expressive meaning in community. Perhaps it is better that way.

9

Taylor, Fullness, and Vitality

WILLIAM E. CONNOLLY

The Distinctive Profile of Charles Taylor

Charles Taylor is a distinctive and inspiring figure in Anglo-American intellectual life. He is so partly because of the breadth and creativity of his work and partly because the projects he undertakes do not fit neatly into any specific field container of academic life.

Is he a historian? Not exactly, though there is a lot of history in his work. Does he offer explanations? Well, yes, in a sense, but these "explanations" do not fit into the usual causal matrix. In both *Sources of the Self* and *A Secular Age*, for instance, he gives us an overview of the intersubjective conditions in which several contending identities, beliefs, and orientations to judgment are formed in late modern life; they include several monotheisms, secularism, and eliminative materialism for starters. He does not exactly "explain" how modernity or secularism came into being. But his discussions of the alternative "sources" available for people to draw upon and the way in which theistic belief has become more "optional" in secular societies do help to set the context of explanation for them. Indeed, when you engage Taylor on this intersubjective matrix your notion of what an explanation looks like is apt to undergo revision. You discern more sharply how the linguistically mediated form of life in which you participate encourages some interpretations, enables others, and makes yet others difficult to formulate without significant creative revision of this dense background.

Is he, then, a normative theorist? Yes, but one of his early essays taught us how every explanatory project, through the possibilities it delineates, the explananda it advances, and the normatively saturated concepts it uses is at once explanatory and normative. Taylor elides the oft-stated dichotomy between these enterprises.

Is he, perhaps, a metaphysician then? Yes, he is. But he teaches us how all theories and interpretations are laden with metaphysical assumptions, even if and when they deny being so. His work challenges both the possibility of being post-metaphysical and the autonomy of metaphysics, for every metaphysical perspective is bound up with distinctive socio-linguistic conditions and experiences, even if it is not simply caused or determined by them. Some possibilities on the edges of that combination may exude creative potential, but they also are very difficult to grasp by carriers of it. Taylor, further, embraces a specific metaphysical perspective. He articulates and defends it while refusing to pretend it has been proven. He acknowledges, even celebrates, the element of faith that resides in his own stance without pretending that he can dispense with some such stance. And he shows, as a corollary, how nontheistic philosophies today are inhabited by their own repositories of faith. In these ways he encourages us to bridge another artificial dichotomy between philosophy and theology that continues to stalk the academy.

Is he a secularist? Well, yes, in a sense, but it is a secularism that many secularists have tried to avoid. It is a secularism that comes to terms with its partial dependence upon some theistic traditions. It is one that also tries to show a variety of strong theists how they are themselves linked to a capacious secular tradition that it may be wise to save in some respects.

I count myself as indebted to Taylor in all these respects. I also agree with him that while an ontology or metaphysic (the two terms have moved close together in contemporary discourse) does not determine an ethic or politics there are complex relays between these dimensions, so that a move in any one of them leans on the others, encouraging some moves in those dimensions and discouraging others. That is why when Taylor addresses an issue, he finds it incumbent to move up and down the historical, ontological, faith, ethical, and linguistic scales in which it is set. As he proceeds in moving up and down these scales, his method must be comparative if it is to locate hidden assumptions and tendencies in his own tradition.

Proceeding this way, Taylor identifies sore points not only in the traditions he challenges but also in those in which he is the most invested by background, faith, and hope. It is as if he thinks that coming to terms with comparative deficiencies and temptations in contending traditions provides the most promising route to encouraging internal modesty within all of them as you also open up promising modes of exchange between them. And reciprocal modesty sets one condition of possibility for the cultural pluralism so urgently needed today.

So when you hear critics say that Taylor does not explore non-Western cultures enough, it might be wise to suggest that they are both right and wrong. He may underplay the ways in which European developments were shocked and crystallized by the New World and even how dependent Euro-American capitalist successes have been on exploitation of other regions as well as constituencies within. To correct these limits is indispensable. But to do so by continuing to apply his general intellectual insights would be to undertake a Herculean task for which few of us may be well prepared today. It could not take simply take the form of either correcting "the West" against some intact tradition in "the East" or the other way around. Such global comparisons omit minority reports and thus actual and potential crosscurrents within and across the regimes under review. Doing so, they may occlude potential cross-fertilizations by treating intersecting traditions in too unilateral and linear ways. Sometimes close, comparative examination of minority reports within and across broad cultural complexes may be a promising way to go; such an agenda allows minorities in one setting to enter into communion and alliance with those in others.[1] The enterprise must also involve complex, if asymmetrical, confessions on both sides about the temptations, ambiguities, and mysteries that haunt its pursuits of unity. To correct this limit in Taylor's approach without forfeiting attention to the minority reports he engages within Euro-American life may require intellectuals of a breadth, depth, and courage unusual in the world today. It may also involve confessions as well as professions.

I find myself influenced by Taylor on the themes listed above. He invests me with ambitions I am certain to fall short in meeting. I am indebted to his idea that a generous ethic does not necessarily issue from a command, a fictive contract, or a transcendental argument. It may well involve the cultivation of opaque sources already circulating within and around you. Indebted to him on this theme I nonetheless try to open up the metaphysical tradition of immanence he squeezes too hard until it, too, becomes a carrier of such an ethic. I will not rehearse here my disagreements with Taylor's readings of nontheistic philosophers of immanence such as Nietzsche, Foucault, and Deleuze, though those issues may peek through.[2]

Fullness and Vitality

Let's take up Taylor's general definitions of fullness and wholeness, said by him to provide aspirational sustenance for both philosophies of transcendence and those of immanence. By a philosophy of transcendence he means, roughly, one that appeals to some notion of the divine, though the notions vary significantly even within the monotheistic tradition. By a philosophy of immanence he means (again, roughly) one that claims to be grounded entirely in natural or earthy processes, though these professions also vary significantly within this tradition. Both, he says, appeal to fullness as an aspiration. Here are a few formulations about fullness from *A Secular Age*:

> Somewhere, in some activity, or condition, lies a fullness, a richness; that is, in that place (activity or condition), life is fuller, richer, deeper, more worthwhile, more admirable, more what it should be. This perhaps is a place of power: we often experience this as deeply moving, as inspiring. Perhaps this sense of fullness is something we just catch glimpses of from afar off; we have the powerful intuition of what fullness would be like if we were in that condition ... The sense of orientation also has a negative slope, where we experience above all a distance, an absence, and exile, a seemingly irremediable incapacity ever to reach this place; an absence of power; a confusion, or worse, the conditions often described in the tradition as melancholy ... These experiences and others which can't all be enumerated here, help us to situate a place of fullness, to which ourselves morally or spiritually. They can orient us because they offer some sense of what they are of: the presence of God, or the voice of nature, or the force which flows through everything, or the alignment in us of desire and the drive to form.[3]

As Taylor says, his description does seem to "tilt toward the believer," leaning toward the idea that fullness is approached in life if and when divine grace becomes infused into it. But he then assures us that "unbelievers" can and do pursue such a condition too. "The unbeliever wants to be the kind of person for whom this life is fully satisfying." Too bad they/we find ourselves visiting therapists so often as we follow this pursuit without an "outside source for the reception of power."[4] They/we pursue multiple, contending strategies to compensate for the lack of fullness, as the traditions of Romanticism, humanism, post-Nietzscheanism, secularism, and a couple of versions of postmodernism reveal.

Quite a category, then, "fullness." It may be worthwhile noting that those who are "unbelievers" from Taylor's vantage point typically adopt an alternative set of positive onto-beliefs of their own. Some of us believe in a cosmos of becoming set on multiple tiers of chrono-time as we identify an outside to every specific human and nonhuman force-field, an outside that periodically helps to set the stage for the creative evolution of a climate, an ocean conveyor system, a glacier flow, a species change, a civilization, a spiritual complex, a human life. The outside is multiple, active, and real; it is merely not divine. Within such a perspective the general definition of fullness as the goal of all traditions worries us. We resist both the universality of its affirmative expressions and its sibling in some versions of critical theory. The latter agree that fullness must be the goal and then support a negative dialectic in which transcendence must always be pursued and must always fail. We also seek to deepen our attachment to an open world that enables us to be, entangles us with multiple forces and species, and is not highly predisposed to humanity in the last instance.

What is the version of transcendence Taylor favours most? It does not seem to be Augustinianism, in which an omnipotent, omniscient god monopolizes all creative power in the universe, denying any portion of positive agency to either humans or to nonhuman force-fields. It is not lodged in the nominalist tradition of the late Middle Ages either. Or Calvinism, though he does offer a powerful interpretation of how Calvinism helped to shape the rise of European modernity.

I am uncertain. But my sense is that Taylor's faith has evolved rather far, perhaps partly in response to his engagements with the sciences and with modes of materialism he resists. He seems to invoke a benevolent, somewhat limited God who does not punish us with devastating natural events, who calls upon us to draw closer to his love, and who provides a gratifying court of appeal and sustenance whenever the worst happens. "Many who are relatively innocent are swept up in this suffering, and some of the worst offenders get off lightly. The proper response to this is not retrospective book-keeping, but making ourselves capable of responding to God's initiative."[5]

This is surely an insufficient rendering of Taylor's faith, partly because it is received from outside it. What is noble within it, even as thus summarized, is Taylor's recognition that its living expression is too often entwined with stringent, punitive Christian traditions that are hard to disentangle definitively from it. In this respect, Taylor is a noble warrior against dangerous tendencies in the tradition he imbibes. Doing so, he sets an example for those of us who care about the world and imbibe other traditions.

The theme I wish to pursue is advanced by a set of thinkers who cut across theistic and nontheistic traditions. William James, Henris Bergson, Alfred North Whitehead, Nietzsche, and Deleuze, while breaking with each other on the issue of God, converge in projecting an open world of becoming that exceeds and includes the human estate. They also transfigure Taylor's pursuit of fullness into an appreciation of vitality. More sharply, they treat the vitality of being as a crucial precondition and aspect of the good life. Today they would almost certainly emphasize the fragility of things for the human estate in both its intercivilizational relations and imbrications with a host of nonhuman force-fields that possess differential powers of metamorphosis. I refer on the latter register to climate patterns, ocean currents, glacier flows, bacterial and viral evolution, hurricanes, soil preservation capacities, and so on.

The vitality of being. Let's follow Whitehead for a moment as he calls upon us to accentuate our sense of belonging to the world by cultivating a simmering sense of vitality already there. Shocked by the quantum revolution that uprooted the Newtonianism he had taken to be apodictic, Whitehead extrapolated creatively from that tradition in a way that diverged from other Euro-American philosophers of his day.

Creativity is an "ultimate term" in his philosophy – meaning, I take it, that you can point roughly to how it happens but not delineate the process in precise explanatory terms. It engenders the "elbow room" in the cosmos. Creativity unfolds amidst preconditions and uncertain constraints that are not known by us with confidence in advance. How could they be, since that would be knowing something that had not yet been created. The constraints are explained in large part by the fact that the universe, at any moment of chrono-time, is composed of "actual entities" of innumerable types which help to set preconditions for new events. An actual entity is any formation that has some tendency toward self-maintenance such as a rock, a cell, a tornado, a system of ocean currents, a continent, a civilization, and so forth.

The creative process unfolds primarily in relations between entities, involving both the excesses that occupy each and their inter-entanglements.

But how? It is through the acceleration of "vibrations" within and between actual entities that novel formations emerge. As Whitehead says,

"Newton would have been surprised at the modern quantum theory and at the dissolution of quanta into vibrations."[6] When elements from one entity press toward another there is the issue of whether, and if so in what ways, they will "ingress" into it, and, then, what new processes of unconscious self-organization or "concrescence" will arise in the latter as it meets the new infusions. Such processes operate in species evolution and even in ocean currents, according to Whitehead, though we will not tarry here to explore his theme of "pan-experientialism."

Let us focus now on the asymmetrical character of the creative process in human relations to sharpen the comparison to Taylor's pursuit of fullness. Whitehead is fascinated by the "scars" of being. A "scar," on this account, is a partially formed tendency from the past that did not become completed in action because another turn was consolidated and taken. *The fork not taken now subsists as a partially crystallized instinct or set of arrested thought imbued energies.* It may fester again as it enters into new vibrations in a situation with vague affinities to the one in which it first subsisted.

Here is how Whitehead puts it: "A feeling bears on itself the scars of its birth; it retains the impress of what might have been but is not. It is for this reason that what an actual entity has [in the past] avoided as a datum for feeling may yet be an important part of its equipment."[7]

Such scars regularly subsist in life as cultural instincts, drives and tendencies set on differing degrees of intensity, stubbornness, and completeness; they fall below the searchlight of consciousness because they are too cloudy and underdetermined to exist. But, nonetheless, they do make a difference. Such patterns of subsistence teach us, Whitehead says, how "the actual cannot be reduced to mere matter of fact in divorce from the potential."[8]

This brief summary is insufficient, of course, to the Whitehead corpus. But it does set the issue of human vitality and sporadic moments of creativity into a larger compass. Human vitality expresses our distinctive and modest participation in larger processes that slide back and forth between accelerated and decelerated vibrations.

Human vitality and a presumptive sense of attachment to the cosmos are thus bonded together, on this reading. Or, at least, the cultivation of care for this world can be readily bonded to vitality because the experience of the latter is one of the things that makes life worthy of value. It all depends upon what other experiences are confronted.

The sense of vitality may be dimly experienced as the excess of life over the specific course of action actually taken; or as a stutter that bursts forth as you search for the appropriate word for an unfolding thought that is not yet in the lexicon; or as you dwell in an uncanny experience of duration in which incipient pressures from a past potential that never became consolidated enter into subliminal exchanges with established habits in a new setting; or as a jazz musician or point guard improvises in the middle of the action; or as participants in a burgeoning social movement allow a new strategy and/or relational conception of themselves to emerge as if from nowhere from their negotiations.

The experience of vitality involves oscillations back and forth between moments of accentuated imbalance and the temporary recovery of a new, yet precarious balance, sometimes set on a new plateau. Such oscillations sometimes move rapidly, as when you start a sentence and find it being adjusted and refined as you proceed. In many cases, the end of that sentence was not simply implicit in its beginning. Focus on the implicit, you might say, is attached to the pursuit of fullness and focus on the incipient to a practice of vitality. Spontaneous humour is connected to the pluripotentiality of incipient activity on the way, too. That's why Nietzsche prized laughter and dance so much, though no one has reported that the near-hermit was a superb ballroom dancer.

How such oscillations work in everyday life can be brought out further by considering a person who has lost the fragile equipoise between a train of thought and periodic triggers that nudge it in new directions. In "Time Regained," the aging hero, Marcel, encounters Charlus, the arrogant intellectual he had known as a young man. The proud Charlus, who now has aphasia, finds that the uncanny process of oscillation I call vitality has become compromised. In the conversation that ensues two de Charluses struggle against each other. "Of the two, one, the intellectual one, passed his time in complaining that he suffered from progressive aphasia, that he constantly pronounced one word or letter by mistake for another. But as soon as he actually made such a mistake, the other M. de Charlus, the subconscious one, who was as desirous of admiration as the first was of pity and out of vanity did things that the first would have despised, immediately, like a conductor whose orchestra had blundered, checked the phrase which he had started and with infinite ingenuity made the end of his sentence follow coherently from the word which had in fact been uttered by mistake ... his vanity impelled him, not without the fatigue of the most laborious concentration, to drag forth this or that ancient recollection ... which would demonstrate to me that he had preserved ... all his lucidity of mind."[9]

The second sentence by Proust consists of phrases that enact in their awkward form the struggle between the two Charluses. The poise that Charlus has lost also discloses something about reciprocal elements in play when you do maintain poise. As Proust knows, perhaps better than others, the unconscious triggers from a past tendency that never became consolidated can jolt a train of thought under new circumstances. Poise amidst vitality is the difference between allowing creativity to be folded into thought and being the victim of odd triggers that disorient thinking. Such is the precariousness of human thinking and vitality. Stutter and stammer as a word or phrase surfaces from a subliminal trigger, but not too much or too often. An excess of triggers overwhelms the element of creativity; their absence freezes it.

Vitality, then, exceeds fullness. It may be closer to the overfullness or abundance of life over identity that Nietzsche talks about in "The Gift Giving Virtue," when you become sensitized to an unfamiliar inflow of experience, absorb and organize it unconsciously, and allow the new energies and altered trajectory that emerge from its digestion to find positive expression in your relations with others. The gift giving virtue involves an unfamiliar inflow, uncanny self-organization of that which is absorbed in relation to that which is already there, and bouts of creative generosity in your relations with other beings and forces. Whitehead, Proust, Bergson, Nietzsche, James, and Deleuze all advance distinctive characterizations of vitality. William James's positive valorization of "litter" in the world, I think, points to uncanny periods of creativity during which something in us responds to energized strands of litter outside us. It always takes two or more to perform the dance of vitality, even when the two are two dissonant trajectories set on differing degrees of consciousness in the same self.

A theory that links agency to vitality, in which intrusions from the outside periodically become catalyzing events, is one in which the active, masterful role of the "agent" gives ground to opaque processes of self-organization that unfold within and between us. You ascertain the outcome as it unfolds rather than before it is enacted. Now it is timely to decide what to do with it. Vitality, agency, creativity, and freedom now become interdefined terms; none dissolves entirely the element of mystery circulating through these connections. How could it, if it is bound to real creativity? That is why the received traditions of both negative and positive freedom in Anglo-American political thought may both need to be worked upon reflectively: the gift and the risk of vitality.

My hope and sense is that some of what has been discussed above resonates with features of Taylor's thought, particularly his notions of reception and responsiveness as key elements in ethics and human agency. Nonetheless, I am not that confident that vitality can be absorbed smoothly within his category of fullness. There are affinities between them, however. When you suffer grief, or a terrible illness, or depression, or an overwhelming loss, or a shocking defeat, vitality becomes drained from life. During such times, a lack of vibrancy is expressed. And also, when you engage in everyday, action-oriented perception, the vital dimension becomes less active or vivid. That must be so, if we are to walk across the street, recognize a friend, or engage precinct monitors on election day. Vitality comes into its own during odd moments of hesitation, dwelling, stuttering, laughter, and uncertainty – during moments when we act like a seer more than an analyst. It has both individual and collective manifestations.

If we are minor participants in a larger cosmos of becoming composed of multiple, interacting force-fields that periodically morph, *part* of our experience of belonging to the world may be tied to that experience of vitality and to those small and large moments of real creativity in which *we* participate. The idea is to cultivate subliminal experiences of vitality further, even as we work to diminish the risks that accompany acting recklessly upon their fruits. In this way we hesitate to embrace either an ideal of fullness through transcendence or a negative dialectic in which "failed transcendence" inevitably accompanies the unavoidable pursuit of fullness. As we contest that pair, we also bear in mind that there are both theistic and nontheistic visions of vitality.

But *does* fullness really contrast that much with vitality? Taylor, I imagine, may say no. Taylor's conception of a limited divinity as a co-presence may point in this direction, as rather similar themes clearly do in James and Whitehead. James celebrates the virtues of a limited god, and Whitehead pursues an impersonal God who presides over the "creative advance of the cosmos" without attending in any personal way to human beings. So we may have a series of different inflections here, amplified by somewhat different images of the cosmos in which each is set.

If Taylor sometimes displaces partial affinities between him and Nietzsche – such as love of this world and presumptive generosity – by emphasizing the themes of aggressive non-theism, violence, and aristocratism also found in the latter, maybe an exchange between Taylor and Whitehead can crystallize the pertinent issues more sharply. Taylor, I admit, has points to make against the Nietzschean tradition; but it is possible that the validity of those points also blinds him to some of the ways that tradition complements and challenges his own thinking. Perhaps one way is the idea that the very preconditions of vitality that enhance our attachment to this world may also pose challenges to the idea that a divinity predisposes the world to us. Or even the Whitehead theme that creativity in the world is strongly linked to the "advance" of the world. During the age of the Anthropocene I may find myself both diverging from Taylor and Whitehead and moving towards Nietzsche on this point.

Charles Taylor and Alfred North Whitehead, on the other hand, may pose delicate challenges to each other on the question of fullness and vitality *because* they move so close to one another before sliding in different directions. They are two inspiring thinkers who care about this world. These indispensable rivals are thus worthy of each other, and more of us must strive to become worthy of them.

PART FIVE

Moral Agency and the Self II

10

Self-Creation or Self-Discovery?

KWAME ANTHONY APPIAH

Beginning with Hume

There's a broadly Humean picture that constrains much modern thinking about normative questions. It's Humean not because Hume actually held it – I am not sure that he did – but because it has so often been ascribed to him that he might as well have. Here is the picture: what people do is driven by two fundamentally different kinds of psychological states. Beliefs – the first kind – are supposed to reflect how the world is. Desires, by contrast, reflect how we'd like it to be. Beliefs are meant to fit the world; the world is meant to fit desires. So beliefs can be true or false, reasonable or unreasonable. Desires, on the other hand, are satisfied or unsatisfied.

Beliefs are supposed to be formed on the basis of evidence, and there are principles of reasoning that determine what it is rational to believe on the basis of what evidence. Desires are just facts about us. Because they are just things that happen to (or in) us, no evidence determines which ones are right. When we act, we use our beliefs about the world to figure out how to get what we desire. Reason, as Hume famously put it in his *Treatise of Human Nature* (1739), "is, and ought only to be the slave of the passions."[1] If our passion is for apples, we go to where our beliefs suggest the apples are. And, once we go looking for the apples we're after, we'll find out whether our beliefs were right.

Because beliefs are about the world, on the other hand, and there's only one world, they can be either right or wrong, and we can criticize other people's beliefs for being unreasonable or simply false. But desires can't be right or wrong, in this sense. Desires are simply not responses to the world; they're aimed at changing it, not at reflecting how it is.

There's a complication to the story, because much of what we ordinarily desire has beliefs, so to speak, built into it. I want the glass because I believe it has the Sauternes in it. No wine, and the desire loses its point. So the desire for the glass is dependent on the belief that there's wine in it. If the belief is wrong, there's a basis for criticizing the desire. On the Humean picture, this is the only way desires can be criticized: by criticizing beliefs they presuppose. Once you remove the conditional element from the specification of a desire, you get to what we might call your basic desires. And since these depend on no assumptions about how the world is, you can't criticize them for getting the world wrong.

Hume himself drew the distinction, in a famous passage, between judgments about how things are and judgments about how things ought to be. Normative judgments naturally come with views about what one ought to think, do, or feel. And this picture is often thought to be Humean in part because Hume insisted that the distinction between "is" and "ought" was, as he said, "of the last consequence."[2] Like desires, oughts are intrinsically action-guiding, in a way that is isn't. And so, in the familiar slogan, "you can't get an ought from an is." Since we are often tempted to move from what is to what ought to be, this move, like many moves philosophers think illicit, has a disparaging name: we call it (following G.E. Moore) the *naturalistic fallacy*.[3]

From Beliefs and Desires to Values

Such a distinction between the way beliefs and desires result in action is the key to the Humean picture of how human beings work. Desires – or, more precisely, basic desires – set the ends we aim for; beliefs specify the means for getting to them. Since these desires can't be wrong or right, you can criticize only the means people adopt, not their ends. Finally, the Humean identifies the truths that beliefs aim at with the facts. If you believe something and your belief is true, it gets one of the facts in the world right.

If that's what facts are on the Humean view, what are values? You could say the Humean thinks that, strictly speaking, there aren't any values. Not, at least, in the world. The world can force us to believe in facts, because if we don't, they'll bump into us anyhow, get in our way. But reality can't force us to desire anything. Where, after all, would one look in the world for the wrongness of a basic desire? What science would demonstrate it? A science might be able to explain why you desire something. It couldn't explain that you should – or shouldn't – desire it. Normativity is never reducible to facts alone.

Talk of values, then, is really a way of talking about certain of our desires. Which ones? Well, when we appeal to what we take to be universal values in our discussions with one another – the value of art or of democracy or of philosophy – we're talking about things we want everyone to want. If we think exposure to art is valuable, then, roughly, we'd like everyone to want to experience it. If we say democracy is valuable, then, roughly again, we want everyone to want to live in a democracy. We might say, as a *façon de parler*, that someone who wants everyone to want x "believes that x is valuable," but that is still just, in reality, a way of talking about a complex desire. Again, some values will subsist upon certain facts. I could value universal vaccination for smallpox, because I wanted to make everyone safer – but give up this "value" once I learned that smallpox had been eradicated. If a value reflects unconditional desires, however, since these basic desires can't be criticized, values can't either. I value kindness. I want to be kind. I want me to want to be kind. I want all of us to want to be kind. As a matter of fact, I want *you* to want everyone to want to be kind. But I don't want this because I believe that all these kindnesses will lead to something else. I value kindness intrinsically, unconditionally. Even if you showed me that some acts of kindness would have effects I didn't want, that wouldn't persuade me to give up kindness as a value. It would only show me that kindness can sometimes conflict with other things I care about.

It may be that there are basic desires like this that everyone has. So it may turn out that there are things that everyone values. Those values will be *contingently* universal; that is, it will turn out that, while there could have been rational people who valued different things from the rest of us, there are, in fact, none. This is a claim to universality that is grounded in human nature: it is the kind of universality claimed by many contemporary defenders of the idea of the "ethical brain." Still, on the Humean view, there remains no universal rational basis on which to establish that they're correct. If someone who lacked such a desire came along, there would be nothing we could say that would provide her with a rational ground for acquiring it.

Against this background something like relative truth looks like the best we can hope for. When I say that kindness is good, we can take this as a reflection of my desires, so that, in that sense, it is "true for me." Or we could suppose, as the philosopher Gilbert Harman[4] did, that such remarks are always implicitly relative to a shared commitment; and then it will be true for the group whose shared commitment it is, reflecting desires they have in common. That will give you a form of moral relativism that is quite recognizable to anthropologists: indeed, many American anthropologists will regard this as a truism.

Turning to Taylor

One way of understanding much of Charles Taylor's work is as a challenge to this Humean picture. Part of the challenge is to insist on a feature of our rational common sense, as G.E.M. Anscombe did in a famous passage in her essay on *Intention*.

> But is not anything wantable, or at least any perhaps attainable thing? It will be instructive to anyone who thinks this to approach someone and say: 'I want a saucer of mud' or 'I want a twig of mountain ash.' He is likely to be asked what for; to which let him reply that he does not want it for anything, he just wants it. It is likely that the other will then perceive that a philosophical example is all that is in question, and will pursue the matter no further; but supposing that he did not realise this, and yet did not dismiss our man as a dull babbling loon, would he not try to find out in what aspect the object desired is desirable?[5]

But Taylor has done more than this. He has offered a picture of our agency that aims to *explain* how our social contexts provide us with the materials for constructing the desirability – characterizations that make our actions intelligible to ourselves and to one another. "A great deal of human action only happens insofar as the agent understands and constitutes himself as integrally part of a 'we,'" he has written.[6] And he has invoked Bourdieu's notion of the "habitus," a "system of durable and transposable dispositions," to flesh out the essentially social nature of the self. Taylor is intent on giving human agency its full glory – he does not want to reduce us to epiphenomena – but insists that we see agency as constituted by the web of practices and collectivities in which it emerges and to which it belongs. It's a perspective, he says, that "runs against the grain of much modern thought and culture, in particular our scientific culture and its associated epistemology" – the kind of naturalism that I began by calling Humean, which has, in his view, deformed "our contemporary sense of self." In its place, he urges us to see the agent "as engaged in practices, as a being who acts in and on a world." What we should take from Bourdieu's notion of the habitus, he says, is that "practice is, as it were, a continual interpretation and reinterpretation of what the rule really means," that the relation between rule and practice is richly reciprocal.[7]

Now I have argued before that Taylor's thesis can seem at odds with its Wittgensteinian underpinnings. "When I obey a rule, I do not choose," Wittgenstein says, in a passage Taylor cites, "I obey the rule *blindly*." Taylor's vision has thus been criticized as being inadequately Wittgensteinian. Doesn't Taylor's emphasis on interpretation – the notion that "we must speak of man as a self-interpreting being, because this kind of interpretation is not an optional extra, but is an essential part of our existence" – invoke the sort of critical reflection and evaluation that Wittgenstein was at pains to call into question? To understand a sign is not to interpret it; to grasp it is *"nicht eine Deutung"* – not an interpretation, but merely a "way of going on." The core of Wittgenstein's remarks on rule-following was to eliminate precisely that interim step – interpretation – that Taylor wants us to take seriously.[8]

As you will see, I am inclined to take Taylor's side here, and I will do so, in a moment, in relation to a question about how we make our selves – also one of Taylor's central topics. But I want first to suggest that we can see the escape from the Humean picture more fruitfully not by challenging it head on – by denying that it is one possible picture – but rather by taking the step that Kant urged on us, when he argued that we can adopt more than one standpoint; and to see the choice between Hume's picture and Taylor's, not as requiring us to take sides, but rather as allowing us to switch between perspectives.

The Sensible and the Intelligible Worlds

For some purposes, as you know, Kant thought we must acknowledge that we are natural beings and regard ourselves and others as part of the natural realm, subject to theoretical explanations in terms of natural causes.

From this standpoint, we belong to the so-called sensible world, the *Sinnenwelt*. But that is not a standpoint we can adopt when we ourselves act as rational agents: "All men think of themselves as having a free will," he noted. Accordingly, "for *purposes of action* the footpath of freedom is the only one on which we can make use of reason in our conduct." Here we situate ourselves in the so-called intelligible world, the *Verstandeswelt*. As he writes in the *Groundwork of the Metaphysics of Morals*, "We can enquire whether we do not take one standpoint when by means of freedom we conceive ourselves as causes acting a priori, and another standpoint when we contemplate ourselves with reference to our actions as effects which we see before our eyes ... when we think of ourselves as free, we transfer ourselves into the intelligible world as members and recognize the autonomy of the will together with its consequence – morality."[9]

Taylor's world is the intelligible world, not the sensible world. And, like Kant, he sees us as inevitably embedded in that world when we contemplate our situation as agents and ask how we shall live, what we shall do. And the world in which we are embedded, Taylor insists, in a way that Kant did not, is always already social.

Our desirability-characterizations of courses of action are rooted in our sense of who we are. But there is a variety of ways of approaching the question, "Who am I?" Here is a canonical formulation of one of them: "And so he who would lead a Christlike life is he who is perfectly and absolutely himself. He may be a great poet, or a great man of science; or a young student at a University, or one who watches sheep upon a moor; or a maker of dramas, like Shakespeare, or a thinker about God, like Spinoza; or a child who plays in a garden, or a fisherman who throws his net into the sea. It does not matter what he is, as long as he realises the perfection of the soul that is within him. All imitation in morals and in life is wrong."[10]

Discovery

We can call this view of the role of the self as a source of reasons *discovery*. It is not surprising that discovery has been an attractive model for those, like the author of this passage, who have felt themselves in some deep way misrecognized in the culture and society in which they lived. And, despite the distracting references to being Christlike, this passage comes, as many of you will know, from Oscar Wilde's "The Soul of Man under Socialism." Discovery's thought is: there is something that I am, let me be *that*. Or, as

Taylor put the position in his well-known essay on *Multiculturalism*, "There is a certain way of being human that is *my* way. I am called upon to live my life in this way, and not in imitation of anyone else's life. But this notion gives a new importance to being true to myself. If I am not, I miss the point of my life; I miss what being human is for *me*."

Now the trouble with discovery is at least twofold. First, it misrepresents the way in which a self is made because it ignores the way in which, as Taylor once put it, a "self exists only within what I call 'webs of interlocution,'" and that "living within ... strongly qualified horizons is constitutive of human agency," so that "stepping outside these limits would be tantamount to stepping outside what we recognize as integral, that is, undamaged human personhood."[11] But second, it ignores the crucial role of invention in the process of making ourselves. Foucault articulated this objection and an alternative picture when he said: "Sartre avoids the idea of the self as something that is given to us, but through the moral notion of authenticity, he turns back to the idea that we have to be ourselves – to be truly our true self. I think the only acceptable practical consequence of what Sartre has said is to link his theoretical insight to the practice of creativity – and not to that of authenticity. From the idea that the self is not given to us, I think there is only one practical consequence: we have to create ourselves as a work of art."[12]

Creativity

This alternative picture of self-making we might call *creativity*. One of Charles Taylor's many useful contributions to contemporary ethics is to show how, once you work through to a plausible version of creativity, it turns out to be a version of discovery. "I can define my identity," he wrote in *The Ethics of Authenticity*, "only against the background of things that matter. But to bracket out history, nature, society, the demands of solidarity, everything but what I find in myself, would be to eliminate all candidates for what matters."[13] This is the point that creativity requires something to work on and with, so that there has to be something given: which is the truth in discovery. So creativity requires discovery. Nietzsche put it this way, famously and, of course, hyperbolically:

> *One thing is needful.* – To "give style" to one's character – a great and rare art! It is practiced by those who survey all the strengths and

weaknesses of their nature and then fit them into an artistic plan until every one of them appears as art and reason and even weaknesses delight the eye. Here a large mass of second nature has been added; there a piece of original nature has been removed – both times through long practice and daily work at it. Here the ugly that could not be removed is concealed; there it has been reinterpreted and made sublime.[14]

But though each of these ways of putting the matter has something to recommend it, they all need supplementation by way of the concept of interpretation – which is why I said earlier that I was going to take Taylor's side against Wittgenstein.

Interpretation

It is worth remembering first, though, that what we are charged with is not making a self but making a life. All of these ways of talking can make it seem as though self-fashioning is our primary practical task. When you start out, you need to make sense of the world into which you are born, which includes the family, the body, and the community you are born into. But that is because you have a life to live. And while family, body, community are in a sense given, to make a life you have to take them up in some particular way: you have to take each of them as something, and there is never just one way to do this. It is this, as Taylor knows, that commends interpretation as a model for what we are doing. For taking an X as a Y is what interpretation is all about.

Your current society provides, for example, models of gender: you can respond to the facts of your sexual body by either (a) adopting pretty much wholesale a "standard" gender identity, or (b) rejecting the standard repertoire, or (c) adapting one or more elements of it. Because it is, as Taylor has always insisted, a dialogical process, you can be shaped into a gender identity without recognizing that that is what is happening. I am living a life; that I am a man – which is something I came to be without much reflection but out of much everyday interaction from infancy – is one source of reasons in living it, explaining, for example, some of why I dress as I do. With different contexts, I would, no doubt, have become a man in a different way, as I would have, too, if I had had a different body or grown into a different sexuality. But we don't want to be too voluntaristic about this.

An interpretation of my situation – like the interpretation of a poem – involves being guided by the materials not simply making something up. Because identities vary in their structures and substrates, the only general thing we can say about this process is that you will be both discovering and inventing all the time. Perhaps there is wisdom to be noted in the etymology of invention, which comes from *invenire*, whose primary sense is "to discover."

I might have discovered all this this for myself, I suppose; but in fact I learned it, as much as from anywhere else, from reading the inventive philosophical work of Charles Taylor.

11

An Explicitative Conception of Moral Theory

JOSEPH HEATH

My goal in this paper is to examine an assumption that is often made by moral philosophers, but which is seldom explicitly stated or defended as such. It is the view that morality has the structure of what Annette Baier refers to as a "normative theory," viz. "a system of moral principles in which the less general are derived from the more general."[1] The most obvious examples are Kantianism and utilitarianism, in which every intermediate or specific moral obligation is (or can be) derived from one overarching, maximally general principle. Many forms of virtue theory and intuitionism have a similar structure – despite not positing a single master principle, they still regard the more specific moral rules (pay your income taxes, give to charity, etc.) as derived from more general ones (be honest, benevolent, etc.). For simplicity, however, I will focus on views that posit an "ultimate principle," with the understanding that much of what I say applies equally to pluralist views that take morality to have the same structure – an ascending pyramid of increasingly abstract normative principles (or goods, or whatever) – but deny that it is unified at the top.

Although philosophers often make the assumption that morality has this structure, they seldom stop to explain why they think it should be so, much less try to justify the claim.[2] There have, of course, always been critics and dissenters (such as Charles Taylor, who describes this "tendency to breathtaking systematization" as essentially unmotivated, and as "a peculiar feature of modern moral philosophy").[3] Philosophers committed to the approach have tended to adopt a "proof is in the pudding" attitude. Rather than provide any sort of independent reason for thinking that morality should have the structure of a normative theory, they have instead simply tried to work out an ultimate principle that "works," in the sense that it permits the derivation of all other duties (and does *not* permit the derivation of non-duties). The thought, generally, seems to be that the success of such a principle would retroactively vindicate the project.

The most obvious objection to this approach appeals to the fact that the everyday person on the street, despite being able to engage in moral judgment, has no access (or at least no conscious access) to any of these more abstract or general principles. Indeed, there appears to be an enormous similarity in the way that people apply moral rules and the way that they apply other norms, such as rules of etiquette.[4] When challenged to defend any particular constraint, they often are not able to offer a very robust justification.[5] (They are, as Jonathan Haidt put it, easily "dumbfounded" by such requests.[6]) More significantly, when confronted with a conflict between two or more of these concrete obligations, most people do not appeal to abstract or general principles to resolve the conflict.[7]

Of course, none of this shows that morality does not have the structure of a normative theory. It does, however, constitute a phenomenon that requires explanation. One way of formulating the issue is to ask what sort of a relationship exists between *conventional morality* – the very specific rules that people apply in order to manage everyday interactions – and what we might refer to, tendentiously, as *morality proper* – the type of abstract principles that moral philosophers have tended to focus on. My primary objective in this paper will be to survey four different ways of thinking about this relationship, each of which enjoys a (largely tacit) following in the philosophical literature. The guiding thread in considering the relationship between conventional morality and morality proper will be the question of how completely or thoroughly mistaken conventional morality can be with respect to either the nature or content of our presumptive moral obligations. In the end, I will argue that the last model, which I refer to as the "explicitative" conception, the one that assigns the most authority to conventional morality, is the most attractive. Thus the more common philosophical view, which regards conventional morality as somehow contingent or as dependent upon morality proper for its validity, represents an inversion of the correct order of logical dependence.

Heuristics

Perhaps the most popular view (or family of views) at the moment regards conventional morality as a set of heuristics – "fast and frugal" rules that we can use in real time to provide solutions to social interaction problems. This view takes its inspiration from the account of psychological heuristics advanced by Daniel Kahneman and Amos Tversky, particularly with respect to judgments of probability. Kahneman and Tversky observed, for instance, that when asked to judge the frequency of a particular type of event, we do not actually try to recall all instances of it over a given period of time. Instead, we employ an automatic process that they refer to as the "availability" heuristic.[8] We try to recall a single instance, then use the ease with which such an instance can be summoned up from memory as a gauge of its relative frequency. One can see this as a clever cognitive adaptation that takes advantage of a pre-existing feature of our long-term memory system. Because events that occur more often can be accessed more quickly (i.e., require less search time to find an instance), speed or ease of retrieval is in most cases a good proxy for frequency of occurrence.

These innate heuristics reside at the level of the so-called "adaptive unconscious."[9] This is reflected in the fact that our higher cognitive faculties have little or no access to the background mechanism through which these judgments are generated. Instead, they present themselves to consciousness only in the form of "outputs," or what are often referred to as intuitive judgments. For example, we have a system of intuitive physics that allows us to predict the trajectory of objects in motion, but most people have no ability to reconstruct the basis of these calculations. Similarly, we have a facial recognition system that tells us when people "look familiar," but we are often incapable of saying what it is that makes them seem familiar.

It is uncontroversial that humans have a range of heuristics, or unconscious responses, that are highly *relevant* to the moral domain. The way that we respond to neoteny (or infantile characteristics) is the most obvious example. The presence of a cute infant evokes a wide range of altruistic behaviours: a suspension of aggression, heightened sympathy, along with the desire to alleviate distress and to protect from harm. There is good reason to think that all of our spontaneous sympathetic reactions are of this sort as well, given the way that they are facilitated through visual representations of suffering, require identification with the victim, and so on.[10] Psychologists have posited even more specific mechanisms in other areas of the moral domain, such as the "violence inhibition module," which has the effect of making physical aggression aversive once the victim begins to exhibit certain distress cues.[11]

It doesn't take any great leap of the imagination to think that conventional morality might be grounded in these sorts of natural intuitions, and that the difference between conventional morality and morality proper might be explicable in these terms. Sophisticated sentimentalists have perhaps been the most eager to latch on to this idea, arguing that what were traditionally called "the moral sentiments" are not just emotional reactions, but are the output of a set of cognitive adaptations that favour various forms of pro-social behaviour.[12] Thus conventional moral judgments reflect our intuitive response to social interactions in the same way that intuitive physics reflects our natural observational response to the movement of medium-sized objects. Morality proper would then be akin to "physics proper," or the probability calculus – it is what we get when we examine a certain set of problems using explicit cognitive procedures, doing the actual calculations needed to produce the correct answer, rather than relying upon some proxy. It winds up being more abstract and parsimonious because the heuristics are essentially a bag of tricks developed by evolution, designed to be triggered in specific circumstances, whereas the explicit principles have cross-situational validity.

A good example of this would be the Westermarck effect, which is what generates the "yuck" response most people have when contemplating sibling incest. It has been shown fairly conclusively that children raised in close proximity over time develop a strong aversion to the thought of sexual relations with one another, regardless of whether they are biologically related.[13] Thus adopted siblings have a strong incest-avoidance response, while biological siblings separated at birth have none. It is not difficult to tell an evolutionary story about how such a mechanism might have developed, or why it would be adaptive. It appears, however, that the mechanism uses "being around each other all the time during childhood," rather than, say, physical resemblance, as a proxy for genetic relatedness. (Furthermore, relatedness is itself just a proxy for "likely to have genetic defects that match one's own.") So while conventional morality may categorically condemn incestuous unions, there is room for morality proper to intervene with a more discerning judgment, pointing out that in the absence of risk to potential offspring, there is no basis for sustaining this judgment.[14]

But it is also a feature of this particular model that conventional moral-ity, while possibly mistaken in the details, cannot be all that wrong. After all, the heuristics that developed had to be heuristics for something. With higher cognition, we can figure out what that something is, and try to act in a way that targets it more directly. But if we follow this procedure, we cannot then decide that morality is about something else entirely. Thus any sort of radical error theory is precluded. Of course, skepticism is still a serious problem – it is not clear why we should not choose to disregard the entire suite of psychological adaptations. However, assuming that we decide to give some authority to the heuristics that generate conventional morality, the obvious procedure to follow when trying to figure out the content of morality proper is to figure out what the heuristics are sup-posed to be an approximation of, with some room for adjustment between the two levels. Thus the "method of reflective equilibrium" makes some sense under this model. Furthermore, unless it can be shown that a par-ticular judgment is being made under anomalous conditions – and thus that there is some reason to suspect a "misfire" – there may be no basis for questioning its normative authority. The details of this, however, depend upon the resources available within the particular account of morality under consideration.

Bounded Rationality

There is a much more cognitivist version of the heuristics view, which holds that conventional morality is a simplified version of morality proper, one that is more suitable for use in real-time practical deliberation. The natural analogy here is to the concept of "bounded rationality," intro-duced by Herbert Simon in an influential critique of the economic model of rational action.[15] Conventional economic theory holds that individuals act in such a way as to maximize their expected utility. Simon expressed doubts about this assumption, on the grounds that the calculations in-volved were unreasonably demanding, such that many individuals could not perform them at all, much less do so in real time. He proposed instead that individuals try to approximate maximization by *satisficing*, whereby they select a (reasonably ambitious) target, strive to achieve it, then quit when they are done.[16] Furthermore, a policy of satisficing often proves to be utility-maximizing given the limited information and computational resources available to agents.

With this sort of a model in mind, one could say that morality proper constitutes the set of resources that we deploy when we have the time and the luxury to sit down and work out a proper solution. Most of the time, however, we are unable to do so, and so we employ a "bounded" set of procedures, such as a set of rules of thumb, that give us a decent approximation of the correct result. These might be similar to the "rule of seventy-two" used to calculate compound interest ("seventy-two divided by the rate of return equals number of years to double an investment"), which doesn't yield exactly the right answer, but is close enough to serve most practical purposes. Note that this rule can be applied by someone who doesn't actually know the correct way to do the calculation. Indeed, it can be passed on from one generation to the next, without anyone actually knowing how to do the exact math.[17] Similarly, "tell the truth" may be a rule that works well enough in most situations, even if it does not constitute an exact statement of our moral obligations. It can also be applied by those who are not able to work out the exact content of their obligations, and it can be passed along from generation to generation, without anyone fully understanding why the constraint should be respected.

In recent philosophical debates one can find the clearest articulation of this view in the work of R.M. Hare, who introduces a distinction between two levels of moral thinking, the "intuitive" and the "critical."[18] Critical morality constitutes the set of principles that we would apply if we had the time, energy, information, and resources to make fully informed decisions in every context. Since we don't, critical morality itself recommends the promulgation of a set of rules for everyday use, which favour the actions that, in general and over time, have proven to promote the outcome that would be endorsed from the standpoint of critical morality. Hare refers to these "prima facie principles" as intuitive morality.[19] The "best set" of such principles "is that whose acceptance yields actions, dispositions, etc. most nearly approximating to those which would be chosen if we were able to use critical thinking all the time."[20]

It is no accident that the substantive conception of critical morality Hare seeks to defend is a species of consequentialism. One of the reasons people find consequentialism counterintuitive is that everyday moral judgment is resolutely deontological in form, and yet consequentialism as such assigns no intrinsic authority to rules (it subordinates the right to the good). So where does our idea that morality is a system of rules come from? The "bounded rationality" perspective provides an attractive answer. Simon's conception of satisficing shows how a teleological form of reasoning winds up being transformed into a set of rules in order to be operationalized. None of this suggests that there is anything wrong with maximization as a characterization of practical rationality, it just means that rule-following is the way that maximization gets implemented, when carried out by cognitively limited, imperfect beings such as ourselves.

Hare applies exactly the same reasoning in the moral realm. Officially, on his view, intuitive morality has no normative authority of its own. It is only valuable if it produces the best outcome over time, as specified by critical morality. In cases of disagreement between intuitive and critical morality, critical morality automatically wins. Indeed, from this perspective any residual attachment we may have to intuitive morality in cases of conflict is a terrible sort of muddle-headedness. It is as though a company manager insisted upon passing up an obviously lucrative trading opportunity on the grounds that it would cause the firm to overshoot its quarterly earnings target. This is why Hare will have no truck whatsoever with the "method of reflective equilibrium," or any other such form of "crypto-intuitionism."[21]

Yet things are not quite so simple. This model of the relationship between conventional morality and morality proper actually requires greater convergence between the two than the heuristics model. With the latter, there is a lot of room for error, given the rough-and-ready character of natural selection, not to mention the differences between modern societies and the environment of evolutionary adaptation. According to the bounded rationality view, however, the rules of intuitive morality are all attempts to approximate the results of critical morality. As a result, the only place that they can be derived from is the latter. Thus in order to show that one's characterization of critical morality is correct, it is necessary to show that it can plausibly be posited as the telos of conventional morality. One cannot claim that conventional morality is a set of prima facie principles aimed at promoting some outcome, then posit as an outcome something that a large number of these rules could not reasonably be thought to promote, not even prima facie. Thus intuitive morality imposes "principle of charity"-like constraints on critical morality. While the normative authority of intuitive morality may be entirely inherited from the level of critical morality, too much divergence between the two begins to cast doubt upon the characterization of critical morality that is being proposed.

Generative Grammar

There are some rather interesting similarities between language and morality, which have served as a source of philosophical speculation for many years.[22] People have a rather extraordinary ability to classify strings of words into one of two categories – grammatical or ungrammatical. They do so near-instantaneously, even when the particular sequence of words is one that they have never encountered before. Furthermore, we have no idea how they do it – for example, no one has yet succeeded in producing a computer program capable of distinguishing grammatical from ungrammatical English sentences with anything close to the level of reliability exhibited by an average speaker. Noam Chomsky argued, famously, that the individual's ability to distinguish grammatical sentences from ungrammatical ones must be the product of some underlying *generative* structure. People cannot simply have memorized a finite list of sentence forms, because they are able to classify (and interpret sentences exhibiting) novel forms as well as familiar ones. Thus they must be using some set of combinatorial and transformational rules, which permit recursive application. Only then would it be possible to explain how individuals are able to interpret new sentence forms despite having only finite linguistic knowledge. Naturally, this competence takes the form of "knowhow" rather than "know-that." Thus the project of producing a "generative grammar" for natural language involves developing an explicit set of rules capable of reproducing the relevant performances. Whether or not such a grammar has any "psychological reality" is controversial – it is clear, however, that some sort of underlying mechanism must be posited, in order to explain linguistic competence, and that the best way to articulate the structure of this mechanism is through a set of generative rules.

There are some interesting parallels between linguistic and moral competence. With morality, people are also able to contemplate an enormous number of actions, in situations that they have never encountered before, and classify them into two categories – moral or immoral (permissible or forbidden, good or evil, etc.) Furthermore, they seem to deploy a set of very general cognitive schemata when making these judgments.[23] Again, we don't really know how they do it, and we certainly don't know how to program a computer to reliably reproduce this system of classification. "Ethical expertise" is a form of know-how.[24] The task of moral philosophy, according to this conception, is to transform this know-how into a type of know-that. Furthermore, many have felt that morality must also have a generative structure – it must consist of some relatively small set of rules, which, when instantiated in various ways, produces the multiplicity of concrete moral judgments. Most importantly, these underlying rules need not bear any obvious similarity to the rules that we apply in everyday life (in the same way that a generative grammar need not look much like the rules of English grammar). They will be "rules for producing rules."

This model of the relationship between conventional morality and morality proper is one that has been particularly attractive to Kantians, partly because Kant's own theory has this structure. The first part of Kant's *Foundations of the Metaphysic of Morals* involved showing that the categorical imperative was already implicit in everyday moral reasoning. His most important claim is that, while common reason does not "think of" the categorical imperative "in such a universal form," it still "uses it" to produce its judgments.[25] Thus the central task of the moral philosopher is the reconstructive one of articulating knowledge that is already implicit in the everyday reasoning of moral subjects. The difference between conventional morality and morality proper, according to this view, corresponds to the distinction between "surface" and "generative" grammar in linguistics.

The most obvious difference between this model and any of the ones previously discussed is that it limits quite sharply the extent to which morality proper can disagree with conventional morality is its judgments. The job of the linguist is to fit theory to data; there is no critical dimension to this form of inquiry. It would not make any sense for a linguist to announce as a "discovery" that certain natural-language sentences are ungrammatical because they violate more fundamental combinatorial or transformational rules. If the results of the theory don't coincide with the judgments of natural-language speakers, it is the theory that must be revised. This is because there is no external foundation for judgments of grammaticality, nothing to give the theorist any independent purchase on the question of whether a particular sentence is well-formed or not. This is in contrast to our judgments of probability, or our ability to anticipate trajectories, where we have not only our heuristics, but also a body of independent evidence against which we can check our intuitions.

Many contemporary theorists who believe that morality is the product of some innate structure underlying everyday moral judgments are quite vague about the nature of this structure. One of the best ways to determine whether they regard it as more of a heuristic, or more like a grammar, is to consider how they treat the potential for divergence between conventional morality and morality proper. Marc Hauser, for instance, despite making all sorts of suggestive references to Chomskian linguistics and describing himself as a "moral grammarian" trying to uncover the structure underlying our "ethicality" judgments,[26] actually winds up treating the "moral organ" more like a heuristic than a generative mechanism. This is because he regards it as corrigible. If it were truly a generative mechanism, then it is not clear how there could be any standpoint from which its outputs could be judged to be mistaken. Unlike a heuristic, a generative mechanism is not a proxy for something else – it just is what it is. Yet Hauser thinks that "it is not only possible but likely that some of the intuitions we have evolved are no longer applicable to current societal problems."[27] Even if this determination could be made in a non-question-begging manner (what makes the "problems" problems?), the only resource we have for producing new intuitions would be the same old (evolved) generative mechanism that was giving us the supposedly wrong answer.

Explicitative Vocabulary

One of the unspoken assumptions widely shared amongst proponents of the generative model is the idea that our ability to formulate robust, generalizable principles from which our conventional moral judgments can subsequently be "derived" reveals something deep about the structure of moral reasoning. For example, if we are able to take a disparate set of norms ("don't lie," "don't cheat," etc.) and show that they can all be derived from some more abstract principle ("treat people as ends, never as means only"), this is taken to suggest that the latter principle is fundamental, and that the normative authority of the more particular rules is inherited from the abstract principle. According to this view, the abstract principles do not simply articulate, or make explicit, the know-how that is being deployed in everyday moral judgment – rather, they tell us "what's really going on" when that judgment is made.

This is not a self-evident claim, however. There is a parallel discussion in the philosophy of logic about whether logical vocabulary should be taken to reveal the "laws of thought," or whether it is just explicitative vocabulary, introduced in a constructivist spirit in order to *talk about* patterns in our practices of inference. The latter was Gottlob Frege's aim in the *Begriffsschrift*, where he attempts "to introduce vocabulary that will let one say (explicitly) what otherwise one can only do (implicitly)."[28] The primary instance of this was his analysis of the conditional, which he regards as a lexical innovation that allows speakers to transform material inference from something that can only be *done* using sentences into the sort of thing that can also represented as the *content* of a sentence. There is no suggestion, however, that this reveals anything about underlying structure. According to Robert Brandom, "the key point is that explicitation is not explanation. Proprieties of inference are not *explained* in terms of something more primitive by being expressed in the explicit form of claims by the use of conditionals."[29]

Logicians, however, have long been tempted by what Brandom calls the "dogma of formalism." Many of our everyday inferential practices involve so-called "material inference licenses." For instance, if we hear thunder, we infer that there must be lightning. If we see rain, we infer that the sidewalks will be wet, and so on. In a language that lacks a way of formulating conditional claims, the movement from premise to conclusion is one that can only be made (and either accepted or rejected by hearers). Introduction of the conditional allows one to rewrite things, in such a way as to make the inference itself the object of a possible judgment.[30] Thus one can ascribe to the reasoner a commitment to a claim of the form "if there is rain, then the sidewalks will be wet." The formalist fallacy occurs when, after having made such an ascription, one begins to think that endorsement of the inference *consists in* a belief in such a conditional. One way this fallacy shows up is in the view that everyday inferences (from, say, p to q) are actually enthymematic (with the conditional "$p \rightarrow q$" being in each case the suppressed premise).[31] The fact that we can, in every case, *add* such a premise does not mean that it was implicit in the inference all along. That it can be added is just a trivial consequence of the way that logical vocabulary is developed.[32]

Consider an analogous situation, this time in the domain of practical rationality. Decision theorists have shown that, as long as the individual's beliefs and desires satisfy certain rather minimal consistency constraints, any rational instrumental action can be represented as the maximization of some utility function. There is, however, an enormous temptation to think, on the basis of this finding, that what individuals are "really" doing when they try to satisfy their various desires is striving to produce some more fundamental psychological state, which renders all of these desires commensurable. The mistake here – as decision theorists have been obliged to point out again and again – lies in thinking that because actions can be represented as maximizing a utility function, that what people have actually been doing (all along, as it were), when they eat supper, or catch a cab, is maximizing their utility. The fact that representation in terms of utility has such generality is not a sign of its being explanatory, it is merely a sign that the vocabulary is "logical," in the explicitative sense of the term.

It is not difficult to see the lessons of this for moral philosophy. Eudaemonistic and perfectionist theories often define "happiness" or "the good" in a way that makes it quite similar to utility. If happiness is defined broadly enough, then it is easy to show that everything anyone does (absent some error of reasoning) promotes happiness. But this does not mean that all of these actions were done in order to achieve happiness, or that happiness is the summum bonum. This is the formalist fallacy – it consists of introducing logical or explicitative vocabulary, then reading it back into the relationship that it was intended to express and thinking that one has uncovered an underlying factor. (For example: Pierre wants to eat cheese. He must think that eating cheese is good. Therefore, he must want to eat it *because he thinks it is good.* "Desiring the good," because of its greater generality, seems to have more explanatory power than "desiring cheese," and so it is taken to be more fundamental. But of course, in this case it is an extra gear, since it is being treated as an analytic truth here that Pierre believes, of that which he desires, that it is good.)

Conventional morality, according to this view, has the same status as the epistemic norms that license material inferences in the explicitative view of logic. It is a cultural artifact, a vast body of very concrete norms (or practices) designed to govern particular types of social interactions. Naturally, it does possess a certain amount of internal structure, and there are regularities within it, which is what allows us to introduce explicitative vocabulary as a way of articulating these patterns. What moral philosophers have been doing, over the years, is developing abstract vocabulary that allows us to represent these patterns, to treat them as the contents of possible judgments. Some of this vocabulary is at an intermediate level of generality, involving second and higher-order categorization (e.g., the concept of "harm," "dignity," or "virtue"), while some is much more abstract (e.g., the notions of "permission" and "obligation" or "right" and "wrong").

This is a conception of moral philosophy that has been advanced most influentially by Jürgen Habermas (with his interpretation of discourse ethics as governed by a "maieutic method.")[33] One can see, however, the explicitative character of normative ethics quite clearly in Kant's work as well (even though this was not Kant's own interpretation of the project). Kant's ambition in developing the categorical imperative was to identify the *form* in virtue of which moral principles might be judged to be correct. The method he employed is quite similar to the one that would later be employed by Frege to discover the *form* in virtue of which inferences are correct. Frege's approach involved distinguishing logical from nonlogical vocabulary by using the "substitutional method" of taking a valid inference, then varying the terms in order to see which changes affected its validity. According to Brandom, the concept of an inference being "good in virtue of its form" follows from this quite directly: "All it requires is a partition of vocabulary into two kinds: those that are to be held fixed and those that are to be regarded as replaceable. Call the kind of vocabulary that is to be held fixed the *K-vocabulary*. The general structure of formality definitions is then that the set of *K-valid* inferences (those that will be understood as good in virtue of their *K-form* alone) comprises those that meet the two conditions of being inferences that (1) are good inferences and (2) cannot be turned into bad inferences by substituting non-*K* for non-*K* vocabulary."[34] Kant's various formulations of the categorical imperative are essentially argument schemata, or proposed items of *K-vocabulary*, that are intended to allow variation of the individual maxim without resulting in the transformation of a correct moral judgment into an incorrect one ("For any p, if you cannot will that p be adopted as a universal law, then p is forbidden," where p denotes an action described in non-*K* vocabulary). There is no doubt that, had there been fewer counterexamples (where substitution of non-*K* for non-*K* vocabulary generates a true premise but false conclusion), many philosophers would have been persuaded that Kant had discovered a piece of machinery *underlying* our everyday moral judgment. Yet this does not follow. Indeed, from the explicitative perspective it is an instance of the same formalist fallacy that logicians commit when they treat the introduction of the conditional as evidence that material inferences are actually enthymemes (and have been all along). As Brandom puts it, "the formal goodness of inferences derives from and is explained in terms of the material goodness of inferences, and so ought not to be appealed to in explaining it."[35]

From this perspective, neither the authority nor the integrity of conventional morality depends on the success of the explicitative endeavour. Because there is no "generative" structure underlying conventional morality, the fact that we often encounter inconsistencies and contradictions at the level of formal moral theory does not threaten to undermine the integrity of conventional morality. There are many patterns of material inference that have also eluded "logical" codification (so far), just as there are a variety of logical paradoxes that have yet to be resolved. Similarly, conventional moral reasoning has elements that no formal system has ever succeeded in expressing systematically. For instance, most people employ a mixture of consequentialist and deontological reasoning, depending on the nature of the problem under consideration. So far, no one has succeeded in reducing one to the other, nor has anyone been able to produce a hybrid system that shows where one stops and the other starts. And yet, people continue to reason morally. Conventional morality remains relatively stable, despite the prevalence of conceptual chaos (and deep disagreement) at the level of "normative ethics."

Which Model Is Best?

When deciding which of these four models (or some other) to adopt, philosophers no doubt have their official reasons for adopting the views that they do, based on an impartial assessment of the facts as they see them. When discussing the issue more informally, however, I find that conversation quickly turns to the *moral reasons* that people have for favouring (or disfavouring) one or another model. Often these are based on the degree of comfort that different philosophers feel with the conventional morality of their own society, with those who are least comfortable favouring views that seem to give them the most critical purchase.

This desire for critical distance, however, generates something of a dilemma. There is, on the one hand, what we might call an "Enlightenment" concern about the inadequacies of conventional morality. We think it is important to maintain some room for reflection and revision, so that individuals – including moral philosophers – are not obliged to endorse whatever the received moral ideas in their society happen to be. There is also a widespread concern that taking conventional morality too seriously will open the door to relativism, simply because social norms differ so greatly from one culture to the next.[36] This tends to push moral philosophers in the direction of wanting a stand-alone conception of morality proper, which could serve as an Archimedean point from which the morality or immorality of any particular practice could be judged. On the other hand, there is a "Burkean" concern about the consequences of straying too far from the tried-and-true precepts of conventional morality, in favour of rules that have been made up from scratch by intellectuals.[37] Revising morality is an endeavour that seems fraught with peril, partly because the process, by its very nature, has a tendency to undermine any moral limitations on how far the revisions can go.

To see the force of the Burkean concern, imagine that individuals could take a pill that would cause them to forget anything they had learned about right and wrong from the ambient culture (e.g., parents, teachers, peers, etc.), and erase any innate heuristics. The result would be to deprive the individual of all know-how, intuitive competence, or prejudices, when it comes to moral questions – it would erase all traces of conventional morality. The person would then be given a selection of the best available work in moral philosophy (perhaps confined to a single school of thought), in order to learn from first principles how to act morally. Would the widespread use of such a procedure be likely to promote any improvement in the human condition? I think most sensible people would find this scenario somewhat terrifying. A real-life Kantian or utilitarian, one who had no independent ability to determine when the application of her preferred principle was generating the wrong answer (and therefore no incentive to gerrymander application of the principle to produce the right answer), would be an extremely dangerous person to be around.[38]

So what most moral philosophers want is a framework that allows them to construe morality proper as an idealized construction, yet at the same time, to keep it *grounded* in conventional morality, so that it doesn't wind up being something unrecognizable. The real question is how to get one without losing the other. The problem is that any gain on one front seems to entail a loss on the other.

When it comes to navigating these shoals, both the heuristics and the bounded rationality models seem to suffer from a very fundamental difficulty. In the case of our intuitive judgments of probability, or physics, the explicit cognitive theory that we can compare them to is both well-developed and widely accepted. In many cases we also have explicit procedures that we can follow in order to determine what the right answer to any given question is. This provides something of a gold standard when it comes to assessing our heuristics. Furthermore, the heuristics them-selves play no essential role in the development of the explicit theory – the "check" on the theory is not its ability to account for our intuitions. However, this is clearly not the case with morality. Various attempts have been made to provide independent foundations for our moral judgments (e.g., by grounding them in a theory of instrumental rationality, linguistic practice, the nature of the good, etc.), none of which have succeeded in carrying general conviction (and all of which generate reasonable Burkean concerns about excessive revisionism with respect to morality).

Thus the overwhelming majority of moral philosophers assign an epi-stemic role to our everyday moral judgments. Yet it is very difficult, from within either the heuristics or the bounded rationality model, to explain why we should do so. Indeed, much of the psychological literature on heuristics in other domains consists of investigators showing just how in-adequate and "rough and ready" these devices are. Our intuitive physics, for instance, suggests that dropped objects go straight down, which gen-erates inept responses when it comes to objects that are being carried by other objects, or that are subject to centripetal force. Why should we think moral heuristics will be any better?[39]

If philosophers were committed to treating *all* of our moral intuitions as authoritative, then there might not be such a problem. Most, however, do not want to do this (for "Enlightenment" reasons), and so wind up adopting some version of Rawls's method of reflective equilibrium, which involves developing a systematic theory on the basis of one's central intuitions, while leaving open the option of revising particular judgments in cases where they conflict with this more systematic view.[40] This is, however, not so much a method as merely the announcement of an intention to bracket a certain set of philosophical difficulties. For example, it offers no guid-ance on which particular judgments are to be treated as fixed points and which ones are to be revised. ("Principle of charity"-like constraints, in the case of the bounded rationality model, suffer from the same difficulty.) Furthermore, whether one relies on the explicit theory or the moral intui-tions in order to decide which judgments are revisable, the entire proced-ure is still moving within a very small, closed circle (even when it is called "wide" reflective equilibrium).

To illustrate the problem, consider the moral intuitions that we have about the treatment of animals. Practices that might seem rather routine to a farmer, such as drowning a litter of barn cats, strike many urban intellectuals as abhorrent. An evolutionary psychologist is likely to side with the farmer. The way that people respond to neoteny is an innate disposition, produced through kin selection, intended to elicit parental investment in one's offspring. Yet the response is fairly generalized – there are specific facial and bodily characteristics that evoke a caring response.[41] Indeed, it is sufficiently general that it can be provoked by juveniles of other species, particularly household pets like cats and dogs, who have evolved adaptations that allow them to exploit the ecological niche provided by the generality of this disposition among humans. From an evolutionary perspective, our reaction is clearly a misfire. Nevertheless, many moral philosophers are inclined to treat it as a fixed point for the purposes of developing a moral theory. Indeed, the urge to assign moral status to animals seems to be one of the most important intuitions leading people to adopt utilitarianism as a comprehensive moral theory. Yet how then is one to adjudicate among different normative-ethical theories, when a single intuition, which seems like a paradigm instance of philosophical error to some, is treated as deal-breaker on philosophical systems by others? Regardless of who is right and who is wrong, it seems obvious that the method of reflective equilibrium is powerless to resolve this conflict.

The alternative would be to nip the problem in the bud, by treating all of our moral intuitions as fully authoritative.[42] This moves the heuristics model in the direction of the generative grammar model. But this seems like an unattractive option as well. Social institutions are often highly unjust, and many people have very disagreeable moral intuitions. Furthermore, there is the sociological fact that conventional morality has changed significantly over time, driven in part by higher-order reflection and critical scrutiny. In the area of sexual morality, for instance, there has been a profound shift over the past hundred years in Western societies, away from a prohibition on non-procreative activities towards a prohibition on non-consensual activities. There are only two ways that the generative model can accommodate this, neither of which are very appealing. The first would be to insist that the earlier views were the result of errors in the application of the generative principles (errors of "performance," as Chomskians would say), which were subsequently corrected. This seems rather unlikely, but is in any case unverifiable. The second option would be to say that these are like changes in "surface grammar," just different instantiations of the same underlying structure. The problem with this response is that it makes the underlying structure extremely indeterminate, certainly far more so than most philosophers attracted to this model have taken it to be. It is difficult to imagine, for instance, that morality proper could simply be agnostic on the question of whether it is appropriate to persecute, tolerate, or encourage homosexuality.

The other aspect of these sorts of changes is the fact that philosophical reflection appears to have played an important role in the transformation of public mores. As Michele Moody-Adams writes, "Much of the moral language that helps shape the economic, social, and political dimensions of the contemporary world is a product of distinctively philosophical efforts to articulate interpretations of the structure of moral experience."[43] It is certainly no accident that the changes in sexual morality came about as part of a broader pattern of liberalization in Western societies, one that involved a shift away from perfectionist towards contractualist ways of thinking about legal and political relations. If moral philosophy involved merely an attempt to codify the generative mechanism that was producing these judgments all along, it seems that it should leave everything in place. Yet the articulation of higher-order concepts – like that of consent, dignity, autonomy, and so forth – appears to have had significant effects on our practices, in part because these concepts are routinely appealed to by those engaged in social criticism.

Thus moral philosophers are clearly doing much more than simple systematization of conventional morality, and yet much less than the construction of an independent, foundational alternative to it. How then to describe the nature of this project? Perhaps surprisingly, I think it is the fourth model, the explicitative conception, that strikes the right balance. The history of philosophical reflection on morality has largely been an exercise in *crafting explicitative vocabulary*. It has involved introducing concepts and terms that will allow us to talk about what we are doing when we make moral judgments. The reason that this exercise has transformative implications with respect to our practices is that it is only by developing an explicit representation of these practices that we can formulate criticisms of them and consciously guide their modification. As Brandom writes, the deployment of explicitative vocabulary "is a way of bringing our practices under rational control, by expressing them in a form in which they can be confronted with objections and alternatives."[44] Explicitation, in other words, is a necessary element of the practice of social criticism.

The idea that "morality proper" represents an idealization of conventional morality turns out to be something of a grammatical illusion, a consequence of the fact that we *use* explicitative vocabulary when criticizing various aspects of conventional morality. This can create the impression that criticizing particular norms involves comparing them to a more abstract or idealized set of rules and showing how they fall short. Again, there are suggestive parallels in the philosophy of logic. Consider, for example, an explicitative analysis of the truth predicate such as the prosentential theory.[45] According to this view, the predicate "is true" is introduced into English in order to overcome the difficulty that we have quantifying over propositions in natural language. Pronouns such as "it" function as variables that can refer to objects (e.g., "I'm not sure what it was, but I deleted it"). We also have pro-verbs, such as "so" (as in, "please do so"). What we lack, however, are single-word prosentences. Thus the "is true" predicate is introduced as a "prosentence-forming operator," which can be used in conjunction with ordinary pronouns such as "it" (e.g., "whatever he said, I'm sure it is true").

The idea that truth discloses an ideal order, standing above relations of belief and justification, occurs as the result of a grammatical illusion. The reason that truth keeps showing up in epistemic discussions is that the only way to *talk about* belief in general, or justification in general, is to quantify over propositions, and this requires the use of a prosentence. To take a simple example, suppose that one wants to express complete agreement with Bill. Using propositional variables, one could say: "For all p, if Bill believes p then p." Substituting "it" for p throughout generates a grammatical anomaly in the third instance of p, and so instead we use the prosentence "it is true" to say "if Bill believes it, then it is true." This still leaves us with a problem articulating the first occurrence of p. One way to solve it is simply to say "everything that Bill believes is true." This is the same as saying "all ravens are black" in lieu of "for all things, if it is a raven then it is black." Yet in the case of Bill's beliefs, the way that this grammatical compression breaks up the prosentence creates the impression that there is a substantive property, "is true," that is being ascribed to each of Bill's beliefs. The explicitative role of the truth predicate is thereby obscured.

With this analysis in hand, it is easy to see how truth could come to be seen, mistakenly, as something that transcends justification. Consider, for instance, what Richard Rorty once called the "cautionary use" of the truth predicate, where we use it to warn people against putting too much stock in the existing evidence for a given proposition: "your belief that p is perfectly justified, but perhaps not true."[46] This is an example of a claim about defeasibility that can quite easily be formulated without the truth predicate, given the use of propositional variables: "for any p, you may be justified in believing p, yet not-p." In order to get this into English, we need to form a prosentence: "for any claim, even if you are justified in believing it, it may turn out not to be true." This can create the impression that truth is some property that justification aims at, and yet is never quite able to obtain. In reality, however, we are not actually talking *about* truth when we use a sentence like this, we are simply *using* the truth predicate to say something very general about justification (viz., that it is defeasible).

This example helps to show how easy it is to hypostatize the explicitative vocabulary that we use, and to imagine that it discloses some special realm, or else a peculiar metaphysical relation between our words and the world. The situation with moral vocabulary is no different. Perhaps the most fundamental piece of explicitative moral vocabulary is the word "ought," which allows us to transform an imperative into an assertion, and thus make it the antecedent of an inference. This is an extremely important explicitative move, because it permits inferential articulation of content that is otherwise indexically bound. Yet some philosophers reverse the order of dependence and present this as evidence that imperatives gain their authority from the fact that the action possesses some quality of "oughtness." (In perhaps the most flagrant act of hypostatization, Francis Patton claimed, in *The Metaphysics of Oughtness*, that "the idea of oughtness is an ethical atom. It cannot be resolved into simpler constituents."[47])

In this way, it is quite easy to see how the fact that we make use of explicitative vocabulary when we critically reflect upon our existing practices can generate the impression that this vocabulary refers to a more idealized version of these practices, and that the only way to criticize our practices is to compare them to this hypothetical alternative, which provides an Archimedean point. But this is an illusion. One need not have access to the inner realm of truth in order to find errors and expose defects in our existing justifications. Our epistemic practices already contain sufficient resources for self-criticism. Similarly, one need not determine the content of morality proper, or the nature of a deontically perfect world, or the essence of "oughtness," in order to criticize conventional morality.

Conventional morality already contains these critical resources. The proof lies in the fact that we do criticize it, routinely, and – in our tradition – have been doing so for thousands of years.

Conclusion

My primary objective in this chapter has been to thematize an issue that is seldom directly addressed in contemporary moral philosophy, concerning the status of conventional morality. Most people can agree that, in everyday practice, we do not employ abstract principles or moral theories to constrain our conduct, but instead rely upon a set of fairly specific, largely taken-for-granted rules. Yet many moral philosophers appear to believe that morality is governed by a normative theory, in Baier's sense of the term, in which the specific rules are derived from more abstract ones.[48] This commits them to adopting a view about the status of conventional morality that assigns it little intrinsic authority. The first three models of the relationship between conventional morality and morality proper are all quite different, and yet they share this feature in common. All three of these models, however, are subject to well-known deficiencies. While, according to the official view, conventional morality has no authority, in practice it winds up having a great deal, simply because there is such deep disagreement among philosophers at the level of abstract normative theory and no obvious place to turn to in resolving these disputes, other than the less controversial judgments we make when considering specific problems.

My goal has been to put a more direct response on the table; to suggest that the order of dependence posited by the ascription of a normative theory to moral agents is backwards. The authority actually rests with conventional morality, and most agreement in moral judgment is due to the fact of shared culture. The more general principles are derived from the specific ones. As Durkheim put it, moral philosophers, with their focus on abstract principles, have taken "for the base of morality that which is in fact only the summit."[49] The weakness of Durkheim's position lay in his inability to explain either the role that abstract principles play or the mechanism through which critical reflection and reform of our practices can occur. The explicitative conception of moral theory outlined here addresses these two issues, by showing how the formulation of abstract principles is what allows us to bring rational scrutiny to bear upon our practices, and thus allows us to deploy the critical resources that are already implicit in our system of conventional morality. It therefore provides an attractive account of the dynamics of moral deliberation. The bounded rationality model, by contrast, gives a bit too much authority to morality proper, and so fails to explain why we would ever modify our more general principles in the face of a recalcitrant intuition. The generative grammar model goes too far in the opposite direction, effectively treating all moral judgments as data points that must be accommodated by the general theory. The heuristics model, by contrast, seems able to give a plausible account of the give and take that occurs between the specific and the general level in the course of philosophical deliberation, but only if one is willing to set aside the skeptical problems raised by the procedure as a whole. The explicitative view, on the other hand, is able to account for the same deliberative dynamics, while providing a more plausible interpretation of the status of the abstract principles.

12

Charles Taylor and Ethical Naturalism

NIGEL DESOUZA

One of the most striking, and strikingly familiar, features of the philosophy of Charles Taylor is his consistency in trying to avoid overly reductivist accounts of human life and action and instead do justice to the phenomenology, as it were. So much of his effort, as he says himself at the very beginning of his first two volumes of collected papers, is to argue against an understanding of human life and action modelled on the natural sciences.[1]

This effort has been front and centre in Taylor's reflections on morality, as contained in several articles and in *Sources of the Self*, especially the first four chapters. Taylor has consistently sought to defend and argue for an understanding of moral agency that is richer than what he feels is implicit in mainstream "procedural moral theories," as he calls them, such as Kantian deontology or utilitarianism. The moral phenomenology which he has sought to work out and which he believes is hidden or ignored by these normative theories is also aimed at meta-ethical theories such as emotivism or quasi-realism and at scientific reductivist accounts which attempt to dispense with or move us beyond the familiar language of morality altogether. The whole apparatus of strong evaluations, goods, hypergoods, constitutive goods, and moral sources laid out in the first four chapters of *Sources of the Self* seeks to uncover how human beings *actually* make sense of their lives, what a genuine moral phenomenology should look like. Taylor's defence of this phenomenology in the face of a skeptical naturalist who sees it as mere projection on to a neutral physical world is, in a word, that it is inescapable.

For the purposes of this chapter, I will not initially delve into the specifics of this phenomenology directly. Rather, I am going to assume a familiarity with it and turn instead to the most recent of Taylor's published reflections on this subject, contained in a little-known paper entitled "Ethics and Ontology," published in 2003 in *The Journal of Philosophy*. This paper raises the issue of naturalism in a way that sees Taylor moving beyond the discussion in *Sources of the Self* and engaging with two thinkers he finds sympathetic to his own objectives, namely John McDowell and David Wiggins. But I want to contend that Taylor does not fully appreciate just how congenial they are to his objectives. For they defend a view of ethical naturalism he should applaud. I will address this first. I will then turn to aspects of Taylor's moral phenomenology which seem to pose a threat to ethical naturalism – in particular, his conceptions of "the incommensurably higher," constitutive goods, and moral sources – and try to show how this need not be the case. Underlying the entire discussion is the question of how best we are to conceive what we may mean by "naturalism."

Two Kinds of Naturalism

As already mentioned, Charles Taylor has consistently opposed attempts to explain the human world in reductivist natural scientific terms. In "Ethics and Ontology," his central concern is to understand how an ethical or moral phenomenology that does justice to how human beings make actual ethical sense of their own and others' lives can be squared with a naturalist ontology. Taylor makes clear that a "naturalist ontology" for him is one that explains things in the terms of post-Galilean natural science, which entails a view of the universe as "devoid of meaning and value."[2] This is the same understanding of naturalism that Taylor targets in *Sources of the Self*.

Now in "Ethics and Ontology," Taylor turns primarily to the writings of John McDowell, and, to a lesser extent, David Wiggins. He rightly finds in these two authors an approach to ethics that is motivated by intuitions similar to those contained in his own work. They do justice to the moral phenomenology, unlike emotivists and quasi-realists. But one of the refreshingly liberating aspects of McDowell's approach, which is arguably also true of Wiggins's, is the innovative understanding of naturalism that they propose and that allows for the kind of reconciliation between the moral phenomenology and a naturalist ontology, between ethics and ontology, that Taylor seems to pass over and that he should in fact endorse. Let me try to flesh this out.

A good place to start is with the notion of values. Both McDowell and Wiggins defend an approach to values that construes our perception of them as analogous to our perception of colours. If we assert that our experience of seeing the colour "red" should really be explained in terms of the primary qualities of the object we are looking at (e.g., its microscopic structure) it follows, quite simply, that we will no longer be explaining the experience itself, as it is *subjectively* experienced. Secondary qualities such as colours, therefore, do have objective reality. While they depend on beings like us to be seen, as long as we ourselves exist, they exist for us and independently of us. We could put it this way: we each subjectively experience them objectively, under favourable conditions (the right lighting, etc.).

McDowell and Wiggins construe values as having an analogous reality, as Taylor observes in his article. Values are not arbitrarily subjective. As Taylor puts it, when I feel a sense of nausea, whatever object it is that causes my nausea is, for me, nauseous. But when it comes to values, my ascription of a value-property to an action or person, while depending on my subjective experience and judgment, can also be criticized and the question as to whether the action or person merits the value-property-ascription can be asked. While values are subjectively experienced, they also have an objectivity to them in so far as we can ask whether someone really is honest or whether that action really was generous. More basically, their objectivity derives from the fact that human beings in a society can perceive the properties of actions or characters in a manner analogous to how they perceive colours. While our sharing the same basic visual perceptual apparatus is the condition of our shared colour perception, an analogous case can be made for the genesis of our shared capacity for value-perception. McDowell and Wiggins provide accounts of this genesis that are similar in important respects. While it is certainly more central to McDowell's account, both of them argue for a naturalistic understanding of this account of the phenomenology of value experience that resists the reductivist terms of what Taylor calls post-Galilean science.

McDowell lays out his candidate for a different understanding of naturalism in *Mind and World* and in his paper "Two Sorts of Naturalism."[3] His objective is to show how human beings' developed ethical (and conceptual) capacities should not have to be explained in the terms of Taylor's post-Galilean science. It is simply erroneous to believe that conceptual monism must prevail, and that natural scientific truth is the only truth there is.[4] Human beings are natural beings and our ethical and conceptual capacities must be seen as ways of actualizing ourselves as animals.[5] In the ethical dimension, our upbringings entail the shaping of our motivational and evaluative propensities such that we come to develop a second nature on the basis of which we become capable of assessing actions and characters and ascribing value-properties to them.[6] For the most part, our ethical action and deliberation occurs in a manner that is non-codifiable, according to McDowell. On the Aristotelian model, if our second nature is one of virtue, then we acquire a complex ethical sensitivity that involves possessing an understanding of all the virtues. And when we determine how to act, the major premise in our practical syllogism, as it were, is not any particular moral rule but rather our conception of the sort of person one should be or of how to live.[7] Assuming all in the community share this second nature of virtue, we can count on there being shared ways of perceiving and responding to values in the actions and characters of the members of that community. This amounts to a logos of the practical and is the basis of ethical objectivity.

Now Taylor does acknowledge that McDowell challenges the ontology associated with the post-Galilean model and that he argues that we must understand the human world on its own terms. Taylor sees McDowell as claiming that with the existence of human beings comes a "whole flock of subjective properties, thick and strong evaluations which needs to be understood on its own terms and which cannot be made transparent to Galilean science."[8] He even claims that "McDowell seems to have done the trick, and to have reconciled the deliverances of phenomenology and the basic concerns of a naturalistic ontology, which cannot allow [ethical] values into the furniture of the universe."[9] But it seems that what Taylor is saying is simply that McDowell has defended the indispensability of such a phenomenology to our accurate and adequate self-understandings. This is a point Taylor himself had made in *Sources of the Self* when he said, "what is real is what you have to deal with, what won't go away just because it doesn't fit with your prejudices ... What you can't help having recourse to in life is real, or as near to reality as you can get a grasp of at present."[10] Taylor construes McDowell as bravely arguing for this in defiance of a post-Galilean naturalist ontology. What we have seen, however, is that McDowell precisely challenges this ontology. What Taylor doesn't

discuss is McDowell's proposal for a revised naturalism which accommodates second nature and rejects a conception of naturalism that equates
nature with what the natural sciences aim to make comprehensible. It is
precisely this way of grounding moral phenomenology that I think advances Taylor's agenda in a novel way.

Wiggins has a similar way of accounting for our shared capacity for
value-perception, which he discusses in "A Sensible Subjectivism" and
"Moral Cognitivism, Moral Relativism, and Motivating Moral Beliefs."[11]
Analogously to McDowell's "shaping of motivational and evaluative propensities," Wiggins shows how a historical social process can lead to the
establishment of shared moral responses to intersubjectively discernible
features that engage our sentiments or feelings. This process "creates a
form of life that invests certain features of people, acts and situations with
the status of values."[12] In growing up within such a form of life, Wiggins
says, our original participation in a general way of feeling and of being
motivated leads to us finding or discovering that x deserves such and such
a response, or has such and such a value. Wiggins also defends this moral
phenomenology by arguing for its naturalist credentials along Humean
but avowedly cognitivist lines – he claims Hume has never deserved the
hostility of moral cognitivists. Wiggins argues, in agreement with Taylor,
that if value properties are not replaceable by physicalistic/scientific explanations, then they are making a difference. He goes on to claim that
value properties reveal how human beings respond not only to natural
features of the world, but "to features that mind itself, as it has taken on a
life of its own, has marked out there. Value properties are properties that
mind critically delimits and demarcates in the world."[13] If these properties
are indispensable and irreducible, Wiggins concludes, "this is surely what
it is for consciousness not merely to arrive in the natural world, but for it
to make itself at home there. By critically determining the presence there
of valuational properties, we colonize that natural world."[14]

This grounding of moral phenomenology in human nature and historical social processes is Wiggins's own version of ethical naturalism that
rejects any post-Galilean scientific view of nature – something Wiggins
explicitly does on several occasions – in favour of a Humean naturalistic
view which "treats human morality as a certain sort of natural phenomenon, a phenomenon of feeling."[15] McDowell and Wiggins, in a word,
broadly agree with Taylor on the structure of the moral phenomenology
that has to be accepted; but they go *further* and try to provide a genetic,

naturalist account of it on the basis of a broader understanding of "naturalism." Taylor even says in his article that a consequence of their accounts is that we "either abandon naturalism or adopt a more sophisticated variant."[16] My point has simply been to highlight that "a more sophisticated naturalism" should in fact be seen as a constitutive element of their accounts and that it is one with which Taylor should find at least partial common cause.[17]

Reconciling Phenomenology and Naturalism

I want now to turn to a few ways in which the ethical naturalism of McDowell and Wiggins appears unable to accommodate Taylor's account of moral phenomenology for the simple reason that his account includes more elements/structures than they seem to allow for. This brings us to the central point of "Ethics and Ontology." Taylor states that he is convinced by McDowell's and Wiggins's accounts, which he says show that "our lives are unintelligible if we try to sideline the human world."[18] As we have seen, but formulating the point a little differently, he feels they have successfully shown that enculturated socialized humans cannot but take as real and objective the web of interrelated values they perceive and use to make sense of their lives analogously to how secondary properties such as colour are real and objective for us (with the proviso that this of course does not mean values are immune to critique – although, as McDowell says, any critique is immanent, like Otto Neurath's boat at sea, which can only be completely rebuilt plank by plank at best[19]). But this agreement notwithstanding, Taylor writes, "I am sorry to trouble a hard-won peace, but it seems to me that there remains an issue here. Some sources of the temptation to undercut the phenomenology of moral life in the name of a post-Galilean 'naturalism' have been perhaps laid to rest, but others remain ... We have not discharged our entire debt to phenomenology once we have laid the ghost of [micro]reductionism to rest. There remains the tension between the phenomenology of the incommensurably higher and a naturalist ontology which has difficulty finding a place for this."[20]

What I take Taylor to be saying here is that the values whose irreducibility and indispensability McDowell and Wiggins have successfully demonstrated relate to social values like generosity, honesty, kindness, and, as he notes in the case of Wiggins, the funny. These are values which relate to human beings in societies interacting and getting along well together.

In this respect, a naturalist ontology can account for most of them in evolutionary terms as serving important survival purposes. These are values that Taylor associates with what in *A Secular Age* he calls "the order of mutual benefit central to exclusive humanism," which depends on the discovery or definition of intra-human sources of benevolence. Taylor links this to attempts in the eighteenth century to ground morality in human sentiments and Hume's tracing of virtues to utility.[21]

Now what is missing from this kind of view of values is what Taylor captures with the expression "the phenomenology of the incommensurably higher." Taylor often uses the example of the Aristotelian *to kallon*, or the noble, to capture one sense of what he means here. A full account of our moral phenomenology cannot just consist of social values and virtues rooted in mutual sympathy and utility. Human beings are also sensitive in their moral lives to higher values like the noble as a source of motivation. And these kinds of values are not obviously amenable to a standard naturalist evolutionary account of morality, Taylor notes. The immediate response to this from the McDowell/Wiggins camp would be that their model can account for this. Let me focus on Wiggins, who would clearly be most sensitive to this kind of criticism, given his desire to defend a Humean cognitivism. Wiggins says that even if moral sensibility has its origin in primitive benevolence, in a primitive system of boo and hurray, "what we have now seems to have transcended its simple origin countless times over" and our responses are now clearly cognitive.[22] Wiggins tries to show how our pairs of value properties and responses develop and generate new ones until we have a whole system of properties and responses which take on a life of their own. There is no reason in principle why the higher values Taylor speaks of should not be able to emerge in this process of cultural evolution. In "Ethics and Ontology," Taylor in fact suggests this emergence of higher values as a possibility that both McDowell and Wiggins may envision, given precisely Wiggins's genetic account of the funny.

He hastens to add, however, that even if this is the case, "emergence in this sense puts a severe crimp in the standard naturalism of today's dominant evolutionary theories."[23] Again, I think we should see both McDowell and Wiggins as simply rejecting the kind of naturalism Taylor is thinking of here. Not only can values not be reduced to primary qualities or neurophysiology, they also cannot be reduced to utility or evolutionary imperatives. For McDowell, our ethical capacities, just like our conceptual capacities, qua second nature, are part of our actualization as organisms,

as the kinds of animals we are, and in this our ethical and conceptual capacities are both essentially natural and each have a logos of their own that
is irreducible. Wiggins makes the same kind of analogy: moral sensibility
may have originated in a primitive system of responses of boo and hurray,
just as the language of consciousness is sometimes supposed to have originated in "the verbalization of reactions of striving towards things (ooh)
or away from them (ouch)" – in each case, there is a development that
follows that far transcends the simple origin.[24] They each take on a life of
their own and become straightforwardly cognitive, in the moral case our
response being to an "intersubjectively discernible feature that engages
with sentiment."[25] Both McDowell and Wiggins argue for the integrity of
the ethical or moral not just as something we cannot do without in making
sense of our lives, but as something as natural to us as our capacity for
language or reason. This is why they would reject Taylor's claim that the
"emergence of higher values" must put a crimp in their ethical naturalism.

Here, however, we come to where Taylor would in fact seem to part
ways with McDowell and Wiggins. For even if Taylor does agree with their
ethical naturalism, there is still a crucial aspect of the phenomenology of
the incommensurably higher that remains unaccounted for. It is a significant step, which Taylor applauds, to demonstrate the irreducibility and
indispensability of values and our moral phenomenology as McDowell
and Wiggins have done. But showing how our evaluative and motivational
propensities are shaped in upbringing and how this is constitutive of our
very existence as ethical agents who thereby acquire the web of interrelated values (norms, behaviours, goods) through which we make sense
of actions and lives is not the whole story. For this only explains the genesis of our nature as ethical creatures. What is missing from this account
of the phenomenology is how articulacy is a crucial part of it. It is one
thing to have a pre-reflective sense of what is generous or noble or even to
possess a reflective concept of what is generous or noble. Equipped with
this sensitivity, I am able to perceive actions that are generous or noble,
analogously to how I can perceive objects as red. But for Taylor my full
sense of the generous and the noble or of my commitment to human
rights is quite another thing, requiring articulacy about what he calls the
"moral source,"[26] i.e., the point behind these values, what gives them their
meaning and power for me, what explains or grounds why they matter to
me, why they move me, e.g., in the case of human rights, why humans are
worthy of respect.

We see here how Taylor's conception of moral phenomenology starts to move beyond what we find in McDowell and Wiggins. Articulacy about the point behind the values we were raised with and subscribe to as adolescents and adults is a crucial aspect of this phenomenology for Taylor. But whether articulated by us or not, this "ontological account"[27] is always there – we have some sense of why we should respect human rights or value generous action: human beings deserve such respect because they are capable of rationality, they possess inherent dignity, etc. These ontological questions underlying the web of values we are raised into are always there for all of us and are part of our moral phenomenology; how and whether we answer them shapes our moral lives. Trying to articulate answers can have a profound impact on my attitude towards these values. For example, from having a merely pre-reflective sense of these values based on my upbringing, articulacy can motivate, move, and empower me in a way that I become consciously committed to pursuing and promoting them. Articulacy about the ontological account underlying and grounding the web of values, however, can be fully accepted by an ethical naturalist, e.g., if one's account has to do with the specialness and dignity of rational nature as articulated by Kant – in Taylor's terminology, this is an example of a constitutive good, a good which underlies and makes sense of all the other goods and values we find meaningful in human life.[28] While not strictly essential to moral agency, articulacy can certainly be seen as a natural aspect of it, at least in as much as language is natural to human beings.

It is thus possible to imagine how the "incommensurably higher" and articulacy about ontological accounts can be plausibly accommodated within ethical naturalism. But for Taylor this is not the whole story. Ontological accounts which refer to human dignity and rational agency both operate within what he calls the "immanent frame," according to which we understand the universe through the natural order that is immanent in it, which we are able to read off it, as it were.[29] Tracing the rise of this immanent frame is one of the main objectives of *A Secular Age*, where Taylor defines religion in Western experience as relating to the transcendent, as opposed to the merely immanent.[30] The latter involves not just a naturalistic account of the universe, but also ontological accounts and constitutive goods which derive from "within," that is, which locate what grounds our web of values in human nature itself (e.g., Kantian rational agency) as opposed to in something external and transcendent, such as the Platonic Idea of the Good or a belief in God.

This is where the strains between Taylor's account of our moral phenomenology and ethical naturalism are greatest. The ethical naturalist account provides a description that remains, for Taylor, squarely within the "immanent frame." Even if it can make room for ontological accounts, these remain within the terms of what Taylor calls "modern exclusive secular humanism" which, by definition, eschews any relation to anything external and transcendent. In *A Secular Age*, Taylor provides what he calls "a phenomenology of moral/spiritual experience,"[31] a crucial aspect of which is the notion of "fullness," which involves our relation to and articulacy about ontological accounts and constitutive goods. Articulacy even within the limits of exclusive humanism brings with it a certain kind of "fullness" or moral empowerment that is important to a full-blooded or robust moral agency. Taylor's conception of moral phenomenology goes even further: an individual's capacity to rise to and experience the greatest "fullness" she is capable of involves some relation to the transcendent and this in turn can undergird a commitment to the highest moral aspirations. Common to all the structures/elements (e.g., ontological accounts, constitutive goods, moral sources) that Taylor adds to the moral phenomenology we find in McDowell and Wiggins is the fact that, arguably, none of them are strictly essential to moral agency; one can be a moral agent without them. (This is arguable because one might interpret Taylor as holding that something is always playing the role in every moral agent of these structures, however implicitly, or even negatively.) But even if not strictly essential, none of them are, for that reason, any less natural. Taylor is not only interested in what is essential to moral agency. He wants to understand what the most robust form of it, i.e., the "fullness" that a human being can achieve, requires. And on this level, ontological accounts and constitutive goods are, according to Taylor, essential and natural.

But Taylor goes beyond this claim, which can plausibly be squared with ethical naturalism, and implies that a relation to the transcendent is essential to the highest level of "fullness." Why isn't a constitutive good within the framework of what Taylor calls modern exclusive secular humanism – e.g., one based on the dignity of human beings – sufficient? Taylor's argument here centres on the role that the reciprocity of love, or lack thereof, plays in moral action and identity. A purely secular humanist ethic committed to universal benevolence, justice, etc. is demanding, and when it encounters obstacles to its realization – which will abound in the messy real world of humanity, such as less than morally enlightened people standing in the way or objects of that benevolence or justice who are ungrateful – it can lead to mutilation and degenerate into fanaticism.[32] Taylor acknowledges that this can also happen and certainly has happened in the case of a religiously inspired ethic. It is thus not just a question of "having the right beliefs,"[33] but rather of having a certain relationship to a transcendent constitutive good and moral source, and this is where the reciprocity of love is key. Taylor frankly admits the admirability and even possible superiority of a secular ethics which is motivated by no hope of reward (such as the "restored life of the Resurrection" that a Christian martyr may hope for) and which persists in the face of a meaningless universe, the example he gives here being of Dr Rieux in Albert Camus's *La Peste*.[34] He asks, however, whether this is in fact the "highest good" human beings can attain, whether the "heroism of gratuitous giving [that] has no place for reciprocity" is what human life is really about.[35] Just as in our most basic experiences of life, of the bond of love between parent and child, perhaps the highest good consists in "communion, mutual giving, and receiving."[36]

Here, fascinatingly, Taylor's ethical naturalism seems to meet up with what – however tentatively and carefully he puts it forth – we can call his conviction on the need for a transcendent moral source. In a word, just as an individual's commitment to her child is based on the bond of reciprocal love, so too must our highest and most abstract universal moral commitments be grounded in a relationship of reciprocal love if we are to achieve the highest form of "fullness" and have a moral source adequate to them. The relationship at this level is between human beings and a God who has love (*agapē*) for them, who can provide "a divine affirmation of the human, more total than humans can ever attain unaided."[37] Having this kind of moral source, and this kind of understanding and relationship to it, Taylor believes, also protects one from the slide to mutilation. Such a relationship to a transcendent moral source is an element – the highest – in a complete account of our moral phenomenology.

Among the many questions that this raises, I will close with just a couple. Does Taylor believe that the relationship to the transcendent as a structure in the phenomenology of the moral/spiritual can be accounted for or reconciled with ethical naturalism, along the same lines as I have suggested one can reconcile other elements in his broader moral phenomenology? Of course, as already stated, such an ethical naturalism would not be confined to what is basically essential to moral agency but would rather try to capture what is necessary for the most robust kind of moral agency human beings are capable of. Another way of asking this question would be: is the basis for the connection Taylor sees between the relationship to the transcendent, on the one hand, and morality and our moral phenomenology, on the other, to be located in his understanding of our moral phenomenology as naturally pointing to the need for a transcendent moral source based on the centrality of relationships of reciprocal love to robust moral agency and identity? Or is the basis to be found in his own religious convictions, and a worldview according to which all that can and should, on one level, be seen as naturalistically unfolding is, on another, but an expression of a divine order which also envelops it and provides it with its ultimate meaning and grounding? I suspect that for Taylor the answer to both these questions is yes. If this is true, then one upshot is that those who do not have a religious faith, but who might agree with the naturalistic argument for a relationship to the transcendent as a structure of our moral/spiritual phenomenology, are consigned to living lives they know can never attain maximum "fullness."

PART SIX

Political Philosophy, Recognition, and Multiculturalism

13

Protecting Freedom of Religion in the Secular Age

CÉCILE LABORDE

I want to start with a paradox. In the secular age, as Charles Taylor has amply illustrated, religious belief no longer structures our social imaginary. Instead it has become one option, one possibility, among others: one of the ways in which we give meaning to our lives. The secular age, then, is characterized by the fact of pluralism – an irreducible pluralism of beliefs, values, and commitments. Yet we secular moderns also give special primacy to freedom of religion, which is standardly presented as the archetypical liberal right. So the paradox is this: how (and why) do we protect freedom of religion in an age where religion is not special?

Here's a plausible solution to this paradox. We could say, roughly, that freedom of religion is in fact a subset of a broader class of freedoms. So instead of seeing religion itself as a special good, we say that religion is one of the ways in which individuals seek the good for themselves. Exercising freedom of religion is one of the ways in which we exercise a more generic freedom – moral freedom. Let us call this an egalitarian solution to the paradox I started with. An egalitarian theory of religious freedom does not deny that religious belief is special and should be respected and protected. What it denies is that religious belief is uniquely special: it can and should be analogized with other beliefs and commitments. Many contemporary liberal philosophers are egalitarians in this sense. John Rawls argues that what the liberal state protects is our ability to form and pursue comprehensive conceptions of the good.[1] Ronald Dworkin sees "ethical independence" as the core value protected by freedom of religion – his last book is entitled *Religion without God.*[2] Martha Nussbaum connects freedom of religion to a conscientious search for "ultimate meaning."[3]

In what follows, I focus on Charles Taylor's version of the egalitarian approach: one he puts forward (with Jocelyn Maclure) in *Secularism and Freedom of Conscience* (originally in French as *Laïcité et liberté de conscience*).[4] In that book, Taylor and Maclure put forward their own egalitarian theory of religious freedom, and a radically inclusive one at that: they argue that all "meaning-giving commitments" should be protected on the same basis as religious commitment. The volume is also fascinating when read as a statement of Taylor's political theory – a normative companion to the more historical, epistemological, and philosophical diagnoses of our contemporary condition found in his *Sources of the Self* and *A Secular Age.*[5]

To put my cards on the table: I agree with Taylor and Maclure that normative egalitarianism is the right response, ethically speaking, to the deep moral pluralism of the secular age. What I shall suggest, however, is that they – like other egalitarian philosophers – have underestimated the profound tensions that beset egalitarian theories of religious freedom. What does it mean, exactly, to treat religious and nonreligious conceptions of the good alike? In virtue of what should nonreligious commitments and lifestyles be analogized with religious beliefs and practices? Equality is attractive, but what is the currency of equality? Equality of *what*?

In seeking to answer these questions, egalitarian philosophers are unavoidably drawn to making the kind of judgments that they would rather avoid: value judgments about the ethical significance of particular beliefs, lifestyles, and preferences. In other words, they cannot merely appeal to a principle of neutrality between conceptions of the good. They must identify, among nonreligious conceptions, those that deserve to be treated on the same plane as religious conceptions. They must, therefore, identify a criterion with which to determine what, within a particular system of beliefs and commitments, deserves to be respected and protected. In the end, these tensions can be traced back to the difficulties of identifying (even a thin) liberal theory of the good in the secular age – in a world where conceptions of the good are irreducibly pluralized, individualized, and subjectivized. In brief, the story I want to tell is also a very Taylorian story, for it is one that – like Taylor's early work – raises questions about liberal neutrality about the good.

An Egalitarian Theory of Religious Freedom

Writing in the context of the Canadian debate about reasonable accommodations, Taylor and Maclure begin by defending the idea that members of
religious minorities have a right, on non-discrimination grounds, to enjoy
similar opportunities to practice their religion as members of the majority.
I have no quarrel with this idea, and have argued along similar lines in
my book on critical republicanism and the hijab controversy in France.[6]
But I'd like to focus on their second main point – namely, that the question of reasonable accommodations raises a more fundamental problem:
in virtue of what are religious believers entitled to special consideration in
the first place? The debate about reasonable accommodations assumes
that religious practice is respectable qua religious, and that existing accommodations of religious beliefs and practices are legitimate – that they
protect a basic, fundamental good or value. But what is this fundamental
good or value that freedom of religion protects? It is important to formulate an answer to that question. The law inevitably creates burdens for
those who have to obey it, and if we are to provide a justification for ex-
empting some citizens from these burdens, it had better be a strong one. A
purely formal egalitarian answer (which analogizes burdens on majority
and minority religious practice, to justify compensating members of minorities for purely external burdens) will not be sufficient. Why is religious
conduct worthy of protection in the first place?

Taylor and Maclure answer that religious belief, for purposes of legal
exemptions, should only be seen as a subset of a broader category of beliefs that deserve protection: "moral beliefs which structure moral identity" – what they call "meaning-giving beliefs and commitments." And
this also covers a broad spectrum of nonreligious beliefs and practices –
from secular pacifism to ecocentric vegetarianism through duties of care
to terminally ill loved ones. The notion of meaning-giving commitments
is broader than that used by other egalitarian philosophers. In contrast to
Rawls, they do not insist that individual beliefs be "comprehensive" in
scope, and they reject Nussbaum's emphasis on "ultimate existential questions." It is a feature of the secular age, they point out, that people's ethical
commitments take the form of "fluid, eclectic set(s) of values" that are not
integrated into a comprehensive whole and are not perceived as "unconditional rules for action." At certain times, however – such as during the

illness of a loved one – the pursuit of certain core values becomes paramount and gives meaning and shape to one's life. In sum, we can say that Taylor and Maclure take the ethical pluralism of the secular age far more seriously than other egalitarian philosophers. Rawls and Nussbaum, it seems, still hold a traditionally religious understanding of the scope (comprehensive) and content ("ultimate questions") of what counts as a morally weighty secular belief.

Drawing on Taylor's rehabilitation of "ordinary life" in *Sources of the Self*, Taylor and Maclure detect pockets of moral depth in ordinary life – in the sudden encounter with finitude in the event of the death of a loved one, or in ecocentric vegetarians' profound convictions about the wrongness of meat consumption, to take their two favorite examples. What makes those commitments particularly weighty is that they allow individuals to act with integrity – where integrity is defined as congruence between one's perceptions of one's duties and one's actual actions. What the end-of-life caregiver and the ecocentric vegetarian have in common is that they both seek to act in accordance with their conscience. "Here I stand, I can do no other," as Martin Luther is thought to have said. Taylor and Maclure note that forcing someone to act against her deep conscientious convictions constitutes a "moral harm" equivalent to the kind of "physical harm" that justifies the special accommodation of citizens with disabilities. Thus, they conclude, citizens with intense, categorical, meaning-giving secular beliefs have a prima facie claim to be considered for exemptions from burdensome laws. The claim is only prima facie because there are limits to accommodation: the rights of others, the interests pursued by the law, the undue hardship caused by accommodations. But even if the claim is not favourably received, what is interesting is that Taylor and Maclure have considerably expanded the range of beliefs and commitments that have a claim to be considered for special protection. They have provided a novel philosophical justification for accommodation itself. To sum up, they reject both the content and the scope criteria for a secular belief to be as morally weighty as a traditional religious belief, but they retain a third criterion, which we could call the categoricity criterion. Secular beliefs are morally weighty when they prescribe duties of conscience.

An Evaluation

Have Taylor and Maclure solved the paradox I started with? Have they developed a plausibly egalitarian definition of morally weighty beliefs that is not biased in favour of religious beliefs yet adequately protects the underlying values expressed by the ideal of freedom of religion? My assessment comes in two parts. In the first, I draw attention to one significant virtue of their account, which is that it implicitly relies on a very Taylorian idea of "strong evaluation." In the second, I cast some doubts about the viability of the individualistic, Protestantized, subjectivist conception of strong evaluation that underpins their account.

Taylor and Maclure get to the heart of a key feature of freedom of religion – one that is strangely neglected by contemporary liberals. It is this: what Taylor said (in an earlier, seminal article) about negative freedoms in general – that they are empty without "strong evaluations" of what they allow the pursuit of – applies with particular acuity to freedom of religion.[7] Freedom of religion, in contrast to more generic freedoms of thought, belief, and association, relies on a moralized distinction between valuable and nonvaluable activities and serves to protect a subset of the former. It is a freedom to pursue a specific end and activity: it refers to the pursuit of a conception of the good with a specific shape, content, and form, rather than the means through which any conception of the good can be pursued. Furthermore, in the case of exemptions and accommodations, which is our focus here, freedom of religion generates demands of positive assistance in pursuing those activities. This means that when adjudicating such claims, it must be decided whether they correctly express the values underpinning the general principle.

Even though they do not explicitly draw on Taylor's earlier writings, Taylor and Maclure are open about the need to make "strong evaluations" about the values that freedom of religion is supposed to protect. This confirms the long-standing Taylorian view that rights protect substantive values: we care about rights because of the good that they protect, which cannot be reduced to individual freedom of choice. So our authors do not shy away from openly perfectionist evaluations, setting "trivial" against "central" commitments and "mere preferences" against "core convictions." Such perfectionist discriminations, it seems to me, are inherent in any serious reflection about the value of freedom of religion. Perhaps this is an obvious point, but it is one that contemporary liberals – punctiliously attached to an ideal of neutrality toward the good – have not fully come to terms with.

Who, then, is to make the strong evaluations required to distinguish between meaning-giving and trivial commitments? Taylor and Maclure's emphatic response to this is: the individual claimant herself. Here they anticipate the charge – often levelled at Taylor's conception of positive liberty – that the idea of "strong evaluation" could give the state the authority arbitrarily to discriminate between better and worse ways to exercise one's freedoms. Instead Taylor and Maclure assert that "the special status of religious beliefs is derived from the role they play in people's moral lives, rather than from an assessment of their intrinsic validity." They defend what they call a subjective conception of freedom of religion, according to which only individuals – not the state, nor religious authorities – are in a position to explain which particular beliefs and commitments are key to their sense of moral integrity. Judges only have to assess whether such claims are made with sincerity (so as to rule out, when possible, fraudulent or pretextual claims). Yet ultimately the subjective conception of freedom points to the sovereignty of private, strong evaluations.

There is much to recommend in this account, to which I am very sympathetic. But it is also plagued by tensions and difficulties. First, Taylor and Maclure effectively collapse religion into conscience and implicitly assume that the latter category is more inclusive than the former. But we may wonder whether this is the case, or whether anything is lost in the redescription of freedom of religion as freedom of conscience. Assume I am a devout Muslim; I observe Ramadan, say my prayers every day, wear the *hijab*, give *zakat* (alms giving or charitable giving), and send my children to Koranic school. Or assume I am a practicing Catholic. I observe Lent, try not to eat meat on Fridays, celebrate Easter, go to church every Sunday, have my children baptized and confirmed. For many Catholics and Muslims (but also other Christians, Jews, Hindus, and Buddhists) the religious experience is fundamentally about exhibiting the virtues of the good believer, living in community with others, and shaping one's daily life in accordance with the rituals of the faith. Those rituals are meaning-giving and are connected to believers' sense of their moral integrity.

Yet they are not duties of conscience, though they are often redescribed as such. The good religious life is a life of constant, difficult, ritual affirmation of the faith against the corrupting influences of the secular world. It is not often one in which one single obligation (say, wearing a particular dress, attending mass) is so stringent as to promise eternal damnation if it is not fulfilled. Taylor and Maclure tend to reinterpret acts of habitual, collective, "embodied practices" of religious devotion as Protestantized duties of conscience. While such a description tallies with the individualization and subjectification of religious experience in contemporary societies, it also has two unanticipated consequences. First, it perversely encourages the most fundamentalist and rigid interpretations of religious dogma. It rewards those Christians who present their objection to homosexuality as a matter of conscience ("here I stand, I can do no other") over and above those habitual believers who seek to accommodate their religious life to a secularizing world, often with considerable unease and forbearance. So here's another paradox: in insisting that only beliefs that are intensely held – and experienced as categorical duties – should be candidates for "reasonable" accommodation, Taylor and Maclure accommodate those with the least "reasonable" beliefs. Of course it can be retorted that only claimants with intense and categorical beliefs are likely to be candidates for accommodation in the first place. But as the dilemma about accommodations is used to identify the values underpinning freedom of religion itself, legitimate questions can be raised about the broader implications of the reduction of religion to conscience.

At this point one may legitimately ask, why did Taylor and Maclure not opt for the weak interpretation of freedom of conscience – which protects all meaning-giving and integrity-constituting commitments – rather than the strong interpretation, which focuses on the more problematic category of conscience? The main concern seems to be about the proliferation of claims. Thus Taylor and Maclure plausibly note that values such as political ideals, professional fulfillment, and artistic creativity are meaning-giving and integrity-constituting. Yet they generally do not generate claims of special accommodation because they are linked to flexible and fluid, not overriding and stringent, obligations. It is only in exceptional cases – the ecocentric vegetarian and the caregiver of a terminally ill parent – that such secular beliefs generate something like an absolute categorical obligation. The strong interpretation of freedom of conscience, then, allows Taylor and Maclure to sketch a manageable theory of accommodations in which only beliefs with a certain degree of categoricity – conscientious beliefs – are accommodated. The administratibility of exemptions is, of course, a legitimate concern. But the singling out of categoricity as the necessary trigger for protection raises its own problems. It draws a normative wedge between two kinds of meaning-giving commitments, those that are inflexible and conscientious and those that are habitual and embodied. This has the effect of singling out individual conscience – as opposed to cultural or community membership – as especially worthy of protection.

In a Canadian context, where cultural identities often feature as the paradigmatic meaning-giving, integrity-constituting commitments, Taylor and Maclure's lack of reference to culture is surprising. In light of Taylor's seminal contribution to the normative theory of multiculturalism, one might have expected that *Secularism and Freedom of Conscience* would take seriously the cultural dimensions of religion instead of proposing a "Protestant" interpretation of what, within religion, is worth protecting. The upshot of their theory is that a sense of communal membership, of cultural identification, of ritualized practice, are not among the values that freedom of religion can be said to protect. Consider the following practices, which currently generate rights to exemption from general laws on grounds of religious freedom in various countries: accommodation of religious dress in the workplace, the ritual killing of animals for halal or kosher meat, tax exemptions for religious charities, church autonomy in the appointment of its leaders. None of these activities is properly described as a conscientious activity, and therefore it is unclear whether they would be entitled to accommodations under Taylor and Maclure's theory. Note that I am not saying that they should; I am simply pointing out this interesting paradox, that a self-proclaimed inclusive theory of freedom of religion actually excludes what most religious believers would take freedom of religion to be about. Religion has been construed as a matter of private conviction rather than of public performance. We could add that, even when freedom of religion relates to actual performances and practices (as it does in accommodation claims), it still draws its moral force from its presumed connection with individual conscience.

Second, let me now raise a connected difficulty with Taylor and Maclure's subjective notion of freedom of religion. While they only consider examples of morally admirable commitments (pacifism, caring for the sick, protecting animal rights) it is not difficult to think of a range of conscientious actions that may be morally trivial, morally wrong, or morally bad. In those cases, should individual strong evaluations be supreme or are different standards called for?

One issue is how to distinguish trivial from morally significant beliefs. Taylor and Maclure assume that there is a consensual understanding of the difference between a morally trivial and a morally significant act. Yet, under conditions of deep moral pluralism, it is precisely those kinds of strong evaluations that are likely to be contested. Consider the standard defence by US courts (following the decision in *Employment Division v. Smith*) of the ingestion of peyote, an otherwise illegal drug. The use of peyote within some Native American rituals is considered by the Supreme Court as a spiritual act falling under the free exercise provision of the First

Amendment (even if it does not generate a right to accommodation – as the court famously declared in the *Smith* case). But what is interesting is this: while ingesting drugs merely to "get high" would count as a trivial, frivolous purpose, ingesting drugs for spiritual purposes rightly falls under the category of a morally significant act deserving of protection. But let's also consider this: what if individuals not belonging to what the courts recognize as a "religion" sincerely claim that they are also using drugs for spiritual purposes? Does "spiritual purpose" extend to dealing with depression, seeking higher truths through controlled intoxication, or dealing with existential pain? In the secular age, how do we draw the line between the spiritual and the trivial, and who is to be the judge of someone else's spiritual integrity?

The other issue is whether freedom of conscience should permit individuals to do bad or unjust things. Taylor and Maclure avoid the difficult question of whether freedom of conscience positively protects a right to do wrong. One very preliminary hypothesis: in the philosophical tradition of thinking about conscience – whether Greek, Buddhist, Muslim, Jewish, Catholic, or Kantian tradition, to name just a few – conscience is respectable and admirable not only as a subjective individual faculty to live in conformity with one's own good; it is, more deeply, respected as the faculty to live in conformity with what one sincerely perceives to be the demands of the good. This is why Antigone's dilemma is so poignant: it vividly pictures a tragic choice between two objectively recognizable moral obligations. In the natural law tradition, conscience is the faculty with which individuals exercise practical judgment about how to apply a general objective moral law to concrete cases. Individuals are fallible, and consciences may err. But conscience is admirable because it is a sincere, though fallible, attempt to find the good. Conscience, therefore, cannot demand us to do evil, inhuman, or outrageous things, even though it can mislead us about the good. But if there is a deep (if complicated) connection between respect for conscience and a nonsubjectivist assessment of its content, then individual strong evaluations will likely be an unreliable guide about what conscience really requires of us.

Where does this leave us? To conclude, I see Taylor and Maclure's succinct but densely argued chapter as the most promising attempt to articulate the morally admirable human faculties traditionally protected by freedom of religion in ways that respect the deep pluralism of the secular age. I have pointed to some problems, which are not so much fatal flaws as unavoidable tensions within the politico-legal philosophy of religious exemptions.

My suspicion is that liberal neutrality about religion ultimately "piggy-backs" on a baggage of ideas, conceptions, and values that originally made sense in a world comprehensively structured by a broadly Christian ethics. In that world, where early liberal ideas of toleration and freedom of religion were articulated, Christian ethics provided the moral framework within which "strong evaluations" – between good and evil, significant and trivial, and so on – were taken for granted. Then it could be coherently assumed that "religion" was a good thing, that any activity pursued under the aegis of religion was therefore also good, and that churches were alternative, self-standing sources of normativity to that of the state. Religion on that view operated as a normative "black box," the content of which the state could try to ignore. It is when this box is thrown open by the egalitarian impulse of the secular age that the need for new "strong evaluations" reappears. Yet those strong evaluations are inherently problematic in a world where there is no publicly validated religious or moral faith, and where the state is expected not to take sides between different ways of conceiving and living the good life.

Egalitarian liberals have struggled to define, in a way that is suitably non-sectarian and evaluative neutral, the morally admirable faculties that traditional freedom of religion can be said to protect. Taylor and Maclure promisingly seek to locate those human faculties in the moral predicaments thrown up by ordinary lives and in the strong evaluations that individuals make in the process. Yet the emphasis on conscience tends to favour a Protestant understanding of what a religion is, and it also relies on an implicit, unarticulated theory of the good. All of this only illustrates one of Taylor's most profound contributions to political philosophy, pointing to the complex ambiguities that beset the liberal ideal of neutrality toward the good life. What I have sought to provide is the sketch of a Taylorian critique of Taylor – a modest testimony of the astonishing fecundity of his thought. In sum, Taylor's recent work points to the formidable challenges that await the still underdeveloped philosophical project of making sense of the ideal of freedom of religion in the secular age. That such a philosophical project is difficult and complex does not imply, of course, that it is not worth pursuing.[8]

14

Two Conceptions of Indian Secularism

RAJEEV BHARGAVA

Charles Taylor is a remarkable thinker – one who has personally influenced me deeply – not least because there are few ideas that he completely rejects or, for that matter, wholly embraces. He is able to do so because though he stands on one side, he helps us to imagine what it's like to be on the other. Taylor almost always helps us to see from both sides of the fence. What he says about the pragmatist philosopher William James is equally true of Taylor himself. He may come down on one side but without leaving us bereft of the force of the other side. Commenting on James's view on the struggle between belief and unbelief in modern Western culture and which Taylor believes is unlikely to end by a decisive victory in favour of the one or the other, Taylor says "James is our great philosopher of the Cusp. He tells us more than anyone else what it's like to stand in that open space and feel the winds pulling you now here now there. It needed someone who had been through a searing experience of morbidity and had come out the other side. But it also needed someone of wide sympathy and extraordinary powers of phenomenological description and one who could feel and articulate the continuing ambivalence in himself." This is true not only of William James but increasingly of the entire philosophical outlook of Taylor who forces us to catch both horns of a dilemma without fully compelling us to let go of either one.

The central purpose of the paper, written to honour him, is to identify two conceptions of Indian secularism and specify their distinctiveness. I begin the paper by explaining why it is important to attend to conceptions of secularism that provide an alternative to mainstream, Western conceptions. In the second section, I outline the structure of political secularism, and bring out its principal differences from perspectives that defend religion-centred states. I then place before the reader three conceptions that fall under the rubric of "Western" secularism. In the fourth section, I identify two conceptions of Indian secularism, the communal harmony model and the principled distance variant. Finally, in the last section, I return to what might be gained from Indian secularisms.[1]

Multiple Secularisms

Wittgenstein's warning that the hold of a particular picture is sometimes so strong that it prevents, even occludes, the awareness of other models of reality is probably more apt about secularism than about other related social and political perspectives. Until recently, the literature on secularism unwittingly assumed that it is a doctrine with a fixed content. The existence of multiple secularisms remained unacknowledged because our imagination was severely constrained by conceptions of secularism developed in parts of the Western world.

It is of course true that the elementary constituents of political secularism are the same throughout the world. Broadly speaking, secularism, anywhere in the world, means a separation of organized religion from organized political power inspired by a specific set of values. Just as without separation there is no secularism, likewise a value-less separation does not add up to secularism. In this sense, secularism is a universal normative doctrine. But it does not follow that these elements are interpreted or related to each other in any one particular way. Many ways exist of interpreting these elements as do different ways of relating them. Each conception of secularism may unpack the metaphor of separation differently or select different elements from the stock of values that give separation its point. It may also place different weights on the same values. So when I talk about conceptions of *Indian* secularism, I do not imply that these have a unique conceptual structure. I only mean that embedded in them is a specific and interestingly different way of interpreting and relating the basic constituents of secularism.

Scholars have also tended to assume that the structure of secularism was timeless, as if it has always existed in the same form. But it does not take much to realize that secularism has multiple interpretations, which change over time. All living doctrines evolve and therefore have a history.

Secularism too has a history made at one time largely by Europeans, then a little later by North Americans and much later by non-Western countries which, incidentally, have histories of other concepts of religio-philosophical coexistence. Non-Western societies inherited specific versions of secularism from their Western counterparts but they did not always preserve them in the form in which they were received. They often added something of enduring value to them and, therefore, developed the idea further. Until recently, Western theorists of secularism did not recognize this non-Western contribution. It may have been earlier adequate for Western scholars to focus exclusively on that part of the history of secularism which was made in and by the West. But today it would be a gross mistake to identify Western variants of secularism with the entire doctrine, if the part was viewed as the whole. For a rich, complex, and complete understanding of secularism, one must examine how the secular idea has developed over time trans-nationally.

Other reasons exist why we must attend to the multiple histories of secularism. There are clear signs that secularism in the predominantly single-religion societies of the west is beginning to be challenged not only from religious believers within but also from recently emigrated believers of other religions. This new multi-religiosity is threatening to throw Western secularism into turmoil. Recall the controversy over the hijab in France. Western societies can no longer take for granted their own current interpretation of secularism, but must re-examine what separation means and what it is for. They must do so because the reasons why secularism is acceptable to the dominant religious majority are not automatically endorsed by religious minorities. For example, on the hitherto dominant interpretation of secularism, it means a strict separation of Church and state for the sake of religious liberty construed individualistically, or, at best, for individualistically construed citizenship rights. However, neither the idea of strict separation nor an individualist defence of religious liberty and citizenship rights may be acceptable to many adherents of non-Protestant, South Asian, or Middle Eastern religions. To convince them of its need and importance, one needs to retrieve the complicated structure of values behind it. Thus, to meet this new challenge to Western secularism, it may be necessary to reconstruct its history or examine the trajectories of secularism in other parts of the world.

In India the issues around secularism arise differently. Religious minorities show no dislike for political secularism but it is questioned by disillusioned critics of modernity and by self-styled spokespersons of the Hindu majority. Critics of secularism point to its alleged links with all kinds of things they dislike: the nation state, instrumental rationality, the hegemony of science, mindless industrialization, and realist statecraft. But both its critics and its defenders appear to have forgotten its constitutive relation with substantive values. They also seem not to recall that "separation" in the early constitutional history of India was never understood to mean the blanket exclusion of religion from the state.

The current crisis of secularism then must compel one to ask why we need it at all. After all, when an idea is widely endorsed, we bother little about its value and purpose. As it is taken for granted, its purpose, as Charles Taylor has reminded us in a different context, recedes into the background, is even forgotten.[2] But when a searching, discomforting scrutiny of it commences, this forgetfulness becomes a nerve-wrecking handicap. This has happened with secularism too. There is a pressing need to remember and retrieve the value-content of secularism. Thus, it is important that we go back in time and to retrieve the complex purposes underlying it, to examine how different secularisms were originally conceived. This would be beneficial not only for us, in India, but also for students of Western secularism. For once we unearth the complicated conceptual structure of Indian secularism, we may find that it has the potential to shape the future of Western secularism. If so, it is not enough for students of Western secularism to look backwards, at the history of its own versions of secularism. They may need to look sideways, at the Indian variant, and discover that in it is reflected not only a compressed version of their own history but also a vision of its future.

This part-retrieval can only be done with the help of a historical account. Providing such a historical account is beyond the scope of this paper. However, it is my guess that such an account would yield the following result. Virtually everywhere the animating principles of a broadly conceived secular perspective is that they encompass an opposition to the hegemony and tyranny of religion, and to religion-based exclusions.[3] The goal of secularism, defined most generally, is to ensure that the social and political order is free from institutionalized religious domination so that there is religious freedom, freedom to exit from religion, inter-religious equality, equality between believers and non-believers, and solidarity, forged when people are freed from religious sectarianism. Thus, religion defines the scope of secularism. The very point of secularism is lost either when religion disappears or if it purges itself from its oppressive, tyrannical, inegalitarian, or exclusionary features. If religion is exhaustively defined in terms of these oppressive features, then the goal of secularism is to eliminate religion altogether. Since religion is a far more complex and ambivalent entity and is not necessarily tyrannical or oppressive, we might see the objective of secularism as the reform, when necessary, of religion but from a vantage point that is partly external and definitely non-partisan or to build a space outside religion. Secularism is not intrinsically opposed to religion and may even be seen as advocating critical respect towards it. Moreover, it invites reciprocal critical respect towards non-religious perspectives.

Political secularism can be defined more narrowly, for it answers the question: what is the appropriate relation between state and religious institutions, given the background purpose that animates secularism more generally, that is, to end religious hegemony, oppression, and exclusion and to foster principled co-existence between followers of religious and non-religious perspectives. The broadest and perhaps the vaguest answer provided by political secularism is that the two must be separated. Here then is the first, initial formulation: political secularism is a normative doctrine for which the state should be separated from religious institutions to check religion's tyranny, oppression, hierarchy, or sectarianism and to promote religious and non-religious freedoms, equalities, and solidarity among citizens. Put schematically, political secularism advocates the separation of state and religious institutions for the sake of values, such as the ones mentioned above.

Religion-Centred and Secular States

To further grasp its structure it is first important to contrast political secularism with doctrines to which it is in one sense related and opposed. Such anti-secular, religion-centric doctrines favour not separation but a union or alliance between religion and state. They advocate religion-centred states. If political secularism advocates a state that separates itself from religion (a secular state), then doctrines which it opposes seek a union with religion (theocracy) or a strong, formal alliance with it (state with an established religion). To understand the distinction between religion-centred and secular states, a further set of distinctions need to be introduced. States may be strongly connected to religion or disconnected from it. Such connection or disconnection may exist at three distinct levels: at (1) the level of ends, at (2) the level of institutions and personnel and at (3) the level of public policy and, even more relevantly, law.[4] A state that has union with a particular religious order is a (a) theocratic state, governed by divine laws directly administered by a priestly order claiming divine commission. A theocratic state is strongly connected to religion at each of the three levels. Hence the use of the term "Union." Historical examples of theocracies are ancient Israel, some Buddhist regimes of Japan and China, the Geneva of John Calvin, and the papal states. The Islamic republic of Iran as Khomeni aspired to run it is an obvious example. A theocratic state must be distinguished from a state that establishes religion. Here religion is granted official, legal recognition by the state and while both benefit from a formal alliance with one another, the sacerdotal order does not govern a state where religion is established. There are different personnel and institutional structures for states and religion. Establishment of religion can take many forms: states with the establishment of single religion that are (b) without the establishment of a church, (c) with the establishment of a single church, and (d) with the establishment of multiple churches. And finally, (e), states with establishment of multiple religions.

Secular states are different from each of these five kinds of states. To further understand this issue and distinguish different forms of secular states, allow me to unfold the structure of the secular state. For a start, we must recognize that a secular state is to be distinguished not only from a theocracy (feature-a) but also from a state where religion is firmly established. But a non-theocratic state is not automatically secular because it is entirely consistent for a state neither to be inspired by divine laws nor run by a priestly order, but instead have a formal alliance with one religion. Second, because it is also a feature of states with established churches, the mere institutional separation of the two is not and cannot be the distinguishing mark of secular states. This second-level disconnection should not be conflated with the separation embedded in secular states, because though necessary, it is not a sufficient condition for their individuation. A secular state goes beyond church-state separation, refusing to establish religion or if religion is already established, disestablishing it. It withdraws privileges that established religion had previously taken for granted. Therefore, a secular state follows what can be called the principle of non-establishment. *This it can do only when its primary ends or goals are largely defined independently of religion.* Thus, a crucial requirement of a secular state is that it has no constitutive links with religion, that the ends of any religion should not be installed as the ends of the state. For example, it cannot be the constitutive objective of the state to ensure salvation, *nirvana*, or *moksha*. Nor can it be a requirement of the state that it increases the membership of any religious community. The conversion of one individual or a group from one religion to another cannot be the goal of the state. Official privileged status is not given to religion. This is largely what is meant when it is said that in a secular state, a formal or legal union or alliance between state and religion is impermissible. No religious community in such a state can say that the state belongs exclusively to it. The identity of the state is defined independently of religion. Furthermore, the non-establishment of religion means that the state is separated not merely from one but from all religions; even all of them together cannot say that it belongs collectively to them and them alone.

To grasp this point at a more general theoretical level, let me distinguish three levels of disconnection to correspond with the already identified three levels of connection. A state may be disconnected from religion at the level of ends (first level), at the level of institutions (second level) and the level of law and public policy (third level).[5] A secular state is distinguished from theocracies and states with established states by a primary, first-level disconnection. A secular state has free standing ends, substantially, if not always completely, disconnected from the ends of religion or conceivable without a connection with them. At the second level, disconnection ensues so that there is no mandatory or presumed presence of religious personnel in the structures of state. No part of state power is automatically available to members of religious institutions. Finally, a secular state may be disconnected from religion even at the level of law and public policy.

Models of Secularism

For many proponents or opponents of political secularism all three levels of separation matter equally. In short, if states are to be fully secular separation must be strict or perfect. I believe the identification of this third level is important, but not because separation at this level is constitutive of political secularism. Rather, differences at this level generate a variety of political secularisms.

In what follows I identify five such models of political secularism, though this list may not be exhaustive. They are picked because of their dominance, world-wide, in the public and intellectual domains. Two of these, one originating in the United States of America that I call the mutual exclusion or the idealized American model (not to be confused with the actual practices of the US federal state) and the other developed first in France called the one-sided exclusion or the idealized French model, have been hegemonic.[6] A third has developed in large parts of Western Europe and has been recently theorized by Tariq Modood, who calls it moderate secularism. Identifying the three "Western" models helps us identify two models of (idealized) Indian secularism, one that might be called the communal harmony model and the other, the least visible publicly, the model of principled distance largely embodied in the Indian Constitution (but practised, in my view, by other states as well).

Recall that given that political secularism is a normative perspective, its broadest formulation is that political institutions or the state should be separated from religious institutions or religion for the sake of some values. The two models that I discuss first interpret this narrowly to mean the separation of state and church/church-based religions.

The One-Sided Exclusion or Idealized French Model

This model holds that the church and church-based religions must be excluded from the state at each of the three levels, that there must be "freedom of the state from religion," but the state retains the power to interfere in church-based religions at level (3). In short, at least at level (3), separation means one-sided exclusion. The state may interfere to hinder and suppress or even to help religion, but in all cases this must be done only to ensure its control over religion. Religion becomes an object of law and public policy but only according to terms specified by the state. Recall that in France the Catholic church was an intrinsic part of the pre-revolutionary regime – the Catholic establishment offered strong support to the monarchy – and continued to play a powerful role in the anti-Republican coalition of the Third Republic. In this long struggle between religious elites bent upon preserving the establishment of Catholicism and secular

Republicans who found the church to be both politically meddlesome and socially oppressive, and who therefore increasingly became profoundly anti-clerical, the anti-establishment advocates of *laïcité* finally emerged victorious. It is not surprising then that this conception, which arose in response to the excessive domination of the church, encourages an active disrespect for religion and is concerned solely with preventing the religious order from dominating the secular. It hopes to deal with institutionalized religious domination by taming and marginalizing religion, by removing organized religion or what the French call *cultes*, from public space more generally and in particular from the official public space of the state. In short, in this conception, organized religion must be privatized. Citizens may enter the public/political domain but only if they leave behind their religious identity or communal belonging. They must enter as "abstract citizens." Rights accrue to them directly as individual citizens unmediated by membership in any community. Thus the principle value underlying separation is our common identity as citizens (and therefore a common, undifferentiated public culture presupposed by it) and a form of equality that springs from such uniformity.[7] I portray this model in this fashion not only because on at least one (perhaps mistaken) interpretation, it is found in the 1905 law of separation but because it has travelled worldwide and informed the practice of many states, such as Turkey and the communist states of USSR and China.

The Mutual Exclusion or Idealized American Model

At least one highly influential political self-understanding in the United States interprets separation to mean mutual exclusion. According to this idealized model, neither state nor church is meant to interfere in the domain of the other. Each is meant to have its own area of jurisdiction. Thus, to use Thomas Jefferson's famous description "a wall of separation" must be erected between church and state. This strict or "perfect separation," as James Madison has termed it, must take place at each of the three distinct levels of ends, institutions and personnel, and law and public policy. The first two levels make the state non-theocratic and disestablish religion. The third level ensures that the state has neither a positive nor a negative relationship with religion. On the positive side, for example, there should be no policy of granting aid, even non-preferentially, to religious institutions. On the negative side, it is not within the scope of state activity to interfere in religious matters even when some of the values professed by the state, such as equality, are violated within the religious domain. This non-interference is justified on the grounds that religion is a privileged, private (i.e., non-state) matter, and if something is amiss within this private domain, only those who have a right to do so within this sphere can mend it. This view, according to its proponents, is what religious freedom means. Thus the freedom that justifies mutual exclusion is negative liberty and is closely enmeshed with the privatization of religion. Of course privatization in this context means not exclusion of religion from the public domain but rather its exclusion from the official domain of the state. The model encourages the state to passively respect religion. Any intervention is tantamount to control. The only way to respect religion is to leave it alone. The two religious clauses of the first amendment may be seen to sum up the meaning of idealized American secularism: "Congress shall make no law respecting an establishment of religion, or prohibiting ... the free exercise thereof." Thus church-state separation exists for the sake of religious liberty plus denominational pluralism.

To understand the main point underlying the idealization of mutual exclusion, it may be pertinent to briefly examine the historical context of its emergence. To begin with the experience of persecution by the early immigrants, mainly Puritans, to the newly discovered continent meant a greater potential understanding of the general value of religious liberty. Secondly, Protestant churches of different hues proliferated and coexisted in different parts of America. To this extent, a limited form of religious diversity was simply a fact. Third, since these newly formed churches were not associated with the *Ancien Régime*, there was no active hostility to them. On the contrary, they were voluntarily created and therefore expressions of religious freedom, not religious oppression. None of this ruled out a strong motivation within members of one church to not only view their own church as more valuable and true but to also seek its establishment. Indeed different parts of the country saw the establishment of one of the many churches in the land. This monopolistic privileging of one over another and the relegation of others to a secondary status continued to be a source of latent or manifest conflict between different churches. Thus mutual exclusion of church and state, at least at the federal level, was deemed necessary to resolve conflicts between different Protestant denominations, to grant some measure of equality between them, and – most crucially – to provide individuals the freedom to set up new religious associations. Religious liberty is deeply valued and so the state must not negatively intervene (interfere) in religion but potential denominational conflict also compelled the federal state to withdraw substantial support to religion.[8]

Modest Secularism (The West European Model)[9]

There are several reasons why European states might be judged to be secular. (a) First, the historical pattern of hostility to church and church-based religions on the ground that they were politically meddlesome and socially oppressive – a pattern that appeared militantly and robustly in the unchurching struggles in France and is also to be found to a significant degree in most West European countries. As a result, the social and political power of churches has been largely restricted. Second, (b) there has over time been a decline not only in church belonging but also belief in Christianity. If there is one place where secular humanism or what Charles Taylor calls exclusive humanism is strong, even naively taken for granted as the only ontological and epistemological game in town, it is surely Western Europe. Both (a) and (b) have had an impact on Europe's constitutional regimes. A fair degree of disconnection exists at level two. More importantly, the ends of the state are delinked from religion to a significant degree (level one disconnection) and so the same basket of formal rights (to different kinds of liberty, and forms of equality etc.) are offered to all individuals regardless of their church-affiliation and regardless of whether they are or not religious. In the dominant political discourse, the self-definition of these states is that they are not religious (Christian) but (purely) liberal-democratic.

However, it is equally true that at both levels one and two, some connection exists between state and religion. Several states continue to grant monopolistic privileges to one or the other branch of Christianity. Examples include the Presbyterian church in Scotland, the Lutheran church in all Nordic countries (except Sweden where it was recently disestablished), the Orthodox church in Greece, and the Anglican Church in England where twenty-four bishops sit in the House of Lords with full voting rights and where the monarch is also the head of the church. Moreover, at level three, at the level of law and public policy, state intervention exists in the form of support for either the dominant church or of Christian churches.

TABLE 14.1 | PERCENTAGE OF WESTERN DEMOCRACIES WITH STATE SUPPORTS FOR RELIGION (EXCLUDING THE UNITED STATES)

Form of State Policies of Support (or monitoring) of Religion	Percentage
Government funding of religious schools or education	100
Religious education standard (optional in schools)	76
Government collects taxes for religious organizations	52
Official government department for religious affairs	44
Government positions or funding for clergy	40
Government funding of religious charitable organizations	36
Established/Official religion	36
Some clerical positions made by government appointment	24

Source: Table from Alfred Stepan, "The Multiple Secularisms of Modern Democracies and Autocracies."[10]

Thus, most European states remain connected to religion (the dominant religion or church) at all three levels. The connection at levels one and two means that they still have some form of establishment, perhaps even elements of theocracy. At level three, there is neither mutual nor one-sided exclusion of religion, but positive entanglement with it. None of this entails that such states are confessional or have strong establishment. Rather, such state-religion connections combined with a significant degree of disconnection mean that these states are at best modestly secular by the standards set by the idealized American or the French model. Indeed, Tariq Modood has called the secularism underpinning these states "moderate secularism" (model three). He has argued that this secularism is compatible with a more than symbolic but weak establishment. The moderateness comes largely from the rejection of exclusion and the adoption of some distance instead. The secularity comes largely from the ends for which states have distanced themselves from and which are largely defined independently of religion.

Two Alternative Conceptions

"Mutual exclusion," "one-sided exclusion," and "moderate secularism" are not the only models of political secularism, however. Other conceptions have emerged outside the West that have transformed the meaning of political secularism. Two of these models have developed in the subcontinent and at least one of these is enshrined in the Indian constitution. (Not to be confused with the actual practices of the Indian state, particularly in recent times.) Perhaps the best way to begin articulating it is by sketching two broad and contrasting pictures of the socio-religious world. In the first, a persistent, deep, and pervasive anxiety exists about the other, both the other outside one's religion and the other within. The other is viewed and felt as an existential threat. So doctrinal differences are felt not as mere intellectual disagreements but are cast in a way that undermines basic trust in one another. The other cannot be lived with but simply has to be expelled or exterminated. This results in major wars and a consequent religious homogenization. Though admittedly skewed, this picture approximates what happened in Europe in the sixteenth century.[11] One might then add that this constitutes the hidden background condition of European ideas of toleration and even its political secularism.

Consider now an entirely different situation. Here different faiths, modes of worship, philosophical outlooks, and ways of practicing exist customarily. Deep diversity is accepted as part of the natural landscape – Syrian Christians, Zoroastrian, Jews, Muslims – Arab traders or Turk and Afghan who came initially as conquerors but settled down – not to speak of a variety of South Asian faiths – all are at home. To feel and be secure is a basic psychosocial condition. All groups exhibit basic collective self-confidence, possible only when there is trust between communities. In short, the presence of the other is never questioned. There is no deep anxiety; instead a basic level of comfort exists. The other does not present an existential threat. This is not to say that there are no deep intellectual disagreements and conflicts, some of which even lead to violent skirmishes, but these do not issue in major wars or religious persecution. There is no collective physical assault on the other on a major scale. This approximates the socio-religious world of the Indian subcontinent, at least until the advent of colonial modernity, and constitutes the background condition of civility and coexistence – perhaps even a different form of "toleration" in India. Indeed, it is not entirely mistaken to say it was not until the advent of colonial modernity and the formation of Hindus and Muslims as national communities that this background condition was unsettled. Religious coexistence could now no longer be taken for granted, doubts about coexistence forced themselves upon the public arena, and religious coexistence became a problematic issue to be spoken about and publicly articulated. An explicit invocation and defence of the idea became necessary that all religions must be at peace with one another, that there should be trust, a basic level of comfort among them, and, if undermined, mutual confidence must be restored. And trust and confidence requires that everyone, particularly the state, has equal regard for all religions. This was put sometimes normatively and sometimes merely affirmed and might be called the communal harmony or "sarva dharma sambhaava" model. This variant of secularism appears to have been derived entirely from its strong link with home-grown traditions. India had therefore worked out its own conception of secularism that is neither Christian nor Western.

The Communal Harmony Model

The source of this conception can be found in Gandhi.[12] Gandhi begins by accepting religious pluralism as the inevitable and healthy destiny of humankind. "There is endless variety in all religions" and "interminal religious differences." "Some go on a pilgrimage and bathe in the sacred river, others go to Mecca; some worship him in temples, others in mosques, some just bow their heads in reverence; some read the Vedas, others the Quran ... some call themselves Hindus, others Muslims." There is, for Gandhi, not only diversity of religions but also diversity within them. "While I believe myself to be a Hindu, I know that I do not worship God in the same manner as any one or all of them."[13] Given this deep religious diversity, "the need of the moment is not one religion, but mutual respect and tolerance of the devotees of different religions," indeed to entertain "equal regard for other religions and their followers."[14] The inescapability of religious diversity morally requires inter-religious toleration and equal respect for all religions. It also necessitates that every religion from the point of view of the religionists themselves.[15]

Gandhi did not find any inconsistency between demanding toleration and equal respect. It is of course true that in the classical seventeenth-century meaning of the term, to tolerate is to refrain from interference in the activities of others even though one finds them morally disagreeable, even repugnant, and despite the fact that one has the power to do so.[16] Here one puts up with, even suffers the morally reprehensible activities of others. The powerless other escapes interference of the powerful because the latter shows mercy towards them, a virtue in the powerful exercised in relation to those who do not really deserve it. Let's call this a hierarchical notion of toleration, given the asymmetry of power between the two groups and the attitude of superiority that one has towards the other. Gandhi's notion of toleration is different. Parents often put up with the blemishes of their children, which they would not suffer in others. We choose to overlook a fault in our lover, even in our close friends, that we would not excuse in others. We might endure deep difference in world-views in fellow citizens because we value fraternity. In all such cases, we put up with dislikeable states of doing or being in others even if we have some power to do something about them simply because we have loving feelings for them. Here one tolerates not despite hate but rather because one loves the other. A mixture of love, friendliness, and fellow feeling is in the background or becomes the ground of a different conception of tolera-tion. So suppose that A accepts the value of many but not all of B's beliefs and practices but recognizes that beliefs and practices he does not accept follow from some of those he does or that some beliefs and practices he is unable to endorse follow inescapably from B's different background, then out of respect for some of his beliefs and practices, A would put up rather than interfere with those with which he disagrees.

Unlike other conceptions that presuppose the idea that oneness with significant others as well as God is achieved by abolishing/ignoring/be-littling the radical other, i.e., by eliminating plurality, here, in the second conception, oneness is attained by accepting all radical others as equally significant because they variously manifest one supreme being or con-cept. Thus to tolerate is to refrain from interfering in the life of others not despite our hatred for them, nor because we are indifferent to them, but because we love them as alternative manifestations of our own selves or deeply care for some basic norm common to all of us. We may not be able to do or be what they are, we may even dislike some of their beliefs and practices, but we recognize that they are translations of our own selves or of gods within each of us. This binds us together in a relationship of lasting affection.

Thus, the moral-practical attitude of equal regard for all religions is a (practical) entailment of a deeper epistemic grasp of the fundamental unity of all religions.[17] For Gandhi, "the soul of religion is one, but it is encased in a multitude of forms. The latter will persist to the end of time. Wise men will ignore the outward crust and see the same soul living under a variety of crusts."[18] The basic reference of all religions is the same: God or Truth. "All religions are true and also that all have some error in them and that whilst I hold by my own, I should hold others as dear as Hinduism, from which it logically follows that we should hold all as dear as our nearest kith and kin and that we should make no distinction between them.[19]

This move towards inclusive monotheism flows directly from the most ancient aspects of Indian polytheistic traditions, a trait they share with other religious traditions of the ancient world. The implicit or explicit theology of these religions allows for translation of gods.[20] In virtually all cultures of classical antiquity, each god performed a function based on his cosmic competence. Thus there are gods of love, war, knowledge, craftsmanship. Likewise, each god embodied an entity of potentially cosmic significance. Hence, gods of fire, rain, earth, time, sun, moon, and sea, or primal gods who create, destroy, preserve, and so on. The god of love in one culture could then also acquire the name of the god of love from another culture. This way differences continue to be viewed as irreducible and yet translatable.[21] One might even call this feature of translatability a theology of recognition – the gods of each culture are recognized within the background of a common semantic universe.[22]

Thus "all worship the same God although under different names."[23] He illustrates this by striking verse from the Grantha Sahib wherein Guru Nanak says that God may be called by the name of Allah, Rahim, and so on. The name does not matter if he is enshrined in our hearts.

This inclusive monotheism permits easy movement across religions. If different names refer to the same god or the same god has different cultural backgrounds, then why create too much fuss about leaving one and embracing another? Indeed why not embrace both, even all? Two more things follow. First, "to revile one another's religion, to make reckless statements, to utter untruth, to break the heads of innocent men, to desecrate temples or mosques *is* a denial of God." Second, "it is wrong for anyone to say that his God is superior to that of another's. God is one and the same for all.[24] At one level, there is a fundamental unity among all religions and precisely because of it they must be regarded as equal. If so, movements of conversion or purification are pointless. "The real Shuddhi movement consist in each one trying to arrive at perfection in his or her own faith. In such a plan character is the only test. What is the use of crossing from one compartment to another, if it does not mean a moral rise?[25] The political implication of this is that "it is the duty of the government to offer protection to all who look up to it, wherever they are and to whatever religion they belong."

Soon after independence, this idea found articulation in public discourse as secularism – strictly speaking, political secularism. The state must show *sarvadharma sambhāv* (be equally well disposed to all paths, god or gods, all religions, even all philosophical conceptions of the ultimate good.) But this should not be confused with what is called multiple establishment, where the state has formal ties with all religions, endorses all of them, and helps all of them, and where it allows each to flourish in the direction in which it found them, to let them grow with all their excrescences, as for example in the Millet system and the imperial British rule. Instead the task of the state as an entity separate from all religions was to ensure trust between religious communities, to restore basic confidence if and when it was undermined. This happens under conditions when there is a threat of interreligious domination, when a majority religion threatens to marginalize minority religions. So here secularism is pitted against what in India is pejoratively called communalism – a sensibility or ideology where a community's identity, its core beliefs, practices, and interests are constitutively opposed to the identity and interests of another community.

To generalize even more, secularism came to be used for a certain comportment of the state, whereby it must distance itself from all religious and philosophical conceptions in order to perform its primary function, i.e., to promote a certain quality of fraternity or sociability, to foster a certain quality of relations among religious communities, perhaps even inter-religious equality under conditions of deep religious diversity.

The Principled Distance Model

A second conception developed too, even more ambitious, that tried to combine the aim of fostering better quality of social relations with an emancipatory agenda, to not only respect all religions and philosophies but to protect individuals from the oppressive features of their own religions or religious communities – or to put it differently, to confront and fight both inter-religious and intra-religious domination simultaneously. This is the constitutional secularism of India, at least on my philosophical interpretation of it.

Several features of this model are worth mentioning.[26] First, multiple religions are not optional extras added on as an afterthought but were present at Indian secularism's starting point as part of its foundation.

Indian secularism is inextricably tied to deep religious diversity. Second, this form of secularism has a commitment to multiple values – namely, liberty, equality, and fraternity (not conceived narrowly as pertaining only to individuals but interpreted broadly to also cover the relative autonomy of religious communities and, in limited and specific domains, their equality of status in society) – as well as other more basic values such as peace, toleration, and mutual respect between communities. It has a place not only for the right of individuals to profess their religious beliefs but also for the right of religious communities to establish and maintain educational institutions crucial for the survival and sustenance of their distinctive religious traditions.

The acceptance of community-specific rights brings me to the third feature of this model. Because it was born in a deeply multi-religious society, it is concerned as much with inter-religious domination as it is with intra-religious domination. Whereas the two Western conceptions of secularism have provided benefits to minority religious groups only incidentally, e.g., Jewish people have benefited in some European countries such as France not because their special needs and demands were met via public recognition but because of a more general restructuring of society guided by an individual-based emancipatory agenda, under the Indian conception some community-specific socio-cultural rights are granted. Common citizenship rights are not seen as incompatible with community-specific rights in limited domains such as education.

Fourth, this model does not erect a wall of separation between religion and state. There are boundaries, of course, but they are porous. This situation allows the state to intervene in religions in order to help or hinder them without the impulse to control or destroy them. This intervention can include granting aid to educational institutions of religious communities on a non-preferential basis and interfering in socio-religious institutions that deny equal dignity and status to members of their own religion or to those of others – for example, the ban on untouchability and the obligation to allow everyone, irrespective of their caste, to enter Hindu temples, as well as, potentially, other actions to correct gender inequalities. In short, Indian secularism interprets separation to mean not strict exclusion or strict neutrality but what I call *principled distance*, which is poles apart from one-sided exclusion or mutual exclusion. When I say that principled distance allows for both engagement with or disengagement from and does so by allowing differential treatment, what kind of treatment do I have in mind? First, religious groups have sought exemptions when states have intervened in religious practices by promulgating laws designed to apply neutrally across society. This demand for non-interference is made on the grounds either that the law requires them to do things not permitted by their religion or that it prevents them from doing things authorized by their religion. For example, Sikhs demand exemptions from mandatory helmet laws and from police dress codes to accommodate religiously required turbans. Muslim women and girls demand that the state not interfere in the religious requirement that they wear the chador. Rightly or wrongly, religiously grounded personal laws may be recognized, and religious persons of different communities be exempted from uniform civil codes. (Elsewhere, Jews and Muslims seek exemptions from Sunday closing laws on the grounds that such closing is not required by their religion.) Principled distance allows a practice that is banned or regulated in the majority culture to be permitted in the minority culture because of the distinctive meaning it has for the minority culture's members. For at least some conceptions of secularism, this variability is a problem because of a simple and somewhat absolutist morality that attributes overwhelming importance to one value – particularly to equal treatment, equal liberty, or equality of individual citizenship. Religious groups may demand that the state refrain from interference in their practices, but they may equally demand that the state interfere in such a way as to give them special assistance so that they are able to secure what other groups are routinely able to acquire by virtue of their social dominance in the political community. The state may grant authority to religious officials to perform legally binding marriages or to have their own rules for or methods of obtaining a divorce. Principled distance allows the possibility of such policies on the grounds that holding people accountable to a law to which they have not consented might be unfair. Furthermore, it does not discourage public justification – that is, justification based on reasons endorsable by all. Indeed, it encourages people to pursue public justification. However, if the attempt to arrive at public justification fails, it enjoins religiously minded citizens to support coercive laws that, although based purely on religious reasons, are consistent with freedom and equality.[27]

Principled distance is not just a recipe for differential treatment in the form of special exemptions. It may even require state intervention and moreover, in some religions more than in others, considering the historical and social condition of all relevant religions. To take first examples of positive engagement, some holidays of each religion, majority and minority alike, are granted national status. Subsidies are provided to schools run by all religious communities. Minority religions are granted a constitutional right to establish and maintain their educational institutions. Limited funding is available to Muslims for *Hajj*. But state engagement can also take a negative interventionist form. For the promotion of a particular value constitutive of secularism, some religion, relative to other religions, may require more interference from the state. For example, suppose that the value to be advanced is social equality. This requires in part undermining caste and gender hierarchies. Thus there is a constitutional ban on untouchability, Hindu temples were thrown open to all, particularly to former untouchables should they choose to enter them. Child marriage was banned among Hindus and a right to divorce was introduced. Likewise, constitutionally it is possible to undertake gender-based reforms in Muslim personal law.

A fifth feature of this model is this: it not entirely averse to the public character of religions. Although the state is not identified with a particular religion or with religion more generally (disconnection at level one), official and, therefore, public recognition is granted to religious communities (at level three). The model admits a distinction between de-publicization and de-politicization, as well as between different kinds of de-politicization. Because it is not hostile to the public presence of religion, it does not aim to de-publicize it. It accepts the importance of one form of de-politicization of religion.

Sixth, this model shows that in responding to religion, we do not have to choose between active hostility and passive indifference or between disrespectful hostility and respectful indifference. We can combine the two, permitting the necessary hostility as long as there is also active respect. The state may intervene to inhibit some practices as long as it shows respect for other practices of the religious community and does so by publicly lending support to them. This is a complex dialectical attitude to religion that I have called critical respect. So on the one hand the state protects all religions, makes them feel equally at home – especially vulnerable religious communities – by granting them community-specific rights. For instance, the right to establish and maintain their own educational institutions and the provision of subsidies to schools run by religious communities. But the state also hits hard at religion-based oppression, exclusion, and discrimination as the constitutional ban on untouchability shows.

Seventh, by not fixing its commitment from the start exclusively to individual or community values and by not marking rigid boundaries between the public and the private, India's constitutional secularism allows decisions on these matters (all matters pertaining to religion at level three) to be made either by contextual reasoning in the courts and sometimes even within the open dynamics of democratic politics. Finally, the commitment to multiple values and principled distance means that the state tries to balance different, ambiguous, but equally important values. This makes its secular ideal more like a contextual, ethically sensitive, politically negotiated arrangement – which it really is – rather than a scientific doctrine conjured by ideologues and merely implemented by political agents.

A somewhat forced, formulaic articulation of constitutional Indian secularism goes something like this. The state must keep a principled distance from all public or private and individual-oriented or community-oriented religious institutions for the sake of the equally significant – and sometimes conflicting – values of peace, worldly goods, dignity, liberty, equality, and fraternity in all of its complicated individualistic and non-individualistic versions.

I hope to have shown that it is inadequate if not mistaken to focus only on currently dominant formulations of Western secularism. To grasp the rich and complicated structure of secularism, it is extremely important to examine the multiple histories of the secular ideal. Modern secularism cannot be understood as growing only in terms of the relationship between the church and the state. The presence in background cultural conditions of other features such as religious diversity (or strife) are equally conducive to the growth of modern secularism. Political secularism today must have a far more complex structure than is available in Western formulations. It must have space for (a) an arena where religion does not matter, (b) another where all religions matter equally and finally (c) where some religious practices matter differently, for the wrong reason, because they adversely affect liberty, equality, and fraternity or communal harmony. The value of the two models of Indian secularism is that they take us in this direction.

15

Memory, Multiculturalism, and the Sources of Democratic Solidarity

MICHELE MOODY-ADAMS

Social Theory, Political Practice, and Democratic Stability

Charles Taylor has produced a remarkably wide-ranging body of work that engages the deepest and most persistent questions of human experience. Whether or not we accept the answers that Taylor provides, we must acknowledge that he has articulated a compelling, richly textured "philosophical anthropology" that greatly enhances and enlarges our understanding of the questions.[1] It is thus a pleasure to join in celebrating his extraordinary contributions to philosophy, intellectual history, and social thought.

Some of Taylor's most important contributions concern the relationship between theory and practice, and he has addressed especially challenging questions about the relationship between social theory (in the broadest sense) and the sometimes-unruly reality of social life. Skeptical critics charge that there are no reliable methods for testing the claims of social theories against the reality they purport to describe and explain, and they ask whether this lack doesn't empty the entire enterprise of social theory of epistemological value. But Taylor rejects the critics' underlying assumption, arguing that the idea that natural science can be a model for argument and inquiry in social theory ignores the "striking disanalogy" between social theories and theories in natural science. On Taylor's view, social theories are about practices that are "partly constituted by ... self-understandings" and that are therefore susceptible of being transformed just by the acceptance of the theories.[2] He acknowledges that "natural science often transforms practice" but insists that "the practice it transforms is not what the theory is about." In science, he contends, practice is "in this sense external to the theory." In social theories, by contrast, "the practice is the object of the theory. Theory in this domain transforms its own object."[3]

It is difficult to overstate the importance of Taylor's account for those of us concerned to defend the methodological vigour and the epistemological "credentials" of moral and political inquiry. His account provides a means of showing that skepticism about the methods and value of social theory misunderstands the relationship between social theory and practice and fails to appreciate how social theory functions as a practice. Taylor acknowledges that social theories can have explanatory and descriptive uses. But he rightly insists that social theories are not primarily "tools" for articulating the "underlying mechanisms" of social practices so as to provide the basis for "more effective" social planning, or for "expert" manipulation of the social environment.[4] Taylor also maintains that what W.V.O. Quine might have called the "empirical foothold" of social theory is not primarily in (allegedly) theory-independent social processes and mechanisms, but principally in the self-understandings of those whose practices the theory seeks to describe or explain. This means that, for Taylor, the "validation" of a social theory has little, if anything, to do with seeking successful predictions about social processes by means of social theories. Instead, and I think rightly, Taylor holds that validating a social theory is about showing that the theory yields "self-definitions" that can withstand sustained and careful scrutiny.[5]

Yet we cannot fully appreciate the value of Taylor's work on social theory and practice if we consider only his contributions to these conceptual disputes. Within the academy as well as outside of it, Taylor's writings have had a profound impact on debates about how to promote stability in multicultural, doctrinally diverse democracies, and about what (if anything) philosophical inquiry and social thought might contribute to this contemporary project. Of course, the problem of political stability is as old as political philosophy itself. Plato's proposal, in *The Republic*, to protect the ideal polis by means of an elaborate myth concerning the "mixture of the metals" in the earthborn, is a reminder of this fact. But contemporary multicultural democracies pose the problem of stability in a new way. In works such as "The Politics of Recognition" (1992), "Nationalism and Modernity" (1997), and "Democratic Exclusion and Its Remedies"

(1999), Taylor has convincingly shown that one of the central questions for contemporary social theory is the fundamentally modern question of how complex democracies – characterized by a profound diversity of doctrines, cultures, and ethnicities – can minimize destructive social conflict and preserve social institutions that promote common purposes. The principal aim of this essay is to explore the merits and the disadvantages of Taylor's claims about how to answer that question.

As with any contemporary discussion of political stability, Taylor's account must be assessed against the background of Rawls's influential treatment of the problem in his *Political Liberalism*. Focusing primarily on doctrinal diversity, and responding in particular to what he called the "fact of reasonable pluralism," Rawls came to think that, in Part III of *A Theory of Justice*, he had wrongly defended an "unrealistic" idea of a "well-ordered society" as one in which citizens endorse fundamental principles of justice on the basis of a "comprehensive philosophical doctrine."[6] According to the more "realistic" account articulated in *Political Liberalism*, the stability of a complex, contemporary democracy depends upon that society's success in achieving an "overlapping consensus" on principles of justice to govern its basic structure.[7] Moreover, only those principles that can be shown to constitute a "political, not metaphysical" conception of justice can be the focus of an overlapping consensus, since a "political conception," as Rawls understood it, draws on central features of democratic political culture without presupposing any particular "comprehensive" doctrine about broader questions of non-political "values and virtues."[8] Rawls thus recast his long-held account of "justice as fairness" as part of a political liberalism that would truly allow philosophy to be both "practical" and "political." He thought that his political liberalism could effectively bridge the gap between social theory and political practice in a doctrinally diverse society because the principles that constitute justice as fairness "might be endorsed ... by all reasonable comprehensive doctrines that exist in a democracy regulated by it."[9] But, perhaps most important, Rawls insisted that a democracy is stable "for the right reasons" only when it is characterized by overlapping consensus on such a conception.[10]

Even sympathetic critics have challenged the political sociology that underwrites Rawls's account.[11] They have also questioned his assumption that democracies are stable in the "right" way only when grounded in agreement on substantive principles of justice.[12] In a compelling critique, Claudia Mills contends that Rawls "overestimates the importance to stability of a shared allegiance to principles," and underestimates "the importance of a shared history of living together."[13] Focusing on overlapping consensus, Mills continues, serves only to focus on "the quality of our endorsement of the rules" when it may actually be more important to focus on "the quality of our shared life together."[14]

Taylor does not explicitly claim to be responding to Rawls's views about the grounds of political stability. But in several relevant writings, Taylor provides compelling reasons to think that many criticisms of Rawls's account have merit. Moreover, Taylor's view differs from Rawls's not just in the fact that Taylor places the challenges of multiculturalism and the "politics of recognition" at the very centre of the contemporary problem of stability.[15] Taylor is also deeply resistant to Rawls's understanding of the role of philosophical reflection in addressing the problem. In a pivotal passage from *Modern Social Imaginaries*, Taylor insists that the basis of political stability is "a question not of philosophy, but of the social imaginary. We need to ask: What is the feature of our 'imagined communities' by which people very often ... accept that they are free under a democratic regime even when their will is overridden on important issues."[16]

I assume that by "philosophy," here, Taylor means to include the Rawlsian project of providing a philosophical account of principles to govern the basic structure of a democratic society, since the passage offers a clear alternative to Rawls's account of the role of such a philosophical account in promoting democratic stability. That alternative involves the claim that what is central to the democratic social imaginary is a "political identity" involving the idea of membership in "an ongoing collective agency" through which each member realizes freedom, whether or not any particular exercise of democratic sovereignty produces an outcome with which every member agrees.[17] Taylor also contends that "whatever is ultimately right philosophically," it is only insofar as people see themselves as sharing membership in a "strong common agency" that democracies can persist over time, and that democratic regimes fail to generate this kind of political identity "at their peril."[18] He maintains, still further, that if widespread identification with a "strong collective agency" is rejected, "the rule of government seems illegitimate in the eyes of the rejecters, as we see in countless cases with disaffected national minorities."[19] His analysis thus confirms Mills's important observation that while concern about the problem of stability most directly raises questions about the motivation to conform to the demands of political institutions (including questions about the source as well as the depth of motivation), it still indirectly raises questions about how we justify institutions.[20] Moreover, like Mills, Taylor suggests that what is most important in addressing the problem of democratic stability is the depth of our motivation to conform, and he offers the notion of the democratic social imaginary as the clue to understanding what underwrites a strong endorsement of democratic institutions.

The Sources of Democratic Solidarity

Taylor's basic understanding of the modern social imaginary builds on Benedict Anderson's view that, like any community larger than a village allowing face-to face-contact, a nation is an "imagined community."[21] Anderson's notion of an imagined community thus informs Taylor's definition of the social imaginary as "that common understanding that makes possible common practices and a widely shared sense of legitimacy." Taylor adds that in the case of the democratic social imaginary, that common understanding involves "accepting a kind of belonging much stronger than that of any chance group that might come together. It is an ongoing collective agency, membership in which realizes ... a kind of freedom."[22]

But for all of its richness, Taylor's account of the political identity that defines the democratic social imagination still seems incomplete. Taylor contends that a democratic people must understand itself as essentially a "collective unit" of decision and deliberation.[23] Yet this way of understanding democratic political identity seems insufficiently attentive to Anderson's observation that even when a nation is composed of a billion people, it is more than just a collective unit of decision and deliberation. Anderson seeks to remind us that even a complex, modern nation is fundamentally a community. As such, even a large, complex democracy always involves a "deep horizontal comradeship" – a "fraternity" – that unites its members regardless of any political and economic inequalities that exist in that community, and regardless of any political oppression that might have involved some members exercising illegitimate power over other members, or simply failing to question the exercise of such power by others. Of course, by the time of *Political Liberalism*, Rawls had come to define a "community" as a group of people "united in affirming one and the same comprehensive doctrine," and he argued that a contemporary democratic society cannot be a community because it would require the oppressive use of state power to make it such.[24] In contrast, Anderson rightly finds evidence of just how strong democratic comradeship – and democratic community – can be, for instance, in the willingness of democratic citizens to sacrifice their lives for their countries. In the same spirit, Taylor has recognized that the strength of democratic comradeship is evident in the willingness of many citizens of democracies to suppress political resentments, even when they "lose out" in the decision-making process on matters of deep and genuine concern to them. Surely, a democratic society in which there is a widespread willingness to display political forbearance must be said to constitute a community.

We thus need a conception of democratic fraternity, and of the political identity bound up with it, that takes seriously the idea that even complex, contemporary democracies persist over time only if they somehow constitute a community. But in virtue of what can a modern democratic society be said to constitute a community? An adequate answer to this question must, first of all, reject the idea (implicit in Rawls's view) that the stability of democracies might be rooted in merely vertical relationships between citizens and the basic institutions that embody their shared principles of justice. That is, if we want to understand the source of, say, a willingness to sacrifice for fellow citizens, or to display forbearance even in the face of political loss, we must appeal to the idea that at least some horizontal relationships between citizens are fundamental to democratic fraternity. But second, although Taylor rightly seeks to define democratic political identity in terms of horizontal relationships between citizens, it seems unlikely that the core elements of democratic fraternity can be captured by Taylor's notion of a common horizontal agency. Taylor has, himself, argued that self-governing societies have a pronounced need for "strong cohesion around a political identity."[25] But I contend that the idea that one is part of a "collective unit" of deliberation and decision is hardly sufficient to provide the kind of cohesion that self-governing societies really need.

The kind of cohesion that is adequate to self-governing societies is a function of two important facts. First, democratic citizenship, like any kind of political membership, is membership in a community of memory that persists through time. As such it will – and indeed must – involve horizontal relationships between citizens that transcend the idea of shared membership in a collective political agency. As Claudia Mills has claimed, democratic citizenship surely involves the appreciation of a shared culture, and of a shared history of living together.[26] But democratic societies make special demands upon their members. In particular, their members must be able to count on their fellow citizens to act in ways that generally preserve that community with minimal reliance on authoritarian or coercive measures. This second feature of democratic life makes it clear that democratic fraternity demands a set of fairly robust civic virtues. Indeed, what constitutes a group of people as a "demos," in a self-governing society, is that they belong to a network of vertical and horizontal relationships that connect citizens to each other by means of a distinctive "civic ethos." This ethos must be shaped not just by the acceptance of a shared history and culture but also, in part, by implicit yet widespread acceptance of certain shared civic virtues, including such virtues as a readiness to display political forbearance and a willingness to make sacrifices both mundane and profound. It is this civic ethos, I contend, around which democratic political identity must cohere.

Of course, as Taylor has cautioned, the challenge of preserving such a cohesive identity means that "democracies are in a standing dilemma." For even though democracies tend towards "inclusion" by virtue of the fact that democracy "is the government of all the people; what makes for exclusion is that it is the government of all the people."[27] Self-governing societies, he observes, have a pronounced need for "strong cohesion around a political identity" and this provides "a strong temptation to exclude those who don't fit easily into the identity which the majority feels comfortable with."[28] Taylor rightly insists on the need to face this dilemma "creatively." Democratic citizens, he contends, must learn to share "identity space," and political identities must be "negotiated" if people want to live together.[29] Still further, the emergence of what Taylor has elsewhere identified as the "politics of recognition" may provide an important counterweight to this tendency towards exclusion.[30] But I will also suggest that the possibility of stability in a complex, multicultural democracy depends on something more: in particular, the willingness of its citizens to balance the need for "cohesion around a political identity" with openness towards a culturally (and doctrinally) rich and varied future. I will show that this is not a utopian demand, since any community – perhaps especially a complex democracy – always has the capacity to submit its current understandings of its history to rational scrutiny, to revise its understandings of its history, and eventually to remake itself in light of that revised understanding.

The effort to understand the civic ethos that allows any society to achieve this balance raises difficult questions. Even a "thin" conception of the horizontal relationships that constitute democratic political identity – like the conception defended by Taylor – cannot be understood in terms of familiar liberal notions of agreement on fair terms of social cooperation. Recall that Taylor stresses the importance, for instance, of the willingness to suppress any resentment that might be generated if we "lose out" in some aspect of the political process. But, surely, what is involved in acting on such a willingness engages a fairly robust democratic virtue.

In the remaining sections of the paper, I want to show in more detail why even though Taylor's notion of the democratic social imagination introduces the idea of horizontal relationships between citizens that connect them to a shared political identity, his conception of that shared identity nonetheless seems insufficient to the task of addressing some central challenges of democratic stability. After all, if I see myself as essentially a member of a collective unit of deliberation and decision, why should I be willing to make even the most mundane sacrifices to preserve institutions and policies that may not express my sincerest hopes and deepest desires for the deliberative outcome? Anderson rightly contends that the willingness to fight and die in combat is the most profound expression of the willingness to make sacrifices in the service of larger, common ends. But more mundane daily sacrifices may, in the long run, be equally important to democratic stability. Thus neither the idea of agreement on principles, nor the idea of cohesion around the idea of identifying with a collective unit of decision and deliberation, is capable of articulating the sources of the democratic solidarity that underwrite even the most mundane sacrifices.

Democratic citizenship involves membership in a stable political community – a community of memory – that protects its citizens against violence and coercion; secures equality of civil, political, and social rights; fosters participation in practices of self-governance; and encourages solidarity by means of a shared but fundamentally "open" national identity.[31] To understand what it means to identify as a member of such a community of memory, we need an account of the habits of mind, modes of action, and patterns of receptiveness toward shared social experiences that make the existence and persistence of such a community possible. What we need, that is, is an account of the virtues that help shape the civic ethos of a stable democracy.

In the rest of this essay, I will discuss three of those democratic civic virtues – three virtues that are in an important sense most fundamental to democratic fraternity. I will show that it is only in and through the preservation of relationships sustained by this civic ethos that a people can collectively constitute a democratic sovereign. I will then offer brief observations about an important subset of civic virtues – a subset of three democratic virtues that we might call the "executive" democratic virtues – that are most closely bound up with the idea of membership in a community of memory.

I will argue, first, that democratic fraternity involves a framework of civic trust that can survive both the inability to predict all the situations in which we need to trust others, and the consequent limits on knowledge about who might be appropriate objects of trust. Second, drawing on Anderson's claims, I will argue that democratic fraternity embodies a readiness to make civic sacrifices in the service of common goals, that must survive the inability to interact directly with most of those who may be called to sacrifice on our behalf, or who will presume our readiness to sacrifice on their behalf. Third, building on Taylor's suggestions about the importance of suppressing political resentment, I will argue that democratic fraternity involves a willingness to extend the civic equivalent of "grace" to people whose interests and commitments may trump ours in democratic decision-making.[32] To be sure, democratic fraternity involves additional civic virtues that I cannot discuss here. It may also depend on what Kurt Baier has called a "constitutional consensus" – that is, an agreement "on the process for adjudication when interests conflict."[33] But these remarks focus on civic trust, civic sacrifice, and civic grace as central components of the political culture that makes democracy possible, and as indispensable elements of the collective self-understanding that promotes political stability.

The Nature and Sources of Civic Trust

Some theorists – particularly those in mainstream liberal political thought – might turn to the idea of agreement on fair terms of cooperation to try to make sense of the idea of civic trust. Moreover, as Annette Baier has noted, in some contexts, contractual agreements may well have a "functional excellence" for any analysis of the grounds of trust. Agreements allow us to make clear what we count on the other to do, what will happen when those expectations are met, and what consequences will follow when they are not.[34] Contractual agreements thus offer the trusting party a remarkable degree of "security," significantly minimizing the risk and vulnerability that typically attend any readiness to trust.[35] But Baier also urges that a great deal of social life involves interactions that are quite unlike situations in which contractual agreements have the potential to minimize risk and vulnerability. Some interactions dramatically limit our ability to form precise expectations, and constrain our capacity to know precisely who is to meet those expectations and when. Baier rightly adds that social life also involves many interactions in which we are connected to others in relationships of "shifting and varying power asymmetry" that increase our vulnerability and enhance the risks of interaction even further.[36] These interactions that are asymmetrical from the point of view of trust seem far less amenable to constructive analysis in terms of the idea of agreement on fair terms of cooperation.

Further, some of these asymmetrical interactions raise problems of social cooperation and solidarity that have profound implications for the stability of complex democracies. Consider the asymmetries in power and knowledge that, in post-9/11 America, affect daily interactions between Muslim Americans (especially if they are observant) and non-Muslim Americans. What transpires as part of the complex networks of trust and trustworthiness at stake in such interactions can have political ramifications that transcend the "local" outcome of any particular interaction. Imagine, for instance, what is at stake when, in a fire emergency, members of a Muslim community in New York City must trust in the professionalism and good will of firefighters still living with the complex psycho-social legacy of the World Trade Center collapse. What makes it likely that, in such situations, some agents will accept their vulnerabilities and take on the risks of trust, and that other agents will meet the demanding expectations of those who trust them? This is essentially a question about what processes and practices can create and sustain civic trust in a complex, doctrinally diverse, and multicultural democracy.

A theorist of "social capital" such as Robert Putnam or Francis Fukuyama might insist that the informal norms that promote the right kind of cooperation will typically arise from participation in voluntary associations and groups.[37] Moreover, it seems reasonable to admit that some of the norms that arise by such processes can sometimes provide the right kind of solution to relevant and important social risks. But, as theorists of multiculturalism have recognized, the kind of comradeship that emerges in at least some small associations and groups can be turned against ethnic, cultural, and national minorities if, and when, they are perceived as outsiders. Thus, in his essay on "Nations and the Cultures of Democracy" Craig Calhoun rightly emphasizes the value of the idea of "we the people" as a means of creating a "collective democratic subjectivity" with the potential to encourage mutual responsibility and trust across internal divisions of ethnicity, class, and region.[38] This is a reminder, in fact, that even if Taylor is right about the "dilemma" that the "dynamic of democracy" often "pushes to exclusion," democratic stability demands a willingness to resist this dynamic at crucial moments.

Moreover, here is where it is crucial to emphasize that being willing to strongly identify with a collective democratic subjectivity usually has to do with being connected to a political society more as a particular community of memory than as a unit of collective deliberation and decision-making. Theorists of multicultural accommodation are therefore right to urge that the reform of education in history is an important vehicle, not only for meeting reasonable demands for minority group recognition, but for broadening the self-understandings of every citizen so as to extend those networks of constructive social interaction and cooperation that are capable of promoting political stability.

Yet formal education in history is not the only means of extending networks of constructive interaction and cooperation. In particular, there are other means of reshaping the way in which democratic citizens think about the communities of memory of which they view themselves to be members. When we participate in debates about the proper focal points for collective memory – perhaps especially, in debates about the meaning and value of public projects of remembrance – we are engaged in debates that respond to emotional and cognitive needs and interests that formal history cannot address. Public projects of remembrance may become embodiments of shared values, objects of collective pride, reminders of shared grief, or promises of hope for a society's future. This is why even at the start of the twenty-first century so many societies continue to create public monuments and memorials, despite the efforts of influential social critics to show that such projects might be obsolete or even anti-democratic.

One means of establishing and affirming a group's place in a community of memory is, in fact, for that group to take an active part in debates about such projects, and political societies must create and protect the conditions in which such debates can be constructively carried out. These debates are not just about the proper understanding of a national past, but also about what a nation can become in a future that embodies the best of its democratic traditions. Such debates both reflect and draw upon the dialogical character of human experience that Taylor has so convincingly described, for instance, in "The Politics of Recognition." Of course, such debates are never easy. A recent controversy in America, surrounding a plan to build an Islamic community centre ("Park 51") a few blocks from the site of the former World Trade Center in lower Manhattan provides important evidence of this fact. But the difficult discussions about that plan effectively foregrounded what was really at stake in charges that the plan was somehow "insensitive" to the losses commemorated at Ground Zero, or that was somehow an "insult" to the victims of 9/11 and their families. What was really at stake was a choice between preserving America's traditions of religious freedom or sacrificing those traditions to the kind of misrepresentation, prejudice, and mistrust that led to the internment of Japanese Americans during the Second World War. If there is to be a repair of the social rifts that emerged in the wake of 9/11, Americans must seriously confront the competing conceptions of collective memory that those events, regrettably, helped to create. The politics of memory is quite different from the politics of equal recognition. The politics of equal recognition is often a politics of difference, while the politics of memory is a politics of solidarity. It asks: "Who are we? What do we stand for? What can we hope for?"

As Gregory Hoskins has argued, this is why the process of collectively working through difficult memories must be recognized as a precondition for "the cross-cultural and transnational empathy" that is essential to stable multicultural democracies.[39] In this context, Taylor has appealed to the value of Gadamer's notion of the "fusion of horizons," a phenomenon through which "what we have formerly taken for granted as the background to valuation" is situated as "one possibility alongside the different background of the formerly unfamiliar culture."[40] But if Hoskins is right, many of the processes that make a fusion of horizons possible are bound up with the requirements we must meet in order to debate difficult memories, and in particular, with the demands such debates make that we suspend our suspicion of the "other" long enough to actually engage in debate. In my view, there is an instructive example of just such a process in the debates that surrounded architect Maya Lin's design for the Vietnam Veterans Memorial (in Washington, DC). These debates, and the memorial they helped to reshape, went a long way toward re-establishing a sense of democratic fraternity in a society that remained deeply divided by doctrinal differences over the justice of the war itself.

The Importance of Civic Sacrifice

Reflecting on the Vietnam Veterans Memorial reminds us that suffering and loss in war are central to projects of public remembrance, and so provides a natural transition to the topic of democracy and civic sacrifice. Anderson rightly emphasizes the "colossal" sacrifices of life and well-being that people have been willing to make on behalf of the nations of which they view themselves as members. But, as I have argued, civic sacrifice is not exhausted by losses in battle. Indeed, a readiness to sacrifice on behalf of others is central to democratic cooperation. For instance, children benefit from public education that is financed, in part, by the taxes of people who may themselves be childless and who may never directly interact with the families who have benefited from their contributions. If citizens of democracies could not count on others to make such sacrifices, much of what is fundamental to democratic cooperation would be impossible.

Yet the sacrifice embodied in death and loss in war is nonetheless an important element of the solidarity that characterizes imagined communities. Think of the role of Pericles's funeral oration in helping revive Athenian solidarity; think of Lincoln's Gettysburg Address as a vehicle for offering a particularly powerful picture of the principles that he believes best expressed the unity and solidarity of the American people. Anderson emphasizes the cultural significance of tombs of unknown soldiers, urging that monuments that are either deliberately empty, or that contain unidentified remains, are "saturated with ghostly national imaginings."[41] But beginning with the First World War – from the memorial to the missing of the Somme in Thiepval with its 72, 337 names, to the Vietnam Memorial in DC with its 58,000 names – national imaginings of sacrifice and loss in war have been increasingly focused on naming the lost whenever possible.[42] Indeed, nearly a century after the dedication of Boston's famous Civil War memorial to Robert Shaw and the Massachusetts 54th regiment, one of the most important debates about collective national memory in

America concerned the reasonableness of adding the recoverable names of African-American soldiers to the base of the memorial statue.

The Massachusetts 54th was the first all-black regiment of the Union army, and it is widely accepted that their sacrifices in a battle for the Confederacy's port in Charleston, South Carolina helped turn the tide in favour of the Union cause.[43] At the 1897 dedication of the memorial to those who died in the battle, William James praised its image of courageous black soldiers fighting alongside courageous white officers as an embodiment of the true meaning of the Civil War, and as an inspiring display of the power of American democratic ideals.[44] Yet for most of the next century, the memorial went through long periods of neglect. This might be traced to the fact that it was dedicated just a year after the 1896 US Supreme Court decision in *Plessy v. Ferguson* that helped give rise to a system of legally sanctioned segregation still being dismantled into the end of the twentieth century. This is why it is so important that in 1980, a group of prominent African-American Bostonians who were aiding in the effort to restore the monument objected to the fact that while the monument bore the names of all the white officers who died in the battle, the monument referred to the fallen black soldiers simply as the "black rank and file." Eventually, in response to their concerns, the recoverable names of sixty-two African-American soldiers were inscribed on the base of the memorial.

Some critics decry the lack of historical accuracy represented by this gesture. But whatever stand we take on that question, this resolution of the controversy that led to the naming of fallen black soldiers inspired new generations of Americans to appreciate the glory and honour in the sacrifices of the Massachusetts 54th, and to acknowledge their importance in shaping the collective national memory. The African Americans who fought to include all the recoverable names thus helped to reshape the democratic social imagination in America, and to strengthen democratic fraternity. Taylor rightly argues that there is an "inner link" between democracy and "strong common agency" that follows "the logic of the legitimacy principle" that underlies democratic regimes.[45] But if we hope to understand the sources of stability in multicultural democracies we must also acknowledge the powerful links between political identity and collective memory, and the importance of the dialogical processes through which various groups have sought to have their sacrifices recognized and honoured.

The Virtue of Civic Grace

But I claimed at the outset that civic sacrifice is not the only evidence of the depth of the fraternity that characterizes stable democracies. So I conclude with a few observations about a notion that I have come to call civic grace (here, adopting from moral philosopher Geoffrey Scarre, an idea that he expressed in the language of "political grace").[46] In my view, it is civic grace that underlies the willingness to relinquish political resentments and bitterness in service of common ideals and goals. Civic grace is different from political forgiveness, which starts from an assumption of blameworthy wrongdoing, and which in practice is thought to require individual, face-to-face interactions between the objects of forgiveness and the wronged party contemplating forgiveness.[47] Civic grace is an extension of civic good will to political opponents one may never meet. It is a willingness to treat them with civility and to assume that most of the disagreements we may have with them do not have to be assumed to be equivalent to disrespect. Further, perhaps more than any other form of political organization, democracies depend upon the widespread possession of civic grace. This is why the steep decline in civic grace in America in the late twentieth and early twenty-first centuries, along with the associated rise in the politics of resentment, poses a profound challenge to the stability of contemporary American democracy.

Yet civic grace emerges at unexpected moments, as it recently did in American debates about health insurance and access to contraception. In the spring of 2012, responding to vitriolic attacks on a Georgetown University law student who took a public stand in that debate, Georgetown President John DeGioia insisted that whether or not Americans agreed with the student's stance they must recognize that she was acting "in the tradition of the deepest values" that Americans share "as a people."[48] He went on to enlist his religious commitments in support of this defense of those values. Citing St Augustine's disdain for arrogance in debate, he argued that protecting space for constructive civil discourse is a way for Americans to respect a "sacred trust" handed down across the generations. But his stance was clearly an expression of civic grace. It was civic grace that allowed him to serve as a moral exemplar, even for those who do not share his faith, by framing a vexing controversy in terms of shared commitment to an important element of America's collective national memory.

Of course, even civic grace cannot suppress the underlying disagreements about the moral dimensions of sexuality, the nature of the family, and the role of women in society that underlie the debate about contraception. Those disagreements reflect the familiar forms of deep diversity that democratic fraternity must acknowledge and respect, even as it affirms social solidarity. Taylor's notion of the modern social imaginary has greatly enriched our understanding of how it might be possible to strike this balance between solidarity and disagreement. But a defensible conception of the democratic social imagination must reflect the important truth that democracies can constructively combine respect for diversity with social solidarity only when the virtues of civic trust, civic sacrifice, and civic grace connect us to complex, constantly evolving communities of memory.

PART SEVEN

Canadian Politics

16

Recognition in Its Place

JEREMY WEBBER

Introduction

Charles Taylor is the most incisive theorist of cultural difference of our time. His 1992 essay "The Politics of Recognition" has been especially influential, so that there is hardly a debate over cultural accommodation that does not take that essay as its starting point.[1] Largely as a result of that essay, recognition has become the master concept through which these issues are considered.

That is a pity. Charles Taylor *is* the most incisive theorist of cultural difference, but not because of recognition. His most important contributions lie in his conception of humanity as self-interpreting animals, his ruminations on the role of language, his invocation of language as an analogy to other forms of cultural difference, and his exploration of the conditions of dialogue across cultures. His most important publication on cultural difference is not "The Politics of Recognition" but the two volumes of *Philosophical Papers*.[2] It is those ideas that lie at the foundation of all the amazing books and papers that have followed. In this chapter, I make the case for the primacy of those hermeneutical contributions, and attempt to put the work on recognition in its place.

This chapter corrects a frequent misinterpretation of "The Politics of Recognition." That essay is generally invoked in a manner independent of its hermeneutical foundations, as though recognition were itself the fundamental concept, entirely self-sufficient, through which cultural conflicts should be understood. Taylor's arguments are assimilated to those of Axel Honneth,[3] perhaps without Honneth's insistent Hegelian overlay, but with recognition nevertheless serving as the master concept. I argue that this is a mistake – it is a mistaken interpretation of Taylor's own arguments and, if we seize upon that interpretation, it disables us from addressing the central issues regarding cultural difference. If we want to address those issues – if we want to understand how language and culture should shape political structure – we should attend to the hermeneutical foundations of Taylor's arguments.

In this chapter, I first note the problems that result from using recognition as a master concept. I then explore the resources that exist within Taylor's hermeneutical theory for understanding cultural difference, communication across cultures, and the structuring of political community. I return to recognition at the end, suggesting its appropriate role.

Recognition as a Master Concept

Recognition is used in at least two ways in the literature. First, it is used as a catch-all term for any situation in which differential rules or institutions are created in order to take account of some form of cultural diversity (Recognition One). Thus one speaks of the recognition of a minority language through the creation of schools in that language, or the recognition of an Indigenous right to self-government. In this first sense, "recognition" can cover a wide range of institutional, political, and economic measures justified on an equally wide range of grounds. It has little justificatory content of its own. It captures the conclusion of a normative argument, not its rationale.

I fully accept recognition in this sense. My criticisms bear instead upon a second conception of recognition, a narrower conception, in which recognition refers specifically to acts of symbolic affirmation in which parties attribute value to other cultures, affirming important facets of their identities (Recognition Two). On this view, people are entitled to have their identities affirmed so that their sense of self-respect is reinforced, not undermined. The focus in Recognition Two is therefore on the effect of statements or actions on the recipient's *amour propre* – the image that the person holds of themselves, the recipient's "relation to self." It is the search for appropriate self-regard that drives the process of accommodation. It is in this second sense that Honneth certainly, and to some extent Taylor in "The Politics of Recognition," uses the term. Indeed, for Honneth, the striving for recognition drives the entire development of our conceptions of justice, in good Hegelian fashion.

There is no doubt that Recognition Two plays a prominent role in some cases of cultural interaction. This is true, for example, when disputes occur over national symbols or parties seek apologies for past injustices.[4] It can also colour disputes over other matters. Taylor wrote "The Politics of Recognition" in the immediate aftermath of the failure of the Meech Lake Accord, a set of constitutional amendments designed to reconcile Quebec to the Canadian constitution. A prominent element of that package was the "distinct society clause," which would have recognized that Quebec constitutes, within Canada, a distinct society. That clause would have had a material effect: the courts were instructed to take Quebec's distinct society into account when interpreting the constitution. But there is no doubt that it was also intended to operate on the symbolic plane, affirming Quebec's uniqueness.[5]

It is wrong, however, to assume that proper self-regard is the primary objective in all cultural conflicts – as, for example, Honneth appears to do. Often the interests at issue are much more tangible. A linguistic minority seeks to have access to government services in its own language, to secure minority-language education, or to use its language in debates within the legislature. A religious minority wants to slaughter meat in the manner stipulated in its texts. Members of an Indigenous people want to govern themselves according to their own norms, through their own institutions, on their own lands. It is wrong and indeed patronizing to treat these demands as though they were simply a minority craving the positive affirmation of the majority. The groups concerned care deeply about the specific measures they are advocating. They would prefer to obtain those measures from a bored and uncomprehending majority than to have generous expressions of respect but no schools, no religious accommodation, and no control over their lands.[6] Minorities do sometimes feel as though their self-esteem is under assault, but that is often a secondary, not a primary, phenomenon: they feel disregarded precisely because their languages are excluded or their religious practices overridden. The first problem with using Recognition Two as a master concept, then, is that it ignores the substance of the minorities' claims, purporting to translate all those claims into one fungible property: a concern with the regard in which one is held by the other party. Recognition Two is relentlessly psychologizing, neglecting the very real demands that cultural minorities make.

Indeed, even symbolic claims often serve ends that cannot be reduced to the reinforcement of individuals' self-image. They enshrine principles that are intended to shape the parties' concrete interactions into the future. That, for example, was the purpose of Quebec's distinct society clause. It was to serve as an acknowledgment that Quebec had a unique cultural role within the Canadian federation, so that that role would be accepted and not undermined in Canada's constitutional law and politics.[7]

Moreover, by treating every conflict as though it were driven by a longing for psychic affirmation, Recognition Two renders their resolution much more difficult. It shifts attention away from the specific measures sought by each group and instead engages in a social alchemy of comparative affirmation and respect.[8] But how, then, does one achieve due respect? How does one recognize one group, or group within a group, or group within that second group, without creating a hierarchy among them – certainly without creating a hierarchy between groups that have already obtained recognition and those that have yet to obtain it? The problem is especially acute precisely because there is always room to contest the definition of what constitutes a group. This was evident when there was a strong possibility that Quebec might secede from Canada. Was the relevant community that was entitled to determine its own future made up of all residents of the province of Quebec? Were Indigenous peoples entitled to secede from a seceding Quebec?[9] Should the boundaries of Quebec be redrawn so that Anglophone-majority areas could remain within Canada? Secession poses such problems of group definition in an especially stark manner, but the linked issues of group definition and parity of treatment arise every time there is a claim to the accommodation of cultural difference. By ignoring the substantive basis of the claims, those relying on Recognition Two disable themselves from offering convincing answers to these questions. Taylor adverts to this problem when he notes the tension between the politics of equal recognition and a politics of recognizing difference.[10]

As long as one's theory of recognition speaks only of achieving self-respect, one's theory will lack sufficient resources to determine what groups should be recognized in what ways. One sees the outcome in Seyla Benhabib's work. She accepts Taylor's view that identity is determined dialogically. She believes that one must acknowledge the role of social interaction in shaping the individual. But, as she rightly notes, individuals participate in an infinite array of dialogical contexts: in families, in linguistic communities, in the workplace, in religious institutions, with people of their own gender, with people of their own ethnicity – indeed ethnicity itself can be defined in a substantial variety of ways drawing on different aspects of one's ancestry or customs. She can see no stable way of distinguishing among the different assertions of identity because each person navigates among the identities in their own way. She therefore appears to conclude that none of these characteristics should form the subject of state recognition.[11] But of course, for a member of a minority language community, even one as populous as the more than seven million Canadians whose mother tongue is French, such a non-conclusion would have a devastating impact on their ability to use their language in political deliberation or interactions with government. The use of their language would be undermined by the inability of the theorist to distinguish between rival identity claims.

There are defensible grounds for distinguishing among groups for the purposes of cultural accommodation. As we will see below, Taylor furnishes tools that help to determine just such grounds; indeed he relies upon them in the relevant passages of "The Politics of Recognition." But those tools extend well beyond the psychological need to have one's identity affirmed. The second problem with using Recognition Two as a master concept is therefore that recognition alone, conceived only in terms of due self-respect, provides insufficient resources to resolve the challenges of cultural accommodation.

This problem is closely related to a third shortcoming. Much of the discussion of recognition falls into an error that Taylor himself decries: it asserts that groups have a right to recognition on the basis of equality. But, as Taylor argues, how can an obligatory recognition amount to a true affirmation of worth?[12] To be anything more than patronizing, it has to involve a substantive judgment, and to have a genuine substantive judgment, it must be possible for that judgment to fail – for the object of recognition to be found wanting. An obligatory recognition, automatically given, is no recognition at all.

Moreover, an obligatory recognition is false to the manner in which a group cleaves to its culture or, in the case of a religious group, to its beliefs. It holds to that culture or those beliefs precisely because it takes them to have real value, to have some claim on truth. An automatic recognition shuts down those truth-claims, treating everything (or nothing) as true.

The third problem with using Recognition Two as a master concept is that, in abstracting from the substantive claims made on behalf of cultures or religions, it has little choice but to treat all claims to recognition as being of equal value, and that approach is false to the basis on which recognition is sought.

A fourth problem with Recognition Two is the extent to which it shifts away from the agency of the claimant group and focuses relentlessly on the agency of the group doing the recognizing. Some Indigenous scholars in Canada have turned against recognition for precisely this reason, preferring the language of resurgence, which emphasizes the agency, the self-determination, of Indigenous peoples.[13] Now, I accept that issues of cultural accommodation are dialogical. Those doing the recognizing inevitably participate in shaping the outcome. A party's agency, its self-determination, is never self-sufficient, but constitutes a contribution to what is inescapably a dialogical relationship in which each party plays a role. Recognition Two, however, is especially poor at taking account of the contributions of the party being recognized. Again, this is because it abstracts from the claimant's actual demands and focuses on the simple conferral of respect, as though the claimant's aspirations were, fundamentally, all about the recognizer. There is little incentive in Recognition Two to listen to a claimant party and engage in depth with its specific claims.[14] What is more, resurgence and response, as opposed to recognition, allow for a broader range of conceivable outcomes, including ones in which there is no perfect agreement between demand and response, no single comprehensive principle by which recognition is conferred. They can comprehend forms of tension and agonistic co-existence that may be truer to our most productive interactions in diverse societies.[15]

Finally, a fifth and related problem is Recognition Two's neglect for relations of power.[16] Entrenched conflicts are treated as though they can be resolved by a simple conferral of respect. Now, the relationship of questions of power to arguments of justice is complex. I address those questions partially elsewhere.[17] My focus here is primarily on the justice side of the equation, specifically how we should understand the relevance of culture to normative argument. But the high abstraction of Recognition Two is especially impervious to questions of power.

The common element in each of these problems is Recognition Two's failure to attend to the substantive foundation of all claims to recognition.

If analysts abstract from that foundation and presume that claimants are simply out to soothe their *amour propre*, they are unable to understand why people might be committed to the preservation of their culture or language, nor are they able to offer any guidance in the resolution of conflicting claims. It is true that an entrenched, forcible denial of due regard does often play a role. Taylor rightly invokes the writings of Frantz Fanon to this effect.[18] Moreover, there may be circumstances in which contending parties fall into an argument for relative precedence – where they too lose sight of the substantive dimensions of their claims. There were times during Canada's constitutional ructions when this seemed to occur, as parties argued over whether a "hierarchy of rights" had been created.[19] But that is the pathology of recognition, not a model for how demands for cultural accommodation ought to be assessed. Real respect can be achieved only by grappling with the substantive claims of the group – with its claims of value, its arguments for change. And to evaluate those claims one requires a richer theory than recognition alone provides.

Hermeneutical Foundations

Charles Taylor has long advanced such a theory. It is evident, though not central, in "The Politics of Recognition" itself. In that essay Taylor is especially concerned with conflicts in which parties argue for express acknowledgment of their identities, seeking to achieve the affirmation of those identities' value. He explores situations in which groups feel undervalued or disregarded ("misrecognized" in Taylor's formulation). At a couple of points he assimilates nationalism to this kind of misrecognition – too simply it seems to me: Taylor, drawing on Herder, has been attracted to an expressivist conception of identity insufficiently mediated by intersubjective deliberation, which can result in an accentuated focus upon the conferral of status.[20] But there is much more than the affirmation of one's self-esteem going on in the essay. For one thing, he specifically denies that one can have a right to respect for one's culture precisely because the affirmation of one's identity, to be effective at all, must involve a genuine attribution of value, not one that is pro forma.[21] Second, a number of his central examples have to do with the substantive claims of parties, not with any desire on their part to reinforce their self-regard. For example, the penultimate section of his essay is entirely concerned with French-speaking

Quebeckers' commitment to *survivance* – their desire to maintain their language and culture into the future.[22] Recognition, in the sense of the affirmation of worth, plays no part in the argument.

But the most telling departure from simplistic theories of recognition occurs in the first section of the essay when Taylor is setting up his argument. He notes that "we become full human agents, capable of understanding ourselves, and hence of defining ourselves," in dialogical relation with others. This relation is not conceived, in the first instance, as a means of bolstering our self-esteem. Our relationships with others enable us to acquire "rich human languages of expression," through which we can define and develop our identities.[23] It is the struggle for meaning, for self-understanding, that is most important, and that struggle is conceived in relational terms precisely because we draw upon the realm of interaction, upon goods that are created and maintained intersubjectively – specifically upon language – in order to understand ourselves and our world.[24]

Even when Taylor turns to our relations with significant others, he does not conceive of those relationships simply with reference to their consolidation of our *amour propre*. Instead, they are conceived in discursive terms, embodying a conversation through which we define ourselves: "We define our identity always in dialogue with, sometimes in struggle against, the things our significant others want to see in us. Even after we outgrow some of these others ... and they disappear from our lives, the conversation with them continues within us as long as we live."[25] Note that on this view identity is dynamic. It is not conceived as a pre-existing datum that is either recognized or misrecognized. It is continually being developed through a process in which the critical comments of others, and our own self-criticism, play important and productive roles. Taylor is here describing a much more robust process than mere affirmation and disaffirmation. Doubtless part of this relation is how we are defined by others and how those definitions correspond to the definitions we assert ourselves. But that process involves a material engagement with others' projections, not simply their repulsion or correction. Moreover, the very process of definition occurs within a sphere of language and conversation that is not reducible to affirmation and disaffirmation or projection and repulsion.[26] Thus we come to the hermeneutical foundations for Taylor's conception of intercultural interaction.

All of Taylor's theorizing, across all subjects, proceeds from the perception that human beings are quintessentially self-interpreting animals, always trying to understand themselves and their world, always striving for meaning.[27] Self-interpretation operates not just at the individual level but also at the level of our communities, as we seek to define what our community stands for – what should be maintained and deepened, what jettisoned. This yearning for meaning, this fashioning of narratives and counter-narratives of who we are and what we might become, and our attempts to realize those images in daily life, are essential dimensions of our action in the world. They are aspects of our individual and social lives that Taylor takes to be foundational, in "The Politics of Recognition" as in his other works.

This process of self-interpretation is conceived in dialogical terms, as the quotations from Taylor above make clear. He emphasizes two fundamental aspects. He notes, of course, the particular exchanges we have with others: the conversations, the criticisms, the "things our significant others want to see in us." Those are immensely important. But he also draws our attention continually to the medium through which dialogue takes place. Our self-understanding and our aspirations are always expressed through a particular language.[28] We use its terms and conceptual structure, formulating our self-understandings in its categories. We conduct our deliberations in a particular language, and over time we accumulate a history of those deliberations – a distinctive set of questions, a catalogue of past answers, memories of past controversies, a history of argumentative interventions – upon which we rely when formulating our positions today. We employ literary and other creations that are expressed within language. And because language serves as the medium for understanding, the accounts within one language differ in significant ways from those in other languages. Those differences are always relative, never absolute, given the commonalities that exist within the range of human experience, the possibilities of apprenticeship into other people's modes of life, and the opportunity for translation among different expressions of the human condition. But the autonomy among languages, though relative, is nevertheless real. It is sustained by the ease of communicating within one language and the difficulty of mastering another.

Indeed, the significance of language is not merely a function of linguistic diversity. Even if there were only one language in the world, its particular character would nevertheless shape our understandings. The salience of language is a result of the fact that we never grasp the world directly, immediately, and completely, but always partially, from a particular perspective, and we then express our understandings through a medium that is itself the product of a particular time and place.

Our languages matter deeply to us. They provide the terms in which we have framed our understandings and aspirations; they carry our most cherished insights. Our particular languages are the media we have mastered; within them, we can say most effectively what we think and can exercise our greatest powers of teaching and persuasion.[29] There is a real benefit to us being able to continue to use them in our communications with our children and grandchildren, in our political deliberations, and so on. There is a corresponding disadvantage if we are forced to work within someone else's terms – if, for example, the languages that make sense to us, the accumulation of insight and reflection through which we have shaped our views, have no currency in the political institutions to which we are subject.

This analysis provides a powerful justification for linguistically-based political autonomy – Taylor's justification for a federal political structure based on language, which is reflected in his discussion of *survivance* in "The Politics of Recognition." Note that this justification has nothing to do with a craving for self-respect – or at least, if respect is in issue it is a function of more substantial interests: the capacity to participate, as full citizens, in political life, as well as the value of having examples and concepts that are intelligible within one's language reflected in the norms by which one is governed.

For Taylor, this linguistically based autonomy need not be absolute. Indeed, he has been a strong advocate for both Quebec's autonomy and a bilingual Canada, perceiving that that combination provides the best fit between Canadians' complex interrelationships and their constitutional structure.[30] This solution points toward another aspect of his invocation of language: language is significant not simply for our ability to understand and accommodate what we generally think of as languages (French, English, Nisga'a, Inuktitut, and so on), but also as a model for other forms of cultural difference: political identities that persist even though they share a language with other polities (England, the United States, Australia, an Indigenous people that now uses English); political identities that exist across different languages (Canada, Switzerland, South Africa, India – or, at a supranational level, Europe); cultural identities that exist at one remove from the aspiration to nationhood (Chinese-Canadian, African-American, regional identities within countries); even religious identities.

All these identities can be understood – perhaps not completely, but at least in significant measure – as being defined by the particular discursive resources they bring to bear on the human condition.[31] They too have their distinctive histories of interaction, their own questions, their own stock of answers, their own literatures, their reference points grounded in their particular histories. The justification for their accommodation is similar to that for languages in the ordinary sense: they furnish the terms through which people understand their participation in the world; the continued capacity to draw upon these languages matters deeply to their adherents. The forms of accommodation may differ substantially among the various identities, not least because the social role of the identities and their ad- herents' aspirations for them often differ greatly. Chinese Canadians, for example, do not seek an autonomous Chinese-speaking polity. On the con- trary, they seek greater inclusion within the Canadian political order. Ac- ceptance of their cultural practices, attention to their distinctive histories and literatures, and a valuing of their ancestral languages are seen by them as indices of their acceptance within Canadian society. It does not make sense to institute, then, identical institutional accommodations for Chi- nese Canadians and for Quebec. Moreover, individuals participate in more than one of these discursive spheres simultaneously: a Chinese Canadian may also be a French-speaking Quebecker, a Canadian, a Roman-Catholic Christian, and so on. Institutional accommodations must therefore aim for some reasonable approximation to the role those languages play within social interaction. The nature of that framework must inevitably be a matter of judgment, adapted to context and responsive to the need to address past inequalities. But the essential point is that Taylor's attention to the intersubjective "languages" within which we understand the world provide us with much better criteria for developing those institutions than does Recognition Two, with its focus on self-respect alone.

This may all seem very complicated. Why shouldn't we just establish a single framework of individual rights and let each individual determine their own identity? Taylor provides the answer to that question as well. It is an illusion to think that we can achieve a framework that is neutral among all identities.[32] All frameworks embody cultural characteristics. All, for example, operate in a determinate language or languages. Those cultural characteristics systematically discourage others. If schools only operate in English, if government services only exist in English, if political participation depends on one mastering English, if the vast majority of the voters in a political community speak only English, then other languages, other literatures, and the forms of life that they interpret and support – French-Canadian, Anishinabek, Nisga'a, or Inuit – will be placed under heavy pressure. Our ability to define our identities is in part a function of the social contexts in which we operate. Those contexts are always imprinted with a cultural character. If we truly care about human freedom, our only option is to incorporate culture into our analysis. Moreover, Taylor's perception that cultures are best understood by analogy to languages allows us to avoid the mistake of identifying cultures with a highly determinate set of commitments and beliefs. Like languages, the resources of cultures can be used to express a wide variety of commitments, to argue over them, to criticize and change them. It is entirely possible both to cherish our culture and to be committed to debate and reform.[33]

As noted above, Taylor not only argues for Quebec's political autonomy based on its cultural distinctiveness. He also argues for the viability of a Canada that crosses cultural boundaries. His theory contains indispensable resources for sustaining such a polity.

Now, one might think that the foundational skill for working across languages would be translation, but Taylor's position is best understood if one begins with the challenge of learning a second language.[34] For Taylor, the foundational skill is the ethnographer's feat of entering into another linguistic community, living within it, and coming to grasp over time how that community's language relates to the broad array of social practices, articulate and inarticulate, existing there. It is only by inhabiting a community's form of life that one begins to grasp its language with any richness – the language's range of uses, its connotations, its resonances, its implications, and the paths it suggests for further development. Indeed, the challenge of mastering a language is never-ending, even for native speakers, precisely because speakers are always striving for better articulation, stretching the language's resources to formulate new understandings.[35] The theoretical literature sometimes treats hermeneutics as though it interprets a world that is entirely made up of linguistic expressions (texts, concepts, ideas expressed in spoken and written languages); it treats hermeneutics, in other words, as though its domain was a self-enclosed world of articulate intellect. Taylor has a much broader conception – much closer to Wittgenstein's understanding – that languages are always embedded within and understandable only in relation to the forms of life of which they are a part.[36]

This conception opens up a broader array of phenomena to the significance of culture. Culture is not a veneer placed over a functionally determined world of power, resources, and production. Cultural understandings are woven into all social practices. Taylor therefore embraces a more expansive conception of culture's relevance than many analysts employ. This in turn has important consequences for cultural accommodation. Cultural difference applies not merely to culture in some narrow sense but to a broad array of social phenomena.[37] Hence Taylor's acceptance that French-speaking Quebeckers have a legitimate interest in the Quebec government controlling dimensions of the province's economic life.[38]

Of course, more than learning a second language is required if one is to sustain a multilingual polity. One also needs some way of bridging linguistic groups, so that each can speak to the other. Taylor suggests how we should understand intercultural communication, illuminating both its possibilities and its difficulties. He says that we should strive for a "language of perspicuous contrast" – not our language, not their language, but new terms "in which we could formulate both their way of life and ours as alternative possibilities in relation to some human constants at work in both ... in which the possible human variations would be so formulated that both our form of life and theirs could be perspicuously described as alternative such variations." Ideally, this would result in a transformation of our terms of self-understanding, not just a perspicuous understanding of the other's.[39] Such a result is conceivable because the forms of life that we inhabit extend beyond linguistic expressions, so that there are overlapping or analogous dimensions of experience upon which we can build. This overlapping lifeworld can serve as the sounding-board for our attempts at mutual understanding.[40]

Gadamer's notion of a "fusion of horizons" (to which Taylor's language of perspicuous contrast is closely related)[41] has been criticized as presuming too much commonality, too much confidence that one can understand another's worldview.[42] But I do not think that Taylor falls into that trap. He and Gadamer are providing pictures of what perfect understanding would look like – pictures of the goal toward which we should strive. Those pictures are compatible with the realization that we can never quite get there. The best we can achieve are better approximations. Other persons always contain a vast reservoir of unknown possibilities.[43]

One great merit of this vision of cross-cultural communication is that it helps us to see what is involved in any attempt to sustain that communication, making clear the effort required to achieve some reasonable understanding. Linguistic differences can be surmounted, but to do so requires commitment and, even then, one's mastery of a new language will be imperfect, always susceptible of further growth. We should strive for cross-cultural communication, but we should never fool ourselves that cultures have been transcended. We need to accommodate the persistence of difference.

The Place of Recognition

The interpretation of cultures set out above is Taylor's great contribution to our understanding of cultural diversity. Where does recognition fit in? Taylor certainly provides an argument for Recognition One. Indeed, he does more. He provides a general account of why cultural difference ought to be taken into account in any significantly diverse society – why accommodation is compatible with a viable theory of justice. Indeed, it will be an essential component of justice if we take four things seriously: 1) the importance to human flourishing of being able to draw upon one's own culture – the culture one has mastered, and in which one has formulated one's deepest commitments; 2) the intersubjective nature – one might even say the ecological nature – of cultures, so that the ability to draw upon our culture does not depend simply on our own efforts but upon the institutional milieux in which we live; 3) the fact that those milieux always have a cultural character; there is no such thing as a neutral milieu; and 4) the fact that different cultures are therefore under differential pressure, and not simply because of the strength or weakness of their members' attachment to the cultures.[44] Taylor therefore provides a cogent rationale for why principles of justice ought, in appropriate circumstances, to be adjusted to cultural difference.

The idea that we have to recognize and accommodate cultural difference is, I suspect, what most political and legal theorists take to be the essence of recognition. In this guise – Recognition One – recognition does not provide a reason to accommodate cultural difference but rather a conclusion: the conclusion that theories of justice ought to take cultural difference into account. Recognition Two's emphasis on the reinforcement of self-esteem as the unique master concept for the analysis of cultural accommodation is, it seems to me, an overdetermined gloss on that essential insight, one that, by focusing on the effect of non-recognition on the individual psyche, reduces cultural accommodation to the purely individualistic focus that many theorists of justice find congenial. Taylor provides a much richer, more complete, and more challenging account of the relevance of cultural difference to theories of justice. Taylor does still more, however. In his exploration of the hermeneutics of social interaction and through his analogy to language, he provides us with tools for analyzing the dynamics of the intersubjective realm of culture. This helps us to see the topography of cultural difference as it relates to normative argument. In doing so, Taylor provides resources for judging how forms of accommodation might be matched to different forms of difference. Recognition Two is unable to do that.

What, then, is Recognition Two's place within his normative theory? One possible answer is that it plays no normative role – that he acknowledges Recognition Two's empirical force in arguments about cultural difference (which he certainly does), but he believes it is relevant only to the pragmatics of cultural conflict, not to the normative reasons for cultural accommodation. There is some ambivalence in Taylor's discussion of Recognition Two, in which he hedges his bets on its normative import.[45] Nevertheless, in the end he does allow that Recognition Two has normative force. The pride of place he gives it in "The Politics of Recognition" suggests that force, and some of Taylor's invocations of Recognition Two clearly go beyond concessions to practical necessity.[46] Moreover, Taylor is attracted to expressivist conceptions of identity more than I would like him to be, and Recognition Two harmonizes closely with those conceptions. Most importantly, Taylor's hermeneutical approach to questions of justice is, in substantial measure, premised on taking human beings as we find them. Thus, the simple fact that people are silenced by persistent disregard does count (rightly) as a normative reason for him. In these last paragraphs, I suggest how we should understand the place of Recognition Two in relation to the central contribution of Taylor described above. On this view, Recognition Two is not free-standing, but occupies a landscape already mapped by Taylor's hermeneutic theory.

One dimension of Recognition Two that is present in Taylor is the recognition that cultures have intrinsic value. This is true in the general Gadamerian sense that the concepts we have inherited, our foreknowledge, our "fore-meanings and prejudices" in Gadamerian terms, are essential to our intellectual engagement with the world. They don't confine that engagement, but they do furnish the indispensable starting-points to understanding.[47] Moreover, for closely related reasons, Taylor values specific cultures, specific traditions of reflection and inquiry, as providing invaluable tools for understanding humanity in its engagement with the world. These reasons for valuing cultures remain at some distance from Recognition Two, however, for they are compatible with an approach that discriminates between cultures, attaching high value to some and no value to others.[48] These reasons lack the peremptory quality that one associates with Recognition Two, where cultures deserve recognition simply as a way of conveying proper respect to the people that hold them.

There is, however, an element of peremptory appreciation in Taylor, one that is grounded in his hermeneutical premises. It is best expressed as a presumption of value, where that presumption is subject to being tested, proven, and the value of the culture fully assessed as one's engagement with the culture proceeds.[49] As we have seen, in Taylor cultures are embedded in particular forms of life and developed through time, driven by individuals' striving for more adequate means of understanding. They carry, then, unique resources for understanding the world, forged in the distinctive experience and language of the people concerned. Given that our intellectual resources are always limited, shaped and tempered within our own culture's practices and history, there is good reason to presume that those working within other cultures will carry insights that we ourselves lack, so that we can always gain by encounter with another's culture. This gain is inherent in the image of the fusion of horizons. It provides powerful reasons for respecting others' cultures even before we know anything about them.[50] Thus, it has the peremptory quality of Recognition Two, albeit a quality that is only vindicated as we engage with the culture.

In principle, the presumption is rebuttable, but even so it is stronger than might at first appear. Cultures are complex things, containing multiple strands, debates, constellations of concepts and practices. Even if aspects of a culture strike us as repugnant, it will be rare that those aspects are so all-encompassing that the culture as a whole should be dismissed out of hand. Moreover, the engagement and apprenticeship necessary to understand a culture mean that our confidence that we have succeeded must often be qualified. Furthermore, the ways in which we can learn from other cultures, which can range from an encounter with features that we want to adopt, through various forms of learning by analogy or adaptation to simply learning by contrast, so that the encounter throws elements of our own tradition into relief, are highly various. Consequently, a comprehensive rejection of another culture is likely to reveal more about our own complacency, parochialism, and lack of rigour than about the merits of the culture concerned.[51]

Nevertheless, this presumptive recognition, while peremptory in a manner similar to Recognition Two, is not based on any concern for the self-regard of the members of the culture. What, then, about self-regard as a driver of recognition? It is true, as Taylor fully acknowledges, that constant denigration of one's culture can undermine one's self-respect. That undermining can in turn impede one's ability to participate in society. Lack of respect, then, can inflict serious damage.[52] The provision of due respect is therefore an element of justice.

But isn't that lack of respect wrong precisely because it is a lack of *due* respect? I suggest that one needs something like the presumption I have just sketched in order to find misrecognition wrong. Otherwise, isn't the much-vaunted recognition truly empty, and doesn't the insistence upon it prevent any serious engagement with another's assertions? Misrecognition is wrong because it fails to account for the substantive value of particular cultures, given a strong presumption of their value, not simply because it undermines people's self-respect. The argument for fostering self-respect is therefore secondary to and derivative from the argument for the value of cultures. And indeed this is how Taylor uses it. In each of his arguments, his assertion of the value of self-respect is nestled within and proceeds from a foundational argument for the importance of cultures.[53] If one drops the latter and focuses only on the value of self-respect, one falls into a condescending pseudo-recognition, which the people who are the objects of recognition will be the first to perceive. Even Recognition Two, then, properly conceived, is founded upon an appreciation of the substantive value of cultures.

Conclusion

Taylor is, then, the most incisive theorist of cultural difference of our time. Much of that contribution is lost, however, if one focuses only upon recognition's role in reinforcing the relation to self of those being recognized. Taylor himself does not do so. Instead he provides us with a rich set of tools for understanding the value of cultures both to their members and to the world at large. In doing so, he not only advances compelling reasons for incorporating cultural diversity into our theories of justice. He also furnishes us with conceptual tools for charting the normative landscape of our culturally diverse societies.

CONCLUSION

A Conversation between Charles Taylor, Jacob T. Levy, Daniel M. Weinstock, and Jocelyn Maclure

McGILL UNIVERSITY, 25 SEPTEMBER 2018

LEVY: The philosophy of social science, and problems and explanations of social and political behaviour, preoccupied you for a long time much earlier in your career. But this hasn't been a direct theme in your more recent work, arising mainly as an implied contrast with your own approach to the study of language and to a lesser degree religion. What do you think about the directions, of economics and empirical political science, your primary targets back then, have taken in recent decades? How do you draw on or think about the social sciences now? Have some parts of the social sciences developed in ways that respond to critiques you offered back then? Is there anything in those critiques that you've reconsidered?

TAYLOR: I think that there are very interesting new ideas that are appearing in various social sciences. And very interesting bad ideas also reappearing in the social sciences. There is a kind of conservation law of reductionism which I've been old enough to observe. For instance, psychology was dominated very powerfully by behaviourism; I wrote my thesis against behaviourism and I published the book[1] and it disappeared. But then Chomsky published his review[2] of Skinner's "Verbal Behaviour."[3] What happened was that Chomsky, or people following Chomsky, offered their computational model of the mind, which allowed reductionists to desert this sinking behaviouralist ship and move over there. And that's what one is constantly seeing. There are big reasons in our culture why reductivism appeals: "We can get a grip on things! And we can get it exactly." So now we have more sophisticated versions. In the language area, we have Steve Pinker, who appeals to both genetic theory and also to a certain kind of mechanistic reductivism in talking about the brain, and the "language of thought" and all those kinds of things, which I'm sure will be discredited a little while down the line, and then something else will happen. In a certain sense all the work I did in the 1960s and 1970s was because I was in a political science department, and because the challenge of reductivism there came from modernization theory, which was applied across all societies as though they faced exactly the same set of stages. So a lot of the work I wrote then was directed against that enemy.

But there's been a continuity of interest in that. I haven't been talking about behaviourism or computer science since my great friend and colleague Hubert Dreyfus did that for us. That's why I could write that book with Bert on language.[4] But the issue I kept raising with the comparative politics of that kind, was that they're ignoring these tremendous differences in culture. Apples and oranges are being compared all the time. You get these cross-cultural questionnaires which ask things like, "What do you think of the place of honour?" and so on. Alasdair MacIntyre is really good on this. You can translate it in various ways in Swahili, and it comes out meaning something very different. And so what I was really looking for through all that was some kind of language to talk about what we sometimes refer to as political culture or what Montesquieu referred to as "les moeurs" and Tocqueville following him, and Hegel referred to as *der objektiver Geist* or Objective Spirit. And in a certain sense the idea, that I really stole from Castoriadis with a little bit of changes, of [the] "social imaginary," was an attempt to do that, particularly when it comes to comparing democracies. I think this has turned out to be fruitful. And people are taking it up. You know, Mukulika Banerjee and also that whole gang in Australia that started this review on social imaginaries. And so there's been [a] certain continuity because I introduced the modern social imaginaries, not just in the book. That was a spin-off from *A Secular Age*.[5] Now I'm working very hard with Craig Calhoun and others on a critique of what's going wrong with democracy. The concept is coming back to the fore. So, in a certain sense since 1960 when I came here – my last contribution to the psychology debate was prior to that – there's been a real building on previous interventions.

LEVY: In that answer you didn't say anything about the multiple modernities thesis, but it sounds like you have modernization in the background of that.

TAYLOR: Absolutely, that's right; the multiple modernities thesis was an attempt to show that there isn't a single process called modernization which is the same everywhere, except it's like a caravan, you know, [with] the US at the head and some African society trudging along in the caravan.

LEVY: Is there anything in recent social science that you find good and interesting and non-reductive in ways that you've been able to draw on?

TAYLOR: There are so many examples. I'm tremendously interested, because of this president, in what people call populism – in people who have, with very ethnographic minds, written about why Trump voters go for Trump. There are two that are fantastic. One is Arlie Hochschild with a tremendous study in South Louisiana.[6] The other is *The White Working Class* by Joan C. Williams.[7] They both really have the same political views as I have, but they're giving us an alternative language to "rednecks" and "deplorables," etc., and ways in which you can take up parts of that identity and make an appeal to it, which gives you some chance of winning some of those people away from the populist movements. We need more stuff like that.

WEINSTOCK: I arrived here in the 1980s, so twenty years later. And my sense was that political science here, and perhaps political science more broadly, was an extremely broad church that went all the way from people who were still presenting predictive models and nomological covering laws, to people who had taken up the more interpretive stance. Both within this department, I would say, but more broadly as well. The readings I would get in different classes were quite ecumenical. The education that I got was both still redolent of the views that you were critiquing, but also a lot of them weren't. Neither position's been beaten back completely. I was thinking, when I was hearing you talk about the Hochschild and *White Working Class*, about views that are becoming quite popular in moral psychology around work by people like Jonathan Haidt, who has tried to understand the reasons that ideas of the left and ideas of the right might appeal to different types of people in terms of very reductive arguments about the brain. So the old wine is coming back.

TAYLOR: Exactly, that's what I mean by the conservation law – that when certain ideas get discredited because they don't work, there are people with a certain temper or basic outlook on life, that are looking for an alternative that is equally reductive and equally clear. Something comes off and somebody invents something like that, and everyone rushes, in this case, from being behaviourist to being computer reductionist – the mind is computation. What is interesting is that when I was younger, twenty years ago, "are you into AI?" meant are you into finding an explanatory theory. Now they have totally deserted that, and it's really "are you into engineering useful robots?" But then you still get people saying, "they're going to take over, they're going to be more intelligent than us, they'll be intelligent enough to make machines that are even more intelligent." But no one is asking themselves, "what is intelligence?"

WEINSTOCK: I don't know if this is a direction that we want to pursue, but I'll mention it and we can let it drop. It's interesting that the most interesting work in AI now, whereas before it was trying to force human intelligence into a model that looked like machines, now it's trying to make machines that really do learn in the way that humans do, so it's realizing that human intelligence is a lot more complex than the old model suggested. And that machine learning is going to be about not assuming that humans are really like machines, but making machines more like humans. Is that progress?

TAYLOR: It's some progress provided they don't misinterpret it, which people do, and think that there aren't levels of human intelligence which require emotions, that require moral and other feelings to make discriminations which just can never be replicated by machines. Or you can only replicate [them] by replacing an emotional state with a series of indicators: you start sweating or you go red or your blood pressure goes up. In a way lie detector tests are at the absolute limit of this. "Are you lying?" There are certain indicators and they're not that certain. And when you get more subtle issues – "what's wrong with Trump?" – well, you have different things to say; some of us say, "lying." All those kinds of evaluative questions are extremely hard to program such that we can have indicators that machines can pick up. They don't really have emotions; it's as simple as that. So, the idea that machines are going to take over all the decisions is absolutely … we're never going to ask a machine whether we should form a coalition with X party, or whether it's more important to fight global warming.

MACLURE: And if we think that from machine learning we can get to something like human level intelligence, or strong AI, or general AI, it's still assuming that the mind or human cognition, even if the approach to AI is very different, is reducible to some more basic properties that machines can have. We now have machines with tremendous computational power, and you basically train the algorithm so it can detect patterns or broad correlations within huge data sets. So we're now reducing the mind to this capacity to extract regularities within large data sets. And computers can do that much better than the human mind, but if we think that we can move from there to general or strong AI, we think that that's the basic property [of human cognition], so that's still a kind of reductionism.

TAYLOR: Yeah, and the mind does it differently. I mean this is where Hubert Dreyfus and his brother Stuart asked all these great chess masters, and after a while the concepts they began to apply, strength over their weaknesses, and in the end they can be beaten, because if you can really count out, "I do this" (all the possibilities) the machine can come across solutions which you could never dream of. And the AI guys went "ooh, Kasparov was beaten by Deep Blue." But that just means [that] if we had the power and the time to count out all [the] possibilities we could arrive at the same thing, but we could never match that. They can have a search of the whole space in seconds.

MACLURE: Your first book was *The Explanation of Behaviour*,[8] which was a critique of behaviourism in psychology and of its influence in the social sciences. In many papers, some collected in the *Philosophical Papers*, you deplored that many researchers in the human sciences imported some of the assumptions and methods of the natural sciences to explain human features (thought, language, action, etc.). A constant theme in your writing in the philosophy of mind, action and language is your dissatisfaction with various reductionist programs which claim that human phenomena such as mental states, actions, and expressive acts can be reduced to more basic natural properties or functions. On the one hand, behaviourism fell in disrepute and the kind of phenomenological analyses of human agency that you put forward with colleagues such as Hubert Dreyfus have been taken up forcefully by younger generations of philosophers of mind and action. On the other hand, "naturalism" or "materialism" appears to remain dominant in many quarters of analytic philosophy. In the philosophy of mind, "physicalism," which claims that the mind can be reduced to more basic physical properties, is the default position. In the broader culture, theories which claim that human character or behaviour is caused by patterns of neural firing or by the coding of specific genes are widespread. It turns out that one of your forthcoming publications is a commentary on a powerful attack on naturalism in the philosophy of mind by a young German philosopher. How do you look back on the past forty years with regard to the influence of the natural sciences in the human sciences and to the fate of the various reductionist programs? Do you think that we are prone to the same kind of distortion and misunderstanding? Did the recovery of philosophical traditions such as phenomenology and Romanticism contribute to a richer understanding of human identity and agency?

TAYLOR: To start from my joking way of putting it, the conservation law, it does appeal to a certain kind of mind – the sense that you really have the same kind of control that you can get over the data, over the phenomena, the same kind of exact computation. Because the most spectacular things that everyone admires of our culture are these great realizations of natural science. You walk in the faculty club if you're just a sociologist or a political [theorist], and you get a sense of, "It would be great to be able to say, 'I've been inventing the cure for cancer.'" All these things mean that a lot of people are deeply attracted to this kind of production. But all the actual formulations in the end show themselves, I believe, to be inadequate. So that's behind the perpetual movement. Sometimes people get so attached to the older forms that they can't bear [change], and that's the cynical side of Thomas Kuhn: paradigms change because the old folks die off. And that's partly true, but it's also true that the younger people get attracted to the new one because they see all too clearly that the old one isn't working. But if you have this basic stance toward life, [this] stance toward science, you're going to look for the next best reductive theory, you see. So, you see that then people say that we're closing the gap, people that Daniel was quoting, because they can do this much more sophisticated stuff. Yeah, but there are obviously big issues of how people choose, which only makes sense if you come to understand that this is where hermeneutics versus natural sciences are the models. And I don't see this debate being clinched for centuries. It's obvious that the nature of modern culture is going to produce some people who are going to have a yen for that reductive form.

MACLURE: And is it more balanced now than it used to be? I was thinking of someone like Tom Nagel, one of his last books is a very powerful, although speculative, critique of naturalism in philosophy and science.[9] You have all the younger generations of philosophers who went back to phenomenology, maybe following people like Dreyfus and yourself in thinking of the embodied mind. But on the other hand, you have scholars like Pinker or Dennett who are very influential in the broader culture as well.

TAYLOR: I think it's a slightly more even playing field now. I think that people like me were looked at more askance, were thought of as more crazy. An example is Bert Dreyfus when he was at MIT. And he really had to leave because a lot of other powerful AI people were at MIT, and they were utterly scandalized. Not just scandalized: they were totally indignant because they were getting a lot of money from the US Air Force. Bert produced this wonderful, short pamphlet. I remember the one image of an ape climbing a tree and saying, "I'm halfway to the moon!" And that circulated around the funding agencies, so Marvin Minsky was absolutely: "Get rid of this guy!" So that meant Bert went to California where he had a great time. But later Minsky kind of relented and they could actually talk to each other. That's a small anecdote which illustrates my feeling that we're not totally, utterly mad off the map, you know ... dreamers!

LEVY: The most traditionally reductionist of the social sciences, economics, is now twenty years into a fascination with behavioural economics and with complexifying the understanding even of what the basic type of human behaviour is. In political science, the methods wars have significantly calmed down and been replaced by an orientation towards multimethods research. The story you tell ethnographically and archivally and historically ought to also make sense in something like choice-theoretic terms. You ought to be able to explain what each other actor was doing, but the interpretation of the actions is something that you want to do beside something like a decision tree. I think we're in a much more balanced moment than in the 1970s.

TAYLOR: That's right, that's right. So, they wanted to claim this as the real relevance of this more reductive stuff, but that you need to feed in more refined and more discriminating data. But there still is this tremendous belief. I mean, rational choice theory is one of the big things that took over for a long time. And there again, you can see what people like me want to say about that.

WEINSTOCK: In a way there's something common from the politics to the philosophy of agency to the philosophy of mind, which you know, one might be tempted to see as a latter-day vindication of the insights of phenomenology, which is to pry away a naturalism from reduction. The idea [is] that the naturalistic stance is something [that] we can't abandon, but that when we look at nature, and humans within it, with non-ideological eyes, eyes that don't assume that nature will work according to this simplistic model, what we see is something that ends up dovetailing some of the insights that were arrived at non-experimentally by yourself, Merleau-Ponty, and others. So now we end up with programs in the philosophy of mind like Thompson at University of British Columbia, Dan Zahavi in Copenhagen, Sean Gallagher, who are all card-carrying naturalists. Here we have our own Ian Gold. They're all on board with the idea that all these things have to be testable. But they have a more open mind about what a real non-ideologically blinkered view of nature will arrive at.

TAYLOR: I've always had worries about the word naturalism – which in my meaning meant, grounding human science or even science of the animate on the natural sciences, on the Galilean type of natural sciences. But if you want to talk about trying to understand how humans behave from human nature, if Aristotle is still on the reading list, then I'm one hundred per cent with that.

MACLURE: So it's more the reductivism than the naturalism.

WEINSTOCK: Or a reductivism to a much broader reductive base than had been the case before. That seems to be something where the balance has definitely shifted across the disciplines and sub-disciplines that we have talked about so far.

MACLURE: Maybe not in analytic philosophy. If you're in philosophy of mind, and you're not a physicalist, it's hard to be taken seriously. Maybe what you're doing is not mature enough. And you still have theories such as eliminativism, where mental states are basically brain states and at some point we will be able to get rid of the level of the mental description because neuroscience will have progressed – so that is still there.

WEINSTOCK: It's still present.

TAYLOR: Well, Dan Dennett is maybe an extreme case, but he has a lot of impact.

MACLURE: Consciousness, qualia, all illusions that we'll one day get rid of.

TAYLOR: Well, even John Searle always used to put it paradoxically: "We don't think, we just think we think."

WEINSTOCK: When I was first at the U de M, I was hired in a position that included philosophy of action, and so I had to school myself in the philosophy of action to teach a course which I taught for a few years and I realized that, when supposedly physicalist philosophers of mind reach for the notion of supervenience rather than reduction, the game has been given up. It was a way of waving one's hands in a vague way, you know, making it sound [like] one was still a reductionist while realizing that the full reductionist program just doesn't to allow us to account for what we need to be accounting for.

LEVY: You have a well-developed political philosophy about, broadly, national and linguistic identities. You also obviously have thought a great deal about social and political theory with respect to religion and secularism. But these projects seem to orbit each other at a distance: there's not much language or nation in *A Secular Age*[10] and not much religion in *Language Animal*.[11] They came together for a moment in the commission report[12]: the security of the French Fact was a premise of the conclusion that French Quebec could be confident enough to afford substantial religious liberty to religious minorities. Is there a general lesson there about how the two themes fit together in your political philosophy? In secular modernity, are linguistic-national identities primary and religious commitments constrained by them, limited by the needs of the linguistic or national community? If not, how *do* you think about these two long-term projects of yours fitting together? How do you think about the religious and the linguistic-national forces shaping political life?

TAYLOR: I think the big thing that links those two is the concept of identity, collective identity, political identity, which I've been trying to think a great deal about and which obviously lay behind the commission report. Many of the actors are in this room right now. Certainly, democracies need very strong, very powerful collective identities that most people subscribe to. For all sorts of reasons. Obviously if you're going to have redistribution, there has to be a sense that we belong together with [the] people from whom, and to whom, the distribution is taking place, and if we're going to trust our fellow deliberators in an electoral deliberation, we have to trust that they're really thinking about us and not just about them. There isn't really a difference here, qua identity, between religious and linguistic ones. Except that in that the present situation in the West, the nature of democratic society is such that there has to be one or two languages, or maybe three in the case of Switzerland, but the languages can't be infinite in number. People have to master enough of them to be able to deliberate together. But in the nature of modern Western society, the religious or metaphysical positions, I think that it's part of the analysis of *A Secular Age* that this multiplicity is galloping; it is increasing all the time.

So that sets [up] the problem of what one asks of people of different religious or metaphysical views in order to be good citizens in a modern republic. And I mean the rest is what we've got worked out in the book Jocelyn and I published[13] that came out of chapter 7 of the Bouchard-Taylor Commission report.[14] That the wrong kind of *laïcité* is if you see it as a kind of marker of a real modern society and then begin to spell it out in terms of *les espaces de la République*, and you must be free of religious signs – all that kind of language you get coming from, unfortunately, France today. The right way is to see that there's a plurality of goals here and that you do have to make trade-offs sometimes, but the basic point that Jocelyn and I were making, and that the report makes, is that there must be neutrality of the public institutions between these different positions, but a maximum freedom of conscience [for] those who hold the multiple positions in society. It's not easy. It's been made a bit more interestingly complex by Cécile Laborde, because she's also identified different contexts in which issues arise about the place of religion, and one of them that we put front and centre in our report, for which she uses the word integrity: you have to not ask somebody to breach their own integrity by not wearing a hijab. But there are other issues concerning what the language of common deliberation is, and a third context in which we're worried about ... "well, if we're giving this possibility to this group but not to that group, is there some problem there that these communities are not equal?" It's even more complex than we maybe made it sound in *Secularism and Freedom of Conscience*.[15] But our basic idea from the beginning was that there are going to be these difficult moments, and I think that is where we now stand. I'm sure there's going to be further movement on this as more people like Cécile Laborde come in and introduce more complications. There'll be further movement on this, but the basic idea will remain the same.

LEVY: Since there are hints here and there in your work that the galloping pluralisation of the comprehensive and religious views might not be a permanent fact and there might be a pendulum swing there, would that have knock-on effects on the linguistic and national part? I have in mind something like [the] relative convergence of religious views from the hundreds in the Anglophone and extremely liberal societies to something like the pillar system as in Germany and the low countries, that say the Roman church could stand as the representative of a plurality of linguistic groups, and you could tolerate more linguistic pluralism because you have an institutionalization of less radical religious pluralism.

TAYLOR: That's certainly logically possible. But I don't see the sociological trends there ... on the contrary, they're all going the other way. For one thing, there's a whole set of problems connected with that, and we'll come to that in a minute; there's immense international migration going on which is diversifying all societies willy nilly, very often it's nilly.

LEVY: But there's some tendency on the part of, say, Britain and France, to want to treat their Muslim immigrant communities as a whole even though those Muslim immigrant communities are incredibly diverse, representing nations all over the world, languages all over the world. And to let there be a public institutional face that is a religious rather than a linguistic face.

TAYLOR: Oh yeah. In France there is very much this idea coming from the Napoleonic epoch that they haven't totally got over, of relating to members of the particular minority religion by creating some organization representing all of them. And then in the UK people are talking about, "why don't we let some Imams in the House of Lords?" These are all in the area of what you might call bridge organizations. So, they in no way amount to the kind of pillarization that's in the Netherlands; demonstrated in its heyday, there were three. And I guess Belgium's the same. That's because there's the internal diversification within religious confessions, which I think is a striking feature of the modern world, which is not about to be reversed either. So, as a matter of fact, already you see these bridge organizations when it comes to Muslims. One sees this in the French case: the Muslims in France and the UK, and I guess in Canada to some extent too, are still grouped in their linguistic, national origin. But even apart from that, Muslims originating from a single nation in any Western nation will have tremendous differences because they relate to different Imams who give different fatwas. So I don't see what could reverse this. And if you get to the third world, the attempts to reverse this are all disastrous. Like Modi in India ... it's terribly painful.

LEVY: I know what you mean, but can you spell out that example?

TAYLOR: Well, that example is that they are trying to make everybody in India identify themselves in some way with the Hindu tradition. Instead of Hinduism it's Hindutva, which is something very vague. Somehow you accept that the culture from the Vedas is the really important culture. The thing is you can't preach that kind of thing without awakening all the old resentments. But what it goes along with is this idea that, "these Muslims came in and there was the burning of the temples and we have to get them," and so on. And "these Christian missionaries are coming here." So, it cannot but deeply divide a society. You see this kind of thing everywhere. So you get Orbán, with his appeal to "Christian civilization!" What you get in these kinds of cases is one of these really great muddles in the modern world, that the concept of religion is getting stretched to its widest extent because it in many cases is stripped of its devotional dimension, its historic dimension. So, a lot of people in Northern Ireland are still wanting to clobber a lot of other people in Northern Ireland, even though a lot of people still do go to church, but a lot of people stopped going to church, and they still want to clobber the other gang because it's all historical. So the actual concept of religion that gets used here is so complex and multi-leveled and multifaceted.

LEVY: Is that a dynamic internal to the kind of mechanisms you talk about in *A Secular Age*?[16] It could be more the dynamic from "The Politics of Recognition"[17] or from "Democratic Exclusion,"[18] where religion becomes a way to organize, when what we need in modern political life are ways to organize categories of us and them.

TAYLOR: Exactly. The extraordinary longevity of what sounds like religious categories covers a deep change in content. So, you know, when there's a question of Turkey bidding to join the EU, which is ancient history now because of Erdoğan and so on, a lot of totally secular politicians actually said, "It was like we'd lost the siege of Vienna! You know the Turks are coming as janitors, not janissaries."

LEVY: That's awful.

TAYLOR: The same thing happens in France, with people who are totally *laïque*, and here too, because there [are] among people who are fiercely *laïque*, [those] who say about the issue of the crucifix in the National Assembly, "Well after all, it is *patrimonie*." So, it's very complex.

WEINSTOCK: One of the ways we could go from here: I'm tempted to push you on something that Jacob says in his question about the commission's report, about the way the commission's report brought together the issues of language and religion in what he describes quite aptly [in] the following way: the security of the French language was a premise of the conclusion that French Quebec be confident enough for substantial religious liberty for religious minorities. So, one of the ways to read the report is, "Relax! Quebec is not going away; we're not going to disappear. The language is secure and we've taken steps to ensure it'll be secure and you the majority can therefore afford, to be a little bit more accommodating of the religious diversity here." So there's a move that not as many people noted as should have, an asymmetry between the way language is treated and the way religion is treated. There's a kind of implicit contract: allow people to live their religious lives as they see fit within limits, but quite broad limits, but the counterpart is that we are going to be with you in defending measures that ensure French is the official language. There are a number of ways of interpreting the way in which language and religion end up being asymmetrically treated. "No, we're not going to impose Catholicism, but we are going to impose French." One is philosophical, which is to say there's just something more fundamental to identity about language than there is about religion. Another is at the opposite end of the spectrum, very pragmatic, which is to say, "we have to throw these insecure majorities a bone. We might as well throw them a bone that is as the opposite of toxic as possible." After all, language is something that anybody can sign on to. A Jew can come into Quebec and learn French and be part of that compact, whereas they can't come in and become Catholic. A third, maybe sociological, in the sense that you talked about a few moments ago. It's not a philosophical point that linguistic identity is more fundamental than religion in some full-blooded philosophical sense; it's just that at this point in our history it has become so. So, I'd like to hear you on that.

LEVY: Or political. Under the fact of that democratic government. There's something about our ability to speak to each other.

TAYLOR: Yeah, it's a bit of all of them. Let's see how it works together here. Because I think it works differently in different societies, but a general tendency you'll observe pretty well everywhere, is when totally new populations come into a given society, where we haven't had any of that kind before, people fear, what? I heard the question as I travelled around the province, "est-ce qu'ils vont nous changer?" The fear they're going to change us, they're going to make it impossible for us to live the way of life we've always understood and that we're attached to. You're certainly right that there are two sides to this way of life. In Quebec, one is the language, the other is a whole lot of other things: sensibility, the way you talk about things, the way you feel about things, and so on. And it's a real fear of *disparaître* surrounding language. It's very powerful. If one [can't] assure, then there's no point in making any kind of bargain. But on the other hand, for a lot of people in Quebec, the great difference that these people represent is definitely threatening. You see this exactly in Germany. Unlike the American case, the French case, or the Dutch case, or the British case, where there's some very important economic deprivation, in fairness, to the motivation in the populist movements, in Germany, there's a relatively successful economy, it's really very largely, "who are these people?" So, a lot of Germans from the very beginning after 1960 and after the wall came up and they couldn't get any fresh new labour from Eastern Germany, they began to bring in Turks, Moroccans, and so on. So, this term "Leitkultur," this "leading culture," they have a kind of fear that if there are too many of them we can't be sure of our culture. So in Quebec this kind of fear exists, but it exists in a very skewed distribution, because for understandable reasons it's much less strong in Montreal [than] it is outside Montreal.

WEINSTOCK: Let's jump into my question. Let me formulate it in a way that flows from this: there are majorities around the world in stable liberal democracies starting to talk and act and make claims that sound a lot like the claims of minorities. *Hillbilly Elegy*,[19] you know, where the white Americans are all of a sudden speaking as if they're threatened. We hear it here in Quebec; we hear it around the world. So, a couple of questions. One of them is: is this something new, are we really in a new moment around the world where majorities are starting to make claims that sound like the claims that twenty years ago we were thinking about minorities making: misrecognition, lack of recognition, culture eroding before forces that even majorities that have control over democratic institutions can't withstand? Is there something morally legitimate about some of this, or is it just the case that for political entrepreneurs, it's the easiest thing in the world to go before the people and tell them, "you're being exploited," "your ways of life are being demeaned," even if there's no empirical reality about it? Or are there forces wrapped up with globalization, whatever that means, that actually do act with respect to majorities the way that majorities sometimes act toward minorities and therefore requiring of some moral response?

TAYLOR: I think what's happening is that we have presumptions now of universality, of non-discrimination and so on, which we didn't have before. But the same kind of emotions are there in the background of all immigration societies, like us and the Americans. During the 1840s the Irish famine sends a whole lot of Irish to New York and Boston. The Know Nothing Party stood up: "they're papists and they don't understand our

Christian Anglo-Saxon way and the way we do politics; the Pope tells them what to do." Which lasts right up to Kennedy being elected. "Is the Pope going to be telling him what to do?"

LEVY: It persists through the era of a Catholic majority on the US supreme court. The suspicion that someone like Antonin Scalia is only problematic-ally integrated.

TAYLOR: So in Canada you see we have a very different situation. The Anglo majority, for a long time, thought they had to really sit on the Franco and Irish minorities, make sure "they don't take too much space, and have schools here," etc. Manitoba schools, not to speak of Aboriginal schools, being pushed down. And what changes is, this massive change comes at the end of the Second World War, partly as a result of the reaction to Nazism. Now the presumption is no longer, this is our country, "we Anglos own Canada, we're going to out of the goodness of our hearts allow these people to speak French." Or "we WASPs, really we're America; we're going to let a few black people in." That presumption has disappeared and there-fore elites are talking about this post-Second World War presumption, and that's what gives them the feeling, "Wow, we're strangers in our own land," to quote the title of Hochschild's book.[20] She worked out this idea of a precedence ladder. Some people will get served first and [some] served second, and what's happening now is people are queue-busting. And you know, she wrote this down and she showed it to them all and they said "Yeah yeah, that's it!" They somehow recognized themselves in this. So, whereas up until well after the Second World War, the big thing was civil rights – the legislation, the ending of lynching and Jim Crow, etc. Which really threw a lot of people back on, "What do you mean? This is the way we've always done it. They've got to keep their place; if they don't keep their place, what's going to happen?" Now there's a terror because all these elites from up there are saying, "They have the same rights as us!" It's a new situation, like the German case, like Merkel. "Berlin is telling us we have to take an infinite number of these people." If that's the new situation then that's what creates the minority sense of "really we're not in power."

WEINSTOCK: The way you just described it makes it sound as though, you know [even if it is] historically, humanly understandable, it has very little moral weight. This is essentially about people reacting to the loss of privilege that they had. And a privilege that was completely unjustifiable when it was happening. Loss of privilege just feels to the person losing that privilege like victimization. But you know, wanting to push it a little bit. One of the things I've been interested in, [in] some of my work in the last few years, has to do with how to react to language shift, the fact that English in particular is sort of this steamroller. It is taking over in a lot of places. Taking over without colonialism or without some noxious political force; it's just the logic of people's choices as they choose which languages to speak that makes it the case [that] in a lot of countries that we visit now, parts of academia in Sweden and Denmark, [are] being carried out almost entirely in English now. And now people are viewing this steamrolling of English as this new lingua franca, as this big force that doesn't necessarily have a huge army behind it; it's just happening as a result of people's choices. Or economic globalization. My own family in France, who worked in the needle trade, which [for] three generations [they] lived quite well off of, are being forced out because they can no longer compete in a globalized economy. That sounds less about the loss of privilege that comes from all of a sudden having to respect other people's rights, but rather from things that are happening in the world that treat even local majorities as if they were minorities that are powerless before these larger forces that aren't democratic majorities lording it over them, but sort of a broader, harder to stop processes.

LEVY: But aren't you looking for something reductionist here? You're looking for an objective macro-social fact, or a few, rather than the interpretations that are being offered. Which might sound substantially similar regardless if the local majority population is or isn't threatened according to one of your big objective stories.

WEINSTOCK: I take it that one of the things we do as political philosophers even in [the] interpretive mode is to try to see whether in the way [in] which political actors express themselves, if there is morally something we can take seriously, perhaps almost to the point of putting in place measures. So, there's a requirement, to that degree, to find a few ways of translating what maybe my cousins in the needle trade wouldn't be expressing exactly in the terms I did. I'm putting it in ways that are maximally sympathetic. Is it all about just basically majorities having to get used to the idea that they have to take other people's rights seriously?

TAYLOR: You're right; if you take Marine Le Pen, and you take Trump, and so on, there's a big globalization component. Globalization is named as something to worry about, competition from all of these other countries, "America's got to be first again;" that was part of Le Pen's argument too. But what is the common thread here? It's what I was saying earlier: something happens whereby your world just isn't familiar anymore. And particularly the unfamiliarity goes along with the conditions being much worse, but it doesn't need to be. It can be just purely cultural crawl. But if it is cultural crawl plus "I don't have a job anymore," what are the forces producing this? And the line-up is usually something more than just the minority, the visual face of this. "It's the minority plus elites that are opening us to competition from everywhere, or so enamoured of these newcomers here, and they're putting them ahead of us."

WEINSTOCK: In a way you mentioned [the] right wing, the Le Pens and the Trumps, but in a way you could make the case that this was also central to the Bernie Sanders appeal.

TAYLOR: Well, no ...

LEVY: The left-wing Brexiters ...

WEINSTOCK: The Lexiters? And to some degree Québec Solidaire. The new discourse on independence that – at least in the week we're doing this, a week before a Quebec election where the sovereigntist party of the left is overtaking the traditional sovereigntist party – especially among the young; the figures among the young are quite staggering. It's not so much independence in order to realize our essence as a people, it is a Scottish kind of thing. Independence so that we can do all of these left-wing things, and amongst these things protect ourselves from globalization.

TAYLOR: Well, that really is the problem, and that is why I see Bernie as different, Bernie isn't saying "I am appealing to the old stock of Americans." He is appealing to everybody who is in this economically disadvantaged position. But what you have in all these societies is certain populations who feel that we had a way of life that was viable and great and now it is being taken away from us, partly by economic change because of globalization, but partly because a lot of people are busting in and taking our space or getting favourable treatment in relation to us. What's good about Bernie is [that] he doesn't have the second. I would like a new vocabulary where populism would mean we think the system is rigged, so we have to mobilize the people to get over that. And then you have a left and a right, a good and a bad variant of it.

WEINSTOCK: There is still a kind of suspicion of elites. Take a popular entertainer like Michael Moore in his last movie. Part of it is, we thought it would be all anti-Trump, but a lot of it is, I would say, the most bitter – where it really hurts – kind of thing is the betrayal of the liberal elites. Of Obama and the Clintons who are taking as much money from Goldman Sachs as the [Republicans]. So that aspect of it seems to me to be shared.

TAYLOR: Well, that's straight-up populism going back to the tradition of progressives and so on. There are "trahisons des chefs des clercs." Chris Hedges is even worse.

MACLURE: Maybe to go back to Daniel's question, something that probably all of us should do now, we know that according to the popular theories explaining the rise of populism and far right movements in Europe and so on, "we find the view that identity politics went too far or is one of the cases of resentment today." You're the author of one of the classic texts on the "politics of recognition."[21] All of us in this room [have] defended versions of multiculturalism or the politics of recognition in political theory. Did we get something wrong; was there something wrong in the ways the politics of recognition or multiculturalism were defended? I know that there are very different ways to defend multiculturalism and identity politics and so on. From your perspective, is there something we need to revise in our theories? And do we need to adapt them to the current situation?

TAYLOR: Well, in a certain sense, we're in the wrong place to ask that question. Because [if] one country seems to have survived this to some degree, you could say it's Canada. But so let's take Canadian practice and Quebec and Europe: yes, there's something they could have done. They weren't prepared mentally, in Europe, for this as an immigration problem. They thought Gastarbeiter, guest workers, and of course a lot of people who came also thought, "I'll make a lot of money [and] I'll go back to Izmir;

I'm going to open a nice little café," etc. So a lot of people shared this illusion. The result was in large parts of Germany, and recently it's got better but only in some Länders ... like us, there is a very important language issue. Here there were the *classes d'accueil* that would try to ensure that the kids who speak Arabic or Swahili at home know enough French that they get into grade school, that they don't get totally behind. It wasn't done in Germany. You have in Kreuzberg, in Berlin, kids that don't speak proper Turkish, they don't really speak proper German, they're heading towards a terrible future of unemployability. And then there are other kinds of things that you need to do, which we don't do in Quebec as much, but which some societies do, which is have all the people from the minority have positions in media, so that there's some sense of familiarization going on. So instead of, first of all, giving the people who come in the tools to function well in society, and instead of trying to make an effort to normalize their presence in a society, you just let everything go without any direction, and that's something that I think pretty well any immigrant society on this side of the Western hemisphere knows is not going to work. And now they do, but the will isn't necessarily there to act on it. The other thing you must not do is precisely have the incoming of all these people coincide temporally with the loss of status and income and so on. I mean that's the "Lexit," the working class in Northern Britain voting "Leave." Because they just can easily buy the idea that it's all foreigners doing this to us, because they've been tremendously let down.

LEVY: Your arguments in political philosophy have often been taken as – and sometimes they clearly were – rejoinders to one or another stylized view of "liberalism" – not only in the years when everything was recast as a liberal-communitarian debate, but in "Atomism"[22] and "Positive Liberty,"[23] in the reliance on Hegel against Kant and Locke, in the sympathetic interest in cultural and nationalist claims in politics, and in your commitment to social democracy or democratic socialism. Mostly you've offered these in a spirit of correction of liberal excess of one kind or another, not in the spirit of "anti-liberalism" that was sometimes attributed to you, but you've had much less to say about what in liberal politics or philosophy seems to you worth preserving. In light of where we are in the second half of the 2010s, and the sense that a kind of liberal political order is under serious threat around the world, I wonder what you'd say about what's worth salvaging or saving from liberalism – however you want to construe liberalism or the idea of a liberal politics.

TAYLOR: Well, I mean, I guess my liberalism goes back to the 1790s. *Liberté, Fraternité, Egalité*. But you can't forget fraternité; that's a big, big problem. That's the criticism I'm just making of societies that have large swaths of the working class, to have a terrible deterioration in their living standards and in their jobs, etc. It's really a total absence of fraternité in the practical sense of solidarity. Solidarity could be the word you could use here. But I also disagree with a certain kind of liberalism. Philosophically I don't think of freedom as simply negative. I argue that out [in] "What's Wrong with Negative Liberty."[24] Secondly, I think that there are various forms of collective identity which are not only not a threat to liberalism properly understood, but are actually essential to it. Like for instance, I have argued all the time [that] there has to be a strong sense of national identity in order precisely for fraternité to work, and therefore for the system to work. And thirdly, I think that you have to count with partial identities, group identities, religious groups, or other such groups that belong in society. People think of themselves in those terms, so we have to have a society which allows some kind of continuous negotiation to go on between them, and continuous exchange, which fosters mutual recognition. So, for all these reasons, there are various kinds of liberalism that have been my target, but it has never been the original trinity that I was mentioning earlier. And as a matter of fact, the communitarian/ liberalism debate I thought was a real muddle. You can tell that by the fact that one sense of the word communitarianism, that of Amitai Etzioni – he's preaching republicanism, that we should have [a] strong sense of obligation to the common good. And yet, *communautarisme* in France is always these partial identities. Particularly religious identities. I really basically agree with Etzioni – perhaps not on this or that detail – but we do want people to have a strong sense of allegiance; same with Montesquieu, what Rousseau said, what Hannah Arendt said, what Aristotle said; you've got to have this strong sense of identity. And yet, the word is used in France to mean something totally different, something thought to be incompatible with France. And I think that kind of community identity certainly isn't necessarily incompatible with that, but there are certain conditions. If you start discriminating against various people, then they're going to turn against the national identity, which is what's happening in France. The jihadi are picking up recruits because of the absurdly self-damaging behaviour [of] people like Vals and so on, going off against the burkini. What is the expression? "Intérêt bien entendu, le libéralisme bien entendu, la laïcité bien entendue, et bien comprise." I'm all for that.

LEVY: But you're still talking about the corrections. You're still talking about, say, the *Fraternité* leg of the trinity. Say something about the liberty part, what it is that didn't have to be corrected, that separates you from, I think, some of the people who still think they are marching under the communitarianism banner.

TAYLOR: The maximum possible liberty – of choice, of conscience, and so on – that's compatible with our having a really functioning democratic society. That's it absolutely, I mean there isn't a reason. There I'm with John Stuart Mill, but not quite for John Stuart Mill's reasons. If I had to write a new theory for everybody to write on their banners, one of the things that would be really important is, don't treat people in virtue of a view of them which is imposed from outside, but in virtue of an understanding of them which really would come from close looking, talking and so on. And I think this is something very important, in all these situations; we live in a very bureaucratic society and necessarily so, we have these big health systems, we have these big education systems, we have all these things we have to deal with, thousands and thousands of people. And it's very easy to slide into treating them all like big general categories, where they're just simply numbers, within that. There has to be – and what's really laudable about a lot of our institutions [is] that within these institutions you have – practitioners, teachers, doctors, who really do the opposite and try to listen to the patient, see what really matters to them. You know, [one of] the best elements of our education system is that they care for your kids who are falling behind and they need some really special treatment, special relations. It's from that point of view that I would talk about the maximum possible liberty, but also maximum possible recognition of what you are – you, as an individual, are. And that's one of the reasons why all of these *Chartes de la laïcité* [are] so infuriating. Because these women are told to take off the hijab, they're being treated by people who have no understanding of what their piety is like, and so [have] a monstrous caricature of them, that they're also a secret jihadi. I would like to erect this to be a primary value in a society – what I consider a really human society would be.

MACLURE: You are known for the views [that] we are "self-interpreting animals" and "strong evaluators." You opposed Lockean theories of personal identity arguing that the basic reason why we can say that a person remains the same through time and change is that her conscious experience is continuous and that she has memories of her past selves. You think that our answers to the questions of what makes a life worthwhile, and of what are the commitments that we need to honour in order to be the person that we want to be – our moral identity – are defining features of our personal identity. You also expressed sympathy for narrativist theories of personal identity – perhaps building on the views of your friend Paul Ricoeur – according to which the interpretation of our experience takes a narrative form. Because of our finitude, we would tend to think that our past, present, and future form a somewhat coherent, albeit revisable, narrative. How do you stand now on these views? Would you agree that one's set of strong evaluations and second-order volitions, although they are defining for the normally functioning human agent, are not the basic criteria of the persistence of personal identity through time? Leaving the science-fiction-inspired thought experiments that are disproportionally popular in analytic philosophy aside, do you think, for instance, that a person who suffers from severe and permanent dementia caused by a neurodegenerative disease is the same person as her previous rational self, or that she became a different person because she no longer has the capacity to form strong evaluations and long-term plans (or, as one is forced to conclude if we take Harry Frankfurt's words literally, that she is no longer a person)? Moreover, are you ready to concede to neo-Humeans that the propensity to interpret one's unfolding existence as a narrative is a contingent rather than necessary dimension of personal identity? Can one be a self-interpreting animal without interpreting our experience as unfolding as a somewhat coherent single narrative?

TAYLOR: Well, you see, it's never entirely coherent, because part of the reason why we all need narrative, we all live on narratives, is that we clarify ourselves, learn, or take certain steps, that seem to us as taking steps forward in understanding ourselves through transitions. There's a way of understanding why I now think this is better than that, because I understand the transition to be removing a confusion, or overcoming or noticing something that I was trying to cover up before. So, it's very hard to grasp what it is to understand oneself. If you say, "well, I understand myself right now!" in reference to the past ... now, might you make such big changes in your life that you would say – people do say these kinds of things – "I've become a different person! You knew me as blah blah person, but now I'm a different person"? But on the other hand, the person who says, [chuck-ling] "I've become a different person," it seems to me that narratively it's something that's awfully hard to imagine. Now, Galen Strawson is a bit contradictory. Now, he claims that … I would have to really sit down and look at examples from life … I could understand someone who thought that his identity was such that he lives in the present, right? But then I bet if you sat Galen down and said, "well, tell me about this," it would be something to the effect that, "I used to buy all this stuff, on a single trajectory, and then I realized that … " so, you see, as long as you have this binary: "I used to think blah blah, then I discovered blah blah," there is some narrative working here. And I find it hard to imagine that Galen, who is kicking against the general view, wouldn't have some such story to tell about himself.

MACLURE: So I guess maybe it's more about the coherence and the linear-ity which we associate with a piece of fiction, that has a beginning and a middle and an end, and that there's some kind of coherence. So perhaps that's what he would challenge.

TAYLOR: Yeah, yeah, of course it's never as coherent as a novel could be. Even if I write an autobiography, I'll be cutting lots of corners. I wouldn't even be able to understand myself in full complex takes – it would go all over the place. And that's certainly a *bémol* you have to put in when you say we understand each other, we understand ourselves, narratively; it hasn't got the total coherence of Tolstoy. Yes, that's true. But my point is that it's such an important role that's played by these transitions that you just can't imagine a human life which doesn't have something of this kind. "I used to think this and now I think that. Now I'm clear what 'loving' really is."

WEINSTOCK: I remember reading an article a long time ago which made an impression on me, after I'd read your articles and thought, "this is clearly right." I read an article by Owen Flanagan that perturbed me the most; it wasn't so much the coherence as the articulacy requirement that seems implicit in your views. So, I remember there being a passage on Tol-stoy's peasants who would somehow not come out as agents in your view because they lack the ability to articulate their second order commitments or their transitions in the way that seems to be implicit in the way you'd originally written those things. Is that a misreading on his part?

TAYLOR: Yeah, I say it's never going to be like Tolstoy himself and never going to be that coherent but, I mean, they have a saying, "You've always been a cheater, ever since you were a kid, and I learnt to stay away from you." They have some sense of the continuity of their lives, of how they're related to their parents. "You've always been a rebel"; "I've always been a rebel, so I told my father when I was very young that I'd take my own path." Or, in the country, "my brother's like that but I'm not." This kind of thing is, in a way, I think it's very condescending to peasantry! But of course, it doesn't have the sophistication.

MACLURE: What about the strong evaluations? So in the first part of *Sources of the Self*[25] when you sketch out these different concepts that were very influential and hugely important, you set out the discussion saying, "well, we have Lockean theories of personal identities that have been quite dominant so far," and I think one of your points is that they're leaving something out: the importance of our basic commitments and answering the question, "Who are we, what's our personal identity?" Is this really the critique of such views, or are we dealing with two different theories that have different objects? It could be [that] for the Lockean what is important are the conditions according to which we can say a person remains the same through time, and this is going to lead us to some very basic properties such as the same body or some form of psychological continuity. And that you're thinking about something else, another dimension of human agency, about what makes me a unique person and gives ethical substance to my identity. But are they incompatible? Do you want to correct these theories or do you think that your view is answering a different question?

TAYLOR: Well, I don't see them asking, I see a view of the person, of what a single person is from the outside. Which is very bodily, you're born now and go on living until ... In the case of the person with dementia – well, there we have this idea of how a person normally functions, an animal functioning. And then suddenly they're prevented from normally functioning; they can't function at all. And then of course they remain a person in the other sense, that they're owed something. How it's proper to treat a person, that remains completely. But they're not capable of functioning normally. But that doesn't mean that it isn't important to understand what the proper functioning of a person is, right? I mean whether we have bought Plato or Aristotle or not, we think in those terms. What's a really fulfilled life, what's a good life, etc. But what I have against the Lockean thing is that it seems to be independent of any kind of moral commitment. My point is that the idea of where you stand, what's important, what's unimportant, is crucial to your identity as we understand it. So, identity is a sense of orientation in this moral world. A sense of moral orientation in the world. Or deep divisions about that, but that issue is always there, see? I mean, this is a Heideggerian move. Where Heidegger defines *Dasein* by a kind of questioning, the Sein of *dasein*, where its own being is a question. I'm saying that you can't just have a blank notion of consciousness. It has to be, for a functioning human being, in a certain space of questions.

NOTES

Chapter One

1 Taylor, "To Follow a Rule," in *Philosophical Arguments*, 165–80.
2 Ibid., 178.
3 Taylor, "Retrieving Realism."
4 Bruner and Kalmar, "Narrative and Metanarrative."
5 Gallagher, "The Socially Extended Mind."
6 Dreyfus, "Everyday Intelligibility."
7 Todes, *Body and World*.
8 Gallagher, "Two Problems of Intersubjectivity" and "The Socially Extended Mind."
9 Young, *Throwing Like a Girl*.
10 Sheets-Johnstone, "Kinetic Tactile-Kinesthetic Bodies."
11 Collins, "Interactional Expertise."
12 McDowell, *Mind and World*.
13 Dreyfus, "Everyday Intelligibility."
14 See Dreyfus, "Everyday Intelligibility."
15 McDowell, *Mind and World*, 341.
16 Ibid., 341–3.
17 McDowell, "What Myth?"
18 Dreyfus, "Myth of the Mental."
19 Ibid.
20 Merleau-Ponty, *Phenomenology*.
21 Jeannerod, *Cognitive Neuroscience*.
22 Robertson and Treisman, "Consciousness," 308.
23 Merleau-Ponty, *Phenomenology*.
24 Bredekamp, *Galilei der Künstler*.
25 McNeill et al., "Neither or Both."
26 Goldin-Meadow, "Role of Gesture."
27 Zahavi, "Mindedness."
28 Gallagher, "Philosophical Antecedents."
29 Csibra and Gergely, "Natural Pedagogy."
30 Taylor, "To Follow a Rule," 171.
31 Ibid.

32 Dreyfus, *Overcoming the Myth of the Mental*, 47.
33 Carruthers, "How We Know."
34 Gopnik and Meltzoff, *Words, Thoughts, and Theories*.
35 Onishi and Baillargeon, "Fifteen-Month-Old Infants."
36 Ibid.; Song et al., "An Agent's False Belief"; Surian, Caldi, and Sperber, "Attribution of Beliefs."
37 Southgate, Senju, and Csibra, "Action Anticipation."
38 Carruthers, "How We Know," 166.
39 Baillargeon et al., "False-Belief Understanding."
40 Perner and Ruffman, "Infants' Insight."
41 This view is similar to the behavioural abstraction hypothesis (e.g., Povinelli and Vonk, "Chimpanzee Minds") stating that infants are able to represent observed behaviour in terms of a more abstract interpretation. For a discussion of this view, see Gallagher and Povinelli, "Enactive and Behavioral Abstraction Accounts."
42 Baillargeon et al., "False-Belief Understanding."
43 Low and Wang, "Long Road to Mentalism."
44 Low and Perner, "Implicit and Explicit Theory of Mind."
45 Bourdieu, *Outline of a Theory of Practice*, 67.
46 Hutto, "Unprincipled Engagements."
47 Merleau-Ponty, *Primacy of Perception*, 119.
48 Southgate, Senju, and Csibra, "Action Anticipation."
49 Buttelmann, Carpenter, and Tomasello, "Eighteen-Month-Old Infants."
50 De Jaegher, Di Paolo, and Gallagher, "Social Interaction."
51 Jacob, "Belief-Ascription."
52 Rubio-Fernández and Geurts, "False-Belief Task."
53 The agent in the duplo task is a Lego toy agent, so interaction here means simply that the child is invited to play with the agent and finish out the scenario of the task. The point is, however, that all of the interaction in this task (between experimenter and child and between child and agent) is designed to facilitate not only the child's ability to track the agent's perspective, but also to enhance the child's enactive responses to the situation.
54 See Gallagher and Hutto, "Understanding Others."
55 Braver, "Thinking of Subjectivity."

Chapter Two

1 Taylor, "Theories of Meaning," in *Philosophical Papers vol. 1*, 248–92.
2 For example in Taylor, "The Importance of Herder," in *Philosophical Arguments*, 79–99; "Heidegger, Language, and Ecology," in *Philosophical Arguments*, 100–26; "Language Not Mysterious?"; and most recently, *The Language Animal*.

3   Taylor, "Theories of Meaning," in *Philosophical Papers vol. 1*, 256; cf. "The Importance of Herder," in *Philosophical Arguments*, 79.

4   Taylor, "Theories of Meaning," in *Philosophical Papers vol. 1*, 290.

5   For example when after a discussion of the constituents necessary for the declarative function of sentences he says: "but *on top of this* we also recognize that speech activity goes well beyond the declarative utterance, and includes questions, orders, prayers, etc." ("Language and Human Nature," in *Philosophical Papers vol. 1*, 240, my italics). On the other hand Taylor convincingly criticizes a "division of labour"-project that thinks it could just add what the expressivist view has to say to the accounts formulated in the Frege-tradition ("Theories of Meaning," 273–82). Cf. my comments on his latest book (*The Language Animal*) in part four, below.

6   Wittgenstein, *Philosophical Investigations*. Quoted henceforward by "*PI*" and paragraph number.

7   Taylor, "The Importance of Herder," in *Philosophical Arguments*, 79–99, 79–83.

8   Wittgenstein, *Tractatus*.

9   For a discussion of the concept of a notation cf. Goodman, "The Theory of Notation," in *Languages of Art*. For an application of Goodman's ideas to Wittgenstein's early thought cf. Schneider, "Satz – Bild – Wirklichkeit."

10 Wittgenstein, *The Big Typescript*, § 30.

11 Dummett, "Can Analytical Philosophy Be Systematic, and Should It Be?" in *Truth and Other Enigmas*, 437–58.

12 Gottlob Frege, *Conceptual Notation and Related Articles*.

13 Frege, *Thoughts*.

14 Wundt, "Völkerpsychologie."

15 "When I use such terms as 'mind,' 'mental representation,' and the like, I am keeping to the level of abstract characterization of the properties of certain physical mechanisms, as yet almost entirely unknown" (Chomsky, *Rules and Representations*, 5).

16 Dummett, "Frege and Wittgenstein."

17 Wittgenstein, *The Big Typescript*, § 46.

18 Wittgenstein, *Philosophical Grammar*, 205.

19 Wittgenstein, *Philosophical Remarks*, 119.

20 Wittgenstein, *Philosophical Grammar*, 202.

21 Ibid., 205.

22 For a discussion of a comparable universality claim for logical forms in the writings of Robert Brandom, cf. Schneider, "Universale Sprachformen?"

23 Rudolf Carnap, "Überwindung der Metaphysik," 219–41, 228.

24 Gottlob Frege, *On Concept and Object*.

25 Stenius, *Wittgenstein's Tractatus*, 212.

26 Schneider, *Religion*.
27 Baker and Hacker, *Frege: Logical Excavations*; Dummett, "An Unsuccessful Dig."
28 Taylor, "Theories of Meaning," *Philosophical Papers vol. 1*, 275.
29 Cf. Crary and Read, *The New Wittgenstein*.
30 Taylor, "Language Not Mysterious?," 32–47.
31 Schneider, *Wittgenstein's Later Theory of Meaning*.
32 Taylor, *The Language Animal*.
33 Ibid., 176.

Chapter Three

1 Arendt, "Action and the Pursuit of Happiness," 1.
2 Popper, "Normal Science and Its Dangers," 56.
3 Taylor, *Dilemmas and Connections*, 326.
4 Walzer, *Just and Unjust Wars*, 99.
5 Taylor, *Multiculturalism and "The Politics of Recognition,"* 59.
6 Ibid., 61 (emphasis added).
7 Taylor, *Dilemmas and Connections*, 24.
8 Taylor, "Interpretation and the Sciences of Man."
9 Ibid., 65.
10 Ibid., 65–6.
11 Ibid., 67–8.
12 Taylor, *Dilemmas*, 24.
13 Ibid., 26.
14 Ibid., 27.
15 Ibid., 25.
16 Ibid., 29.
17 Ibid., 32–3.
18 Ibid., 138.
19 Ibid., 140.
20 Ibid., 144.
21 Taylor, *A Secular Age*, 3 (emphases added).
22 Ibid., 3. Although Taylor's canvas is extremely broad, he is primarily concerned with the historical transformations in Latin Christendom. Although he thinks that most Western societies are secular in his sense (including the United States), he says: "Clear contrast cases today would be the majority of Muslim societies, or the milieux in which the vast majority of Indians live" (Taylor, *A Secular Age*, 3). Consequently, he is not claiming that all modern existing societies are secular.
23 Taylor, *A Secular Age*, 19 (emphasis added).
24 Ibid., 18.

25 Ibid., 510.
26 I develop this argument more fully in Bernstein, "The Uneasy Tensions of Immanence and Transcendence." See also Philip Kitcher's defence of secular humanism in Philip Kitcher, *Life after Faith*.
27 Taylor, *A Secular Age*, 3.
28 Bernstein, "Pragmatism, Pluralism, and the Healing of Wounds," in *The New Constellation*, 336.
29 Taylor, "Afterward," 318–19.

Chapter Four

1 I am grateful for written comments on a previous draft from Cécile Laborde, Jean Cohen, Matteo Bonotti, and Sune Laegaard. This chapter was first published in J.L. Cohen and C. Laborde, eds, *Religion, Secularism, and Constitutional Democracy* (New York: Columbia University Press, 2015). I am grateful to Columbia Press for its republication here.
2 Modood, *Multiculturalism* and *Essays on Secularism and Multiculturalism*.
3 Modood, "Is There a Crisis of Secularism?," 131, and Bhargava, "Is European Secularism Secular Enough?"
4 Kymlicka, *Multicultural Citizenship*.
5 Kymlicka, "Historic Settlements and New Challenges."
6 Laborde has argued in *Critical Republicanism* that in doing so I am guilty of "status quo partiality." My commitment to political secularism as practiced in Western Europe is comparable to a commitment to democracy as practiced in those states: it is not a commitment to an existing set of institutions or to one particular time, namely to a narrow status quo.
7 For further details see Modood, "Moderate Secularism, Religion as Identity."
8 Though see Stepan, "Religion, Democracy, and the 'Twin Tolerations.'"
9 Bhargava, "Political Secularism: Why It Is Needed," 88; and see also Bhargava, "Is European Secularism Secular Enough?"
10 Bhargava, "Political Secularism: Why It Is Needed," 88.
11 Bhargava's theoretical position has become more difficult as while still holding on to his tripartite analysis of the secular state (ends, institutions, laws/policies) he has come to accept moderate secularism as a distinct West European form of secularism (Bhargava, "Can Secularism Be Rehabilitated?" and "Is European Secularism Secular Enough?") even though moderate secular states cannot be analyzed in terms of state-religion *institutional* separations.
12 Laborde, "Political Liberalism and Religion."
13 Dworkin, *Is Democracy Possible Here?*, 62.
14 Ibid., 57.
15 I assume that is what he means by saying that Britain is a secular nation. Nevertheless, he simultaneously thinks of Britain as an ambiguous example

of a "moderate religious state," while for me Britain is a primary example of a moderate secular state.

16   In relation to the last point I would point to how, for example, the Bishop of Bradford played a leading role in leading a local dialogue with Muslims who angrily burnt copies of the novel *The Satanic Verses* in 1989; since then this inter-faith role has come to have government involvement, especially through the creation at one time of a government department, the Department of Local Government and Communities, and one of its most developed recent manifestation is the policy of "Near Neighbours," in which central government funds are distributed to local community initiatives but applications have to be initially validated by a local priest of the Church of England.

17   "Weak establishment" is not a flattering term and perhaps "thin" or "minimal" might be substituted for "weak" but I continue to use the latter as it refers to power and it is clear that secularism is about relations of power.

18   Fetzer and Soper, *Muslims and the State.*

19   Laegaard, "Unequal Recognition, Misrecognition and Injustice."

20   Modood and Kastoryano, "Secularism and the Accommodation of Muslims in Europe."

21   "Symbolic establishment" is discussed by Brudney, "On Noncoercive Establishment," and Laborde, "Political Liberalism and Religion," and allowed as consistent with liberalism.

22   Cf. Rawls, "The Idea of Public Reason Revisited," and Habermas, "Religion in the Public Sphere."

23   Taylor, "The Meaning of Secularism"; Bouchard and Taylor, *Building the Future*; and Maclure and Taylor, *Secularism and Freedom of Conscience.*

24   Bader, "The Governance of Religious Diversity," 52.

25   Baubérot, "The Evolution of Secularism in France."

26   Akan, "*Laïcité* and Multiculturalism."

27   In relation to Finland, see Tuomas Martikainen, "Muslim Immigrants, Public Religion and Developments," 98.

28   In Modood, "Moderate Secularism, Religion as Identity and Respect for Religion," I offer five different reasons why the state may be interested in religion, of which truth is just one, and of course is one that lost considerable legitimacy in the twentieth century in western Europe.

29   See Modood, *Multiculturalism.* I am presenting a conception of multiculturalism that is based on the pioneering work of Will Kymlicka, Bhikhu Parekh, Charles Taylor, and Iris Marion Young, without being identical to the views of any one of them.

30   Cf. Taylor, *Multiculturalism and "The Politics of Recognition"*; Maclure and Taylor, *Secularism.* The latter's focus on conscience and protection of negative liberty, of exemptions from the state seems to supplant the ideas of Recognition and the harms of misrecognition, of alienation and symbolic equality,

which are central to Taylor's famous earlier work. My own view is much closer to the "non-procedural liberalism" that Taylor argues for in *Multiculturalism*, centred on recognition and that "judgement about the good life can be enshrined in laws and state action" as long as they are consistent with Liberal Democratic Constitutionalism (LDC) without being confined to LDC.

31 Cf. the discussion on the role of "operative public values" in Parekh, *Rethinking Multiculturalism*.

32 Rawls, "The Idea of Public Reason Revisited."

33 Taylor, "The Meaning of Secularism."

34 I owe this point to a discussion with Sune Laegaard.

35 Bader, *Secularism or Democracy?*

36 After years of arguing that the appropriate liberal response to diversity is neutrality, Christian Joppke now argues that a liberal state may have a Christian identity, though he restricts this to a Christian cultural heritage identity, but interestingly believes it may be more inclusive of religious diversity than a narrowly "liberal" state identity (Joppke, "A Christian Identity for the Liberal State?")

37 Dworkin, in *Is Democracy Possible Here?*, denies that religion is special in the "moderate" secular state's view of religion, which is odd because the whole point of secularism is that religion has to be treated specially and as a unique problem.

38 It is specifically in relation to my advocacy of "equalizing upwards" that Laborde, in *Critical Republicanism*, believes I fall into the error of "status quo partiality."

39 Similarly, in the case of how to extend equality to gays and lesbians in relation to marriage, few have suggested that it should be done by abolishing the institution (one way of placing heterosexuals and homosexuals on the same level).

40 Patti T. Lenard, "What Can Multicultural Theory Tell Us," 317.

41 As established in Zelman v Simmons-Harris (2002) http://en.wikipedia.org/wiki/Zelman_v._Simmons-Harris (last accessed 9 January 2014).

42 Rajeev Bhargava, "States, Religious Diversity and the Crisis of Secularism" and "Is European Secularism Secular Enough?"; Laborde, "Political Liberalism and Religion."

43 Casanova, "Immigration and the New Religious Pluralism"; Kymlicka, *Historical Settlements*; Foner and Alba, "Immigrant Religion in the US and Western Europe."

44 Bhargava, "States, Religious Diversity and the Crisis of Secularism," "Can Secularism be Rehabilitated?," and "Is European Secularism Secular Enough?" For a fuller discussion of why I think Bhargava misunderstands Western European secularisms, see Modood, "Moderate Secularism, Religion as Identity and Respect for Religion" and "Moderate Secularism: A European

Conception," though I note that in "Can Secularism be Rehabilitated?" and in this volume he now accepts that Western European moderate secularisms are distinct from and additional to his contention that the American and the French models are the mainstream Western models. See also endnote 11.

45 Kymlicka, "Historic Settlements and New Challenges," 548; cf. Bhargava, "Is European Secularism Secular Enough?"

46 Foner and Alba, "Immigrant Religion in the US and Western Europe," 379.

47 Heath and Roberts, *British Identity*.

48 Wind-Cowie and Gregory, *A Place for Pride*, 41.

49 Modood, *Essays on Secularism and Multiculturalism*.

50 See Modood, *Church, State and Religious Minorities*.

51 Casanova, "Immigration and the New Religious Pluralism," 141.

52 A point recognized by Casanova, "Immigration and the New Religious Pluralism" and offered as a factor by Foner and Alba, "Immigrant Religion in the US and Western Europe."

53 In relation to inflammatory politics around the "Ground Zero Mosque," "Shariah Law," public burnings of the Qur'an, and how these controversies should be dealt with, see Nussbaum, *The New Religious Intolerance*.

54 Murray, "Norwegian Killer."

55 Sune Laegaard has usefully made a distinction between alienation and symbolic inequality and argued that it is the latter that is at stake in "What's (un)Problematic About Religious Establishment?"

56 Karl Marx, *The Economic and Philosophic Manuscripts of 1844*.

57 de Latour, "Is Multiculturalism Un-French?"

58 For more on this see *Essays on Secularism and Multiculturalism*.

Chapter Five

1 Kymlicka, *Politics in the Vernacular*, 252.

2 For a powerful challenge to theocratic politics as it played out in the 2012 US presidential election, see Wills, "Contraception's Con Men." In "My Problem with Christianism," Andrew Sullivan suggests a helpful distinction between Christianity and "Christianism" (i.e., theocratic Christianity), intended to parallel the already familiar distinction between Islam and Islamism.

3 Andersen, "How American Lost Its Mind."

4 What does it mean to say that not expressing contempt for the beliefs of fellow citizens is a civic duty but not a moral duty? If one really thinks that a particular belief is nonsense (for instance, religiously motivated rejection of the theory of evolution), it's not obvious that one shows respect for other people by displaying more respect for their beliefs than one thinks those beliefs actually merit. Perhaps feigned respect of this sort is simply patronizing. On the other hand, it's hard to see how one can sustain healthy civic relations

within a political community if groups of citizens are denouncing each other not only for embracing the wrong policies but also for being credulous fools. But perhaps this betrays insufficient trust in the capacity of citizens to be honest about their philosophical differences. Perhaps here too, feigned respect is merely patronizing. That is to say, I'm less confident than adherents of Rawls's political liberalism (as well as multiculturalists) tend to be about what respect for the beliefs of fellow citizens truly requires. For a good discussion of this issue, see Eagleton, *Reason, Faith, and Revolution*, 147–8.

5 See Stolberg, "For Romney."

6 As Taylor nicely expresses it, the original impulse in Rawls's political liberalism idea was for "religious views [to be left] in the vestibule of the public sphere" (Taylor, "Why We Need a Radical Redefinition of Secularism," 49; cited hereafter as "Radical Redefinition"). And since this was a manifestly non-neutral requirement put upon *certain* citizens, Rawls felt impelled to require that *all* "comprehensive doctrines" be left in that same vestibule. Taylor goes on to write ("Radical Redefinition," 53) that Rawls entertained such an idea (namely the idea of leaving the religious comprehensive doctrines in the vestibule) only "for a time"; cf. Maclure and Taylor, *Secularism and Freedom of Conscience*, 110. However, without some version of this doctrine, political liberalism would not be political liberalism.

7 For a fuller version of this critique, see Beiner, *Civil Religion*, chapter 23.

8 An expanded version entitled "What Does Secularism Mean?" has been published in Taylor, *Dilemmas and Connections*, 303–25.

9 Taylor, "Radical Redefinition," 35.

10 Ibid., 37: Atatürk's regime is not "genuinely secular" because it is "fixated on" (i.e., discriminates against) religion. That is, it doesn't leave people at liberty in their chosen religious identities, but aggressively challenges those identities. Hence secularism "in its polemical sense of non- or antireligious" (39) is not really secularism.

11 For the reference to "Jacobin" *laïcité*, see "Radical Redefinition," 35; cf. Maclure and Taylor, *Secularism and Freedom of Conscience*, 17. In "Radical Redefinition," Taylor calls this "hyper-Republicanism" (40).

12 Taylor, "Radical Redefinition," 39. Cf. Maclure and Taylor, *Secularism and Freedom of Conscience*, 14: "The temptation to make secularism the equivalent of religion is generally stronger in countries where secularism came about at the cost of a bitter struggle against a dominant religion [such as France or Turkey]. It may be because of the fairly widespread sense that secularism was achieved in Quebec in a pitched battle against the Catholic church that some Quebecers today are sympathetic toward a certain version of French and Turkish secularism." Bill 21 ("An Act respecting the laicity of the State"), passed in June of 2019 by the Coalition Avenir Québec government of Quebec Premier François Legault – with the support of a majority of

Quebeckers – clearly aligns contemporary Quebec with the modes of secularism rejected by Taylor; and Taylor has been very vocal (rightly so) in his repudiation of this particular manifestation of militant *laïcité*.

13   However, unlike Taylor, I do think that it is reasonable to ask the question: in a country like the UK, where by law only an Anglican can be head of state, why *doesn't* that impugn the civic status of non-Anglicans?

14   Maclure and Taylor, *Secularism and Freedom of Conscience*, 13. Of course, this is a co-authored book, so with respect to any particular sentence there is uncertainty about whether it is a Taylor sentence or a Maclure sentence. However, all the ideas in the book that are of interest to me in this chapter are affirmed by Taylor in a *New Statesman* interview cited below (note 26) to be ideas to which he's committed; and the same ideas occur also in the single-authored "Radical Redefinition" essay. Therefore, I consider the book to be Taylor's book, however unfair this might be to Maclure.

15   Cf. Maclure and Taylor, *Secularism and Freedom of Conscience*, 20: "the state must be the state for all citizens."

16   Cf. Taylor, "Radical Redefinition," 37. I have explained in *Civil Religion*, chapter 23, why I do not find Rawls's assimilation of religious and non-religious comprehensive doctrines to be persuasive. See especially 299, n. 37. Taylor, in his debate with Habermas (Habermas and Taylor, "Dialogue"), carries a step forward Rawls's suggestion inscribed in the very notion of comprehensive doctrines that there is in principle no difference between basing one's view of life on religious beliefs and basing it on a secular philosophy. This is another aspect of Taylor's Rawlsian turn.

17   Rawlsian categories are appealed to throughout *Secularism and Freedom of Conscience* (see, for instance, 86, 97, and 107); and they figure equally prominently in the "Radical Redefinition" essay: see, for instance, Taylor, "Radical Redefinition," 37, on "state neutrality" (citing "the value of the late-Rawlsian formulation for a secular state"); and 48, on "overlapping consensus." Taylor tends to present Rawls, and Habermas too, as having modified their earlier harder-line philosophical rationalism in a way that brings them closer to Taylor's views (Taylor, "Radical Redefinition," 35 and 53; Maclure and Taylor, *Secularism and Freedom of Conscience*, 110). But I think this tells only half the story. If Rawls has moved closer to Taylor, Taylor has also moved closer to Rawls.

18   Taylor, "Radical Redefinition," 47; Maclure and Taylor, *Secularism and Freedom of Conscience*, 14–15.

19   Maclure and Taylor, *Secularism and Freedom of Conscience*, 112, n. 4.

20   Since it is obviously my view that referring to "the neutral state" is misleading, my suggestion would be just to call it "the liberal state." See Maclure and Taylor, *Secularism and Freedom of Conscience*, 16–17, which acknowledges limits to the idea of state neutrality while remaining committed to the language of neutrality.

21 It was Taylor-inspired in the fairly obvious sense that contestation over "the priority of the right to the good" became central to Michael Sandel's critique of Rawls. (Sandel, like me, was a student of Taylor's at Oxford.) The basic Rawlsian idea was that as philosophers we shouldn't attempt to *adjudicate* competing conceptions of the good, because we know in advance that this will never lead anywhere. Instead, we should content ourselves with formulating principles of civic co-existence that will help to advance our individual ends, whatever our ends turn out to be. It is hard to see any difference between that Rawlsian view, and the Taylorian view expressed in texts on secularism that we have been examining.

22 This more radical neutralism is captured in familiar Rawlsian slogans of "apply[ing] the principle of toleration to philosophy itself," "stay[ing] on the surface, philosophically speaking," etc. For relevant citations, see *Civil Religion*, 296, n. 28 and 298, n. 34. My view of these aspects of Rawls's later thought can be summed up like this: Rawls feels that in the interests of civic peace, he needs to emasculate philosophy as the pursuit of ultimate truth about the ends of life, and this in turn has the consequence that he ends up emasculating his own version of liberalism. Putting it like this should help make clear why I don't regard Rawls as a political-philosophical model. I have pursued this critique further in Beiner, *Political Philosophy: What It Is and Why It Matters*, ch. 13.

23 Beiner, *Civil Religion*, 298–9.

24 This conception is developed in three places: in Beiner, "Citizenship as a Comprehensive Doctrine"; in chapter 23 of Beiner, *Civil Religion*; and in Beiner, "Secularism as a Common Good."

25 Surely the rise of right-populism since 2016, both in the US and elsewhere, has put paid to any confidence that liberalism is reliably founded on a stable and enduring society-wide consensus. One hopes that a liberal vision of civic life survives the current crisis, but whether it does or not, these recent challenges to liberal self-understanding have probably permanently shaken the Rawlsian presumption that liberal commitments are a historical *achievement* rather than something that's ever-vulnerable to illiberal setbacks.

26 The phrase "hard-line secularist" comes from a personal communication from Taylor to Akeel Bilgrami, the text of which Bilgrami published in his article "Secularism: Its Content and Context," 95. Taylor's text then gets discussed between Taylor and his interviewer in Derbyshire, "The Books Interview." Taylor emphatically endorses the interviewer's interpretation of Taylor's conception of secularism according to which Richard Dawkins and Christopher Hitchens do "not count as secularists." That, I have to say, is a very implausible suggestion. In a debate with Will Hutton (Dawkins and Hutton, "What Is the Proper Place for Religion in British Public Life?"), Dawkins makes perfectly clear that he understands the meaning of secularism in exactly the way that

Taylor does. To be sure, he has anti-theistic arguments to which he is commit-ted in addition to his pro-secularism arguments. But that doesn't mean that Dawkins himself views the two sets of arguments as one and the same.

27 It is important to note that the kind of illegitimate clerical power in need of being pacified or liberalized is not limited to theocratic control of the state, for one can have oppressive, priest-dominated forms of social life even where the state is not in any direct sense a theocracy. In that sense, the idea of a liberal regime encompasses both political and social norms; that is, norms intended to protect individuals against clerical oppression both at the level of the state and within society itself. Such concerns about coerced religious practice partly animate the "republican" conception of secularism that Tay-lor rejects.

28 For an extended discussion, see Beiner, "Hermeneutical Generosity."

29 I'm of course not opposed to mutual understanding between different reli-gions, and between believers and non-believers. How could one be opposed to that? But this strikes me as a civic task, not a philosophical task. Related to this, let me propose another possible way of characterizing the parallel between Taylor and Rawls. The task of philosophy is the pursuit of truth. And pursuing truth uncompromisingly is as likely to lead to intractable limits to mutual understanding as to the promotion of mutual understanding. This indeed is why a theorist like Rawls (for civic reasons not unlike those that ani-mate Taylor) is concerned to invent a way of doing political philosophy that (paradoxically) actually moves away from the preoccupation with truth char-acteristic of philosophy as such. I'd be inclined to say that for both Rawls and Taylor, the tasks of liberal citizenship are imported into philosophy, thereby diminishing the radicality of philosophy in its proper vocation. Hence both Taylor and Rawls, surprising as this may be, belong to a common movement that is content to see the proper purposes of philosophy trumped, or sub-sumed, by what is thought to be the more urgent business of promoting better and more tolerant citizenship.

30 The original version of this essay was written for "Charles Taylor at 80," a con-ference held in Montreal 29–31 March 2012. I'm very grateful for responses received from conference participants, not least those from Charles Taylor himself.

Chapter Six

1 See Taylor, "What is Wrong with Negative Liberty?," in *Philosophical Papers* vol. 2, 211–29.

2 See, e.g., Mills, "Ideal Theory as Ideology," and Simmons, "Ideal and Non-Ideal Theory."

3   See, e.g., Kramer, *The Quality of Freedom*; Carter, *A Measure of Freedom*; Steiner, "How Free: Computing Personal Liberty"; and Flathman, *The Philosophy and Politics of Freedom*.

4   There is much discussion of whether constraints on freedom must come directly or indirectly from the actions of other persons or, alternatively, they can merely be things for which persons are somehow responsible. For discussion see Carter, "Positive and Negative Liberty."

5   Kramer, *Quality of Freedom*, 15. This is the core of Kramer's view whose details are discussed at length in his book.

6   See the works listed in note 3. Kramer, however, insists that value qualifiers should be added that tie the extent of freedom to the value the actions one is free to do has for the agent. See Kramer, *Quality of Freedom*, 425–43.

7   Berlin, "Two Concepts of Liberty," in *Four Essays on Liberty*, 135.

8   See, e.g., my "Liberalism and Individual Positive Freedom."

9   See the exchange among Carter, Kramer, and Dowding and Van Hees: Carter and Kramer, "How Changes in One's Preferences Can Affect One's Freedom," and Dowding and van Hees, "Counterfactual Success Again."

10 Both Carter and Kramer accept that freedom in the negative sense can expand or contract because of a change in a person's desires, though it will not be merely from such a change ("How Changes in One's Preferences Can Affect One's Freedom"). But in my example, the change in desire is the only reason a person is moved from one classification to another, and if we are not bothered by such a shift in this case, I'm not sure why we should be so worried generally about making reference to a person's value perspective in our accounts.

11 Taylor, "What Is Wrong with Negative Liberty?," in *Philosophical Papers vol. 2*, 182–3.

12 Carter, *A Measure of Freedom*, ch. 6.

13 Kramer disagrees with Carter and Steiner on this point: see Kramer, *Quality of Freedom*, 425–43, for discussion.

14 See, e.g., Carter, *A Measure of Freedom*, ch. 2.

15 Kramer, *Quality of Freedom*, 425ff.

16 For a helpful analysis of the problem, see Arneson, "Freedom and Desire."

17 See Carter, *A Measure of Freedom*, 130–40.

18 See, e.g., Hirschmann, *The Subject of Liberty*. Also, see Christman, "Can Positive Liberty Be Saved?" and Carol Gould, *Rethinking Democracy: Freedom and Social Cooperation in Politics, Economy, and Society* (Cambridge: Cambridge University Press, 1988).

19 Sen, *Inequality Reexamined*, chs 3–4.

20 See Sen, "Well-Being, Agency, and Freedom," and Carter, *A Measure of Freedom*, 56–8.

21 Again, see Berlin, "Two Concepts," in *Four Essays on Liberty* for discussion of this worry. For broader discussion of the intellectual history of notions of this sort, see Taylor, *Sources of the Self*; see also Taylor, *The Ethics of Authenticity*.

22 I have attempted to defend such a notion under the rubric of autonomy. See Christman, *The Politics of Persons*, ch. 7.

23 Carter, *A Measure of Freedom*, 155–6.

24 Harry Frankfurt, "The Faintest Passion"; Taylor, *Sources of the Self*, 91–110.

25 For discussion of the complexities that social conceptions of agency introduce into accounts of freedom, see Christman, "Freedom and the Extended Self."

26 Matthew Kramer has the most expansive account of this constraint, arguing that barriers count as restraints of freedom if they are the product of human action, directly or indirectly, to whatever degree (*Quality of Freedom*, 313).

27 People stuck in a mineshaft, on such a view, are unfree to leave, strictly speaking, only if their being trapped resulted from human action. (One is tempted to stop the presses right there, since it leads to the rather discomfiting conclusion that we have to inform those stuck minors that the verdict about whether they are in fact free or not free while in the cave must await the completion of an official inquiry concerning fault!) I mentioned at the outset that perspective mattered, and here one wonders why the source of the physical barriers I face matters to my experience of freedom. Kramer argues that if one carelessly throws an apple off the side of a cliff that (unbeknownst to the person) causes an avalanche that traps another person, then that is sufficient to count as a human source (Kramer, *Quality of Freedom*).

28 This is partly the reason that David Miller claims that constraints count as limitations on freedom if human beings are responsible for them (or their removal) in some way. See Miller, *Markets, State, and Community*, 23–46.

29 Kramer, *Quality of Freedom*, 362 ff.

30 Douglass, *Narrative*, 59.

31 Ibid., 60.

32 I acknowledge that this case could be described as Douglass's grandmother being prevented from seeing her family and that this is captured in negative accounts. Perhaps, but this merely brings us back to the need to classify particular losses of freedom with reference to people's value perspectives and, in this kind of case, the social nature of those perspectives.

33 For Taylor's version of this approach, see *The Ethics of Authenticity*, 32–3.

34 Catriona Mackenzie, "Relational Autonomy, Normative Authority, and Perfectionism."

35 Phillip Pettit, *A Theory of Freedom*, 87.

36 Ibid., 73. Pettit goes on to say that being treated as worthy of address occurs when one's avowal interests are properly tracked in the interaction.

This last point connects freedom as discursive control with freedom as non-domination, the political notion of freedom Pettit develops in his republican view (see Pettit, *Republicanism*).

37 Anderson and Honneth, "Autonomy, Vulnerability, Recognition, and Justice," 137. See also Honneth, *The Struggle for Recognition*. On the concept of recognition, Honneth writes: "social recognition represents the necessary condition for subjects being able to identify with their valuable qualities and, accordingly, develop genuine autonomy" (Axel Honneth, "Grounding Recognition," 515).

38 This makes this view consistent with the position taken by Nancy Fraser in her exchange with Honneth over the issue of whether recognition must be seen as an invariant, metaphysical component of agency or a contingent and variable requirement growing out of particular social struggles. See Fraser and Honneth, *Redistribution or Recognition?*

39 See Haque, "Ambiguities and Confusions in Migration-Trafficking Nexus: A Development Challenge," in *Trafficking and the Global Sex Industry*, edited by Karen Beers and Delila Amire (Lanham, MD: Lexington Books, 2006), 3–21.

40 I discuss these phenomena in more detail in "Human Rights and Global Wrongs: The Role of Human Rights Discourse in Responses to Trafficking," in *Poverty, Agency and Human Rights*, edited by Diana T. Meyers (Oxford: Oxford University Press, 2015), 321–46. See also, Md. Shahidul Haque, "Ambiguities and Confusions," and Rhacel Parreñas, Maria Cecilia Hwang, and Heather Ruth Lee, "What is Human Trafficking? A Review Essay," in *Signs* 37, no. 4, Sex: A Thematic Issue (Summer 2012): 1015–29. For a journalistic account of such phenomena, see Nicholas Kristoff and Cheryl WuDunn, *Half the Sky: Turning Oppression into Opportunity for Women Worldwide* (New York: Knopf, 2009), chs 1–2.

41 See Taylor, *Multiculturalism and "The Politics of Recognition,"* 68f.

42 Ibid., 32f.

43 Topics in this discussion were also developed in Christman, "No Longer A Slave but Not Yet Free," and Christman, "Analyzing Freedom from the Shadows of Slavery."

Chapter Seven

1 Charles Taylor, "What's Wrong with Negative Liberty?," in *Philosophical Papers* vol. 2, 211–29.

2 Taylor, *Sources of the Self*, 47.

3 Flathman, *The Philosophy and Politics of Freedom*; Kateb, *Emerson and Self-Reliance*.

4 Taylor, "What's Wrong with Negative Liberty?," 221.

5 Foddy and Savulescu, "A Liberal Account of Addiction."
6 Taylor, "Foucault on Freedom and Truth," and Taylor, "Connolly, Foucault, and Truth."
7 Taylor, "What Is Human Agency?," in *Philosophical Papers vol. 1.*
8 Taylor, "Politics of Recognition," in *Multiculturalism and "The Politics of Recognition."*
9 Taylor, "Politics of Recognition," 34.
10 Ibid., 26.
11 de Beauvoir, *The Second Sex.*
12 Ferguson, *The Man Question*, 129.

Chapter Eight

1 Taylor, *A Secular Age.*
2 Ibid., 212–18.
3 Ibid., 595.
4 Ibid., 61.
5 Jean-Jacques Rousseau, in the *Profession de foi du vicaire Savoyard*, makes the extraordinary claim that all evil is human in origin – that death would be no evil and physical suffering of small significance – were it not for the baneful influence of human vanity on our judgment and experience. But this is a very unusual view.
6 Taylor, *A Secular Age*, 306.
7 How striking is the contrast with the classical doctrine of Christianity, for which human embodiment – particularly its "concupiscence" – testifies to our fallen natures.
8 Locke, *The Second Treatise of Civil Government*, §183.
9 Kant, *Religion and Rational Theology*, 8:257.
10 Ibid., 8:258.
11 Ibid., 6:490.
12 Kant, *Lectures on Ethics*, 6:97–8.
13 Johann Gottlieb Fichte, "Concerning the Scholar's Vocation," 144–84, 168–9.
14 Sergey Nechayev, "Revolutionary Catechism."

Chapter Nine

1 One version of such an approach, pitched at the level of Taylor's work, is Viveiros de Castro, *Cannibal Metaphysics*. There de Castro compares the perspectivism of Amazonian cultures to the minor European tradition of perspectivism advanced by Gilles Deleuze, allowing each tradition to illuminate the other.

2 One version of that engagement can be found in Connolly, "Catholicism and Philosophy."

3 Taylor, *A Secular Age*, 5–6.

4 Ibid., 7, 10.

5 Ibid., 655.

6 Whitehead, *Process and Reality*, 94.

7 Ibid., 226–7.

8 Ibid., 227.

9 Marcel Proust, "Time Regained," in *In Search of Lost Time*, 247–8. I also draw upon this instance from Proust in Connolly, *A World of Becoming*, ch. 4.

Chapter Ten

1 Hume and Selby-Bigge, *A Treatise of Human Nature*, 415.

2 Ibid., 469.

3 Moore, *Principia Ethica*, 12.

4 Harman, "Moral Relativism Defended."

5 Anscombe, *Intention*, 70–1.

6 Taylor, "To Follow a Rule," in *Philosophical Arguments*, 168, 173.

7 Ibid., 168, 170, 178.

8 Tully, "Wittgenstein and Political Philosophy," 193, 195.

9 Kant, *Groundwork for the Metaphysics of Morals*, 118.

10 Oscar Wilde, *The Soul of Man under Socialism*, 137.

11 Taylor, *Sources of the Self*, 36, 27.

12 Foucault, *Ethics: Subjectivity and Truth*, 262.

13 Taylor, *The Ethics of Authenticity*, 40.

14 Nietzsche, *The Gay Science*, 232.

Chapter Eleven

1 Baier, *Postures of the Mind*, 232.

2 It is clear why many philosophers would *like* it to be so – in order to provide a principled resolution to conflicts of obligation. But wanting something to be true falls very much short of demonstrating that it is true.

3 Charles Taylor, *Sources of the Self*, 76–7.

4 See Bucciarelli, Khemlaniand, and Johnson-Laird, "The Psychology of Moral Reasoning."

5 As Susan Dwyer puts it: "Common experience suggests that human beings are not particularly adept at providing justifications for their moral judgments: either they cannot provide reasons for those judgments or the reasons they offer are only weakly associated with the judgments themselves." See Dwyer's "Moral Dumbfounding and the Linguistic Analogy."

6 Haidt and Bjorklund, "Social Intuitionists Answer Six Questions." See also Haidt, "The Emotional Dog."

7 The major focus of Lawrence Kohlberg's program was to investigate moral reasoning by examining how people responded to conflicts of duty. See Kohlberg, *Essays on Moral Development*.

8 Tversky and Kahneman, "Availability."

9 Wilson, *Strangers to Ourselves*.

10 For more extensive discussion, see Heath, "Three Evolutionary Precursors to Morality."

11 Nichols, *Sentimental Rules*, 11–16.

12 See, e.g., Joyce, *The Evolution of Morality*, 108–18.

13 Shepher, "Mate Selection," and Wolf, *Sexual Attraction and Childhood Association*.

14 For discussion, see Prinz, *The Emotional Construction of Morals*, 30.

15 Simon, "A Behavioral Model of Rational Choice."

16 Ibid., 109–10.

17 Alisdair Macintyre famously proposed in *After Virtue* that a "Riddley Walker" scenario of this sort existed in the domain of ethics.

18 Hare, *Moral Thinking*, 25.

19 Ibid., 38.

20 Ibid., 50.

21 Ibid., 75–6. See also Hare, "Rawls' Theory of Justice," 82–4.

22 See Dwyer, Huebner, and Hauser, "The Linguistic Analogy."

23 See, for instance, Hauser, *Moral Minds*, 171–8; Mikhail, "Universal Moral Grammar."

24 Lenny Moss, "Ethical Expertise and Moral Maturity."

25 "Within the moral knowledge of common human reason we have attained its principle. To be sure, common human reason does not think of it abstractly in such a universal form, but it always has it in view and uses it as the standard of its judgment … Without in the least teaching common reason anything new, we need only to draw its attention to its own principle, in the manner of Socrates, thus showing that neither science nor philosophy is needed in order to know what one has to do in order to be honest and good, and even wise and virtuous." Kant, *Foundations of the Metaphysic of Morals*, 20 [403–4].

26 Hauser, *Moral Minds*, 37, 43.

27 Ibid., xx.

28 Brandom, *Making It Explicit*, 108.

29 Ibid., 112. I will be using the term "explicitative" instead of "expressive" in what follows, in part to avoid confusion with Taylor's concept of "expressivism," which is quite different from Brandom's.

30 Ibid., 108.

31 Ibid., 98.

32 Ibid., 104.

33 Habermas, *Moral Consciousness and Communicative Action*, 97. Thus "the description we employ to pass from knowing how to knowing that is a hypothetical reconstruction that can provide only a more or less correct rendering of intuitions" (ibid.).

34 Brandom, *Making It Explicit*, 104.

35 Ibid., 105.

36 There are some very useful reminders of this in Prinz, *The Emotional Construction of Morals*.

37 The subtitle of John Mackie's book *Ethics: Inventing Right and Wrong* articulates quite nicely the feature that scares most people off of views like his own.

38 Naturally, *pur et dur* Kantians and utilitarians will object to this, on the grounds that their principle, correctly interpreted, never produces the wrong answer. But this just sets off more Burkean alarm bells. Part of being dangerous is not being able to see the limitations of one's own principles.

39 Cass Sunstein, for one, has suggested that moral philosophers have been "inadvertently and even comically replicating the early work of Kahneman and Tversky, by uncovering situations in which intuitions, normally quite sensible, turn out to misfire." See Sunstein, "Moral Heuristics"; see also Doris and Stich, "As a Matter of Fact."

40 Rawls, *A Theory of Justice*, 18.

41 Cf. Boukydis, "Adult Perception of Infant Appearance."

42 As does, in effect, de Waal, *Primates and Philosophers*.

43 Moody-Adams, *Fieldwork in Familiar Places*, 194.

44 Brandom, *Making It Explicit*, 106.

45 Grover, *A Prosentential Theory of Truth*.

46 Richard Rorty, "Pragmatism, Davidson and Truth," 334 (variable name changed).

47 Patton, *The Metaphysics of Oughtness*, 1.

48 Baier, *Postures of the Mind*, 232.

49 Durkheim, *Les Règles de la méthode sociologique*, 24 (my translation).

Chapter Twelve

1 Charles Taylor, *Philosophical Papers vol. 1*, 1ff.

2 Charles Taylor, "Ethics and Ontology," 306.

3 John McDowell, *Mind and World*; "Two Sorts of Naturalism," in *Mind, Value, Reality*, 167–97.

4 McDowell, "Précis of *Mind and World*," 238.

5 McDowell, *Mind and World*, 78.

6 McDowell, "Two Sorts of Naturalism," in *Mind, Value, Reality*, 184ff.

7 John McDowell, "Virtue and Reason," in *Mind, Value, Reality*, 53ff.

8 Taylor, *Ethics and Ontology*, 312.
9 Ibid., 314.
10 Taylor, *Sources of the Self*, 59.
11 Wiggins, "A Sensible Subjectivism," *Needs, Values, Truth*, 185–214; Wiggins, "Moral Cognitivism."
12 Wiggins, "Moral Cognitivism," 79.
13 Ibid., 84.
14 Ibid.
15 Ibid., 68.
16 Taylor, *Ethics and Ontology*, 316.
17 Interestingly, in *Sources of the Self* (67ff.) Taylor does discuss what he calls a "sophisticated naturalism" but which he associates there with Bernard Williams's discussion in chapter 8 of *Ethics and the Limits of Philosophy*. That naturalism overlaps interestingly, but only partially, with McDowell's and Wiggins's naturalism discussed here.
18 Taylor, *Ethics and Ontology*, 315.
19 McDowell, "Two Sorts of Naturalism," in *Mind, Value, Reality*, 189.
20 Taylor, *Ethics and Ontology*, 314, 316.
21 Taylor, *A Secular Age*, 256, 258.
22 Wiggins, "Moral Cognitivism," 70.
23 Taylor, *Ethics and Ontology*, 319.
24 Wiggins, "Moral Cognitivism," 70.
25 Ibid.
26 Taylor, *Sources of the Self*, 91ff.
27 Ibid., 8.
28 Ibid., 92ff.
29 Taylor, *A Secular Age*, 542.
30 Ibid., 16.
31 Taylor, *A Secular Age*, 780.
32 Taylor, *Sources of the Self*, 516ff.; *A Secular Age*, 695ff.
33 Taylor, *A Secular Age*, 697, 701.
34 Ibid., 702.
35 Ibid.
36 Ibid.
37 Taylor, *Sources of the Self*, 521.

Chapter Thirteen

1 Rawls, *A Theory of Justice*.
2 Dworkin, *Religion without God*.
3 Nussbaum, *Liberty of Conscience*.
4 Maclure and Taylor, *Secularism and Freedom of Conscience*.

5   Taylor, *Sources of the Self; A Secular Age.*
6   Laborde, *Critical Republicanism.*
7   Taylor, "What's Wrong with Negative Liberty?," in *Philosophy and the Human Sciences: Philosophical Papers.*
8   This essay was presented at "Charles Taylor at 80: An International Conference" held in Montreal on 31 March 2012. I have since refined the critique, and tried to develop my own version of an egalitarian theory of religious freedom in *Liberalism's Religion.*

Chapter Fourteen

1   The term "secularism" can be used in at least three senses. First, it is used as a shorthand for secular humanism and more particularly for a de-transcendentalized version of it, which Taylor calls exclusive humanism. This secularism describes a general view of the world and the place of humans within it but need not have an explicit normative content. In contrast, secularism in the second sense specifies the ideals, even ultimate ideals, which give meaning and worth to life which its followers strive to realize. In an article published in 1994, I called it ethical secularism. Ethical secularism tells one how best to live in the only world and only life we have, this one, here and now, and what the goals of human flourishing are conceived independently of God, gods, or some other world. I distinguished this ethic from political secularism, the third sense of the term. Here it stands for a certain kind of polity in which organized religious power or religious institutions are separated from organized political power or political institutions for specific ends. One idea behind this distinction was to argue that both those who believe in ethical secularism and those who believe in or practice various religions can come to agree on the constitutive principles that underlie political secularism. Political secularism neither entails nor presupposes ethical secularism. To believe that in order to be a political secularist one had to be an ethical secularist is simply false. I shall say no more about the first two senses of secularism and in what follows will focus only on political secularism (henceforth, simply called secularism).
2   I owe an understanding of this issue to my reading of Taylor's "Philosophy and Its History."
3   I am making a distinction here between religiosity, piety, faith, and religious experience on the one hand and religion on the other. By religion, I mean what Smith meant in his *The Meaning and End of Religion* (see also foreword by John Hick), i.e., a modern Western invention that leads men and women to think of themselves as members of one exclusive group with a well delineated mode of realizing ultimate ends, including a way of achieving salvation. It is a particular system of belief, a system of doctrines, embodied in a

bounded community often pitted against others. In this sense, even "secular philosophies" can be called religion.

4 See Bhargava, "Political Secularism." Also see Bhargava, "Secular Politico-Legal Regimes."

5 As we shall see, this would also open up the possibility of distinguishing forms of secular states.

6 I call them idealized because they are theoretical, not empirical entities. They are ideal types. Thus real laws and policies in America or France do not always correspond to the idealized versions mentioned here. Even idealized versions are contested in the countries where they originated. It is even possible that a model is born in a particular country or region and disappears from there very quickly.

7 It is important to reiterate that what actually happens on the ground in France might be different from what the model would have us believe. Nonetheless it cannot be denied that this conception is part of the French political imaginary and as an abstract ideal has been transmitted, sometimes successfully, to many parts of the world – Kemalist Turkey, Communist Russia, and China, to name just a few countries – and has fed the political imagination of Francophile intellectuals in virtually every corner of the world.

8 In addition to potential denominational conflict was the continuing disagreement between evangelicals who saw some forms of state-church entanglements as corrupting and undermining religion and, correspondingly, disestablishment as a tool for a flourishing religious ethos and the more Republically minded people such as Jefferson who wished to protect the political domain from religious excesses and therefore saw religious liberty and political liberty as two distinct values, each requiring separation. In short, mutual exclusion was believed necessary primarily for religious liberty but also for the more general liberties, including political liberty of individuals.

9 By European, I here mean West European minus France.

10 Table taken from Alfred Stepan, "The Multiple Secularisms of Modern Democracies and Autocracies." All data are collected from the "Religion and State Dataset" gathered by Jonathan Fox, Department of Political Studies, Bar Ilan University. The data are reported in Fox and Sandler, "Separation of Religion and State." For a more detailed analysis of this data see Fox, *A World Survey of Religion and State*. The countries comprising the non-US Western democracies are the following: Andorra, Australia, Austria, Belgium, Canada, Cyprus, Denmark, Finland, France, Germany, Greece, Iceland, Ireland, Italy, Liechtenstein, Luxembourg, Malta, The Netherlands, New Zealand, Norway, Portugal, Spain, Sweden, Switzerland, and the United Kingdom.

11 Religious homogenization was not absolute in Europe, of course, which is why I have used the term "predominantly single-religion societies" above. I

say this also keeping in mind the presence of Jews in Europe. It should not be forgotten that the end of the fifteenth century witnessed waves of expulsion of Jewish people in many parts of Europe. Although members of the Jewish community subsequently remigrated, by "the 1570s, there were few openly professing Jews left in Western or Central Europe." See Kaplan, *Divided by Faith*, 314.

12 Gandhi, *The Way*.

13 Ibid., 39.

14 Ibid., 40–1.

15 Ibid., 41.

16 See, for example, Susan Mendus, *Toleration and the Limits of Liberalism*.

17 "Amidst the endless variety in all religions, one can discern a fundamental unity" (Gandhi, *The Way*, 4).

18 Ibid., 41.

19 Ibid., 57. "My Hindu instinct tells me that all religions are more or less true. All proceed from the same God but are imperfect because they have come down to us through imperfect human instrumentality" (ibid., 58).

20 On the distinction between implicit and explicit theology, see Assmann, *Of Gods and Gods*, 13.

21 Ibid., 54–8.

22 Eventually, this theological mode of coping with diversity can be enlarged to include soteriologies that do not depend on gods. One can deploy the more general term "ethic of self-realization" that includes both god-dependent and god-free ethics pertaining to humans and even non-human selves. Each of these ethics can be treated as a way of being or relating to the ultimate, in whichever way the latter is defined or understood.

23 Ibid., 42.

24 Ibid., 43.

25 Ibid., 58.

26 Rajeev Bhargava, "How Should States Deal with Deep Religious Diversity?"

27 Eberle, *Religious Convictions in Liberal Politics*.

Chapter Fifteen

1 Taylor argues that the idea of a "philosophical anthropology" best unifies the "tightly related agenda" that has characterized a great deal of his work in philosophy. See Taylor's Introduction to his *Philosophical Papers vol. 2*, 1.

2 Charles Taylor, "Social Theory as a Practice," in *Philosophical Papers vol. 2*, 101. I develop a similar argument in Moody-Adams, *Fieldwork in Familiar Places*, ch. 3.

3 Taylor, "Social Theory as a Practice," in *Philosophical Papers vol. 2*, 101.

4 Ibid., 92.

5 Ibid., 104–15.
6 Rawls, *Political Liberalism*, xv–xvi.
7 Ibid., 15. Here Rawls offers an especially straightforward definition of "overlapping consensus."
8 Ibid., 13–14. Here Rawls defines a "comprehensive doctrine." For evidence of Rawls's almost exclusive focus on doctrinal conflict, and his expression of confidence that it can produce a view still appropriate to societies where cultural and ethnic diversity are also important, see the introduction to the expanded edition of *Political Liberalism*, xxv–xxix.
9 Ibid., 375.
10 Ibid., xxxix.
11 See Klosko, "Rawls's 'Political' Philosophy and American Democracy."
12 See Baier, "Justice and the Aims of Political Philosophy."
13 Mills, "'Not A Mere Modus Vivendi,'" 192.
14 Ibid.
15 See Taylor, "Politics of Recognition," in *Multiculturalism and "The Politics of Recognition."*
16 Taylor, *Modern Social Imaginaries*, 189.
17 Taylor, "Democratic Exclusion (and Its Remedies?)," in *Dilemmas and Connections*, 124–46, 124–5; see also Taylor, *Modern Social Imaginaries*, 89–190.
18 Taylor, *Modern Social Imaginaries*, 190.
19 Ibid.
20 Mills, "'Not a Mere Modus Vivendi,'" 193–4.
21 Anderson, *Imagined Communities*.
22 Taylor, *Modern Social Imaginaries*, 190.
23 Taylor, "Nationalism and Modernity," in *Dilemmas and Connections*, 81–105, 92.
24 Rawls, *Political Liberalism*, 37 and 40–3.
25 Taylor, "Democratic Exclusion," in *Dilemmas and Connections*, 138.
26 Mills, "'Not a Mere Modus Vivendi,'" 192.
27 Taylor, "Democratic Exclusion," in *Dilemmas and Connections*, 124.
28 Ibid., 138.
29 Ibid., 140.
30 Taylor, "Politics of Recognition."
31 This draws on an unpublished paper of mine entitled "Cultural Diversity, Globalization and the Future of Democratic Citizenship."
32 Here I build upon an idea articulated in the work of Scarre, "Political Reconciliation, Forgiveness and Grace." Scarre develops a notion that he calls "political grace" to be distinguished from the notion of forgiveness (which presupposes a reaction to wrongdoing). My notion of "civic grace" is meant to be broader, still, in scope – as I develop in the final section of this paper.
33 Baier, "Justice and the Aims of Political Philosophy," 775.
34 Baier, "Trust and Antitrust," 250.

35 Ibid., 251.

36 Ibid., 252. My remarks, here, are concerned with the nature of the kind of horizontal trust in democracies that is an element of democratic fraternity, and leaves aside the quite different challenges of understanding the sources of "vertical" trust in government institutions and processes that is another important component of democratic stability.

37 Putnam, *Bowling Alone*; see also Fukuyama, "Social Capital and Civil Society."

38 Calhoun, "Nationalism and the Cultures of Democracy," 153.

39 Hoskins, "The Politics of Memory," 242.

40 Taylor, "Politics of Recognition," 67.

41 Anderson, *Imagined Communities*, 9.

42 One of the most instructive accounts of the importance of including the names is offered by the architect Maya Lin in "Making the Memorial."

43 Blatt, Brown, and Yacovone, *Hope and Glory*.

44 William James, "Robert Gould Shaw: Oration by Professor William James," in *Essays in Religion and Morality*.

45 Taylor, *Modern Social Imaginaries*, 190.

46 Scarre, "Political Reconciliation, Forgiveness and Grace."

47 Here I adapt Scarre's intuition that it is important to distinguish the idea of extending some kind of "grace" to another and claiming to extend forgiveness for wrongdoing.

48 DeGioia, "A Message to the University Community."

Chapter Sixteen

1 Taylor, "Politics of Recognition," in *Multiculturalism and "The Politics of Recognition."* Taylor's essays have generally been republished many times. When citing individual essays from collections, I will give the essay's title and original year of publication.

2 Taylor, *Philosophical Papers vol. 1*; Taylor, *Philosophical Papers vol. 2*. Taylor's more recent writing on these issues, Maclure and Taylor, *Laïcité et liberté* (*Secularism and Freedom of Conscience* in English translation), is less characteristic, embodying Maclure's Rawlsianism (this work was published in the wake of the report of the Bouchard-Taylor Consultation Commission on Accommodation Practices Related to Cultural Differences, for which Taylor was co-commissioner and Maclure was expert analyst).

3 Honneth, *The Struggle for Recognition*.

4 See, for example, Minow, *Between Vengeance and Forgiveness*, 110–17; James, "Politics and Canadian Citizenship."

5 See Taylor, "Politics of Recognition," 52ff; Taylor, "Shared and Divergent Values" (1991), in *Reconciling the Solitudes*, 168–71; Webber, *Reimagining Canada*, 125–62; Russell, *Constitutional Odyssey*, 133–53.

6 See, for example, Indigenous scholar Glen Coulthard's criticism of analyzing Indigenous claims in terms of "recognition" in part precisely because it diverts attention from Indigenous peoples' entitlement to the land: Coulthard, "Place against Empire"; Coulthard, *Red Skin, White Masks*.

7 On the symbolic dimensions of constitutions, see Webber, "Constitutional Poetry."

8 The phrase is used by James, "Politics and Canadian Citizenship," 257, drawing on Bourdieu, *Outline of a Theory of Practice*, 192.

9 See Grand Council of the Crees, *Sovereign Injustice*.

10 Taylor, "Politics of Recognition," 37–44, 51ff.

11 Benhabib, *The Claims of Culture*, 71–80. See Kompridis, "Normatizing Hybridity/Neutralizing Culture," who carries a line of argument very similar to mine, although his entry point is the concept of culture.

12 Taylor, "Politics of Recognition," 68–70.

13 Alfred, *Wasa'se*; Simpson, *Dancing on Our Turtle's Back*; Coulthard, *Red Skin, White Masks*, 154–79; Simpson, *Mohawk Interruptus*, 11.

14 Taylor, "Politics of Recognition," 70–1.

15 See Eisenberg et al., *Recognition versus Self-Determination*; Webber, *The Constitution of Canada*, 261–4.

16 This is a major feature of the Indigenous critiques cited above.

17 Webber, "The Mediation of Ideology"; Webber, "Relations of Force and Relations of Justice."

18 Taylor, "Politics of Recognition," 64–5; Fanon, *The Wretched of the Earth*.

19 Webber, *Reimagining Canada*, 135.

20 Taylor, "Politics of Recognition," 25, 30–2, 64; Taylor, *Sources of the Self*, 414–16. For Taylor's debt to Herder, see Taylor, "The Tradition of a Situation" (1988) in *Reconciling the Solitudes*, 136; Taylor, *Hegel*, 13–29. I don't doubt the historical role of expressivism in nationalism, but I don't want it to overshadow a more open and meritorious nationalism grounded in the role of language in our political lives. This nationalism seeks to secure peoples' ability to use their own linguistic and cultural resources in their political engagement. The value of this ability is well recognized in Taylor, "Nationalism and Modernity" in *Dilemmas and Connections*, 95–6, and its link to democratic participation is also seen (92–3), although Taylor nevertheless emphasizes the "register of dignity" throughout this paper. In my view, the emphasis on dignity diverts attention from the foundation of an open and individual-respecting nationalism that is not reducible to dignity. For that foundation see Webber, *Reimagining Canada*, and the arguments made by Taylor in "Why Do Nations Have to Become States?" (1979) in *Reconciling the Solitudes*, 53–6, and "Democratic Exclusion (and Its Remedies?)" (1999) in *Dilemmas and Connections*, especially 127–31.

21 Taylor, "Politics of Recognition," 68–70.

22 Ibid., 51–61; see also 41, n. 16.

23 Ibid., 32.

24 Taylor extensively explores the constitutive quality of language in *The Language Animal*.

25 Taylor, "Politics of Recognition," 32–3.

26 See also his unpacking of "black is beautiful": "Self-Interpreting Animals" (1977) in *Philosophical Papers vol. 1*, 69.

27 Ibid., 45–76; Taylor, "Interpretation and the Sciences of Man" (1971) in *Philosophical Papers vol. 2*, 26–7; Taylor, *Sources of the Self*, 34–5.

28 See also Taylor, "Self-Interpreting Animals," in *Philosophical Papers vol. 1*, 68–75; Taylor, "Language and Human Nature" (1978) in *Philosophical Papers vol. 1*, 230–7; Taylor, *Sources of the Self*, 34–9.

29 Taylor, "Why Do Nations Have to Become States?," 48–9; Taylor, *Sources of the Self*, 27–32.

30 Taylor, "Why Do Nations Have to Become States?," 57–8.

31 See, e.g., Taylor, "Interpretation and the Sciences of Man," 39.

32 See his two foundational essays that demonstrate that the idea of a choosing subject is itself dependent on broader intersubjective meanings sustained by institutions and associations: "Atomism" (1979) and "What's Wrong with Negative Liberty" (1979), both in *Philosophical Papers vol. 2*, 187–229, especially 205–6. Taylor's *Sources of the Self* is, in large measure, a history of the emergence and contours of those meanings.

33 Taylor, "Interpretation and the Sciences of Man," 39.

34 See especially ibid., 24.

35 Taylor, "Theories of Meaning" (1980) in *Philosophical Papers vol. 1*, 256–8.

36 Taylor, "Interpretation and the Sciences of Man," 15–57 (see especially 21–4, 32ff); Taylor, "To Follow a Rule" (1992) in *Philosophical Arguments*, 165–80; Taylor, *The Language Animal*, 21, 42–4.

37 See Webber, "Culture, Legal Culture, and Legal Reasoning."

38 Taylor, "Why Do Nations Have to Become States?," 49–52.

39 Taylor, "Understanding and Ethnocentricity" (1981), in *Philosophical Papers vol. 2*, 125–30. For other expressions of this possibility of cross-cultural argument, see "Explanation and Practical Reason" (1989), in *Philosophical Arguments*, 55–9; "Comparison, History, Truth" (1990), 148–52; "Understanding the Other: A Gadamerian View on Conceptual Schemes," in *Dilemmas and Connections*, 24–38. In "Conditions of an Unforced Consensus on Human Rights" (1999), 105–23, Taylor invokes John Rawls's notion of an "overlapping consensus" as one possible form of normative collaboration short of full dialogue. My sense is that this and the "language of perspicuous contrast" speak to different aspects of the process – the latter to the nature of cross-cultural dialogue and "overlapping consensus" to the relationship between justifications and a particular institutional form (see the concession by Taylor at 118).

40 Taylor, "Interpretation and the Sciences of Man," 15–57; Taylor, "To Follow a Rule," 165–80; Taylor, "Explanation and Practical Reason," 49–50.

41 Gadamer, *Truth and Method*, 304–6; Taylor, "Understanding and Ethnocentricity," 126; Taylor, "Comparison, History, Truth," 148–51; Taylor, "Understanding the Other," 24–38.

42 Taylor, "Understanding as Metaphoric," 104.

43 Lévinas, *Totalité et Infini*. See Taylor, *Sources of the Self*, 60–2; Taylor, "Comparison, History, Truth," 150–1.

44 Each of these themes can be teased out of the latter sections of Taylor, "Politics of Recognition," 52ff.

45 Note, for example, Taylor's emphasis on recognition as a need, rather than an obligation, in the first pages of "Politics of Recognition" (26, 34–6); his acknowledgment that the equation of non-recognition with oppression might be exaggerated (36–7); his use of the language of empirical description rather than normative prescription when introducing the politics of recognition (37–44, 64–6); the doubts he expresses even about a right to a presumption of recognition, let alone a right to recognition itself (68); and even, at the very end of the essay, the diffident language he uses for the moral quality of the right to have one's culture presumed valuable (73).

46 See, e.g., ibid., 42–3, 72–3.

47 Gadamer, *Truth and Method*, 268–306. See also Taylor, "Explanation and Practical Reason," 42ff.

48 This appears to be what Alasdair MacIntyre does in his otherwise excellent description of the rationality of traditions, for he tends to close in upon one clearly superior anti-liberal tradition: MacIntyre, *Whose Justice?*, especially 395ff.

49 This is manifestly how Taylor interprets it: "Politics of Recognition," 66–73.

50 Ibid.; Webber, "A Two-Level Justification."

51 Taylor, "Politics of Recognition," 73.

52 Ibid., 25–6, 36.

53 See Taylor, "Why Do Nations Have to Become States?," 48–53; Taylor, "Politics of Recognition," 32–7, 58–9.

Conclusion

1 Taylor, *The Explanation of Behaviour*.

2 Chomsky, "A Review of Skinner."

3 Skinner, *Verbal Behaviour*.

4 Dreyfus and Taylor, *Retrieving Realism*.

5 Taylor, *A Secular Age*.

6 Hochschild, *Strangers in Their Own Land*.

7 Williams, *White Working Class*.

8   Taylor, *Explanation of Behaviour*.

9   Nagel, *Mind and Cosmos*.

10 Taylor, *A Secular Age*.

11 Taylor, *The Language Animal*.

12 Bouchard and Taylor, *Building the Future*.

13 Maclure and Taylor, *Secularism and Freedom of Conscience*.

14 Bouchard and Taylor, *Building the Future*.

15 Maclure and Taylor, *Secularism and Freedom of Conscience*.

16 Taylor, *A Secular Age*.

17 Taylor, "Politics of Recognition," in *Multiculturalism and "The Politics of Recognition,"* 25–75.

18 Taylor, "The Dynamics of Democratic Exclusion."

19 Vance, *Hillbilly Elegy*.

20 Hochschild, *Strangers in Their Own Land*.

21 Taylor, "Politics of Recognition."

22 Taylor, "Atomism," in *Philosophical Papers vol. 2*, 187–211.

23 Taylor, "What's Wrong with Negative Liberty?," in *Philosophical Papers vol. 2*, 211–30.

24 Taylor, "What's Wrong with Negative Liberty?"

25 Taylor, *Sources of the Self*.

BIBLIOGRAPHY

Akan, Murat. "Laïcité and Multiculturalism: The Stasi Report in Context." *British Journal of Sociology* 60, no. 2 (2009): 237–56.

Alfred, Taiaiake. *Wasa'se: Indigenous Pathways of Action and Freedom*. Peterborough: Broadview, 2005.

Anderson, Benedict R. *Imagined Communities: Reflections on the Origin and Spread of Nationalism*. London: Verso, 1991.

Andersen, Kurt "How America Lost Its Mind." *Atlantic* (Sept 2017), https://www.theatlantic.com/magazine/archive/2017/09/how-america-lost-its-mind/534231/.

Anderson, Joel, and Axel Honneth. "Autonomy, Vulnerability, Recognition, and Justice." In *Autonomy and the Challenges to Liberalism: New Essays*, edited by John Christman and Joel Anderson, 127–49. Cambridge: Cambridge University Press, 2005.

Anscombe, Gertrude E.M. *Intention*. Oxford: Basil Blackwell, 1958.

Arendt, Hannah. "Action and The Pursuit of Happiness" (1962). Reprinted in *Thinking Without a Banister: Essays in Understanding, 1953–1975*, edited by Jerome Kohn, 201–19. New York: Schocken Books, 2018.

Arneson, Richard J. "Freedom and Desire." *Canadian Journal of Philosophy* 15, no. 3 (1985): 425–48.

Assmann, Jan. *Of God and Gods*. Madison: University of Wisconsin Press, 2008.

Bader, Veit. "The Governance of Religious Diversity: Theory, Research and Practice." In *International Migration and the Governance of Religious Diversity*, edited by Paul Bramadat and Mathias Koenig, 43–72. Kingston: Queen's Policy Studies, 2009.

– *Secularism or Democracy? Associational Governance of Religious Diversity*. Amsterdam: Amsterdam University Press, 2007.

Baier, Annette. *Postures of the Mind*. Minneapolis: University of Minnesota Press, 1985.

– "Trust and Antitrust." *Ethics* 96, no. 2 (January 1986): 231–60.

Baier, Kurt. "Justice and the Aims of Political Philosophy." *Ethics* 99, no. 4 (July 1989): 771–90.

Baillargeon, Renée, Rose M. Scott, and Zijing He. "False-Belief Understanding in Infants." *Trends in Cognitive Sciences* 14, no. 3 (2010): 110–18.

Baker, Gordon P., and Peter M.S. Hacker. *Frege: Logical Excavations*. Oxford: Blackwell, 1984.

Baubérot, Jean. "The Evolution of Secularism in France: Between Two Civil Religions." In *Comparative Secularisms in a Global Age*, edited by Linnel E. Cady and Elisabeth Shukman Hurd, 57–69. Basingstoke and New York: Palgrave, 2012.

de Beauvoir, Simone. *The Second Sex*. Translated by Constance Borde and Sheila Malovany-Chevallier. New York: Alfred A. Knopf, 2010.

Beiner, Ronald. *Civil Religion*. Cambridge: Cambridge University Press, 2011.

– "Citizenship as a Comprehensive Doctrine." *Hedgehog Review* 10, no. 3 (2008): 23–33.

– "Hermeneutical Generosity and Social Criticism." In *Philosophy in a Time of Lost Spirit: Essays on Contemporary Theory*, 151–66. Toronto: University of Toronto Press, 1997.

– "Secularism as a Common Good." In *Citizenship and Multiculturalism in Western Liberal Democracies*, edited by David Edward Tabachnick and Leah Bradshaw, 37–55. Lanham, MD: Lexington Books, 2017.

Benhabib, Seyla. *The Claims of Culture: Equality and Diversity in the Global Era*. Princeton: Princeton University Press, 2002.

Berlin, Ian. *Four Essays on Liberty*, 1st ed. Oxford: Oxford University Press, 1969.

Bernstein, Richard J. *The New Constellation*. Cambridge: Polity Press, 1991.

– "The Uneasy Tensions of Immanence and Transcendence." *International Journal of Politics, Culture and Society* 21, nos 1–4 (2008): 11–16.

Bhargava, Rajeev. "Can Secularism Be Rehabilitated?" In *Secular States and Religious Diversity*, edited by Bruce J. Berman, Rajeev Bhargava, and André Laliberté, 69–97. Vancouver: University of British Columbia Press, 2013.

– "How Should States Deal with Deep Religious Diversity? Can Anything Be Learned from the Indian Model of Secularism?" In *Rethinking Religion and World Affairs*, edited by Timothy Samuel Shah, Alfred Stepan, and Monica Duffy Toft, 73–84. Oxford: Oxford University Press, 2012.

– "Political Secularism." In *A Handbook of Political Theory*, edited by John Dryzek, B. Honnig, and Anne Philips, 636–55. Oxford: Oxford University Press, 2006.

– "Political Secularism: Why It Is Needed and What Can Be Learnt from Its Indian Version." In *Secularism, Religion and Multicultural Citizenship*, edited by Geoffrey B. Levey and Tariq Modood, 82–110. Cambridge: Cambridge University Press, 2009.

– "Secular Politico-Legal Regimes in Religiously Homogenous and Diverse Societies." In *Law, Religion, State and Society*, Routledge Handbook of Law and Religion, edited by Silvio Ferrari, 229–44. Abingdon-on-Thames: Routledge, 2015.

– "States, Religious Diversity and the Crisis of Secularism." *Open Democracy* 22 (March 2011) http://www.opendemocracy.net/rajeev-bhargava/states-religious-diversity-and-crisis-of-secularism-0.

Bilgrami, Akeel. "Secularism: Its Content and Context." *Economic and Political Weekly* 47, no. 4 (2012): 89–100.

Blatt, Martin H., Thomas J. Brown, and Donald Yacovone, eds. *Hope and Glory: Essays on the Legacy of the 54th Massachusetts Regiment*. Amherst: University of Massachusetts Press, 2000.

Bouchard, Gérard, and Charles Taylor. *Building the Future: A Time for Reconciliation (Commission de consultation sur les pratiques d'accommodement reliées aux différences culturelles*/Consultation Commission on Accommodation Practices Related to Cultural Differences, 2008). Quebec: Gouvernement du Québec, 2008.

Boukydis, Zachariah. "Adult Perception of Infant Appearance: A Review." *Child Psychiatry and Human Development* 11 (1981): 241–54.

Bourdieu, Pierre. *Outline of a Theory of Practice*. Translated by Richard Nice. Cambridge: Cambridge University Press, 1977.

Brandom, Robert. *Making It Explicit*. Cambridge, MA: Harvard University Press, 1998.

Braver, Lee. "Never Mind: Thinking of Subjectivity in the McDowell-Dreyfus Debate." In *Mind, Reason, and Being-in-The-World: The McDowell-Dreyfus Debate*, edited by Joseph K. Schear, 143–62. London: Routledge, 2013.

Bredekamp, Horst. *Galilei der Künstler: Die Zeichnung, der Mond, die Sonne*. Berlin: Akademie-Verlag, 2007.

Brudney, Daniel. "On Noncoercive Establishment." *Political Theory* 33, no. 6 (2005): 812–39.

Bruner, Jerome, and David A. Kalmar. "Narrative and Metanarrative in the Construction of Self." In *Self-Awareness: Its Nature and Development*, edited by Michael Ferrari and Robert J. Sternberg, 308–31. New York: Guilford Press, 1998.

Bucciarelli, Monica, Sangeet Khemlaniand, and Philip N. Johnson-Laird. "The Psychology of Moral Reasoning." *Judgment and Decision Making* 3 (2008): 121–39.

Buttelmann, David, Michael Carpenter, and Melinda Tomasello. "Eighteen-Month-Old Infants Show False Belief Understanding in an Active Helping Paradigm." *Cognition* 112 (2009): 337–42.

Calhoun, Craig. "Nationalism and the Cultures of Democracy." *Public Culture* 19, no. 1 (2007): 151–73.

Carnap, Rudolf. "Überwindung der Metaphysik durch logische Analyse der Sprache." *Erkenntnis* 2 (1932): 219–41.

Carruthers, Peter. "How We Know Our Own Minds: The Relationship between Mindreading and Metacognition." *Behavioral and Brain Sciences* 32, no. 2 (2009): 121–82.

Carter, Ian. *A Measure of Freedom*. Oxford: Oxford University Press, 1999.

– "Positive and Negative Liberty." *Stanford Encyclopedia of Philosophy*, 2003. http://plato.stanford.edu/entries/liberty-positive-negative/.

Carter, Ian, and M.H. Kramer. "How Changes in One's Preferences Can Affect One's Freedom (and How They Cannot): A Reply to Dowding and Van Hees." *Economics and Philosophy* 24, no. 1 (2008): 81–96.

Casanova, José. "Immigration and the New Religious Pluralism: A European Union – United States Comparison." In *Secularism, Religion and Multicultural Citizenship*, edited by Geoffrey B. Levey and Tariq Modood, 139–64. Cambridge: Cambridge University Press, 2008.

Chomsky, Noam. "A Review of B.F. Skinner's *Verbal Behaviour*." *Language* 25, no. 1 (1959): 26–58.

– *Rules and Representations*. Oxford: Blackwell, 1980.

Christman, John. "Analyzing Freedom from the Shadows of Slavery." *Journal of Global Slavery* 2, nos 1–2 (2017): 162–84.

– "Can Positive Liberty Be Saved?" In *Political Philosophy in the 21st Century: Essential Essays*, edited by Steven M. Cahn and Robert B. Talisse, 155–68. Boulder: Westview Press, 2013.

– "Freedom and the Extended Self." *Ethical Perspectives* 21, no. 2 (2014): 225–54.

– "Liberalism and Individual Positive Freedom." *Ethics* 101 (1991): 343–59.

– "No Longer a Slave but Not Yet Free: Freedom and Social Dislocation." In *Freedom and Its Enemies: The Tragedy of Liberty*, edited by Renata Uitz, 171–88. The Hague: Eleven Publishers, 2015.

– "Human Rights and Global Wrongs: The Role of Human Rights Discourse in Responses to Trafficking." In *Poverty, Agency and Human Rights*, edited by Diana T. Meyers. Oxford: Oxford University Press, 2015.

– *The Politics of Persons: Individual Autonomy and Socio-Historical Selves*. Cambridge: Cambridge University Press, 2009.

Collins, Harry M. "Interactional Expertise as a Third Kind of Knowledge." *Phenomenology and the Cognitive Sciences* 3, no. 2 (2004): 125–43.

Connolly, William E. *A World of Becoming*. Durham: Duke University Press, 2011.

– "Catholicism and Philosophy: A Nontheistic Appreciation." In *Charles Taylor*, edited by Ruth Abbey, 166–86. Cambridge: Cambridge University Press, 2004.

Coulthard, Glen. "Place against Empire: The Dene Nation, Land Claims, and the Politics of Recognition in the North." In *Recognition versus Self-Determination: Dilemmas of Emancipatory Politics*, edited by Avigail Eisenberg, Jeremy Webber, Glen Coulthard, and Andrée Boisselle, 147–73. Vancouver: UBC Press, 2014.

– *Red Skin, White Masks: Rejecting the Colonial Politics of Recognition*. Minneapolis: University of Minnesota Press, 2014.

Crary, Alice, and Rupert Read, eds. *The New Wittgenstein*. London: Routledge, 2000.

Csibra, Gergely, and György Gergely. "Natural Pedagogy." *Trends in Cognitive Sciences* 13 (2009): 148–53.

Dawkins, Richard, and Will Hutton. "What Is the Proper Place for Religion in British Public Life?" *Guardian*, 18 February 2012.

DeGioia, John J. *"A Message to the University Community on Civility and Public Discourse,"* 2 March 2012. https://president.georgetown.edu/message-civility-public-discourse.html.

De Jaegher, Hanne, Ezequiel Di Paolo, and Shaun Gallagher. "Can Social Inter-action Constitute Social Cognition?" *Trends in Cognitive Sciences* 14, no. 10 (2010): 441–7.

de Waal, Franz. *Primates and Philosophers*. Princeton: Princeton University Press, 2006.

Derbyshire, Jonathan. "The Books Interview: Charles Taylor." *New Statesman*, 23 February 2012.

Dreyfus, Hubert L. "The Return of the Myth of the Mental." *Inquiry: An Interdisciplinary Journal of Philosophy* 50, no. 2 (2007): 352–65.

– "What Could Be More Intelligible than Everyday Intelligibility? Reinterpreting Division I of *Being and Time* in the Light of Division II." *Bulletin of Science, Technology and Society* 24, no. 3 (2004): 265–74.

Dreyfus, Hubert L., and Charles Taylor. *Retrieving Realism*. Cambridge, MA: Harvard University Press, 2015.

Doris, John M., and Steven Stich. "As a Matter of Fact: Empirical Perspectives on Ethics." In *The Oxford Handbook of Contemporary Analytic Philosophy*, edited by Frank Jackson and Michael Smith, 138–46. Oxford: Oxford University Press, 2005.

Douglass, Frederick. *Narrative of the Life of Frederick Douglass an American Slave*. New York: Penguin Classics, 2014.

Dowding, Keith, and Martin van Hees. "Counterfactual Success Again." *Economics and Philosophy* 24, no. 1: 97–103.

Dummett, Michael. "Frege and Wittgenstein." In *Perspectives on the Philosophy of Wittgenstein*, edited by Irving Block, 31–42. Oxford: Blackwell, 1981.

– *Truth and Other Enigmas*. London: Duckworth, 1978.

– "An Unsuccessful Dig." *Philosophical Quarterly* 34 (1981): 377–401.

Durkheim, Emile. *Les Règles de la méthode sociologique*. Paris: PUF, 1998.

Dworkin, Ronald. *Is Democracy Possible Here? Principles for a New Political Debate*. Princeton: Princeton University Press, 2006.

– *Religion without God*. Cambridge, MA: Harvard University Press, 2013.

Dwyer, Susan. "Moral Dumbfounding and the Linguistic Analogy: Methodological Implications for the Study of Moral Judgment." *Mind and Language* 24 (2009): 274–96.

Dwyer, Susan, Bryce Huebner, and Marc D. Hauser, "The Linguistic Analogy: Motivations, Results, and Speculations." *Topics in Cognitive Science* 2 (2010): 486–510.

Eagleton, Terry. *Reason, Faith, and Revolution*. New Haven: Yale University Press, 2009.

Eberle, Christopher J. *Religious Convictions in Liberal Politics*. Cambridge: Cambridge University Press, 2002.

Eisenberg, Avigail, Jeremy Webber, Glen Coulthard, and Andrée Boisselle, eds. *Recognition versus Self-Determination: Dilemmas of Emancipatory Politics*. Vancouver: UBC Press, 2014.

Fanon, Frantz. *The Wretched of the Earth*. Translated by Constance Farrington. New York: Grove Weidenfeld, 1963.

Ferguson, Kathy. *The Man Question: Visions of Subjectivity in Feminist Theory*. Berkeley: University of California Press, 1993.

Fetzer, Joel S., and J. Christopher Soper. *Muslims and the State in Britain, France, and Germany*. Cambridge: Cambridge University Press, 2004.

Fichte, Johann Gottlieb. "Some Lectures Concerning the Scholar's Vocation." In *Early Philosophical Writings*, edited and translated by Daniel Breazeale. Ithaca: Cornell University Press, 1988.

Flathman, Richard E. *The Philosophy and Politics of Freedom*. Chicago: University of Chicago Press, 1987.

Foddy, Bennet, and Julian Savulescu. "A Liberal Account of Addiction." *Philosophy, Psychiatry, and Psychology* 17, no. 1 (2010): 1–22.

Foner, Nancy, and Richard Alba. "Immigrant Religion in the US and Western Europe: Bridge or Barrier to Inclusion?" *International Migration Review* 42: 360–92.

Foucault, Michel. *Ethics: Subjectivity and Truth*. New York: The New Press, 1998.

Fox, Jonathan. *A World Survey of Religion and State*. Cambridge and New York: Cambridge University Press, 2008.

Fox, Jonathan, and Shmuel Sandler. "Separation of Religion and State in the Twenty-First Century." *Comparative Politics* 37, no. 3 (April 2005): 317–55.

Frankfurt, Harry. "The Faintest Passion." In *Necessity, Volition, and Love*, 95–107. New York: Cambridge University Press, 1998.

Fraser, Nancy, and Axel Honneth. *Redistribution or Recognition? A Political-Philosophical Exchange*. Translated by Joel Golb, James Ingram, and Christiane Wilke. New York: Verso, 2003.

Frege, Gottlob. *Conceptual Notation and Related Articles*. Edited and translated by Tevell Ward Bynum. Oxford: Clarendon, 1972.

— "Thoughts." In *Collected Papers on Mathematics, Logic, and Philosophy*, edited by Brian McGuinness, 351–72. Oxford: Blackwell, 1984.

– "On Concept and Object." In *Collected Papers on Mathematics, Logic, and Philosophy*, edited by Brian McGuiness, 182–94. Oxford: Blackwell, 1984.

Fukuyama, Francis. "Social Capital and Civil Society IMF Working Paper (April 2000): 1–19.

Gadamer, Hans-Georg. *Truth and Method*, 2nd ed. Translated by Joel Weinsheimer and Donald Marshall. London: Continuum, 1989.

Gallagher, Shaun. "Philosophical Antecedents to Situated Cognition." In *Cambridge Handbook of Situated Cognition*, edited by Phillip Robbins and Murat Aydede, 35–51. Cambridge: Cambridge University Press, 2009.

– "The Socially Extended Mind." *Cognitive Systems Research* 25–6, nos 4–12 (2013). doi:10.1016/j.cogsys.2013.03.008.

- "Two Problems of Intersubjectivity." *Journal of Consciousness Studies* 16, nos 6–8 (2009): 289–308.

Gallagher, Shaun, and Daniel D. Hutto. "Understanding Others through Primary Interaction and Narrative Practice." In *The Shared Mind: Perspectives on Intersubjectivity*, edited by Jordan Zlatev, Timothy Racine, Chris Sinha, and Esa Itkonen, 17–38. Amsterdam: John Benjamins, 2008.

Gallagher, Shaun, and Rebecca S. Jacobson. "Heidegger and Social Cognition." In *Heidegger and Cognitive Science*, edited by Julian Kiverstein and Michael Wheeler, 213–45. London: Palgrave-Macmillan, 2012.

Gallagher, Shaun, and Daniel J. Povinelli. "Enactive and Behavioral Abstraction Accounts of Social Understanding in Chimpanzees, Infants, and Adults." *Review of Philosophy and Psychology* 3, no. 1 (2012): 145–69.

Gandhi, Mohandas K. *The Way to Communal Harmony*. Ahmedabad: Navajivan Publishing House, 1963.

Goldin-Meadow, Susan. "The Role of Gesture in Communication and Thinking." *Trends in Cognitive Sciences* 3 (1999): 419–29.

Goodman, Nelson. *Languages of Art: An Approach to a Theory of Symbols*. Indianapolis: Hackett Publishing Company, 1968.

Gopnik, Alison, and Andrew N. Meltzoff. *Words, Thoughts, and Theories*. Cambridge, MA: MIT Press, 1997.

Gould, Carol. *Rethinking Democracy: Freedom and Social Cooperation in Politics, Economy, and Society*. Cambridge: Cambridge University Press, 1988.

Grand Council of the Crees (of Quebec). *Sovereign Injustice: Forcible Inclusion of the James Bay Crees and Cree Territory into a Sovereign Québec*. Nemaska, QC: Grand Council of the Crees, 1995.

Grover, Dorothy. *A Prosentential Theory of Truth*. Princeton: Princeton University Press, 1992.

Habermas, Jürgen. *Moral Consciousness and Communicative Action*, translated by Christian Lenhardt and Shierry Weber Nicholson. Cambridge, MA: MIT Press, 1991.

- "Religion in the Public Sphere." *European Journal of Philosophy* 14, no. 1 (2006): 1–25.

Habermas, Jürgen, and Charles Taylor. "Dialogue." In *The Power of Religion in the Public Sphere*, edited by Eduardo Mendieta and Jonathan VanAntwerpen, 60–9. New York: Columbia University Press, 2011.

Haidt, Jonathan. "The Emotional Dog and Its Rational Tail: A Social Intuitionist Approach to Moral Judgment." *Psychological Review* 108 (2001): 814–34.

Haidt, Jonathan, and Frederik Bjorklund. "Social Intuitionists Answer Six Questions about Moral Psychology." In *Moral Psychology, vol. 3: The Neuroscience of Morality*, edited by Walter Sinnott-Armstrong, 181–217. Cambridge, MA: MIT Press, 2008.

Haque, Md. Shahidul. "Ambiguities and Confusions in Migration-Trafficking Nexus: A Development Challenge." In *Trafficking and the Global Sex Industry*, edited by Karen Beeks and Delila Amir, 3–21. Lanham, MD: Lexington Books, 2006.

Hare, Richard M. *Moral Thinking*. Oxford: Oxford University Press, 1981.

– "Rawls' Theory of Justice." In *Reading Rawls*, edited by Norman Daniels, 81–107. Stanford: Stanford University Press, 1975.

Harman, Gilbert. "Moral Relativism Defended." *Philosophical Review* 84, no. 1 (1975): 3–22.

Hauser, Marc. *Moral Minds*. New York: HarperCollins, 2006.

Heath, Anthony, and Jane Roberts. *British Identity: Its Sources and Possible Implications for Civic Attitudes and Behaviour*. London: Department of Justice, HMSO, 2008.

Heath, Joseph. "Three Evolutionary Precursors to Morality." *Dialogue* 48 (2009): 717–52.

Hirschmann, Nancy. *The Subject of Liberty: Towards a Feminist Theory of Freedom*. Princeton: Princeton University Press, 2003.

Honneth, Axel. "Grounding Recognition: A Rejoinder to Critical Questions." *Inquiry* (February 2001): 499–519.

– *The Struggle for Recognition: The Moral Grammar of Social Conflicts*. Cambridge, MA: MIT Press, 1996.

Hochschild, Arlie. *Strangers in Their Own Land: Anger and Mourning on the American Right*. New York and London: New Press, 2016.

Hoskins, Gregory. "The Politics of Memory and the World Trade Center Memorial Site." *Journal of Social Philosophy* 38, no. 2 (2007): 242–54.

Hume, David, and L.A. Selby-Bigge. *A Treatise of Human Nature*. Oxford: Clarendon Press, 1896.

Hutto, Daniel D. "Unprincipled Engagements: Emotional Experience, Expression and Response." In *Radical Enactivism Intentionality, Phenomenology, and Narrative: Focus on the Philosophy of Daniel D. Hutto*, edited by R.A. Menary, 13–38. Amsterdam: J. Benjamins, 2006.

Jacob, Pierre. "A Puzzle about Belief Ascription." Paper presented at *Understanding Others: An International Workshop on the Philosophical Problem of Other Minds*. St Hilda's College, Oxford. 12 March 2013.

James, Matt. "Politics and Canadian Citizenship." In *Canada: The State of the Federation 1998/99: How Canadians Connect*, edited by Harvey Lazar and Tom McIntosh, 247–81. Montreal: McGill-Queen's University Press, 1999.

James, William. *Essays in Religion and Morality*. Cambridge, MA: Harvard University Press, 1982.

Jeannerod, Marc. *The Cognitive Neuroscience of Action*. New York: Wiley-Blackwell, 1997.

Joppke, Christian. "A Christian Identity for the Liberal State?" *British Journal of Sociology* 64, no. 4: 597–616.

Joyce, Richard. *The Evolution of Morality*. Cambridge, MA: MIT Press, 2006.

Lévinas, Emmanuel. *Totalité et Infini: Essai sur l'extériorité*. Paris: Librairie Générale Française, 1994.

Kant, Immanuel. *Groundwork for the Metaphysics of Mortals*. Translated by H.J. Paton. New York: Harper & Row, 1964.

– *Foundations of the Metaphysic of Morals*. Translated by Lewis White Beck. Indianapolis: Bobbs Merrill, 1959.

– *Lectures on Ethics*. Edited by Peter Heath and Jerome B. Schneewind, translated by Peter Heath. Cambridge: Cambridge University Press, 1997.

– *Religion and Rational Theology*. Translated and edited by Allen W. Wood and George Di Giovanni. Cambridge: Cambridge University Press, 1996.

Kaplan, Benjamin. *Divided by Faith*. Cambridge, MA: Harvard University Press, 2010.

Kateb, George. *Emerson and Self-Reliance*. New York: Rowman & Littlefield Publishers, 2002.

Klosko, George. "Rawls's 'Political' Philosophy and American Democracy." *American Political Science Review* 87, no. 2 (June 1993): 348–59.

Kohlberg, Lawrence. *Essays on Moral Development*, vol. 1. New York: Harper & Row, 1981.

Kompridis, Nikolas. "Normatizing Hybridity/Neutralizing Culture." *Political Theory* 33 no. 3 (2005): 318–43.

Kramer, Matthew. *The Quality of Freedom*. Oxford: Oxford University Press, 2003.

Kristof, Nicholas, and Cheryl WuDunn. *Half the Sky: Turning Oppression into Opportunity for Women Worldwide*. New York: Knopf, 2009.

Kymlicka, Will. "Historic Settlements and New Challenges." *Ethnicities* 9, no. 4 (2009): 546–70.

– *Multicultural Citizenship*. Oxford: Oxford University Press, 1995.

– *Politics in the Vernacular*. Oxford: Oxford University Press, 2001.

Laborde, Cécile. *Critical Republicanism: The Hijab Controversy and Political Philosophy*. Oxford: Oxford University Press, 2008.

– "Political Liberalism and Religion: On Separation and Establishment." *Journal of Political Philosophy* 21, no. 1 (2013): 67–86.

Laegaard, Sune. "Unequal Recognition, Misrecognition and Injustice: The Case of Religious Minorities in Denmark." *Ethnicities* 12, no. 2 (2012): 197–214.

– "What's (un)Problematic about Religious Establishment? The Alienation and Symbolic Equality Accounts." Paper presented at the Centre for the Study of Equality and Multiculturalism, University of Copenhagen, 21 September 2012, at: http://cesem.ku.dk/papers/What_s__un_problematic_about_religious_establishment.pdf/.

de Latour, Sophie Guérard. "Is Multiculturalism Un-French? Towards a Neo-Republican Model of Multiculturalism." In *Liberal Multiculturalism and the Fair Terms of Integration*, edited by Peter Balint and Sophie Guérard de Latour, 139–56. Basingstoke: Palgrave, 2013.

Lenard, Patti T. "What Can Multicultural Theory Tell Us about Integrating Muslims in Europe?" *Political Studies Review* 8 (2010): 308–21.

Lin, Maya. "Making the Memorial." *New York Review of Books* (2 November 2000): https://www.nybooks.com/articles/2000/11/02/making-the-memorial/.

Locke, John. *The Second Treatise of Civil Government and A Letter Concerning Toleration.* Oxford: Blackwell, 1948.

Low, Jason, and Josef Perner. "Implicit and Explicit Theory of Mind: State of the Art." *British Journal of Developmental Psychology* 30, no. 1 (2012): 1–13.

Low, Jason, and Bo Wang. "On the Long Road to Mentalism in Children's Spontaneous False-Belief Understanding: Are We There Yet?" *Review of Philosophy and Psychology* 2, no. 3 (2011): 411–28.

MacIntyre, Alisdair. *After Virtue.* Notre Dame: University of Notre Dame Press, 1981.

– *Whose Justice? Which Rationality?* Notre Dame: University of Notre Dame Press, 1988.

Mackenzie, Catriona. "Relational Autonomy, Normative Authority, and Perfectionism." *Journal of Social Philosophy* 39, no. 4 (2008): 512–33.

Mackie, John. *Ethics: Inventing Right and Wrong.* London: Penguin, 1977.

Maclure, Jocelyn, and Charles Taylor. *Laïcité et liberté de conscience.* Montreal: Boréal, 2010.

– *Secularism and Freedom of Conscience.* Cambridge, MA: Harvard University Press, 2011.

Martikainen, Tuomas. "Muslim Immigrants, Public Religion and Developments towards a Post-Secular Finnish Welfare State." *Studies in Contemporary Islam* 8, no. 1 (2013): 78–105.

Marx, Karl. *The Economic and Philosophic Manuscripts of 1844 and the Communist Manifesto.* New York: Prometheus Books, 1988.

McDowell, John. "Précis of *Mind and World.*" *Philosophical Issues* 7 (1996): 231–9.

– *Mind and World.* Cambridge, MA: Harvard University Press, 1994.

– *Mind, Value, Reality.* Cambridge, MA: Harvard University Press, 1998.

– "What Myth?" *Inquiry* 50, no. 4 (1994): 338–51.

McNeill, David, Susan Duncan, Jonathan Cole, Shaun Gallagher, and Bennett Bertenthal. "Neither or Both: Growth Points from the Very Beginning." *Interaction Studies* 9, no. 1 (2008): 117–32.

Mendus, Susan. *Toleration and the Limits of Liberalism.* London: MacMillan, 1989.

Merleau-Ponty, Maurice. *Phenomenology of Perception.* Translated by Colin Smith. London: Routledge and Kegan Paul, 1962.

– *The Primacy of Perception.* Edited by James M. Edie. Evanston: Northwestern University Press, 1964.

Mikhail, John. "Universal Moral Grammar: Theory, Evidence, and the Future." *Trends in Cognitive Sciences* 11 (2007): 143–52.

Mills, Charles. "Ideal Theory as Ideology." *Hypatia* 20, no. 3 (2005): 165–83.

Mills, Claudia. "'Not A Mere Modus Vivendi': The Bases for Allegiance to a Just State." In *The Idea of Political Liberalism: Essays on Rawls*, edited by Victoria Davion and Clark Wolf, 190–203. Lanham: Rowman & Littlefield, 2000.

Miller, David. *Markets, State, and Community.* Oxford: Clarendon Press, 1989.

Minow, Martha. *Between Vengeance and Forgiveness: Facing History after Genocide and Mass Violence.* Boston: Beacon Press, 1998.

Modood, Tariq, ed. *Church, State and Religious Minorities.* London: Policy Studies Institute, 1997.

– "Is There a Crisis of Secularism in Western Europe?" Paul Hanly Furfey Lecture, *Sociology of Religion* 73, no. 2 (2012): 130–49.

– "Moderate Secularism: A European Conception." *OpenDemocracy* 8 (April 2011): http://www.opendemocracy.net/tariq-modood/moderate-secularism-european-conception.

– "Moderate Secularism, Religion as Identity and Respect for Religion." *Political Quarterly* 81, no. 1 (2010): 4–14.

– *Multiculturalism: A Civic Idea*, 2nd edition. Cambridge: Polity Press, 2013.

Modood, Tariq, and Riva Kastoryano. "Secularism and the Accommodation of Muslims in Europe." In *Multiculturalism, Muslims, and Citizenship: A European Approach*, edited by Tariq Modood, Anna Triandafyllidou, and Ricard Zapata-Barrero, 162–79. London: Routledge, 2006.

Moody-Adams, Michele. *Fieldwork in Familiar Places: Morality, Culture and Philosophy.* Cambridge, MA: Harvard University Press, 1997.

Moore, G.E. *Principia Ethica.* Cambridge: Cambridge University Press, 1993.

Moss, Lenny. "Ethical Expertise and Moral Maturity: Conflict or Complement?" *Philosophy and Social Criticism* 16 (1991): 227–35.

Murray, Craig. "Norwegian Killer Linked to Tea Party and EDL." (23 July 2011): http://www.craigmurray.org.uk/archives/2011/07/norwegian-killer-linked-to-tea-party-and-edl/.

Nagel, Thomas. *Mind and Cosmos: Why the Materialist Neo-Darwinian Conception of Nature is Almost Certainly False.* New York: Oxford University Press, 2012.

Nechayev, Sergey. "Revolutionary Catechism." http://www.marxists.org/subject/anarchism/nechayev/catechism.htm.

Nichols, Shaun. *Sentimental Rules.* New York: Oxford University Press, 2004.

Nietzsche, Friedrich. *The Gay Science.* Edited and translated by Walter Kaufmann. New York: Vintage, 1974.

Nussbaum, Martha. *Liberty of Conscience: In Defense of America's Tradition of Religious Equality.* New York: Basic Books, 2008.

– *The New Religious Intolerance: Overcoming the Politics of Fear in an Anxious Age.* Cambridge, MA: Harvard University Press, 2012.

Onishi, Kristine H., and Renée Baillargeon. "Do 15-Month-Old Infants Understand False Beliefs?" *Science* 308 (2005): 255–8.

Parekh, Bhikhu. *Rethinking Multiculturalism: Cultural Diversity and Political Theory.* Cambridge, MA: Harvard University Press, 2000.

Parreñas, Rhacel, Maria Cecilia Hwang, and Heather Ruth Lee. "What is Human Trafficking? A Review Essay." *Signs* 37, no. 4 (Summer 2012): 1015–29.

Patton, Francis L. *The Metaphysics of Oughtness*. Mannipay: Strong and Asbury, 1887.

Perner, Josef, and Ted Ruffman. "Infants' Insight into the Mind: How Deep?" *Science* 308 (2005): 214–16.

Pettit, Phillip. *Republicanism: A Theory of Freedom and Government*. New York: Oxford University Press, 1997.

– *A Theory of Freedom: From the Politics to the Psychology of Agency*. Oxford: Blackwell, 2001.

Popper, Karl. "Normal Science and Its Dangers." In *Criticism and the Growth of Knowledge*, edited by Imre Lakatos and Alan Musgrave, 51–8. Cambridge: Cambridge University Press, 1970.

Povinelli, Daniel J., and Jennifer Vonk. "Chimpanzee Minds: Suspiciously Human?" *Trends in Cognitive Sciences* 7, no. 4 (2003): 157–60.

Prinz, Jesse. *The Emotional Construction of Morals*. Oxford: Oxford University Press, 2007.

Proust, Marcel. *In Search of Lost Time*. Translated by Andreas Mayor and Terence Kilmartin. New York: The Modern Library, 1993.

Putnam, Robert D. *Bowling Alone: The Collapse and Revival of American Community*. New York: Simon & Schuster, 2000.

Rawls, John. "The Idea of Public Reason Revisited." *University of Chicago Law Review* 64, no. 3 (1997): 765–807.

– *Political Liberalism*, expanded edition. New York: Columbia University Press, 2005.

– *A Theory of Justice*, 2nd ed. Cambridge, MA: Belknap, 1999.

Robertson, Lynne C., and Anne Treisman. "Consciousness: Disorders." In *Encyclopedia of Perception*, edited by E. Bruce Goldstein, 304–9. New York: Sage, 2010.

Rorty, Richard. "Pragmatism, Davidson and Truth." In *Truth and Interpretation*, edited by Ernest Lepore, 333–68. Oxford: Blackwell, 1986.

Rubio-Fernández, Paula, and Bart Geurts. "How to Pass the False-Belief Task before Your Fourth Birthday." *Psychological Science* 24, no. 1 (2013): 27–33.

Ruffman, Ted, and Josef Perner. "Do Infants Really Understand False Belief? Response to Leslie." *Trends in Cognitive Sciences* 9, no. 10 (2005): 462–3.

Russell, Peter H. *Constitutional Odyssey: Can Canadians Become a Sovereign People?*, 3rd ed. Toronto: University of Toronto Press, 2004.

Schneider, Hans J. *Phantasie und Kalkül: Über die Polarität von Handlung und Struktur in der Sprache*. Frankfurt: Suhrkamp, 1992.

– *Religion*. Berlin: de Gruyter, 2008.

– "Satz – Bild – Wirklichkeit: Vom Notationssystem zur Autonomie der Grammatik im Big Typescript.'" In *Wittgensteins 'große Maschinenschrift': Untersuchungen zum philosophischen Ort des Big Typescripts (TS 213) im Werk Ludwig Wittgensteins*, edited by Stefan Majetschak, 79–98. Bern: Peter Lang, 2006.

- "Universale Sprachformen? Zu Robert Brandoms 'expressiver Deduktion' der Gegenstand-Begriff-Struktur." In *Die Öffentlichkeit der Vernunft und die Vernunft der Öffentlichkeit, Festschrift für Jürgen Habermas*, edited by Lutz Wingert and Klaus Günther, 151–91. Frankfurt: Suhrkamp, 2001.
- *Wittgenstein's Later Theory of Meaning: Imagination and Calculation.* Chichester: Wiley Blackwell, 2014.

Scarre, Geoffrey. "Political Reconciliation, Forgiveness and Grace." *Studies in Christian Ethics* 24, no. 2 (2011): 171–82.

Selinger, Evan M., and Robert P. Crease. "Dreyfus on Expertise: The Limits of Phenomenological Analysis." *Continental Philosophy Review* 35 (2002): 245–79.

Sen, Amartya. *Inequality Reexamined.* Oxford: Oxford University Press, 1992.
- "Well-Being, Agency, and Freedom." *Journal of Philosophy* 82 (1985): 169–221.

Sheets-Johnstone, Maxine. "Kinetic Tactile-Kinesthetic Bodies: Ontogenetical Foundations of Apprenticeship Learning." *Human Studies* 23 (2000): 343–70.

Shepher, Joseph. "Mate Selection among Second Generation Kibbutz Adolescents and Adults: Incest Avoidance and Negative Imprinting." *Archives of Sexual Behavior* 1 (1971): 293–307.

Simmons, John A. "Ideal and Non-Ideal Theory." *Philosophy and Public Affairs* 38, no. 1 (2010): 5–36.
- *Inequality Reexamined.* Oxford: Oxford University Press, 1992.

Simon, Herbert A. "A Behavioral Model of Rational Choice." *Quarterly Journal of Economics* 69 (1955): 99–118.

Simpson, Audra. *Mohawk Interruptus: Political Life across the Borders of Settler States.* Durham, NC: Duke University Press, 2014.

Simpson, Leanne. *Dancing on Our Turtle's Back: Stories of Nishnaabeg Re-creation, Resurgence, and a New Emergence.* Winnipeg: Arbeiter Ring Publishing, 2011.

Skinner, Burrhus F. *Verbal Behaviour.* New York: Appleton-Century-Crofts, 1957.

Smith, Wilfred Cantwell. *The Meaning and End of Religion.* London: McMillan, 1963.

Song, Hyun-Joo, Kristine H. Onishi, Renée Baillargeon, and Cynthia Fisher. "Can an Agent's False Belief Be Corrected by an Appropriate Communication? Psychological Reasoning in 18-Month-Old Infants." *Cognition* 109, no. 3 (2008): 295–315.

Southgate, Victoria, Coralie Chevallier, and Gergely Csibra. "Seventeen-Month-Olds Appeal to False Beliefs to Interpret Others' Referential Communication." *Developmental Science* 13, no. 6 (2010): 907–12.

Southgate, Victoria, Atsushi Senju, and Gergely Csibra. "Action Anticipation through Attribution of False Belief by 2-Year-Olds." *Psychological Science* 18, no. 7 (2007): 587–92.

Steiner, Hillel. "How Free: Computing Personal Liberty." In *Of Liberty*, edited by Allen Phillips-Griffiths, 73–89. London: Cambridge University Press, 1983.

Stenius, Eric. *Wittgenstein's Tractatus: A Critical Exposition of Its Main Lines of Thought.* Oxford: Blackwell, 1960.

Stepan, Alfred. "The Multiple Secularisms of Modern Democracies and Autocracies." In *Rethinking Secularism*, edited by Craig Calhoun, Mark Jeurgenseyer, and Jonathan VanAntwerpen, 114–44. New York: Oxford University Press, 2012.

– "Religion, Democracy, and the 'Twin Tolerations,'" *Journal of Democracy* 11, no. 4 (2000): 37–58.

Stolberg, Sheryl G. "For Romney, a Role of Faith and Authority." *New York Times*, 15 October 2011. https://www.nytimes.com/2011/10/16/us/politics/for-romney-a-role-of-faith-and-authority.html/.

Sullivan, Andrew. "My Problem with Christianism." *Time* (15 May 2006), 74.

Sunstein, Cass. "Moral Heuristics." *Behavioral and Brain Sciences* 28, no. 4 (2005): 531–42.

Surian, Luca, Stefania Caldi, and Dan Sperber. "Attribution of Beliefs by 13-Month-Old Infants." *Psychological Science* 18, no. 7 (2007): 580–6.

Taylor, Charles. "Afterward: Apologia pro Libro suo." In *Varieties of Secularism in a Secular Age*, edited by Michael Warner, Jonathan VanAntwerpen, and Craig Calhoun, 300–25. Cambridge, MA: Harvard University Press, 2010.

– "Connolly, Foucault, and Truth." *Political Theory* 13, no. 3 (1985): 377–85.

– *Dilemmas and Connections: Selected Essays.* Cambridge: Belknap Press, 2011.

– "The Dynamics of Democratic Exclusion." *Journal of Democracy*, no. 4 (1998): 143–56.

– "Ethics and Ontology." *Journal of Philosophy* 100, no. 6 (2003): 305–20.

– *The Ethics of Authenticity.* Cambridge, MA: Harvard University Press, 1992.

– *The Explanation of Behaviour.* Abingdon: Routledge Keagan Paul, 1964.

– "Foucault on Freedom and Truth." *Political Theory* 12, no. 2 (1984): 152–83.

– *Hegel.* Cambridge: Cambridge University Press, 1975.

– "Interpretation and the Sciences of Man." In *Interpretive Social Science*, edited by Paul Rabinow and William M. Sullivan, 25–73. Berkeley: University of California Press, 1979.

– *The Language Animal: The Full Shape of the Human Linguistic Capacity.* Cambridge, MA: Harvard University Press, 2016.

– "Language Not Mysterious?" In *Reading Brandom, On "Making It Explicit,"* edited by Bernhard Weiss and Jeremy Wanderer, 32–47. London: Routledge, 2010.

– "The Meaning of Secularism." *Hedgehog Review* 12, no. 3 (2010): 23–34.

– *Modern Social Imaginaries.* Durham: Duke University Press, 2003.

– *Multiculturalism and "The Politics of Recognition."* Princeton: Princeton University Press, 1992.

– *Philosophical Arguments.* Cambridge, MA: Harvard University Press, 1995.

– *Philosophical Papers vol. 1: Human Agency and Language.* Cambridge: Cambridge University Press, 1985.

– *Philosophical Papers vol. 2: Philosophy and the Human Sciences.* Cambridge: Cambridge University Press, 1985.

– "Philosophy and Its History." In *Philosophy in History: Essays in the Historiography of History*, edited by Richard Rorty, Jerome B. Schneewind, and Quentin Skinner, 17–30. Cambridge: Cambridge University Press, 1984.

– *Reconciling the Solitudes: Essays on Canadian Federalism and Nationalism.* Montreal and Kingston: McGill-Queen's University Press, 1993.

– "Retrieving Realism." In *Mind, Reason, and Being-in-The-World: The McDowell-Dreyfus Debate*, edited by Joseph K. Schear, 61–90. London: Routledge, 2013.

– *A Secular Age.* Cambridge, MA: Harvard University Press, 2007.

– *Sources of the Self: The Making of the Modern Identity.* Cambridge, MA: Harvard University Press, 1989.

– "Why We Need a Radical Redefinition of Secularism." In *The Power of Religion in the Public Sphere*, edited by Eduardo Mendieta and Jonathan VanAntwerpen, 34–59. New York: Columbia University Press, 2011.

Taylor, George H. "Understanding as Metaphoric, Not a Fusion of Horizons." In *Gadamer and Ricoeur: Critical Horizons for Contemporary Hermeneutics*, edited by Francis J. Mootz III and George H. Taylor, 104–18. London: Continuum, 2011.

Thomas, Alan. "Kant, McDowell and the Theory of Consciousness." *European Journal of Philosophy* 5, no. 3 (1997): 283–305.

Todes, Samuel. *Body and World.* Cambridge, MA: MIT Press, 2001.

Tully, James. "Wittgenstein and Political Philosophy: Understanding Practices of Critical Reflection." *Political Theory* 17, no. 2 (May 1989): 172–204.

Tversky, Amos, and Daniel Kahneman. "Availability: A Heuristic for Judging Frequency and Probability." *Cognitive Psychology* 5 (1973): 207–32.

Vance, J.D. *Hillbilly Elegy: A Memoir of a Family and a Culture in Crisis.* New York: Harper, 2016.

Viveiros de Castro, Eduardo. *Cannibal Metaphysics.* Minneapolis: University of Minnesota Press, 2014.

Vonk, Jennifer, and Daniel J. Povinelli. "Social and Physical Reasoning in Human-Reared Chimpanzees: New Data from a Set of Preliminary Studies." In *Perception, Causation, and Objectivity: Issues in Philosophy and Psychology*, edited by Johannes Roessler, Hemdat Lerman, and Naomi Eilan. Oxford: Oxford University Press, 2011.

Walzer, Michael. *Just and Unjust Wars.* New York: Basic Books, 1992.

Webber, Jeremy. *The Constitution of Canada: A Contextual Analysis.* Oxford: Hart Publishing, 2015.

– "Constitutional Poetry: The Tension between Symbolic and Functional Aims in Constitutional Reform." *Sydney Law Review* 21, no. 2 (1999): 260–77.

– "Culture, Legal Culture, and Legal Reasoning: A Comment on Nelken." *Australian Journal of Legal Philosophy* 29, no. 27 (2004): 27–36.

– "The Mediation of Ideology: How Conciliation Boards, through the Mediation of Particular Disputes, Fashioned a Vision of Labour's Place within Canadian Society." *Law in Context* 7, no. 2 (1989): 1–23.

– *Reimagining Canada: Language, Culture, Community and the Canadian Constitution*. Montreal: McGill-Queen's University Press, 1994.

– "Relations of Force and Relations of Justice: The Emergence of Normative Community between Colonists and Aboriginal Peoples." *Osgoode Hall Law Journal* 33, no. 4 (1995): 623–60.

– "A Two-Level Justification of Religious Toleration." *Journal of Indian Law and Society* 4, no. 1 (2014): 1–29.

Whitehead, Alfred North. *Process and Reality*. New York: The Free Press, 1978.

Wiggins, David. "Moral Cognitivism, Moral Relativism, and Motivating Moral Beliefs." *Proceedings of the Aristotelian Society* 91 (1990–91): 61–85.

– *Needs, Values, Truth*. Oxford: Clarendon Press, 1987.

Wilde, Oscar. *The Soul of Man under Socialism and Selected Critical Prose*. New York: Penguin Books, 2001.

Wills, Garry. "Contraception's Con Men." *NYR Daily* (15 February 2012). https://www.nybooks.com/daily/2012/02/15/contraception-con-men/.

Williams, Joan C. *White Working Class: Overcoming Class Cluelessness in America*. Boston: Harvard Business Review Press, 2017.

Wilson, Timothy. *Strangers to Ourselves*. Cambridge, MA: Harvard University Press, 2004.

Wind-Cowie, Max, and Thomas Gregory. *A Place for Pride*. London: Demos, 2011.

Wittgenstein, Ludwig. *The Big Typescript*. German-English Scholar's Edition. Edited and translated by C. Grant Luckhardt and Maximilian A.E. Aue. Oxford: Blackwell, 2005.

– *Philosophical Grammar*. Edited by Rush Rhees, translated by Anthony Kenny. Oxford: Blackwell, 1974.

– *Philosophical Investigations*. The German text, with an English translation by G.E.M. Anscombe, P.M.S. Hacker, and Joachim Schulte, revised 4th ed. Chichester: Wiley-Blackwell, 2009.

– *Philosophical Remarks*. Edited by Rush Rhees, translated by Raymond Hargreaves and Roger White. Oxford: Blackwell, 1975.

– *Tractatus Logico-Philosophicus*. Translated by Charles K. Ogden. Mineola: Dover, 1999.

Wolf, Arthur P. *Sexual Attraction and Childhood Association*. Stanford, CA: Stanford University Press, 1995.

Wundt, Wilhelm. "*Völkerpsychologie: Eine Untersuchung der Entwicklungsgesetze von Sprache, Mythus und Sitte*." Bd. 2: Die Sprache, Teil 2, Leipzig 1912, ch. 7, I, 222–56. Leipzig: Die Sprache, 1912.

Young, Iris M. *Throwing Like a Girl and Other Essays*. Bloomington: Indiana University Press, 1990.

Zahavi, Dan. "Mindedness, Mindlessness and First-Person Authority." In *Mind, Reason, and Being-in-The-World: The McDowell-Dreyfus Debate*, edited by Joseph K. Schear, 320–40. London: Routledge, 2013.

CONTRIBUTORS

KWAME ANTHONY APPIAH, FRSL, is professor of philosophy and law at New York University. His books include *Cosmopolitanism: Ethics in a World of Strangers* (2006), *The Ethics of Identity* (2007), *The Honor Code: How Moral Revolutions Happen* (2010), and *The Lies that Bind: Rethinking Identity* (2018). He has served as president of the PEN American Center and the Modern Language Association, and chair of the American Philosophical Association and the American Council of Learned Societies. Professor Appiah writes the *Ethicist* column for the *New York Times*.

RAJEEV BHARGAVA is director of the Institute for Indian Thought at the Centre for the Study of Developing Societies, Delhi. His books include *Individualism in Social Science* (1992), *The Promise of India's Secular Democracy* (2010), and *What Is Political Theory and Why Do We Need It?* (2010). His edited books include *Secularism and Its Critics* (1998) and *Politics and Ethics of the Indian Constitution* (2009). Since February 2017, he has written a fortnightly column in the Indian national daily, the *Hindu*.

RONALD BEINER, FRSC, is professor of political science at the University of Toronto. His books include *Political Judgment* (1983); *What's the Matter with Liberalism?* (1992); *Philosophy in a Time of Lost Spirit* (1997); *Liberalism, Nationalism, Citizenship* (2003); *Civil Religion* (2011); *Political Philosophy: What It Is and Why It Matters* (2014); and *Dangerous Minds: Nietzsche, Heidegger, and the Return of the Far Right* (2018). He is also editor of Hannah Arendt's *Lectures on Kant's Political Philosophy* (1982), published in sixteen foreign-language editions.

RICHARD J. BERNSTEIN is Vera List Professor of Philosophy at the New School for Social Research. His books include *Why Read Hannah Arendt Now* (2018), *Ironic Life* (2016), *Pragmatic Encounters* (2016), and *The Pragmatic Turn* (2010).

JOHN CHRISTMAN is professor of philosophy, political science, and women's studies and director of the Penn State Humanities Institute at Pennsylvania State University. His books include *Social and Political Philosophy: A Contemporary Introduction* (2018); *The Politics of Persons: Individual Autonomy and Socio-Political Persons* (2009); and *The Myth of Property: Towards an Egalitarian Theory of Ownership* (1994).

WILLIAM E. CONNOLLY is Krieger-Eisenhower Professor of Political Science at Johns Hopkins University. His newest book is *Climate Machines, Fascist Drives and Truth* (2019).

NIGEL DESOUZA is assistant professor of philosophy at the University of Ottawa. His articles have appeared in *Ethical Theory and Moral Practice*, *The British Journal for the History of Philosophy*, *Intellectual History Review*, *Herder Yearbook*, and the *Herder Handbuch* (2016). He is co-editor, with Anik Waldow, of *Herder: Philosophy and Anthropology* (2017).

SHAUN GALLAGHER is Lillian and Morrie Moss Chair of Excellence in Philosophy at the University of Memphis and professorial fellow at the Faculty of Law, Humanities and the Arts, University of Wollongong (AU). He is also honorary professor of health sciences at Tromsø University (Norway). He was the Humboldt Foundation Anneliese Maier Research Fellow (2012–18). His publications include *Action and Interaction* (2020); *Enactivist Interventions: Rethinking the Mind* (2017); *The Neurophenomenology of Awe and Wonder* (2015); *Phenomenology* (2012); *The Phenomenological Mind* (with Dan Zahavi, 2012); *How the Body Shapes the Mind* (2005); *Hermeneutics and Education* (1992); and he is editor-in-chief of the journal *Phenomenology and the Cognitive Sciences*.

JOSEPH HEATH, FRSC, is professor of philosophy at the University of Toronto. He is the author of several books, including *Communicative Action and Rational Choice* (2001); *Following the Rules* (2008); and *Morality, Competition, and the Firm* (2014). His most recent book, *The Machinery of Government*, is forthcoming from Oxford University Press.

NANCY J. HIRSCHMANN is Stanley I. Sheerr Term Professor in the Social Sciences at the University of Pennsylvania. Her books include *The Subject of Liberty: Toward a Feminist Theory of Freedom*; *Gender, Class, and*

Freedom in Modern Political Theory and *Disability and Political Theory* (edited with Barbara Arneill). She has recently held fellowships from the American Council of Learned Societies, the National Humanities Center, and the European University Institute, and is completing a book on the idea of freedom from the perspective of disability.

CÉCILE LABORDE, FBA, holds the Nuffield Chair of Political Theory at the University of Oxford. She is the author of *Pluralist Thought and the State* (2000); *Critical Republicanism* (2008); and *Liberalism's Religion* (2017). Edited volumes include *Republicanism and Political Theory* (2007) and *Religion in Liberal Political Philosophy* (2017).

JACOB T. LEVY is Tomlinson Professor of Political Theory, founding director of the Yan P. Lin Centre, and coordinator of the Research Group on Constitutional Studies at McGill University. He is the author of *Rationalism, Pluralism, and Freedom* (2015) and *The Multiculturalism of Fear* (2000). He is a senior fellow of the Niskanen Center.

JOCELYN MACLURE is professor of philosophy at the University of Laval. His publications include, with Charles Taylor, *Secularism and Freedom of Conscience* (Harvard University Press, 2011). He served as an expert analyst on the Bouchard-Taylor Commission on reasonable accommodation, and is the current president of the Quebec Ethics in Science and Technology Commission.

TARIQ MODOOD, MBE, FBA, FAcSS, FRSA, is professor of sociology, politics, and international studies and founding director of the University Research Centre for the Study of Ethnicity and Citizenship at the University of Bristol. He served on the *Commission on Multi-Ethnic Britain*, the UK *National Equality Panel*, and the *Commission on Religion and Belief in British Public Life*. His books include *Essays on Secularism and Multiculturalism* (2019); *Multiculturalism: A Civic Idea* (2013); *Multiculturalism Rethought* (2015, as co-editor); *Multiculturalism and Interculturalism: Debating the Dividing Lines* (2016); and *The Problem of Religious Diversity: European Problems, Asian Challenges* (2017).

MICHELE MOODY-ADAMS is Joseph Straus Professor of Political Philosophy and Legal Theory at Columbia University, where she has also served as dean of Columbia College and vice-president for undergraduate education. She has been a Marshall Scholar, a National Endowment for the Humanities Fellow, and she is a lifetime Honorary Fellow of Somerville College, Oxford. She is the author of *Fieldwork in Familiar Places: Morality, Culture and Philosophy* and is currently at work on a book entitled *Renewing Democracy.* She has published numerous articles on moral psychology, justice, gender and race, academic freedom, and democratic disagreement.

MICHAEL ROSEN is Senator Joseph S. Clark Professor of Ethics in Politics and Government at Harvard University. He is the author of *Hegel's Dialectic and Its Criticism* (1982); *On Voluntary Servitude: False Consciousness and the Theory of Ideology* (1996); and *Dignity: Its History and Meaning* (2012).

HANS J. SCHNEIDER is emeritus professor at the Institute for Philosophy, University of Potsdam. His main fields of interest are philosophy of language, philosophy of religion, and the philosophy of Ludwig Wittgenstein. His books include *Pragmatik als Basis von Semantik und Syntax* (1975); *Phantasie und Kalkül* (1992) [revised partial translation with a foreword by Charles Taylor: *Wittgenstein's Later Theory of Meaning: Imagination and Calculation* (2014)]; and *Religion* (2008).

CHARLES TAYLOR, CC, GOQ, FRSC, FBA, is emeritus professor of philosophy at McGill University, and has also been professor of political science at McGill, Chichele Professor of Social and Political Theory at All Souls College University of Oxford, and Board of Trustees Professor of Law and Philosophy at Northwestern University. He has been awarded the Kyoto Prize, the Templeton Prize, the Berggruen Prize for Philosophy, and the John W. Kluge Prize.

JEREMY WEBBER, FRSC, is professor of law at the University of Victoria. He is the author of *Reimagining Canada: Language, Culture, Community and the Canadian Constitution* (1994); *The Constitution of Canada: A Contextual Analysis* (2015); and *Las gramáticas de la ley: Derecho, pluralismo y justicia* (2017) and co-editor of *Recognition versus Self-Determination: Dilemmas of Emancipatory Politics* (2014); *Storied Communities: Narratives of Contact and Arrival in Constituting Political Community* (2011); and

Between Consenting Peoples: Political Community and the Meaning of Consent (2010).

DANIEL M. WEINSTOCK is James McGill Professor of Law and director of the Institute for Health and Social Policy at McGill University. He has published extensively on challenges posed by religious and ethno-cultural diversity for liberal-democratic theory and practice.

INDEX